Business Valuation Update Yearbook 2017

BVR
What It's Worth
1000 SW Broadway, Suite 1200, Portland, OR 97205
(503) 291-7963 • www.bvresources.com

BVR
What It's Worth

Editor: Andy Dzamba

Publisher: Sarah Andersen

Managing Editor: Monique Nijhout-Rowe

Senior Copy Editor: David Solomon

Chair and CEO: David Foster

President: Lucretia Lyons

Chief Revenue Officer: Lisa McInturff

Customer Service Manager: Retta Dodge

Print/PDF ISBN: 978-1-62150-103-9

EPUB ISBN: 978-1-62150-104-6

Library of Congress Control Number: 2017932820

Table of Contents

Introduction

For over 20 years, *Business Valuation Update* has presented the latest thinking in methodologies as well as up-to-date news and analysis, changes in regulations and professional standards, leading conferences, publications of interest, and practice-building ideas. We have continued this tradition, and here are some highlights of what you'll see in this yearbook.

Section I. Business Valuation Approaches, Methods, and Entity-Specific Issues

Business Valuation Update is committed to the idea that, if the business valuation profession is to advance, it must be open to new ideas, techniques, and methodologies. There must also be challenges to conventional thinking and a fostering of healthy debates.

The debate over the discount for lack of marketability heated up over the application (or misapplication) of a DLOM in New York statutory appraisal actions. An article, "NY's Unfair Application of Shareholder-Level Marketability Discounts," triggered comments by readers who agree the problem lies with judges who lack training in valuation concepts and often build their value determinations on questionable or stale precedent. A number of follow-up articles appeared, including "Definitional Problem Underlies N.Y. Courts' Unfair DLOM Stance" and "DLOMs in N.Y. Fair Value Cases: Private Company Discounts Are Not Caused by Lack of Marketability."

This debate triggered a call for action for the profession to speak with one voice and eliminate the confusion over the use of discounts. One valuation expert offers up some nomenclature and—more importantly—a framework that he hopes will help in developing a common language that could be used in valuation reports in an article titled "Adjustment Mapping and the Public-vs.-Private-Company Discount Debate."

BVU followed the continued interest in the implied private company pricing line (IPCPL), a model designed to better estimate the cost of capital for small private companies (those with revenues below $150 million). The model was first introduced in 2012, and *BVU* ran a series of articles starting in 2013. An article titled "Debate Rekindles Over Private Company Cost of Capital Model" covers certain aspects of the model that have been called into question and the responses by the IPCPL developers.

Other new methodologies and approaches were highlighted in several articles, such as "A Quantitative Model Evolves for Determining Passive Appreciation," "Multifactor Scorecard Analysis Helps With Debt-Versus-Equity Problem," and "Simplified MUM for Determining Personal Goodwill."

As the year came to a close, the most talked about issue was the issuance of the controversial proposed IRC Section 2704 regulations designed to curb estate valuation discounts for minority interests. The valuation community was shocked over the scope of the proposed rules, which would apply to family-owned operating businesses as well as asset-holding entities that are perceived to be pushing the envelope in terms of discounts. Appraisers were also stunned over how the regs essentially redefined long-accepted definitions of "fair market value," "marketability," and "control." Two articles cover this: "Proposed Sec. 2704 Regs Fly in the Face of BV Theory and Tax Law" and "Groundswell Builds as IRC Sec. 2704 Regs Sink In."

Other articles of note deal with cost of capital, damages, ESOPs, internet domain valuation, economic obsolescence, and determining reasonable compensation. Attendance at the valuation conferences was brisk over the past year, and several articles provide recaps as well as some detailed coverage.

Section II. Industry-Specific Valuation

A challenge to traditional thinking on valuing hotels was presented in "Hotel Valuation: Breaking the Rules—But Getting it Right!" This article explains why the dominant method for the appraisal of hotels is contrary to the main methods used for the appraisal of other real estate-centered enterprises (RECEs) and is therefore flawed.

In terms of emerging industries, the legal marijuana business took the spotlight as eight new states approved marijuana initiatives amid the presidential election. That brings the total to 28 states and jurisdictions that now allow legal marijuana business in some capacity. The article titled "Coping With the Challenges of Valuing a Cannabis-Related Firm" discusses the nuances of appraising these firms.

A lot has been going on in healthcare, and *BVU* attended the AICPA's conference devoted to this industry (see "AICPA Conference Covers Healthcare Valuation Challenges and Opportunities"). A different approach to measuring the fair market value of physician compensation is designed to help ward off a crackdown by the government, which has been winning False Claims Act (FCA) lawsuits against a number of hospitals, reaping hundreds of millions of dollars in fines. The lawsuits have emerged out of the trend of hospitals acquiring medical practices, and the FMV of physician compensation is a key element of these cases. Instead of paying physicians the median compensation, hospitals could set fair market value compensation based on the resource-based relative value scale (RBRVS). This is covered in "New Approach to FMV of Physician Pay Could End Hospital Woes."

Other healthcare-related articles of interest include "How to Avoid Harsh HIPAA Penalties When Doing Healthcare Valuations," "Valuation Characteristics and Methodologies for Urgent Care Centers," and "IRS Reasonable Compensation Job Aid: Healthcare Perspective."

A number of articles discuss particular valuation aspects of specific industries, including accounting firms, oil and gas, franchises, architectural/engineering firms, veterinary practices, and wealth management firms.

Section III. From the Courtroom

There was an ongoing stream of business valuation-related court case, and the most notable cases are identified in an article titled "10 Best Valuation Cases for 2015." Litigation is an important and growing area for many valuation practices, and several articles provide advice in this area, such as "Attorneys Reveal Seven Surprising Views on Expert Depositions," "Pitfalls for Expert Witnesses Doing a Valuation Report Review," and "Recent Case Points Up Danger of the Discovery Trap."

BVU was fortunate to be at a conference session that featured U.S. Tax Court Judge David Laro, whose remarks always deserve a great deal of attention (see "Judge Laro Toplines Panel on Hot Issues in Tax Valuation").

Section IV. Business Valuation Profession and Practice Management

A number of articles reveal insights into valuation firm performance and practice development. For example, the article titled "Most BV Firms Expect 2016 Revenues to Top Last Year" points out that two-thirds of business valuation firms say they expect to do more business than the previous year. Most of the revenue is coming from certain areas, the top area being tax, gifts, and estates, which represents about one-third of total revenue on average. Other articles further examine the mix of practice revenue and the research sources that valuation firms prefer.

Other articles include a recap of developments in the valuation profession and several interviews with leading practitioners. A look at the profession outside the U.S. was revealed in "What Is the Practice of BV Like in the Middle East?" which features an interview with a local expert.

Section V. Reviews of Data Sources and New Books

The cornerstone book in the Duff & Phelps handbook series on cost of capital, the *Valuation Handbook - Guide to Cost of Capital,* went through a number of refinements and additions for its 2016 edition, such as an expanded Chapter 12, which provides detailed answers to questions practitioners submitted. For a review, see "What's New and Noteworthy in the DP 2016 Valuation Handbook."

There was a significant expansion to private-company business transaction data in *Pratt's Stats,* and also a number of new features added, including 45 additional data fields, including fields dedicated to purchase price allocation, franchise designation, and real estate asset value. There's also an enhanced ability to find more comps as transactions can now include up to three SIC or NAICS codes to reflect multiple lines of business. The search functionality was also improved, and you can now search by region, EBITDA, seller's discretionary earnings, and more. An article titled "Appraiser Review: How *Pratt's Stats* Upgrades Improve Your Search for Comps" gives more details. Private transactions outside the U.S. are summarized in "Latest Data on Private-Company Transactions in the United Kingdom."

Several new books of note were reviewed, including one on economic damages ("Book Review: *The Comprehensive Guide to Economic Damages,* Volume 1 and 2, 4th ed.," and see also "Fannon and Dunitz Bridge the Gap in the Practice of Economic Damages."). Three top valuation thought leaders (Shannon Pratt, Jay Fishman, and James Hitchner) released a book in Q&A format ("Book Review: *A Consensus View—Q&A Guide to Financial Valuation*"). In the healthcare area, a preview of a new edition of a valuation guide was provided ("Sneak Preview of New Material in the *BVR/AHLA Healthcare Valuation Guide*").

Section VI. Data

Each month, *BVU* publishes the Cost of Capital Center, with selected general data such as the 20-day Treasury yield, long-term inflation estimate, Dow Jones Industrial P/E ratio on current earnings, and other data. Also published is Duff & Phelps premiums over the long-term risk-free rate.

Relatively new to the Cost of Capital Center are data related to a model that is designed to better estimate cost of capital for small private companies. This model uses the implied private company pricing line 2.0 (IPCPL), which is based on *Pratt's Stats* data and is indexed directly to the IPCPL cost of capital. Published monthly is a private-company cost of capital index based on four company sizes (in terms of revenue). The index represents the after-tax cost of capital (calibrated for 35% tax rate and midperiod convention) for an average/typical risk company to be used on unlevered, after-tax expected free cash flows.

The yearbook amalgamates the monthly data from the Cost of Capital Center and presents it in tabular and chart form.

Many more articles of interest are in the yearbook than those mentioned above, many of which top valuation experts and thought leaders contributed. BVR thanks them for their contributions, and we look forward to keeping you posted on important developments in the business valuation profession.

Sincerely,

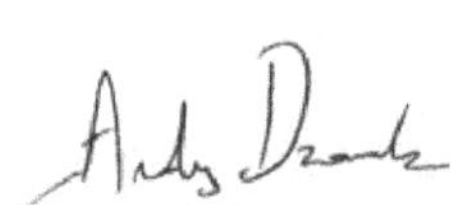

Andrew Dzamba
Executive Editor
Business Valuation Update

Section I.
Business Valuation Approaches, Methods, and Entity-Specific Issues

Some Key Takeaways From the AICPA FVS Conference

Over 1,100 attendees converged on Las Vegas for the AICPA Forensic and Valuation Services Conference 2015. *BVU* was there and heard some outstanding speakers and topics. Covered below are just a few of the takeaways. Future issues will cover these—and more—in greater detail.

AICPA doings. The chair of the FVS executive committee, Carol Carden (PYA PC), updated attendees on several key issues the AICPA is monitoring. One is the forthcoming proposed regulations from the IRS on discounts for family limited partnerships (FLPs) and family businesses. It was originally thought that these regs would limit the discounts and thus have a significant impact on valuation. However, the IRS appears to be easing up on this matter.

"The IRS officials working on the section 2704(b) regulations recently told the AICPA trust, estate, and gift tax technical resource panel that they are still working on the regulations. The regulations will rely on the statute, not follow the Treasury's green book proposals," says Carden. Does this mean that the regulations may not have as big an impact as was expected—or maybe no impact at all? "I think we won't know the answer until the regulations are released," says Carden. "As of now, it does not appear to be as impactful as we first thought." In any event, a special AICPA panel will analyze the proposed rules when they are released.

Another key issue is The Appraisal Foundation's exposure draft on control premiums (MPAP) that was issued for public comment. The AICPA submitted comments on the draft, which, when adopted, will become valuation advisories through TAF's Appraisal Practices Board.

The chair of the BV committee, Randie Dial (CliftonLarsonAllen), mentioned the four valuation and forensic practice aids the AICPA issued during the past year (a "phenomenal accomplishment"): economic damages, estate/gift tax, fraud, and expert witnesses and consultants. A new practice aid is in the works for determining the fair value of public equity/venture capital (PE/VC) investments, and a working draft will be released in spring 2017.

Dial also spoke about a new college program being rolled out where students can take a valuation course that prepares them for the ABV exam, which they would take in two three-hour class sessions. If they pass, the students would have the ABV "on hold" until they get their CPA, at which point the ABV would kick in.

AICPA senior technical manager Eva Simpson gave an update of the new credentials to be issued for fair value. The new credential for fair value related to business and intangibles will roll out in spring 2016, and the new credential for financial instruments will launch in fall 2016. A draft of the mandatory performance framework will be issued for exposure in early 2016. The AICPA, ASA, and RICS will issue this new credential under a common framework, but the individual will be bound by the issuing group's professional and ethics standards. It is unclear whether the new credential will be a new set of letters or some special mark added to a person's existing BV credential, such as an asterisk or other symbol.

Cost of capital. There were a number of sessions on cost of capital, a topic that has evolved into a very complex area with a voluminous amount of published material. Naturally, it triggers a great deal of discussion and debate. Interestingly, one of the keynote speakers, Professor Aswath Damodaran (New York University Stern School of Business), feels that too much time is spent on figuring out a discount rate and too little time is spent on developing cash flows. True, the "D" in DCF is important, but most mistakes occur in forecasting the "CF," he says. Plus, Damodaran argues that most experts misunderstand what the cost of capital measures and they consistently make fundamental errors in how the inputs are estimated. This is understandable, given how complex it has become, possibly by design. One well-known leading valuation expert commented: "It took me seven years to understand it."

Here are some comments and remarks from a number of the sessions on cost of capital:

- The build-up method and modified CAPM are still valid methods for developing cost of capital; one speakers says, "We do both all the time";
- A poll of session attendees reveals that the build-up method with Duff & Phelps data is the method most used;
- Most valuation experts don't use modified CAPM for valuing smaller private companies; however, they don't automatically avoid it because some industries will have smaller public companies;
- One well-known expert with a lot of court experience says that he never goes into court with a Greek letter (meaning beta) because the judge's eyes glaze over;
- Try using the implied private company pricing line (IPCPL) as a sanity check alongside other methods; this is a newly developed tool that uses data from *Pratt's Stats*, and, although it's not ready for court, "it's of interest" and "may have some merit," speakers say;
- The annual Pepperdine report on private capital markets is "very interesting"—a survey of business appraisers, brokers, banks, private equity groups, business owners, and investors

that have benchmarked the current climate and projected outlook for lending, investing, and acquiring capital; however, no actual transaction data are in the report;

- For the equity risk premium, most appraisers use the ex post approach (historical information); Damodaran and Dr. Ashok Abbott (West Virginia University) use the ex ante approach. A show of hands reveals that most experts use the Duff & Phelps handbook for the ERP;[1] and

- The "component detail method" is "great fodder" for cross-examination; it implies precision when precision doesn't exist.

Personal injury damages. A session on personal injury/wrongful death damages calculations, an area of increasing interest to valuation experts, attracted a big crowd. Holly Sharp and Michele Avery (both with LaPorte CPAs & Business Advisors) was the presenter. A few tips:

- Ask for tax return transcripts from the IRS when determining the lost earnings base—don't simply rely on return copies you're given;

- If subject was earning cash compensation, don't include it—courts say it's too speculative;

- Lost retirement benefits (other than Social Security) should be included, such as 401(k) plans (including the lost employer match) and defined benefit plans (becoming less prevalent, though);

- As for Social Security, courts in many jurisdictions don't allow it because it's too speculative; if using it, the government's website has a formula for figuring benefits (don't offset it with survivor benefits in certain jurisdictions—check with the attorney);

- The issue of projected medical costs is due to big changes under the ACA; consult with the attorneys as to how to approach it (e.g., use billed cost? out-of-pocket costs? charged costs?);

- Realize that work-life tables are not age-related nor based on calendar years, e.g., a 30 year-old with 30 more years of work life does not mean work until age 60—it means years in the work force;

- The attorney may say to project out earnings until full retirement age—that's OK to do as an alternative scenario;

- Tax affecting projected earnings is an issue—some jurisdictions say you must do it;

- Selecting the discount rate for future losses is simple—courts say use the best and safest investment, e.g., for 30 years of losses, use the 30-year U.S. Treasury rate; and

1 *Annual Valuation Handbook: Cost of Capital,* Duff & Phelps; available from BVR (www.bvresources.com).

- The fee for a damages calculation plus the report is typically $1,500 to $2,500 on average, say the speakers for their area; this is for a basic wage-earner report, but it can hit $5,000 if more complex (e.g., lots of fringes, multiple compensation sources, etc.).

The speakers also report that the courts have not yet addressed the issue of damages in the context of the ACA's mandate on insurance. In the past, a defendant could not benefit because of the plaintiff's insurance picture. That is, the defendant doesn't pay less damages because the plaintiff had good insurance. Now, with the ACA's requirement that all must have insurance, it's not clear yet what will happen to that argument.

Regression analysis for lost profits. Statistics, particularly regression analysis, can "perhaps" be used to do the "but for" forecast for calculating lost profits, say Michael Crain (Financial Valuation Group) and G. William Kennedy (Berkeley Research Group LLC). They did a double session on this, and they are contributing a chapter on this in a forthcoming book, *Calculation of Lost Profits Damages: Theory and Practice,* to be published by Valuation Products and Services (VPS).

Regression analysis may be used for identifying relationships between key business drivers in order to quantify lost profits damages. The "before" data (prior to the damage incident) is used to forecast it out to be able to state, for example, "there's a 95% degree of certainty that here's what the profits would have been but for the damages." However, there are many complications and pitfalls when using this and other statistical methods. Attack points in the analysis will be over the violation of OLS assumptions. You'll need to detect and correct heteroscedasticity, serial correlation, and multicollinearity, which may render your model unreliable. One attendee asked: "Does Excel do the assumption testing?" No, say the speakers, but you can purchase a third-party add-on to do it.

The use of statistical methods to quantify lost profits is an emerging and interesting topic that deserves further investigation.

Judge Laro speaks. A panel discussion on valuation in tax featured Judge David Laro of the U.S. Tax Court. He gave the following advice and views (his views, not the views of the court):

- The final chapter has yet to be written about tax affecting pass-through entities; the existing opinions that say no tax affecting are TC memo opinions and not binding on other judges;

- Take a second look at *Mandelbaum* (his case) as guidance for doing a DLOM; he's bothered by restricted stock and pre-IPO studies because they're "old";

- Consult the attorney about whether you can consider subsequent events in your valuation analysis; some circuits allow it;

- Failure to comply with USPAP does not disqualify you as an expert; and

- Communication between the valuation expert and the attorney is all discoverable, so be aware that anything can show up in court.

This session—which included another U.S. Tax Court judge, an attorney, and a law professor—had a great amount of interesting material. For more details see the separate article elsewhere in this issue.

IP litigation. There's been an uptick in patent litigation in 2015, after a downturn in 2014, according to a panel on IP litigation that included damages experts Glenn S. Newman (Baker Tilly Virchow Krause LLP), who served as moderator, Jeffrey M. Buchakjian, Joseph W. Lesovitz (both with EisnerAmper LLP), and an intellectual property lawyer, Steve G. Schortgen (K&L Gates). They offered other valuable observations.

Experts are divided over the continued importance of *Georgia-Pacific*. Some worry that a failure to discuss the factors in a reasonable royalty analysis spells exclusion of their testimony. Others say it's become less important over time. What's clear is that experts only have to discuss the factors relevant to their case. Of course, experts must know the legal principles, but, most importantly, they must tie the law to the facts of the case. Time and again, courts find the link is missing and discredit a damages analysis.

The entire market value rule (EMVR), which comes into play in a lost profits and reasonable royalty calculation, is an exception to the rule that an expert must apportion damages according to the value the patented feature contributes to a product that also contains nonpatented features. EMVR allows basing damages on the entire value of a product only if "the patent-related feature is the basis for customer demand." Courts interpreting EMVR have created confusion as to damages proof. Plaintiffs' experts don't know how deep to go in their analysis to show "customer demand." The calculation gets increasingly more complicated because high-tech devices contain so many components beside the patented feature. Better to ask yourself: What value does the protected feature add to what component of the accused device?

The panel cautions valuation experts to select the royalty base carefully to reflect only the value the patented feature adds to the infringing product. Do not count on being able to adjust an improperly high royalty base by lowering the royalty rate.

Courts generally frown on the use of rules of thumb, including the Nash bargaining solution, in part because experts don't explain a particular rule's applicability to the facts of the case (see above). Courts also tend to be skeptical about the use of surveys to support damages claims because of the potential for biased questions.

Finally, clients today are scrupulous about litigation costs, the lawyer on the panel says. Therefore, it's tempting for the attorney on the case to rein in costs whenever possible. But limiting an expert to a tight budget may be penny-wise and pound-foolish. The last thing the attorney wants is to hear the expert testify he or she would have done a more thorough damages calculation but for budget constraints.

Healthcare valuation. There have been a number of notable recent whistleblower cases in which the government sued hospitals, challenging the fair market value of medical practice acquisitions. The thrust of these cases is the measurement of the fair market value of physician compensation. In his session devoted to "fraud" in healthcare, Mark O. Dietrich explained that the current use of physician compensation surveys to establish fair market value is based on several false premises.

Dietrich has developed a new valuation method for determining the FMV of physician compensation designed to be more accurate than the current use of faulty survey data, which are "guaranteed to indicate a loss." The existence of losses on doctors and acquired practices is a key element of all the recent cases where the government says there's fraud and violations of the Stark Law. The government has been winning these cases and reaping hundreds of millions of dollars in fines against hospitals. This new valuation method—if given the chance—could alter the course of these cases, which are sure to continue.

For more details on this and other healthcare valuation issues, see the article elsewhere in this issue on the AICPA's Healthcare Conference, which took place right after the FVS event.

Marijuana firms. Over a third (39%) of experts would not accept a marijuana business for a valuation engagement, according to a poll taken at a session on valuation issues in this industry conducted by Hilary Bricken (Harris Moure PLLC) and James Marty (Bridge West CPAs and Consultants LLC). A larger percentage (55%) say they would not accept a marijuana business client for tax and accounting work.

The industry's relatively short history, high level of risk, high volatility, and complex, quickly evolving regulatory structure are unique considerations that can make valuations tricky. As a result, purchases and sales are "all over the map," Bricken says. Especially problematic is the determination of the subject company's proper risk-adjusted discount rate and the valuation multiple to apply to cash flow and EBITDA, notes Marty. Regardless, the legal marijuana business is an "an accountant's dream." Marty started up a separate accounting firm devoted to this industry and quickly grew the practice to over 100 clients.[2]

2 Jim Marty is a contributor to a BVR special report, *Marijuana Dispensaries: A Budding Industry Brings Opportunities and Challenges for Business Appraisers.*

NY's Unfair Application of Shareholder-Level Marketability Discounts

By Gilbert E. Matthews, CFA, and Michelle Patterson, JD, Ph.D.

The statutory standard of value in dissenting shareholder cases in most states is "fair value."[1] New York and 47 other states use the "fair value" standard in appraisals. As a valuation measure, most states interpret fair value as the shareholder's pro rata portion of the value of a company's equity with no discount for lack of marketability or for minority interest. "Fair value" does allow adjustments for marketability at the entity level, and most states permit it. However, in contrast to the other states, New York applies marketability discounts at the shareholder level in fair value determinations, which harms dissenters by transferring value to continuing shareholders.

A core principle of fair value is equal treatment of all shareholders in the same entity. Because a discount for lack of marketability (DLOM) at the *entity level* impacts all shareholders equally, it does not impact a dissenter's right to receive a pro rata share of equity value.[2] Thus, most states permit fair value adjustments to entity value to reflect company-specific factors that may affect the liquidity of the company as a whole. In contrast, when New York applies a marketability discount at the *shareholder level,* the minority shareholder is penalized because he or she receives treatment unequal to other shareholders in the same entity. Most states, recognizing fair value principles, reject discounting a departing shareholder's interest in favor of controlling or continuing shareholders. In some states, an occasional court may, under specific circumstances, impose such a discount, and a few states are nonaligned because they have not formally addressed the issue. New York's position, however, is unique: It stands alone in that it *favors* (and some lower courts believe *requires*) the imposition of a marketability discount on dissenting shareholders in fair value determinations.

When a DLOM—a liquidity discount—is placed on the entire company, it is often reflected by adjustments to valuation inputs. For example, the court may accept lower multiples in a guideline

1 Ohio and California use "fair market value" in statutory appraisals. California does, however, use "fair value" in oppression cases. Wisconsin generally uses "fair value" but uses "market value" for certain related party transactions approved by a two-thirds vote of unaffiliated shareholders.

2 Discounts at the entity level are applied to the equity value of the corporation or partnership as a whole. Discounts at the shareholder level are applied to specific equity interests.

company analysis or an increase in the discount rate in a discounted cash flow (DCF) calculation. A New York appellate decision (affirmed by the Court of Appeals[3]) noted the use of a higher discount rate to adjust for marketability and said:

> The expert testified that lack of marketability was a risk factor that he included in his determination of the appropriate capitalization rate. He ... insisted that lack of marketability was a consideration in his formulation of the capitalization rates used in his valuation method.[4]

MBCA and ALI reject DLOMs at the shareholder level. The Model Business Corporation Act (MBCA), created by the American Bar Association and which has been adopted as the basis for corporate law in most states, explicitly opposes discounts at the shareholder level in determining fair value. The MBCA's 1999 definition says:

> "Fair value" means the value of the corporation's *shares* determined ... *without discounting for lack of marketability* or minority status except, if appropriate, for [certain] amendments to the articles. [emphasis added][5]

Sixteen states have adopted the MBCA fair value definition forbidding the application of a DLOM to a dissenter's shares, and courts in many other states have been influenced by the MBCA's definition.

The American Law Institute (ALI) also rejects the application of discounts in fair value determination and explains its reasoning:

> [T]he fair value of shares should be the value of the eligible holder's proportionate interest in the corporation, without any discount for minority status or, absent extraordinary circumstances, lack of marketability.[6]

It proceeds to define "extraordinary circumstances" narrowly:

> Such [extraordinary] circumstances require more than the absence of a trading market in the shares; rather, the court should apply this exception only when it finds that the dissenting shareholder has held out in order to exploit the transaction ... so as to *divert value to itself that could not be made available proportionately to other shareholders.* [emphasis added][7]

Most states reject DLOMs at the shareholder level. Although 30 years ago, many states permitted DLOMs at the shareholder level, most now reject them in both appraisal and oppression cases,

---

3 New York's highest court is the Court of Appeals, the intermediate level is the Appellate Division, and the trial court is called the Supreme Court.

4 *Matter of Seagroatt Floral Co.*, 167 A.D.2d 586, 588 (N.Y. App. 1990); *aff'd*, 583 N.E.2d 287 (N.Y. 1991).

5 MBCA § 13.01(4) (1999).

6 ALI, Principles of Corporate Governance: Analysis and Recommendations §7.22(a) (1994).

7 Id., Comment e. The Colorado Court of Appeals interpreted this exception when it rejected a DLOM:

> [I]t is apparent that, in [the ALI's] view, the marketability discount should be limited to those situations in which the likely appraised "fair value" of a dissenter's share would exceed the value of a remaining share in the corporation.

Pueblo Bancorp. v. Lindoe, Inc., 37 P.3d 492, 498 (Colo. App. 2001); *aff'd*, 63 P.3d 353 (Colo. 2003) ("*Pueblo Bancorp*").

either by statute[8] or by state supreme or appellate court decisions.[9] Thirty-five states reject marketability discounts outright as contrary to the concept that fair value is the shareholder's proportional share of a company's equity value. Sixteen of these follow the MBCA and bar discounts by statute, while the other 19 have barred DLOMs under case law. Seven states allow an exception to permit an "equitable" application of a DLOM to a minority interest on the basis of minority opportunism, aggrandizement, or self-dealing.[10] Five states have not yet addressed the DLOM issue.[11] New York is the only state that generally applies marketability discounts in fair value cases to specific shareholder interests.

New York's long-standing position on DLOMs. The New York courts rely on a long history of judicial interpretation of §623(h)(4) of its corporate code, which makes no reference to discounts in its text. It reads:

> In fixing the fair value of the shares, the court shall consider the nature of the transaction giving rise to the shareholder's right to receive payment for shares and its effects on the corporation and its shareholders, the concepts and methods then customary in the relevant securities and financial markets for determining fair value of shares of a corporation engaging in a similar transaction under comparable circumstances and all other relevant factors.

In the 1995 *Beway* case, New York's highest court, the Court of Appeals, confirmed that, although minority discounts are unacceptable in New York fair value cases, a DLOM at the shareholder level is not only permitted but must be considered in all fair value cases.[12] *Beway* cited the 1985 *Blake* appellate decision, which said:

> [A] minority interest in closely held corporate stock should not be discounted solely because it is a minority interest.
>
> However, a discount recognizing the lack of marketability of the shares of Blake Agency, Inc., is appropriate. ... A discount for lack of marketability is properly factored into the equation because the shares of a closely held corporation cannot be readily sold on a public market. Such a discount bears no relation to the fact that the petitioner's shares in the corporation represent a minority interest.[13]

Although the Court of Appeals in *Beway* clearly understood the error of applying minority discounts in dissenter fair value determinations, it misconstrued the conceptual basis for the marketability discount. The court, in affirming *Blake*, failed to see that a marketability discount on minority or departing shares was essentially another form of minority discount. *Beway* and *Blake* thus established the legal precedents for the application of marketability discounts at the shareholder level in New York fair value cases. The recent *Ferolito* decision (2014), which involved the AriZona beverage company,

8 E.g., Illinois (which had used DLOMs frequently), Louisiana, Nevada, and North Carolina.

9 E.g., *Blitch v. People's Bank*, 540 S.E. 2d 667 (Ga. App. 2000); *Wenzel v. Hopper & Galliher, P.C.*, 779 N.E.2d 30 (Ind. App. 2002); *Pueblo Bancorp.*; *Shawnee Telecom Resources, Inc. v. Brown*, 354 S.W.3d 542, 562 (Ky. 2011) ("*Shawnee*").

10 Connecticut, Florida, Michigan, Minnesota, Missouri, New Jersey (in oppression cases but not appraisals), and Wisconsin.

11 Alaska, Hawaii, New Hampshire, North Dakota, and Tennessee.

12 *Friedman v. Beway Realty Corp.*, 87 N.Y.2d 161, 166 (N.Y. 1995) (*Beway*).

13 *Matter of Blake v. Blake Agency*, 107 A.D.2d 139, 149 (N.Y. App. 1985) (*Blake*).

spoke to the continued strength of these precedents when it noted that "nearly all courts in New York that have considered the question whether to apply a DLOM have answered in the affirmative."[14]

Most New York cases use a 25% DLOM. Most New York courts have followed *Beway* in accepting a DLOM at the shareholder level. Because some New York decisions are not clear as to whether the marketability discount was applied at the entity level or at the shareholder level, we will address only those cases where the DLOM has explicitly been at the shareholder level.[15] Numerous New York decisions have applied a 25% DLOM at the shareholder level, commonly without explanation. *Ferolito* said, "The Court concludes that a 25% DLOM is appropriate, which even one commentator opposed to application of a DLOM in most if not all cases admits 'hover[s] in the range' of the DLOM typically applied."[16]

Some courts, however, have weighed the specific facts of their case and, in light of New York's preference for minority DLOMs, have decided to apply the discount but to utilize a lower rate, such as 15%[17] or 10%.[18]

Some New York judges appear to understand the criticisms. A few New York trial courts have declined to apply marketability discounts. *In re Walt's Submarine Sandwiches,* a 1990 decision denying a DLOM, was upheld on appeal.[19] In 2000, *Academe Paving* rejected the 30%-to-35% discount for lack of marketability proposed by respondents' expert and ruled that no discount should be applied.[20] More recently, the Appellate Division, while reversing some parts of a 2012 decision, did not reverse the trial court's ruling in *Chiu* that no DLOM should be applied.[21] In the 2012 *Zulkofske* decision, the judge awarded a 50% shareholder half of the value of the corporation, rejecting the respondent's argument that there should be a 30% liquidity discount at the shareholder level.[22]

Several other cases have explicitly applied a DLOM at the entity level while refusing to apply the marketability discount to minority shares.[23] In the *Seagroatt* case, a DLOM was applied to the com-

14 *Ferolito v. AriZona Beverages USA LLC,* 2014 N.Y. Misc. LEXIS 4709 (N.Y. Supr., Oct. 14, 2014) at *46.

15 "The DLOM is not designed to discount the value of the corporation ... but to reflect the lack of marketability of the shares of the corporation." *Application of Jamaica Acquisition, Inc.,* 2009 N.Y. Misc. LEXIS 2773 (Sept. 29, 2009) at *16.

16 *Ferolito* at *50-*51, quoting Peter Mahler, "The Marketability Discount in Fair Value Proceedings: An Emperor Without Clothes?" July 11, 2011, available at www.nybusinessdivorce.com/2011/07/articles/valuation-discounts/the-marketability-discount-in-fair-value-proceedings-an-emperor-without-clothes/ (Mahler, "Emperor Without Clothes?").

17 E.g., *Quill v. Cathedral Corp,* 215 A.D.2d 960 (N.Y. App. 1995) (15% for business retained, zero for business sold before trial); *Murphy v. U.S. Dredging Corp.,* 74 A.D.3d 815, 818 (N.Y. App. 2010).

18 E.g., *Matter of Joy Wholesale Sundries,* 125 A.D.2d 310 (N.Y. App. 1986); *Matter of Raskin v Walter Karl Inc., Inc.,* 129 A.D.2d 642, 644 (N.Y. App. 1987); *Matter of Carolina Gardens, Inc.,* 238 A.D.2d 189 (N.Y. App. 1997); *Cortes v 3A N. Park Ave. Rest. Corp.,* 2014 N.Y. Misc. LEXIS 4693 (N.Y. Sup., Oct. 28, 2014).

19 *In re Walt's Submarine Sandwiches, Inc.,* 173 A.D.2d 980 (N.Y. App. 1991).

20 *O'Brien v. Academe Paving, Inc.,* No. 99-2594 (Sup. Ct. Broome Co., N.Y., Sept. 25, 2000), slip op. at pp. 12-14.

21 *Man Choi Chiu v. Chiu,* 125 A.D.3d 824 (N.Y. App. 2015). *See* Mahler, "Appellate Court Upholds 0% Marketability Discount in LLC Fair Value Case" (2015), available at www.nybusinessdivorce.com/2015/02/articles/llcs/appellate-court-upholds-0-marketability-discount-in-llc-fair-value-case/.

22 *Application of Zulkofske,* 2012 N.Y. Misc. LEXIS 3088 (N.Y. Supr., June 28, 2012) at *7, *11.

23 *E.g., Matter of Dissolution of Bambu Sales, Inc.,* 672 N.Y.S.2d 613, 617 (N.Y. Sup. 1997); *Hall v. King,* 265 A.D.2d 244, 245 (N.Y. App. 1999); *Matter of Vetco, Inc.,* 292 A.D.2d 391, 392 (N.Y. App. 2002); *Matter of Beattie v. PlanData Systems Corp.,* 2009 N.Y. Misc. LEXIS 3971 (N.Y. Sup. Jan. 15, 2009) at *7. Each of these decisions used a 25% DLOM.

pany as a whole but not to the dissenter's shares. In *Adelstein,* the court applied a 5% DLOM to the valuation at the entity level, but no discount was applied to the plaintiff's one-third interest.[24] In addition, the Appellate Division sustained the trial court's rejection of a DLOM in its 2012 *Giaimo* decision,[25] awarding the minority shareholder a pro rata portion of equity value net of entity-level selling costs.

***Zelouf* describes a DLOM as tantamount to a minority discount.** In the recent *Zelouf* case, the judge considered the facts of the case and rejected the respondents' argument for a DLOM on the petitioner's shares. She opined that "application of a DLOM here would be tantamount to the imposition of a minority discount."[26]

Zelouf International Corp. is a private company whose shareholders are all members of the founder's family. When the court appraised the 25% interest owned by Nahal Zelouf, the widow of a shareholder, it decided to apply a zero DLOM. It commented that, because "the soul of the business [is] personal relationships, it seems unlikely that the company would or could ever actually be sold" and concluded that "the rationale for a applying a DLOM breaks down when one considers that any liquidity risk ... is more theoretical than real."[27]

The company, without Nahal and her family, will always remain under the control of the Zelouf family. This makes the company's illiquidity irrelevant, mooting the concern for which a DLOM accounts. If the other Zelouf family members will never pay a price for the company's theoretical illiquidity, then there is nothing "fair" about artificially depressing Nahal's recovery due to a hypothetical sale that will never occur. To impose such a cost on Nahal is tantamount to levying the very sort of minority penalty that New York law prohibits. Liquidity risk only manifests into real cost in an actual sale and should not be imposed here where there will never be a sale and, thus, no real cost.[28]

When the case was reargued before the same judge, the respondents asserted that New York required a DLOM. The judge, however, reiterated her rejection of a DLOM in the case and explained:

> In effect, applying a DLOM here would be the economic equivalent of imposing a minority discount—that is, Nahal realizing less for her shares because she is being forced to sell while Danny gets to realize their full value by staying in control. It is well settled that minority discounts are not permitted under New York law. Indeed, it is the tension between the application of a DLOM, which is done in most cases *but is not legally required* [emphasis added], and the practical effect of a DLOM here serving as a minority discount, repugnant to New York courts and never allowed, that drives the court's ruling.[29]

24 *Adelstein v. Finest Food Distrib. Co., N.Y., Inc.,* 2011 N.Y. Misc. LEXIS 5956 (N.Y. Sup., Nov. 3, 2011) at *12, *21; *aff'd,* 116 A.D.3d 850 (N.Y. App. 2014).

25 *Giaimo v. Vitale,* 101 A.D.3d 523, 525 (N.Y. App. 2012).

26 *Zelouf Intl. Corp. v. Zelouf,* 999 N.Y.S.2d 731, 735,737 (N.Y. Sup. 2014) (*Zelouf* II).

27 *Zelouf Intl. Corp. v. Zelouf,* 2014 N.Y. Misc. LEXIS 4341 (N.Y. Sup., Oct. 6, 2014) (*Zelouf* I) at *22.

28 *Zelouf* I at *23.

29 *Zelouf* II at 735.

The *Zelouf* court discussed several cases in other states that had rejected DLOMs. It acknowledged that it would be incompatible with New York precedent to decide that a DLOM was "legally inappropriate"[30] but commented:

> The court begins by noting that no New York appellate court has ever held that a DLOM must be applied to a fair value appraisal of a closely held company. On the contrary, the Court of Appeals has held that "there is no single formula for mechanical application." Indeed, the Court of Appeals recognizes that "[v]aluing a closely held corporation is not an exact science" because such corporations "by their nature contradict the concept of a market value." As set forth in the Decision, since Danny [Zelouf] is not likely to give up control of the Company, Nahal should not recover less due to possible illiquidity costs in the event of a sale that is not likely to occur.[31]

Thus the court not only ruled against a shareholder-level DLOM, but it also rejected an entity-level discount.

Long-standing critiques of New York's position. Barry Wertheimer's authoritative 1998 article on appraisal criticized the New York Court of Appeals' reasoning in continuing to permit the use of DLOMs:

> A "lack of marketability" discount is another form of minority discount in that, if permitted, the dissenting shareholder receives less than a proportionate share of the value of the corporation as a whole. It therefore should be rejected for the same reasons minority discounts should be rejected.... The New York position is particularly difficult to understand. [*Beway*] provides a powerful rejection of minority discounts for all of the correct reasons, yet permits a lack of marketability discount.... *Hopefully, the New York Court of Appeals will rethink this issue when it next arises.* [emphasis added][32]

Unfortunately, the Court of Appeals has not addressed the DLOM issue since *Beway*, other than ruling in 2001 that the DLOMs for two minority shareholders should be equal.[33]

The *Beway* court, in affirming *Blake*, failed to see that although a DLOM may be appropriate at the entity level (with some form of valuation adjustment), permitting a DLOM to be utilized at the shareholder level would be "further discount[ing] ... a minority shareholder's stock ... because of its minority status."[34] They failed to recognize that the result would be to deprive minority shareholders of their proportionate interest in the corporation as a going concern. Also, it would result in shares of the same class being treated unequally. Instead of treating both the minority and controlling interests equally so as not to penalize the minority—which *Beway* agrees is the intention of fair value adjudications—*Beway's* affirmation of a DLOM on minority shareholders in

30 *Zelouf* II at 737.

31 *Zelouf* II at 735, quoting *Seagroatt*. The court commented, "[E]ven if this court were required to apply a DLOM, the evidence submitted at trial does not justify a DLOM of 25% or higher. If it had applied a DLOM, the court would have applied a 10% DLOM." (*Zelouf* II at 737, fn. 5).

32 Barry M. Wertheimer, "The Shareholders' Appraisal Remedy and How Courts Determine Fair Value," 47 *Duke L. J.* 613, 641 (1998) at fn. 136.

33 *Matter of Penepent Corp.*, 750 N.E.2d 47, 49 (N.Y. App. 2001).

34 *Penepent* at 51.

fact resulted in an unfair transfer of value from the diminished minority interest to the continuing shareholders.[35]

Peter Mahler, a New York lawyer specializing in shareholder disputes who has published many articles in his blog discussing New York's practice, has pointed out in a 2011 article:

> In many states outside New York, ... DLOM and DLOC [discount for lack of control] both have been banished from fair value determinations based on a policy decision that to apply either works an injustice against oppressed or dissenting minority shareholders and represents a windfall to the controlling shareholders.[36]

Mahler's article questioned whether "*Blake, Beway* and their progeny [were] predicated on flawed, internally inconsistent assumptions that effectively compute fair value at the non-marketable *minority interest* level of value rather than proportionate interest in the company's going concern value at a control level." [emphasis in original][37] In support of his position, Mahler discussed Chris Mercer's opposition to DLOMs in New York, both in his writings and in his trial testimony in the *Giaimo*[38] case. Mercer, a well-known and authoritative valuation expert and author, also testified for a 0% DLOM in the *Ferolito* and *Chiu* cases.

In his recent thoughtful discussion of the *Ferolito* case, Mercer argued, "The case law logic supporting a minority discount of 0% in selected New York cases would also, if applied consistently, support a 0% marketability discount for an attractive, salable company like AriZona."[39]

Kenneth Weinstein, a New York lawyer, and Joel Rakower, a New York valuation practitioner, summarize the problem. They wrote, "The application of a discount for lack of marketability to a dissenting minority ownership's position runs afoul of the very statute meant to protect the oppressed shareholder."[40] They conclude:

> The *Beway* Court's holding *in Blake*, recognizing and supporting the existence of marketability discounts, ... tends to run afoul of current financial theory. Thus, application of a marketability discount cannot normally be justified ... and is merely a secondary discount to a minority position, disallowed by legislative intent and interpretation.[41]

Conclusion. With respect to marketability discounts, New York continues to be out of line with the MBCA and the ALI, as well as the widely accepted view in other states and in legal literature.

35 *See, e.g.,* Z. Christopher Mercer, "New York's Largest Corporate Dissolution Case—AriZona Iced Tea" (2015), p. 17, available at mercercapital.com/article/new-yorks-largest-corporate-dissolution-case-arizona-iced-tea/ (Mercer, "New York's Largest Corporate Dissolution Case"); Gilbert E. Matthews and Michelle Patterson, "How the Court Undervalued the Plaintiffs' Equity in *Ferolito v. AriZona Beverages*—Part II: *Ferolito* and the Application of DLOM in New York Fair Value Cases," *Financial Valuation and Litigation Expert*, April/May 2015.

36 Mahler, "Emperor Without Clothes?"

37 Id.

38 *Giaimo v. Vitale*, 2011 N.Y. Misc. LEXIS 1866 (N.Y. Sup. 2011) at *11-*12.

39 Mercer, "New York's Largest Corporate Dissolution Case," p. 17.

40 Kenneth J. Weinstein and Joel Rakower, "Marketability Discount and Dissenting Minority Ownership," *N.Y.L.J.*, July 8, 2011, pp. 7-9, at p. 7.

41 Weinstein and Rakower, p. 9.

There is broad consensus that DLOMs should seldom, if ever, be permitted in appraisal or oppression cases. New York's approach is based on outdated valuation approaches that were utilized three decades ago or more. Weinstein and Rakower wrote:

> Determination of "fair value" under [N.Y.] BCL [§] 1118 has become the subject of increased litigation, and grows more complicated with the increasing sophistication of the appraisal industry, effectively in its infancy in the 1980s, when defining case law pertaining to same evolved. Despite proliferation of new studies and greater understanding of financial theory within the appraisal community, a court's ability to accept and recognize these changes is limited at best, if principal reliance is upon cases determined in the 1980s.[42]

Wertheimer recommended in 1998 that the Court of Appeals reconsider New York's view of DLOMs. Since then, several other states that had previously accepted DLOMs at the shareholder level have changed their positions, leaving New York as the outlier.[43]

Mercer's article on *Ferolito* commented that because of the post-trial settlement of the case, "the Court of Appeals in New York will miss an excellent opportunity to reexamine the marketability discount issue."[44] A reexamination of New York's obsolete position on DLOMs is long overdue.

Gilbert E. Matthews, *CFA, is senior managing director and chairman of the board of Sutter Securities Inc. (San Francisco) and can be reached at* gil@suttersf.com. *He has more than 50 years of experience in investment banking and has spoken and written extensively on fairness opinions, corporate valuations, and litigation relating to valuations.*

Michelle Patterson, *J.D., Ph.D., is a consultant to Sutter Securities. She was an associate in litigation with Gibson, Dunn & Crutcher and has taught at Brandeis, UC Santa Barbara, Mills College, and San Francisco State University.*

42 Id.

43 A 2009 decision noted that "*Blake* is considered the seminal New York case in upholding the use of DLOM." *Application of Jamaica Acquisition, Inc.*, 901 N.Y.S.2d 907, 2009 N.Y. Misc. LEXIS 2773 (N.Y. Supr. 2009) at *17. The sole case cited in *Blake* supporting a DLOM was *Ford v. Courier-Journal Job Printing Co.*, 639 S.W.2d 553 (Ky. App. 1982). In 2011, the Kentucky Supreme Court's *Shawnee* decision overruled that 1982 appellate decision.

44 Z. Christopher Mercer, "New York's Largest Corporate Dissolution Case," p. 17.

When to Consult a Compensation Expert During a Valuation

Determining reasonable compensation can be a challenging issue in a business valuation—and it can represent the largest earnings adjustment. Sometimes, the valuation analyst can establish reasonable compensation. Other times, you need to call in a compensation consultant. Mark Higgins, ASA, president of Higgins, Marcus & Lovett, a business valuation and litigation consulting firm based in Los Angeles, lays out the thought process he uses in deciding when to call in extra help.

How much is at stake? The first issue to look at is the potential impact of a compensation adjustment. "You need to determine if an adjustment will have a material impact on the value conclusion or the outcome of the particular matter," says Higgins. An adjustment will have a different impact depending on the size of the subject company and the magnitude of the potential adjustment. For example, if you make a $50,000 adjustment to the earnings of Company A (see exhibit), the earnings and value double. If you make the same adjustment to Company B, earnings increase by only 5%. In the second example, "[s]uddenly, the significance of the compensation adjustment gets lost in the noise of all of the other inputs and judgments you'll have to make in the case," he says.

What is the context? The context of the valuation work can influence the importance of the compensation issue and your decision to bring in an expert. Is the engagement in the context of litigation or a matter that may lead to litigation, such as a divorce? Does it involve a large taxable estate that is likely to attract an audit—or maybe there's an IRS audit already underway? Reasonable compensation may already be considered a key issue in the case, so that may warrant an outside expert.

Uniqueness factor. A key decision factor might be the uniqueness of the business or the unique skills of the owner/executive. "The more unique the business or the more unique the individual's role, the more likely you are going to find that published industry data will be less helpful to you," he says. In such a case, it's more likely that you will need to get a focused expert involved in establishing reasonable compensation.

Has the cost been coordinated with the client? This needs to be considered as you are scoping out the potential compensation issues on the front end of an engagement. Try to get as much data as possible to identify whether you think the engagement will have compensation issues that would indicate the need to get an outside expert involved. "Talk to the client and their advisors about that on the front end, so you can clearly establish if a compensation analysis is going to be a part of the project and then get a reasonable budget in place for that."

How much analysis is needed? Once the above questions are addressed, the decision to bring in a compensation expert will depend on the level of review and analysis that will be required. Higgins views this as four levels:

1. Internal review by appraiser;
2. Internal analysis and adjustment by appraiser;
3. High-level report from outside data source; and
4. Focused analysis by retained outside expert.

The first level is an internal review conducted by the appraiser that results in no explicit analysis or adjustment contained in the report. The valuator has concluded that compensation is clearly reasonable and no adjustment is warranted. There are two ways to handle this in the report, according to Higgins. One way is to simply be silent about it and include nothing. The other way is to state in the report that you have considered the level of compensation and have concluded that no adjustment is warranted. However, you are simply stating this opinion without including any data that you may have relied upon in reaching that conclusion.

Impact on Value of a Compensation Adjustment	
Company A	
Revenue	1,000,000
Exec Compensation	200,000
Other Expenses	750,000
Net Income	50,000
Compensation Adjustment	50,000
Impact on Value	100%
Company B	
Revenue	20,000,000
Exec Compensation	300,000
Other Expenses	18,700,000
Net Income	1,000,000
Compensation Adjustment	50,000
Impact on Value	5%
(Source: Higgins, Marcus & Lovett Inc. Pipis Consulting Inc.)	

The second level is also an internal analysis conducted by the appraiser, but there is an adjustment being made to compensation. This would involve the use of data already routinely in the possession of the appraiser, such as industry ratio publications or published compensation surveys. In the report, there should be a narrative description of the analysis conducted, the data relied upon, and the calculation of the adjustment.

The third level is where the outside expert may first come into the picture, perhaps informally to point you in the direction of appropriate subscription or fee-based compensation databases. "This level of investigation is typically economical enough that you would not need client approval," he says. "The cost would be absorbed within the typical out-of-pocket expenses that you can pass through." The input that you are providing when using these databases is typically limited to: (1) the position/title that you are assessing; (2) the industry; (3) the size of the company; and (4) its location. At a relatively modest cost, this approach can add credibility to your opinions and report. While not comparable to a full study by a compensation expert, this level of analysis brings an objective review of market data that is tailored to the specific characteristics of the subject business and the position in that business.

As an example, Higgins refers to a printout from a popular compensation data source. The example provides data on base salaries and incentive compensation for the CEO position in metals wholesalers in Southern California with $15 million in revenue. The information presents total compensation as a 25th percentile of $235,000, a mean of $352,000, and a 75th percentile of $495,000. It gives you a range of data that may help you to determine the level of reasonable compensation and whether an adjustment is warranted. "This is fast and inexpensive data, but it provides a range of comparative data rather than a single estimate of what appropriate compensation is for the individual's role that you are analyzing," says Higgins. This may be enough for your particular engagement. But it may not be enough, particularly if the potential earnings adjustment is relatively large or the circumstances are particularly unique or contentious.

The fourth level is when you find that the information that you get with limited and inexpensive research is insufficient. This is often the case if reasonable compensation is a central issue in the engagement. That's when you need to bring in a compensation expert to do a focused analysis of the individuals involved. "Of course, in virtually every case, that requires some separate client approval and typically a separate engagement letter," he says.

For more information: Higgins, along with Mark Lipis (Lipis Consulting), recently conducted a webinar, Determining Reasonable Compensation: How to Deal With the Data. Mark Lipis is a compensation consultant who has served as an expert witness involving reasonable compensation. To access a recording of the webinar, go to www.bvresources.com/dlc.

Simplified MUM for Determining Personal Goodwill

By Thomas Gillmore, CPA, CFE, CVA

Editor's note: The author is a valuation expert and forensic accountant in Florida who uses the multiattribute utility model (MUM), but not in its full form. He uses a streamlined version that has been accepted in court and that may reduce the exposure to severe cross-examination. In this article, he gives some background on the relevant legal landscape in Florida and describes his version of MUM based on a recent engagement.

In a number of different contexts, the valuation analyst may need to evaluate the fair market value of a business interest for the purpose of equitable distribution or shareholder settlement. This evaluation may include breaking out goodwill into its two components: personal and enterprise goodwill.

In Florida, the state Supreme Court's instruction in *Thompson v. Thompson* to the business valuation analyst was to seek out and evaluate the various goodwill attributes of a subject business and determine (or opine on) whether each attribute is in the nature of personal or enterprise goodwill:

> We therefore answer the certified question with a qualified affirmative: If a law practice has monetary value over and above its tangible assets and cases in progress which is separate and distinct from the presence and reputation of the individual attorney, then a court should consider the goodwill accumulated during the marriage as a marital asset. *The determination of the existence and value of goodwill is a question of fact and should be made on a case-by-case basis with the assistance of expert testimony.*[1] (emphasis added)

In *Schmidt v. Schmidt,* the 4th District Court of Appeal reversed the trial court's valuation of the subject business and remanded for the trial court to ascertain the personal goodwill remaining in the marital portion of the business, which can be determined by analyzing what the value of the business would be if the business owner did not sign a covenant not to compete (CNC).[2]

The trial court in *Schmidt,* when pressing the valuation expert to quantify the business value with and without a CNC, would have benefited by the expert's reference to *Thompson v. Commissioner,* T.C. Memo 1996-468 (1996), where the Tax Court lists 11 factors to determine the economic reality of

1 *Thompson v. Thompson,* 576 So. 2d 267, 270 (Fla. 1991).

2 *Schmidt v. Schmidt,* 120 So. 3d 31, 33-34 (Fla. 4th DCA 2013).

a CNC including the following: grantor's business expertise, grantor's intent to compete, grantor's economic resources, potential damage to the grantee, grantor's network, duration and geographic scope of the CNC (limited to seven years in Florida), enforceability by state law, age and health of grantor, payment terms, payment duration, and fairness of negotiations. Having considered these factors, the analyst could opine on the likelihood and degree of moral turpitude of the seller and weight of countervailing actions from the buyer.

The analyst's failures in *Schmidt* are evidenced when the court assigns extraordinarily undifferentiated significance to a CNC as if the personal goodwill of a plastic surgeon is similar or even identical to the personal goodwill of an insurance broker or plumber, by stating, "Because the $2,520,562 value requires execution of a non-compete agreement, it is clear that such valuation still includes a personal goodwill component."

The *Schmidt* court appears frustrated by the lack of guidance the expert witness offered then rightly remands the case.

Parity unraveled. It is critical to distinguish between: (1) the requirement or existence of a CNC; and (2) the quantification of personal goodwill.

In *Held v. Held*, the 4th District Court of Appeal found that, "for purposes of separating enterprise goodwill from professional goodwill, there was no distinction between a non-compete agreement and a non-piracy agreement."[3] Similarly, there is no distinction between a CNC between the seller and buyer of: a physician's practice, an insurance broker's book of business, a plumber's geographic operating area, or a Kentucky Fried Chicken location. A plumber with over 100 employees who signs a CNC cannot to himself then be allocated 100% of the enterprise value (as personal goodwill).

Regardless of the type of enterprise, the strength of a noncompete assures the buyer that he or she will acquire and hold unimpeded access to the enterprise cash flows being purchased in good faith. The CNC, although critical to the buyer's future success, does not in any way accurately portray the full spectrum of personal goodwill monetary value, which varies greatly between a plastic surgeon and the skilled plumber as shown in this example. For example, I will actually "wear" the plastic surgeon's goodwill on my face or body part; however, I will not wear the goodwill of a plumber on my face or body. Thus, in my opinion, the plumber's personal goodwill attributes, when considered altogether, rise to a value considerably less than the attributes associated with a plastic surgeon's personal goodwill attributes.

Two important points emerge from this:

1. The analyst should take care to not mistakenly focus on the existence of a CNC as if that is the sole determinant of whether personal or enterprise goodwill exists, or the analyst may fail to even consider the CNC as part of the valuation; and

3 *Held v. Held*, 912 So. 2d 637 (Fla 4th DCA 2005).

2. Even experienced valuation analysts frequently and mistakenly focus on the personalized name of a subject entity as if that is the sole determinant of whether personal or enterprise goodwill exists.

The errant analyst may go further with these mistaken thought processes by stripping away *all* enterprise value from cash flows and then assign a "fair market value" to the business consisting of some cumulative variant of cash, other assets, plus accounts receivable minus debts. Some analysts will also mistakenly toss in a 10%-to-20% liquidity/marketability discount against the cumulative resultant value, thus "quantifying" a supposed difficulty in liquidating cash, which of course is a spurious notion. All or any part of this misguided process will expose the errant analyst to tough cross-examination on the stand or at deposition.

The analyst should be familiar with the AICPA reference material[4] in which Robert Cimasi, the author, states, "[The appraiser shall] identify, distinguish, disaggregate, and allocate the relevant portion of existing goodwill to either professional or personal goodwill." Mr. Cimasi goes on to say, "[P]rofessional or personal goodwill results from the charisma, education, knowledge, skill, board certification, and reputation of a specific physician practitioner."

The expert may want to be familiar with the work of David Wood, CPA, ABV, CVA, who developed the multiattribute utility model (MUM),[5] which "recently received ratification" by the court in *Lieberman v. Lieberman.*[6] Many of the goodwill attributes both Cimasi and Wood identified are listed here:

- Ability, skills, and judgement;
- Age and health of the owner;
- Closeness of contact with clients or patients;
- Comparative personal success in the subject industry;
- Marketing and branding associated with the individual;
- Marketing and branding associated with the subject entity;
- Personal in-bound referrals;
- Personal reputation;
- Personal staff;

4 Robert James Cimasi, MGA, ASA, AVA, CM&AA, *The Advisor's Guide to Healthcare – Consulting With Professional Practices,* AICPA.

5 For example, see "'MUM's the Word': A Formal Method to Allocate Blue Sky Value in Divorce," *Business Valuation Update,* March 2007.

6 *Lieberman v. Lieberman,* Case No. FD-2008-956 (Tulsa, Okla.), Judge Funderburk presiding. The expert witness in *Lieberman* relied on the Illinois case *In re Marriage of Alexander* (2006 Ill. App. Lexis 836) to defend against a *Daubert*-like challenge.

- Work habits;
- Ancillary services;
- Assets in use;
- Business name;
- Business reputation;
- Repeating revenue streams;
- Systems and organizational structure;
- Workforce in place;
- Location of business; and
- Barriers to entry.

Simplified MUM. Having reviewed *Daubert* challenges, Florida courts admonished expert analysts who failed to defend their positions with scientific methods and who relied on subjectivity and speculation.[7] Thinking proactively, an analyst may be able to preempt or prevent the *Daubert* challenge altogether by removing entirely the subjective "utility" of each goodwill attribute, e.g., those Wood and Cimasi identified, thus relying solely on the existence of an attribute in binary terms. In other words, the attribute either exists or it does not, which alleviates debate on "just how important is each specific attribute's utility."

True, whether the attribute rises to the level of "making a difference" may be discussed, but this threshold is far less extenuous than the burden of convincing someone that the utility of an attribute rises to a specific level of, for example, "4" on a scale of 1 to 10, an obvious response being "why does the utility of that attribute not rise to a level of 7 or 8, and how does your subjective choice of a level 4 differ from a subjective choice of 7 on your conclusion of fair market?" The experienced counsel or trier of fact could have a field day with a utility level of 3, or 2, or 8, finally proclaiming that your method is too subjective to be reliable.

Case example. The following workflow analysis is an excerpt of the author's valuation report narrative developed in contemplation of relevant Wood/Cimasi goodwill attributes on a startup clinical laboratory (clinic) offering on-site collections. To generate a level playing field/fairness in the analysis, the author uses an equal row count of personal attributes to enterprise attributes as shown in Exhibit 1.

7 See *The Value Examiner*, May/June, 2015 referencing these cases: *Hedges v. Klaus Doup, PA*, *Perez v. Bell South Telecommunications, Inc.*, and *Giamo v. Florida Autosport, Inc.*

Exhibit 1. Simplified MUM Schedule

Enterprise Attributes	Add to Scale (0, 1)	Personal Attributes	Add to Scale (0, 1)
Assemblage of assets	0	Ability, skills, judgment	0
Barriers to entry	0	Age and health of practitioner	0
Business location (GEO preferred)	0	Closeness of contact	0
Business locations (multiple)	1	Comparative professional success	0
Business name	0	Marketing and branding	1
Business reputation	0	Personal referrals	1
Patient base	1	Personal reputation for judgment, skills, knowledge	1
Repeating revenue stream	0	Personal staff	0
Systems and organization	1	Personalized business name	0
Workforce in place	1	Work habits	0
Total enterprise attributes	4	Total personal attributes	3
Enterprise: 57% Personal: 43% Total: 100%			

The subject business is 3.5 years old as of August 2015, owned by three shareholders with a 40/40/20 voting rights, and employs 1,099 contractors who perform the phlebotomy work on-site at nursing homes, residences, and the like. Gross revenues are approaching $800,000 and are scheduled to reach $2 million in the coming years.

A discussion of each attribute related to enterprise and personal goodwill follows. Those attributes marked with a "-" do not exist, so value allocation is not appropriate. Attributes marked with a "+" are those that do exist, so value allocation is appropriate.

Enterprise goodwill. A total of 10 attributes were considered related to enterprise goodwill in the case.

1. *Assemblage of assets* (-). The analyst considered the following premises of value when contemplating whether the assemblage of assets can be differentiated from the mere fact that certain assets exist.

Premise 1: Value in continued use as part of a going-concern business enterprise;

Premise 2: Value in place, but not in current use in the production of income;

Premise 3: Value in exchange, as part of an orderly disposition;

Premise 4: Value in exchange as part of a voluntary liquidation; and

Premise 5: Value in exchange, as part of an involuntary liquidation.

The assemblage of assets of the clinic is in place and is used to generate revenue as described in Premise 1. However, the assets are easily replicated, i.e., tables, chairs. Therefore, *value allocation is not appropriate.*

2. *Barriers to entry* (-). Depending on the specialty and location, it can be difficult and or may take considerable time for new entrants in this industry to establish a referral base and other relationships with other physicians, hospitals, and the local community.

However, the clinic, only 3.5 years in existence, has developed insufficient differentiating factors such as size, presence, long-term relationships, and cost differentiators in this industry and in its geographic operating area to create difficulties (or barriers) to competitors entering the marketplace. Therefore, *value allocation is not appropriate.*

3. *Business location* (-). A business that is easily accessible and ideally located may have more enterprise goodwill. Convenience and recognition may be important factors to a particular business. Alternatively, a hard-to-find location may indicate that consumers are returning for other reasons, such as personal attention, price, or customer support.

The clinic's physical location is not relevant to the homebound patient base, which comprises approximately 98% of revenues. Therefore, *value allocation is not appropriate.*

4. *Business locations—multiple (+).* If a business has multiple locations, it may mean that goodwill is more associated with the enterprise and less with the individual, i.e., an individual cannot be in all locations at the same time and consumers' satisfaction is more likely to be associated with factors other than personal.

The clinic's revenues are derived from on-site visitation to the patient's location. Therefore, *value allocation is appropriate.*

5. *Business name* (-). If the name of the business carries the name of the individual, a greater level of personal goodwill may be present, which may be more difficult to transfer.

The clinic has roughly 3.5 years of activity to assess, meaning it is still in the development phase and is not yet well established in the marketplace. The clinic is still reliant on the personal efforts of the owners to gain new business, i.e., the business name itself is not recognized well enough to entice new business activity. Therefore, *value allocation is not appropriate.*

6. *Business reputation* (-). Business reputation is frequently a factor in determining the attraction of new business and a consumer's likelihood to return for future business. If the reputation is more directly related to the business in general, as opposed to the individual providing the service, then the goodwill is more likely enterprise goodwill.

The clinic has roughly 3.5 years of activity to assess, meaning it is still in the development phase. The clinic is still reliant on the personal efforts of the owners to gain new business, i.e., the business name itself is not recognized well enough to entice new business activity. Therefore, *value allocation is not appropriate.*

7. *Patient base* (+). Where a practice has a large, established patient base that requires recurring care, a greater business value is likely to exist. The patient base can be examined by reviewing the following data:

- Direct contracting customer lists;
- HMO enrollment lists; and
- Patient lists.

The clinic patients do not as a rule require recurring care similar to that which brought them in first place. The clinic interacts with a transient patient base. However, those patients are likely to need annual or more frequent recurring care. Therefore, *value allocation is appropriate.*

8. *Repeating revenue stream* (-). The nature of some businesses is that the consumer finds a need for the service on a regular or even scheduled basis. Vaccinations of pets, routine dental cleanings, and annual physicals are examples of specific services that generate repeat business. A consumer relationship that generates revenues through the year or years, although not necessarily on a scheduled basis, could also generate repeat business.

Although the clinic interacts with a transient patient base, there is a continued relationship with the nursing homes. However, the clinic is still reliant on the personal efforts of the owners to retain current business, i.e., the business itself is not yet well established in the marketplace. Therefore, *value allocation is not appropriate.*

9. *Systems and organization* (+). The systems and organization attribute refers to all of the decisions management makes that create the structure of the business. It is broader than computer systems and encompasses policies, manuals, procedures, methodology, and forms and documents developed to support the operations.

Systems and organization attributes include but are not limited to:

- Treatment plan/care mapping;
- Procedures and manuals;
- Laboratory notebooks;
- Computer and software integration; and
- Maintenance and support relationships.

The transferrable value of necessary systems and organization exists with the clinic, with the fulcrum being an established patient base. Therefore, *value allocation is appropriate.*

10. *Workforce in place* (+). Based on the economic principle of substitution, i.e., the cost to create a substitute workforce. The following aspects of workforce cost should be considered:

- Replacement cost new—the cost to create the ideal workforce;
- Reproduction cost new—the cost to re-create the actual current workforce;
- Four cost components:
    - Direct costs—recruitment/relocation fees;
    - Indirect costs—interview/hiring/training time;
    - Developer's profit—return on direct and indirect costs;
    - Entrepreneurial incentive—lost income during the workforce assemblage period (i.e., an opportunity cost).

The clinic has a workforce in place that would be transferrable to a buyer. Therefore, *value allocation is appropriate.*

Personal goodwill. Professional (or personal) goodwill is not transferrable. Even with long transition periods of introduction for a new acquiring physician owner, the charisma, skills, reputation, and personal attributes of the seller cannot, by definition, be transferred. Personal goodwill is that which would make a doctor's patients follow him or her even if he or she changed location, staff, and phone number.

A total of 10 attributes were considered related to personal goodwill in the case.

1. *Ability, skills, and knowledge* (-). There are insufficient factors in this category to distinguish the owners from their competition in this industry. Therefore, *value allocation is not appropriate.*

2. *Age and health* (-). There is likely less personal goodwill in the case of an older or unhealthy practitioner, since expected future earnings are not expected to continue for a long period of time. The age and health of the individual is considered when weighing the likely longevity of the continuing goodwill. This could be particularly important if the individual's health is poor and/or the age is advanced.

There are insufficient differentiating factors in this category to distinguish the owners from their competition in this industry. Therefore, *value allocation is not appropriate.*

3. *Closeness of contact* (-). When the individual performs a service or offers a product, the closeness of contact generally increases the likelihood that the goodwill generated will be personal. For example, an anesthesiologist may have little or no personal contact, while an ophthalmologist can have substantial personal contact.

The clinic is still reliant on the personal efforts of the owners to gain new business, i.e., the business name itself is not recognized well enough to entice new business activity. However, the owners themselves do not generally perform the on-site work.

There are insufficient factors in this category to distinguish the owners from their competition in this industry. Therefore, *value allocation is not appropriate.*

4. *Comparative professional success* (-). There are insufficient factors in this category to distinguish the owners from their competition in this industry. Therefore, *value allocation is not appropriate.*

5. *Marketing and branding* (+). Name recognition for the individual, as opposed to the product or service that is established through marketing efforts to tie the individual's name to the business, may indicate a higher level of personal goodwill. This might involve the individual's direct involvement in media advertisements and other marketing efforts.

The clinic is still reliant on the personal efforts of the owners to gain new business, i.e., the business name itself is not recognized well enough to entice new business activity. Therefore, *value allocation is appropriate.*

6. *Personal referrals* (+). A personal in-bound referral is defined as a referral from an outside source, such as a patient or a referring physician that has been made to a *particular individual.* The person making the referral is aware of some trait that makes the individual an appropriate referral. Typically, referrals are made because an individual has a specialized skill, talent, or reputation and has inspired confidence in the referral source.

The clinic is still reliant on the personal efforts of the owners to gain new business, i.e., the business name itself is not recognized well enough to entice new business activity. Therefore, *value allocation is appropriate.*

7. *Personal reputation* (+). If the reputation of the individual whose personal goodwill is being assessed is positive and strong, then the likelihood increases that the resulting goodwill is personal. For example, the best plastic surgeons are internationally renowned in their field and can attract patients from around the world. On a smaller scale, word-of-mouth recommendations from satisfied clients go a long way toward drawing new business.

The clinic is still reliant on the personal efforts of the owners to gain new business, i.e., the business name itself is not recognized well enough to entice new business activity. Therefore, *value allocation is appropriate.*

8. *Personal staff* (-). Personal staff employees work for the business because of the personal reputation or knowledge of the individual whose personal goodwill is being assessed. If employees of a business chose to work for the business specifically to have the opportunity of working with and learning from this individual, they are more inclined to leave if this individual is no longer associated with the business.

There are insufficient factors in this category to distinguish the owners from their competition in this industry. Therefore, *value allocation is not appropriate.*

Exhibit 2. Valuation of 40% Interest Net of Personal Goodwill		
Gross profits valuation		$393,038
Net sales valuation		$496,153
Indicated value by market		$444,595
Market comparable valuation		$444,595
Value of personal goodwill	43%	$191,176
Value of enterprise goodwill	57%	$253,419
Enterprise goodwill		$253,419
Minority discount 10%		-$25,342
Brokers' fee 10%		-$25,342
Prepare for sale (mgmt. time)		-$15,000
Liabilities		TBD
Recapture of funds		-$24,000
Transferrable value		$163,736
40% allocation to shareholder		**$65,494**

9. *Personalized business name* (-). If the name of the business carries the name of the individual, a greater level of personal goodwill may be present. The goodwill may be more difficult to transfer, particularly if a name change is anticipated. Therefore, *value allocation is not appropriate.*

10. *Work habits* (-). When comparing two business owners working the same amount of hours in the same specialty, for example, the physician that works more efficiently is likely to have more personal goodwill. Increased time spent per patient is also likely an indicator of personal goodwill.

There are insufficient factors in this category to distinguish the owners from their competition in this industry. Therefore, *value allocation is not appropriate.*

Conclusion of value. The clinic sought to buy out or push out a 40% shareholder who had allegedly misappropriated funds, which caused EBITDA to be unreliable. In summary, the author compared the clinic's gross profits and net sales to known market transaction of similar companies, applied the goodwill ratio, and then added in discounts and premiums for a conclusion of value (see Exhibit 2).

In family law and commercial litigation settings, the author has found many physician-owners, business owners, spouses, attorneys, and judges to be accepting of the goodwill ratio approach, commonly referred to by the author as a simplified MUM. I have used this method for firms with enterprise gross revenues ranging up to $2.5 million.

***Tom Gillmore,** CPA, CFE, CVA, is a self-employed forensic accountant serving the Central Florida legal community, business owners, and individuals from his office in Winter Park, Fla., since January 2009. He can be reached at www .FloridaValuationCPA.com.*

Seven Tips on Cost of Capital From the AICPA FVS Conference

There was great interest in the several sessions on cost of capital at the AICPA Forensic and Valuation Services Conference 2015 in Las Vegas. Speakers acknowledged that this is a topic that has evolved into a very complex area with a voluminous amount of published material that can be "daunting." Here are some of the notable pieces of advice and insights that can kick your cost of capital estimates up a notch—and make them more defensible.

1. Don't avoid MCAPM. The build-up method and modified CAPM (MCAPM) continue to be valid methods for developing cost of capital. Some speakers say they frequently—or always—use both methods on an engagement. The most prevalent method, based on a poll of conference attendees, is the build-up method using Duff & Phelps data. The data are contained in the *Valuation Handbook - Guide to Cost of Capital,*[1] which one speaker called a "great contribution to the valuation profession." Most valuation experts don't use MCAPM for valuing smaller private companies. However, the method should not be automatically avoided because some industries will contain smaller public companies.

2. Consider normalizing the risk-free rate. Speakers and attendees alike say they typically use a spot rate for the risk-free rate. Historically, valuators utilized the 10-year or 20-year U.S. government bond yield as of the valuation date. However, in the past few years, utilizing a normalized rate that more likely reflects sustainable risk-free returns has been considered.

Beginning in late 2008, the government, together with the Federal Reserve Bank, implemented actions that effectively lowered interest rates in an attempt to stimulate the economy, similar to that done during and after World War II. Because of this, the use of a normalized risk-free rate may be appropriate. The Duff & Phelps handbook has calculated a recommended normalized risk-free rate to be used as of various time periods. The book also discusses the logic and methodology of calculating the normalized risk-free rate. If a normalized risk-free rate is used, a normalized ERP should also be used.

3. Revisit ERP approach. For the equity risk premium, most appraisers use the ex post approach (historical information). A show of hands during one conference session revealed that most experts

1 The 2016 edition is available from BVR (www.bvresources.com).

use the Duff & Phelps handbook for the ERP. New to the historical ERP data in the book is the addition of an adjustment for "WWII interest rate bias." As mentioned above, the Fed lowered interest rates between 1942 and 1951. Some analysts believe this time period should be excluded from the historical return data because the rates were manipulated.

Speakers also point out that some renowned experts such as Aswath Damodaran (New York University) and Ashok Abbott (West Virginia University) consider the ex ante approach. Damodaran's website offers "very rich" data on ERP that he published each year (typically in March) under the title "Equity Risk Premiums (ERP): Determinants, Estimation and Implications." This material is free and is available on his blog.[2]

4. Beware of the 'component detail method' for CSR. When developing the company specific risk (CSR) to be added into whichever method you're using, some analysts consider separate components of CSR and then place a risk factor (positive or negative) on each detailed component. For example, "management depth" may be +0.05%, "supplier pricing leverage" may be -0.10%, and so on, all adding up to an overall CSR percentage. There could be several dozen factors to the analysis. The trouble is, this is "great fodder" for cross-examination, speakers say. It implies precision when precision doesn't exist. No empirical evidence can back up the assignment of specific risk percentages for each individual component.

A variation of this method uses simple observation of a component and does not specify a percentage for each. This method merely indicates whether each component increases, decreases, or has a neutral effect on the CSR. But this can be attacked pretty much the same as the percentage method, speakers say. What may be easier to defend is a simple list of the CSR components—without individual percentages or any indication of effect. Of course, no matter what method is used, if the analysis is done properly, you come to the same overall conclusion.

5. Try IPCPL. The implied private company pricing line (IPCPL) is a newly developed tool that uses data from *Pratt's Stats* and is designed to better estimate the cost of capital for a small private company. It's not ready for court, but speakers urged attendees to take a look at it. One suggestion: use it as a sanity check alongside other methods. The IPCPL developers would welcome comments.[3]

6. Look at Pepperdine studies. The annual Pepperdine report on private capital markets is "very interesting," speakers say. It is a survey of business appraisers, brokers, banks, private equity groups, business owners, and investors that benchmarks the current climate and projected outlook for lending, investing, and acquiring capital. They point out, however, that no actual transaction data are in the report.[4]

2 aswathdamodaran.blogspot.com.

3 For more information, there is an IPCPL section in BVR's Cost of Capital Resource Center (www.bvresources.com).

4 Pepperdine University Private Capital Markets Project (bschool.pepperdine.edu/).

7. Use a strong visual aid. Trying to explain how you developed a cost of capital figure can be quite a challenge. Some speakers say they use a chart in both their reports and in court that lays out the broad range of rates of return in the market. At the low end of the spectrum (less than 1%) are U.S. Treasury rates (e.g., 30-day bills, five-year notes) and at the high end are rates required by venture capitalists (up to 60%). The analyst can then more easily explain where the subject company falls within this spectrum based on its relative risk. This kind of exercise should be done anyway, as a way of stepping back to see whether a conclusion of value makes overall sense.

Of course, you can't simply point to a chart such as this and expect to be finished. It's a good sanity check, but you still must provide objective support for the discount rate you choose. For example, in one case, the analyst explained that he chose a discount rate of 35%, which he called "conservative," saying that venture capitalists generally require a 30%-to-60% return. However, the analyst "did not provide any objective support, either at trial or in his expert report, for selecting a discount rate in this range."[5]

5 *Morton v. Comm.*, T.C. Memo 1997-166. Available at *BVLaw* (www.bvlibrary.com/bvlaw).

DLOMs in N.Y. Statutory Fair Value Cases—A Follow-Up to Matthews

By William C. Quackenbush, MBA, ASA, MCBA, BCA, ABAR

As an appraiser, I have had the opportunity to prepare many valuations for New York statutory fair value cases, and I have testified in some of them. I'd like to weigh in on the topic of discounts for lack of marketability (or DLOMs) as a follow up to the recent *BVWire* posting (see sidebar) and the article by Gil Matthews on the topic.[1]

In the 1985 *Blake v Blake Agency, Inc.* decision,[2] the court stated that the statute designed to "afford a minority shareholder the right to bring a proceeding to dissolve the corporation and to distribute its assets among the shareholders ... was enacted for the protection of minority shareholders, and the corporation should therefore not receive a windfall in the form of a discount because it elected to purchase the minority interest pursuant to [statute]. Thus, a minority interest in closely held corporate stock should not be discounted solely because it is a minority interest." Unfortunately, while in the same decision the court rightly rejected a discount for lack of control, it allowed a discount for lack of marketability without much discussion.

Gil picks up the story in 1995's *Beway* case and brings the reader up-to-date on the issue, rightly describing a nearly schizophrenic trail of decisions over the past 20 years regarding DLOMs. I would argue that in this case schizophrenia is contagious, with the court infected by BV testimony with the same symptoms. It is no wonder that Peter Mahler wishes that the BV community would speak with one clear voice on the issue. Indeed, in this instance, poor case law is often the result of bad or weak appraisal work creating poorly informed triers of fact.

I would suggest the following "valuation-speak" in appraising a minority interest under statutory fair value:

> To determine the value of a non-control interest not burdened with the penalties, if any, regarding the subject interest's lack of control vis-à-vis a control level value, including any illiquidity or lack

1 Gil Matthews (Sutter Securities), "NY's Unfair Application of Shareholder-Level Marketability Discounts," *Business Valuation Update*, January 2016. The article is reprinted on page 21.

2 107 A.D.2nd 139 (1985).

> of marketability attributable to the lack of control nature of the oppressed interest—essentially the value of a pro-rata share of the whole.

Yet it seems that the New York courts have had trouble accomplishing this goal, in good part because of the valuation work presented to them in expert testimony. I suggest that two issues are in play here that stir up the pot.

First, there continues to be some debate in the BV profession as to whether some DLOM is ever appropriate at the enterprise level. Is a 100% equity ownership interest in a privately held company less liquid than the underlying publicly traded stock data upon which the value is calculated in an income approach (discount rates) or market approach (market multiples) that must be addressed through some sort of valuation adjustment?

Both Shannon Pratt and John Stockdale consider such a possibility in their writings. Pratt[3] states:

> The rationale for a marketability discount on controlling interests of closely held companies is that the controlling owner of a closely held business who wishes to liquidate his or her controlling ownership interest generally faces the following transactional considerations:

- Uncertain time horizon to complete the offering or sale;
- Cost to prepare for and execute the offering or sale;
- Risk concerning the eventual sale price;
- Noncash and deferred transaction proceeds; and
- Inability to hypothecate (that is, the inability to borrow against the estimated value of the stock).

> All of the above considerations make the sale of the controlling interest in a closely held business risk difficult and costly. For this reason, many valuators believe that such controlling interests suffer from some measure of lack of marketability that needs to be represented via a discount adjustment to value.

And both Pratt[4] and Stockdale[5] make reference to studies focused on control-level interests such as the following:

> *DiMattia* (2008):[6] examined public stock prices for companies that have received tender offers and the merger arbitrage that resulted from these offers. Merger arbitrage is the practice of betting on the outcome of a merger. Since some mergers are never completed, and some chance that the final price could change from the offer price during the time between the announcement

3 Shannon P. Pratt, "Business Valuation: Discounts and Premiums," 2nd Edition, 2009, p 201.

4 Ibid., pp. 207-210.

5 John Stockdale Sr., *BVR's Guide to Discounts for Lack of Marketability, Volume 1, 5th ed.* p 317ff.

6 Ronald D. DiMattia, *"Controlling Interests – Discount for Lack of Marketability: The Empirical Evidence,"* CPA Expert, Summer 2008, 1-6.

> and closing, trading prices for these company stocks tend to be less than the tender offer price. Referenced in the DiMattia article were two studies: (1) Branch and Yang (2006),[7] who found an average spread between price and tender offer one day after the announcement; and (2) Micah Officer (2007),[8] who found an average spread between price and tender offer of failed mergers one day after the announcement.
>
> *Loeplin, Sarin and Shapiro study:*[9] Published in 2000, the Loeplin study of matched pairs of private- and public-company acquisitions between 1984 and 1998 (excluding financial companies and regulated utilities) showed that there was evidence of a discount for private companies over public companies.
>
> *DeFranco, Gavious, Jin, and Richardson study:*[10] In 2007, these researchers compared private-company acquisitions from *Pratts Stats* to acquired public companies from Compustat. They performed a multifactor regression analysis to control for differences in size, sales, growth, R&D expenditures, and EBITDA (the latter two as a percentage of revenues) and found a discount when comparing EBITDA multiples.

However, Chris Mercer (Mercer Capital) takes the position that no discount for lack of marketability is appropriate:

> The argument against the existence of a marketability discount applicable to controlling interests is simple. If enterprise value is determined based on expected cash flows, expected growth of those cash flows, and the riskiness of those cash flows, then what additional factors would support a discount from this value?[11]

Further, the New York statute itself suggests an "either-or" option: liquidate and pay out pro rata or buy out pro rata. Are adjustments concerning marketability or liquidity necessary to create equivalency in the two value options? It is ostensibly this thinking that has led jurists in New York to rule that real estate holding companies are less likely to require DLOM adjustments than operating companies, attributing illiquidity to more ethereal "goodwill."[12]

My first point here is not to state my unambiguous opinion on the topic in this short space, but rather to suggest that the valuation profession needs to continue its discussion regarding control-level DLOMs.

Second, and I have opposition reports in my files to document this, some business appraisers and accountants who have provided expert witness work for statutory fair value in New York have

7 Ben Branch and Taewon Yang, "Merger Deal Structures and Investment Strategies," *The Journal of Alternative Investments*, Winter 2006.

8 Micah Officer, "Are Performance Based Arbitrage Effects Detectable? Evidence From Merger Arbitrage," working paper, Feb. 20, 2007, 15.

9 John Koeplin, Atulya Sarin, and Alan C. Shapiro, "The Private Company Discount," *Bank of America Journal of Applied Corporate Finance* 12, no. 4 (Winter 2000): 94-101.

10 Gus DeFranco, Ilanit Gavious, Justine Yiquing Jin, and Gordon D. Richardson, "The Existence and Explanations for the Private Company Discount," working paper, April 27, 2007.

11 Z. Christopher Mercer and Travis W. Harms, *Business Valuation: An Integrated Theory*, 2nd ed., Wiley 2008, p. 95.

12 See *Vick v. Albert*, 47 AD3d 482 [1st Dept 2008], *CINQUE v. Largo Enters. of Suffolk County, Inc.*, 212 AD 2d 608 - N.Y.S.2d 735, and *Giaimo (EGA Associates, Inc.)*, 2011 NY Slip Op 50714(U) (Sup Ct NY County Apr. 25, 2011). Note, however, that in *Murphy (United States Dredging Corp.)*, 74 AD3d 815, 2010 NY Slip Op 04794 (2d Dept June 1, 2010), the court essentially overruled 15 years of precedent and expanded DLOM's applicability beyond just goodwill. (These cases are available at *BVLaw* (www.bvlibrary.com/bvlaw).)

Call for Change in New York's DLOM Stance Gains Steam

New York's out-of-step position with respect to the discount for lack of marketability in fair value proceedings is a hotly debated issue—and it's getting even hotter. A "new note" in the debate was sounded in an article in the January issue of *Business Valuation Update*, according to a blog post, "The DLOM Debate Heats Up," by attorney Peter Mahler (Farrell Fritz) in the New York Business Divorce blog (www.nybusinessdivorce.com).

Stands alone. In the article "NY's Unfair Application of Shareholder-Level Marketability Discounts" (page 21), Gil Matthews (Sutter Securities) writes that New York "stands alone in that it *favors* (and some lower courts believe *requires*) the imposition of a marketability discount on dissenting shareholders in fair value determinations. There is broad consensus that DLOMs should seldom, if ever, be permitted in appraisal or oppression cases." Matthews points out that New York is out of line with both the Model Business Corporation Act (MBCA) and the American Law Institute (ALI) "as well as the widely accepted view in other states and in legal literature."

Mahler gives his perspective on the issue and says that it "would be nice if the business valuation community could speak with one, clear voice on the issue, which would then facilitate consideration by legislators or, should they defer to the courts, appellate judges, of any needed changes to New York's policy toward DLOM in fair value proceedings."

Stay tuned for more on this issue!

Note: See the *BVWire* for continuing coverage of this and all key business valuation topics. Go to www.bvresources.com and click on Free Ezines (registration required).

applied DLOMs based on their analysis of restricted stock studies and pre-IPO studies, both of which generate evidence for DLOMs *for noncontrol* interests. This issue is more problematic.

None of the studies referenced in these valuations provide any evidence for lack of marketability for control-level interests—the adjustment that might be appropriate in New York statutory fair value cases. Thus decisions made based on this evidence are flawed. Applying non-control-level DLOMs continues, in Blake's words, to fail to protect the minority interest.

These flawed reports typically derive DLOMs of 30% to 50% based solely on the evidence of discounts attributable to noncontrol, minority interests with no discussion or empirical evidence connecting the studies referenced to the subject at hand: the pro rata share of the whole. This misapplication of market evidence has been, and continues to be, unhelpful to triers of fact.

To help Peter Mahler (Farrell Fritz) with clarification (see sidebar), the BV profession needs to discuss more rigorously the issue of illiquidity and lack of marketability for control interests in privately held companies. Also, the profession may need to police itself more on the second, as well as help educate the legal community and the triers of fact on these issues.

***William C. Quackenbush,** MBA, ASA, MCBA, BCA, ABAR, is a director at Advent Valuation Advisors (Newburgh, N.Y.). He served as the chair of the ASA's Business Valuation Committee and writes and speaks regularly on business valuation issues.*

Complications With Event Studies in Securities Litigation

By Adrian M. Cowan, Ph.D., and Paul J. Seguin, Ph.D.

Editor's note: This is an excerpt from a chapter in the 4th edition of The Comprehensive Guide to Economic Damages, *edited by Nancy Fannon and Jonathan Dunitz. The entire chapter gives a primer on event studies, how they are used in securities litigation, robustness tests, complications, and more. The book, formerly titled* The Comprehensive Guide to Lost Profits and Other Commercial Damages, *is available from BVR (www.bvresources.com).*

In this section, a number of frequently encountered complications a researcher may face and how one can address them in a statistically robust fashion is addressed. Confounding events can be particularly problematic. In addition, other important considerations for the expert are the subjective nature of event studies and the type of security under investigation.

The *event window* is readdressed first. In Section 2 (earlier in the full chapter), it was assumed that: (i) the asset traded in a liquid and informationally efficient market; and (ii) there were no "confounding" firm-specific news events during the trading day. Under these assumptions, a single (close-to-close) trading day was used as the event window. However, as with the estimation window width, the width of the event window involves a trade-off. First, the window must be of a width sufficient to allow the news to be fully incorporated into the price of *f*. However, as this width increases, the amount of confounding news likewise increases. The first set of complications addresses alternative choices of event window widths.

Confounding events. As was discussed above, one key decision involves the choice of the *event window* and the inherent trade-off. As above, the event window should be sufficiently long to allow the asset price to fully reflect the at-issue information but sufficiently narrow to reduce the impact of confounding events.

As an example, before the opening of trading on December 5, it is announced that an analyst has initiated coverage of *f* with a "strong buy." However, the at-issue event occurred at 2 p.m. during the trading day when a strategic partner of *f* announces it has cancelled a contract with *f*. Had we used a one-day event window as we did in Example 1 above, the close-to-close (December 4-to-December

5) return would contain or reflect both pieces of information. Thus, if possible, we would select an event window that included the cancelled contract but would exclude the analyst upgrade.

In this example, two solutions are plausible. First, one can choose to use consecutive *opening* prices to compute an open-to-open return ($R_{f,t}$ is calculated using the opening prices of December 5 and December 6). As the coverage initiation should be incorporated in both these prices, *differences* in these prices will not reflect this confounding event.

Assume the researcher decides that the estimation period will contain 120 close-to-close (total, or with dividend) returns to both the firm, *f*, and the market index, *m*. Using these returns, a regression is run, and, after appropriate specification testing and remedial measures, the resulting estimates of α and β are -0.002% and 0.870, but the t-statistic associated with the estimate, "a", is insignificant.[1] Economically, this means that, if the index doesn't change over an interval and the return to *m* is zero, it is *expected* that the return to *f* will likewise equal zero.

Using the open-to-open return for both *f* and *m*, which are $R_{m,t} = 1.1\%$ and $R_{f,t} = -1.5\%$, the abnormal return is calculated as:

$$AR_{f,t} = R_{f,t} - \{a + bR_{m,t}\}$$

$$= R_{f,t} - \{0 + [0.87 \times 1.1]\}$$

$$= -1.50\% - \{0.957\%\} = -2.457\% \approx -2.5\%$$

As above, the researcher can induce that losses to shareholders due to the contract cancellation were roughly 2.5% of the preannouncement market cap.

An alternative approach for choosing an event window that focuses on the at-issue announcement involves using *intraday* returns. For example, assume the researcher concludes, perhaps based on an analysis of contemporaneous volume, that news of the cancelled contract was fully incorporated within one hour from the intraday announcement. So, by 3 p.m. on December 5, the price of *f* fully reflects or incorporates the news of the cancelled contract. Thus, to compute the one-hour abnormal return, the researcher would continue to use estimates of α and β from before (-0.002% and 0.870) even though they were estimated using daily and not hourly data. As above, the estimate associated with α is insignificant.[2] The only change would be to use the corresponding *one hour* returns to both *f* and the index. Assuming the researcher finds that the return to the S&P 500 and the firm for the 2 p.m.-to-3 p.m. hour are 0.320% and -1.645%, respectively,

1 As this parameter represents the expected return to holding the equity for one period assuming the index does not change, this parameter can be expected to be close to zero.

2 Should one find a significant estimate of α even after performing diagnostics, one would prorate this estimate if the event window interval differs from the estimation period interval. Although exact pro rationing can be nontrivial, it rarely has a meaningful impact on estimates of abnormal returns.

$$AR_{f,t} = R_{f,t} - \{a + bR_{m,t}\}$$

$$= -1.645 - \{0 + [0.870 \times 0.320\%]\}$$

$$= -1.645\% - \{0.278\%\} = -1.923\%.$$

Now the researcher will conclude that losses were roughly 1.9% of the preannouncement market cap.

Confounding factors are particularly problematic and require a significant attention to detail on the part of the expert. In *In re Omnicom Group, Inc. Securities Litigation,*[3] defendants successfully argued for summary judgment based in part on the failure of the plaintiffs' expert to disaggregate confounding factors. The court noted that identifying *some* confounding factors is not sufficient to determine the portion of loss attributable to the misrepresentations. The plaintiffs' expert in *In re Scientific Atlanta, Inc. Securities Litigation*[4] failed to identify a new characterization of previously known information as a confounding factor and segregate the loss associated with this factor as opposed to the alleged fraudulent act. The plaintiffs in this case alleged that defendants engaged in channel stuffing and improper accounting practices for the purposes of hiding declining product demand. The plaintiffs failed to prevail at summary judgment in part as the court held that insufficient evidence was presented that allowed for a disaggregation of the loss related to fraud-related and non-fraud-related causes. This again highlights the import of identifying all confounding factors in the development of the event study.

Trading halts/trading delays. In previous sections, it has been assumed that trading in the at-issue firm, *f*, is continuous around the announcement. A more likely scenario is that the announcement occurs during nontrading hours, i.e., "after hours" or "preopening," and leads to a *trading delay,* or the news is released during the trading day but causes *a trading halt.* Briefly, a trading *halt* is enacted when news impacting an exchange-listed equity cannot be delayed until the end of a trading session (a *regulatory* halt), or the news causes an imbalance between buy and sell orders so great that market makers cannot absorb it (a *nonregulatory* halt). In either case, trading is suspended in the impacted equity until news is disseminated and a new price can be established.[5] However, tempting as it may be to use the change in price during the halt or delay, it is an open question whether the resultant price is an equilibrium one or whether it fully captures the information. Indeed, expanding the window beyond the halt/delay in both directions can be justified. First, informational leakages may occur before the actual announcements. Second, as opening or reopening trading may be the primary objective of market makers, the post-announcement price may not fully reflect the news. Again, the researcher should define the event window based on examination of contemporaneous levels of volume.

3 *In re Omnicom Group, Inc. Securities Litigation,* 541 F. Supp. 2d 546 - Dist. Court, SD New York 2008.

4 *In re Scientific Atlanta, Inc. Securities Lit.,* 754 F. Supp. 2d 1339 - Dist. Court, ND Georgia 2010.

5 Lee, Ready, and Seguin.

Subjectivity of event studies. Experts need to make many subjective decisions in the development of an event study. A knowledgeable expert will limit the subjectivity in the study to a minimum.

In analyzing event studies at the class certification stage, courts have acknowledged that "many decision points in designing an event study require some subjectivity."[6]

Therefore, it is incumbent upon the expert to justify the decision process as reliable and reasoned and take the steps necessary to minimize the subjectivity.

For example, the very identification of news events and the determination of which events are material are subjective. When news should be reflected in the market price is a function of when that news becomes available. The more specific the guidelines for the definition of the event and the expected impact period of the event, the more likely any impact of the event will be captured. Thus, it is important not only to clearly define the event, but also to clearly establish the period during which the defined event will influence security prices.

The courts argue that subjectivity should be minimized and that the expert articulate objective criteria in the selection process. There are two key components to this objectivity. First, the criteria used by the expert needs to be clearly articulated. Second, the objective criteria must be articulated *before* the selection of the event dates. Unfortunately, despite the need for clarity, the identification of surprise events, i.e., events that would warrant a market movement in the price of the stock, is not always easy as a practical matter.

'Alternative' securities. As securities litigation based on fraud on the market has not been limited to highly traded equities listed on a national exchange, so too event studies have been applied to alternative securities including, but not limited to, corporate bonds, preferred stock, options, and other derivative securities. Three factors that the type of security under investigation influence are: (i) the evaluation of efficiency under the *Cammer* and *Krogman* factors; (ii) the interpretation of the market response to information; and (iii) the type of prices available to conduct the study. Here, we discuss three classes of securities where the above three factors may meaningfully vary, i.e., nonequities, illiquid assets, and newly listed equities.

Despite the presence of peer-reviewed, reliable academic research conducted using event studies for both bonds and preferred stocks, class action lawsuits that involve these financial instruments require care to show that they trade in efficient markets. Unfortunately for an expert, rulings have not been consistent in this area. For example, in *In re American Int'l Group, Inc. Sec. Litigation,*[7] the U.S. District Court found that there was insufficient support to find that AIG's bonds traded in an efficient market. The more recent trend appears to recognize differences in the stock and bond markets as evidenced by recent rulings that bonds do operate in efficient markets. In *In re Bennett*

6 *Diamond Foods,* citing *Countrywide,* 273 F.R.D. at 618.

7 *In re American Int'l Group, Inc. Sec. Litigation,* 265 F.R.D. 157 (S.D.N.Y. 2010).

v. Sprint Nextel Corp.,[8] *In re Winstar Communications Securities Litigation,*[9] and *In re HealthSouth Corp. Securities Litigation,*[10] courts found that the bonds did trade in efficient markets. The courts appear to apply the *Cammer* factors but in a nuanced framework to address differences between the markets between stocks and bonds as discussed in *Plumbers & Pipefitters v. Burns.*[11] In addition, additional factors are under consideration, e.g., reports of bond rating agencies.

Further, one cannot expect a news event to impact the various securities of a company in exactly the same way (Hartzmark, Schipani, and Seyhun, 2011), so it is incumbent on an expert to delineate any anticipated influence of news on the at-issue security. The importance of this was highlighted in the motion for class certification in *Bennett v. Sprint Nextel Corp.,* 298 F.R.D. 498 (D. Kan. 2014), which dealt with Sprint bonds and the alleged violation of the Securities Exchange Act of 1934 as the result of false and misleading statements. That court found that, "unless the statement disclosed information that altered Sprint's likelihood of default, the price of the Sprint Bonds would not be expected to change in any meaningful way." The failure of the defendant's expert to evaluate the substance of the information released on event days caused the court to find that the event study was unreliable.

Illiquidity also requires care by the expert, and more effort is required to show efficiency. The mere fact that a security trades on a national exchange is not conclusive evidence of efficiency: In *In re Federal Home Loan Mortgage Corp. (Freddie Mac) Securities Opinion Litigation,* No. 09-832, the court found that "Plaintiff has not shown by a preponderance of the credible evidence that the market for Freddie Mac's Series Z preferred shares was efficient during the class period." Thus, an expert would be required to evaluate the trading characteristics of that particular issue with respect to the *Cammer* factors to determine efficiency.

Illiquidity also increases the complexity of any analysis as prices that are both current and reliable may not be readily available. For example, because corporate bonds may not trade on a daily basis, historical price quotations for bonds will often be a so-called matrix price. Rather than a transaction price, a matrix price is derived from the prices of other bonds with similar characteristics, i.e., similar credit ratings, durations, options, etc. Given that it is not a transacted price, the courts generally require that matrix prices must be shown to be consistent with the general direction of movement in the price of the security. (See, for example, *Teamsters Local 445 Freight Div. Pension Fund v. Bombardier, Inc.,*[12] *Plumbers and Pipefitters, National Pension Fund v. Burns.*[13]) Thus, although transaction prices are always the preferred price to use in an event study, matrix prices may be used if shown to be consistent and reliable proxies.

8 *Bennett v. Sprint Nextel Corp.,* 298 F.R.D. 498 (D. Kan. 2014).

9 *In re Winstar Communications Securities Litigation,* 290 F.R.D. 437 (S.D.N.Y. 2013).

10 *In re HealthSouth Corp. Securities Litigation,* 261 F.R.D. 616 (N.D. Ala. 2009).

11 *Plumbers & Pipefitters, Nat'l Pension Fund v. Burns,* 967 F. Supp. 2d 1143 (N.D. Ohio 2013).

12 *Teamsters Local 445 Freight Div. Pension Fund v. Bombardier Inc.,* 546 F.3d 196 (2nd Cir. 2008).

13 *Plumbers & Pipefitters, National Pension Fund v. Burns,* 967 F. Supp. 2d 1143 (N.D. Ohio 2013).

Finally, there exists the situation where historical prices simply do not exist. Such is the case with newly issued equities (IPOs). In some of these cases, courts have recognized a "fraud *created* the market" theory.[14] Under this theory, reasonable investors, absent the fraud, would not have initially invested in the security. Although circuit courts disagree on the acceptance of this theory, it is an avenue in the support of the presumption of reliance in a new issues market.[15]

***Adrian M. Cowan, Ph.D.**, is co-founder of Analytic Focus LLC, a national statistics, finance, and economics consulting organization. She is a former associate professor in finance in the Business School at St. Mary's University. **Paul J. Seguin, Ph.D.**, is a senior affiliate consultant for Analytic Focus LLC.*

14 Michael Kaufman, "Fraud Created the Market," 63 *Ala. L. Rev.*, 2012, 275, 282.

15 See, for example, *Eckstein v. Balcor Film Investors*, 8 F.3d 1121, 1130 (7th Cir. 1993), and *Ross v. Bank South, N.A.*, 885 F.2d 723, 729 (11th Cir. 1989).

How to Avoid Tripping Up Over Subsequent Events

If you're not considering events that happen after a valuation date, you may be compromising your valuation report. Worse, if you're in court, your report could be tossed out. "Hold on," you might be saying. "Events subsequent to the valuation date should be excluded from a valuation analysis." Yes, that's generally true, but there are exceptions. The trick is knowing when you should—and should not—take this information into account.

At the recent AICPA FVS conference in Las Vegas, David Laro, a senior judge of the U.S. Tax Court made it a point to say that some courts have examined subsequent events that are relevant to the taxpayer's perceptions at that time. In some cases, subsequent events were reasonably foreseeable as of the valuation date, so they are relevant to the valuation.

Two categories. There are two categories of subsequent events or information: (1) those that affect value; and (2) those that do not affect value but that do give evidence of value that existed at the valuation date. In general, those that affect value should not be considered—unless they are foreseeable. On the other hand, those events that give evidence of value that existed as of the valuation date may indeed be considered.

This concept is explained very well in several key court cases:

> A distinction may be usefully drawn between later-occurring events which *affect* fair market value as of the valuation date, and later-occurring events which may be taken into account as *evidence* of fair market value as of the valuation date. When viewed in this light—as evidence of value rather than as something that affects value—later-occurring events are no more to be ignored than earlier-occurring events.[1]
>
> Subsequent events or conditions which affect the value of the property can be taken into account only if they are reasonably foreseeable on the valuation date. Conversely, subsequent events which merely provide evidence of the value of the property on the valuation date can be taken into account regardless whether they are foreseeable on the valuation date.[2]

1 *Estate of Jung v. Commissioner,* 101 T.C. 412, 101 T.C. No. 28 (U.S. Tax Ct., Nov. 10, 1993). Available at *BVLaw* (www.bvlibrary.com/bvlaw).

2 *Morton v. Commissioner,* T.C. Memo 1997-166, 73 T.C.M. (CCH) 2520 (U.S. Tax Ct., April 1, 1997). Available at *BVLaw* (www.bvlibrary.com/bvlaw).

In practice. You will typically come up against three broad scenarios during an engagement: (1) the subject company follows its historical path, which can be either normal growth or decline; (2) foreseen or predictable changes or events affect the company; and (3) the company is hit with changes or events that are unforeseen or unpredictable.

When the company is sailing along as historically expected, it is certainly appropriate to use the company's financial information for the year following the valuation date. This is especially true when financial information preceding the valuation date is missing or not available. It is also appropriate to use the company's financial information for the year following the valuation date if it reflects changes caused by foreseen or predictable events. For example, the company may have launched a great new product, landed a big new client, or is modernizing its plant to increase efficiency.

However, it is *not appropriate* to use the company's financial information for the year following the valuation date if it reflects changes caused by unforeseen or unpredictable events. For example, the surprise loss of a key customer or supplier, an act of Mother Nature that significantly interrupts operations, or an unforeseen change in government regulations that affect the business.

'Knowable' interpretation. Every valuation expert knows that for information to be taken into account it must be "known or knowable." This is sometimes interpreted to mean that financial results through the valuation date that haven't yet been published as of the valuation date are not usable. But a reasonable interpretation is that this unpublished information—although it's not officially compiled—meets the criterion of "knowable." In reality, most CEOs and CFOs have a pretty good idea of what their results were, even though they have not been formally compiled or published.

This same interpretation can also hold true for guideline public company data. For example, if the valuation date is a calendar year, some appraisers would only use data through September 30 for the guideline companies because year-end results would not have been released. However, it would be reasonable to use actual year-end results for the guideline companies. Reasons: The information coincides with the company's year-end, and analysts' predictions of year-end results are available.

What to do. Use professional judgment to determine when it is appropriate to use subsequent events or information as part of the valuation process. If a subsequent event is significant, consider disclosing it in your valuation report, but make it clear that the information was not used to determine value as of the valuation date. If you're involved in a court case, consult the attorney to see whether the particular jurisdiction allows the consideration of subsequent events.[3]

3 For a full discussion on subsequent events, see *Understanding Business Valuation: A Practical Guide to Valuing Small- to Medium-Sized Businesses*, 4th edition, by Gary Trugman and also *Business Valuation and Federal Taxes: Procedure, Law and Perspective*, 2nd edition, by David Laro and Shannon Pratt. Both books are available from BVR (www.bvresources.com/publications).

Multifactor Scorecard Analysis Helps With Debt-Versus-Equity Problem

By J. Richard Claywell, CPA ABV, ASA, CBA, CVA, ICVS, CM&AA, MAFF, CFD, ABAR

Editor's note: A divorce case from last year illustrated how the debt-versus-equity issue can skew a valuation [Freihage v. Freihage, *2015 Ill. App. Unpub. LEXIS 14 (see the April 2015 issue of* Business Valuation Update*)]. In this article, the author presents a scorecard analysis based on the* Mixon *case and others that analysts can use to help make a determination of whether money transferred to a company represents debt or equity.*

When valuing a closely held business, it is common to have debt on the financial statements. When questioning the debt, it often becomes apparent that the owners of the business have not adequately documented the debt. When that happens, the question becomes: Is it debt or is it equity? This can become problematic in litigation cases where the adjusted book value is used or goodwill is being determined from a base using the net asset value of the company.

If there is no supporting evidence or there is a disagreement as to how the "debt" should be classified, the valuation analyst will have to make an informed opinion as to the character of the liability. The courts have developed guidelines for determining the debt-versus-equity question in a number of cases.[1]

In the *Mixon* case, the court performed a detailed analysis and provided very insightful information that the valuation analyst can use in determining the debt-versus-equity issue. This particular case stressed at least 13 factors that merit consideration in determining this issue:

1. The name given to the certificate;

1 This issue has often been considered by the 5th Circuit. *Berkowitz v. United States,* 5th Cir. 1969, 411 F.2d 818; *Curry v. United States,* 5th Cir. 1968, 396 F.2d 630, cert. denied, 393 U.S. 967, 89 S.Ct. 401, 21 L.Ed.2d 375; *Harlan v. United States,* 5th Cir. 1969, 409 F.2d 904; *Tomlinson v. The 1661 Corporation,* 5th Cir. 1967, 377 F.2d 291; *United States v. Snyder Brothers Company,* 5th Cir. 1966, 367 F.2d 980, cert. denied, 386 U.S. 956, 87 S.Ct. 1021, 18 L.Ed.2d 104; *Aronov Construction Company v. United States,* M.D.Ala.1963, 223 F.Supp. 175, aff'd, 5th Cir. 1964, 338 F.2d 337; *Montclair, Incorporated v. Commissioner of Internal Revenue,* 5th Cir. 1963, 318 F.2d 38; *Campbell v. Carter Foundation Production Company,* 5th Cir. 1963, 322 F.2d 827; *Rowan v. United States,* 5th Cir. 1955, 219 F.2d 51, *Estate of Mixon v. United States,* 5th Cir, 1972, 464 F2d 394.

2. The presence or absence of a fixed maturity date;
3. The source of payments;
4. Right to enforce payment of principal and interest;
5. Participation increase in management;
6. Subordination;
7. Intent of the parties;
8. Thin or adequate capitalization;
9. Identity of interest between creditor and stockholder;
10. Payment of interest only out of dividend income;
11. Ability to obtain loans from outside lending institutions;
12. The extent to which the advance was used to acquire capital assets; and
13. The failure of the corporation to repay on the due date.

These factors are presented in scorecard form in Exhibit 1 and are explained below, based on the appellate court opinion in the *Mixon* case, which involved funds advanced to a bank.

Name or type of certificate. The thrust of this factor is that the court looked to the type of certificate the parties used in considering the debt-versus-equity question. The issuance of a stock certificate indicates an equity contribution; the issuance of a bond, debenture, or note is indicative of a bona fide indebtedness. The district court found that the advance was not evidenced by any formal, unconditional promise to pay. Although the complete absence of any specific evidence of indebtedness might on first blush appear to reveal little about the quality of the transaction, the real issue for tax purposes has long been held to be the extent to which the transaction complies with arm's-length standards and normal business practice.[2]

Focusing on this as a factor, a payment to the corporation by a shareholder-director without provision for terms of repayment, interest, and consideration would undoubtedly indicate that the advances were equity bound and intended. In this case, the only conclusion discernible from the record is that the deposit was placed in a unique temporary account, and no one knew exactly what it was in an accounting sense or what to call it.

2 *Nassau Lens Company v. Commissioner*, 2d Cir. 1962, 308 F.2d 39.

The client may instruct the accountant as to where the debt or equity needs to be placed on the balance sheet. However, when the liabilities are being adjusted to fair market value, a more in-depth analysis of the debt versus equity should be performed. It may become a matter of professional judgment as to how to classify the debt versus equity.

The presence or absence of a fixed maturity date. The presence of a fixed maturity date indicates a fixed obligation to repay, which is a characteristic of a debt obligation. On the other hand, the absence of a fixed maturity date indicates that repayment is in some way tied to the fortunes of the business, which is indicative of an equity advance. In this case, there was no fixed date of repayment expressly provided, but it was beside the point. There was uncontradicted "evidence that all concerned anticipated repayment within two years and the fact that the contributors were limited in their actions by the emergency situation existing at the time of the advance and the coercive influence of the banking authorities."[3]

The valuation analyst must have a firm understanding of any terms and repayment of any and all obligations of the company.

The source of payments. The court did not directly consider this factor, but the significance of it is that, if repayment is possible only out of corporate earnings, the transaction has the appearance of a contribution of equity capital. But if repayment is not dependent upon earnings, the transaction reflects a loan to the corporation.[4]

In this case, repayment was tied to strengthening the bank's capital account through improvement in its surplus accounts. Repayment could only be made from the surplus accounts, and, when the advances were repaid, the balance sheet indicated a decrease in the capital section of the balance sheet. These facts would appear to support an equity characterization of the transaction. "The court, however, finds otherwise here. Unlike most other cases, even those in which a debtor-creditor relationship has been found, the source of repayment in the instant case was without question not earnings or profits. It cannot be seriously disputed that the source of the repayment to taxpayer was the cash generated by the collection of the bond claim and collection of the charged-off loans. These collections had no effect on the bank's earnings. The [defendant] government's reliance on mere labels in contending that the source of repayment was an increase in the capital accounts, which normally results from an earnings increase, is not persuasive where, as here, the source of the capital increase was without doubt something other than earnings."[5]

Right to enforce payment of principal and interest. The court noted that, if there is a definite obligation to repay the advance, the transaction would take on some "indicia of a loan."[6] In the case, the government contended that repayment was solely within the "unfettered discretion of

3 *Estate of Mixon v. United States*, 5th Cir, 1972, 464 F2d 394.

4 This factor is somewhat anomalous in view of the fact that the majority of bona fide loans are likewise repaid out of earnings.

5 *Estate of Mixon*, op. cit.

6 *Campbell v. Carter Foundation Production Company*, 5th Cir.1963, 322 F.2d 827.

state and federal banking authorities" and that the directors would have had no recourse against the bank in the event of default.

But the court disagreed, noting that, although repayment was dependent on collection of the bond claim and the charged-off loans, it was not dependent on the "success of the business" as that phrase is ordinarily used. "Repayment was conditioned on reasonably foreseeable events, which could almost be characterized as events certain. The only real uncertainty in the collection was a matter of 'when' rather than 'whether.' In this case, there was nothing to contradict that 'all parties involved did not consider the advance as providing permanent capital financing, which is ordinarily derived from equity advances, but rather temporary working capital to meet what was thought to be, and what proved to be, a temporary emergency. Once the determinable conditions were met, the court had little doubt that the bank was legally obligated under general principles of creditors' rights to return the funds.'"[7]

Participation increase in management. In the *Mixon* case, the contributors were not granted any increased voting power or participation in the bank's affairs by virtue of the advance. This fact served as cumulative evidence that the advances were loans, rather than a contribution of equity.

Subordination. In any determination of whether a party is dealing as a shareholder or a creditor, it is important to determine whether the advance has a status equal to or inferior to that of regular corporate creditors.[8] "The fact that an obligation to repay principal is subordinate to claims of other creditors does not, however, necessarily indicate that the purported debt is in reality an equity contribution, especially where the advance is given a superior status to that of other equity contributions."[9]

In the *Mixon* case, it was not clear where the advance stood on the preference scale. In some cases, there will be a provision for express subordination, but there was no such provision in this case.

Intent of the parties. The court noted that the parties' intent to create either a debt or equity relationship is, "in a sense, the ultimate issue to be determined here." However, the government failed to distinguish between subjective and objective intent, the court said.

It noted the case of *United States v. Snyder Brothers Company,* which quoted language from *Kraft Foods Company v. Commissioner of Internal Revenue,* 2d Cir.1956, 232 F.2d 118:

> We think the problem is not one of ascertaining "intent," since the parties have objectively manifested their intent. It is a problem of whether the intent and acts of these parties should be disregarded in characterizing the transaction for federal tax purposes (367 F.2d at 982-983).

7 See *Clark v. Boston-Continental National Bank,* D. Mass. 1936, 9 F.Supp. 81; *Binns v. First National Bank,* 367 Pa. 359, 80 A.2d 768 (1951); *State ex rel. Gordon v. Trimble,* 318 Mo. 341, 300 S.W. 475 (1927).

8 See *Tomlinson v. The 1661 Corporation,* 5th Cir. 1967, 377 F.2d 291; *United States v. Henderson,* 5th Cir. 1967, 375 F.2d 36; *United States v. Snyder Brothers Company,* 5th Cir. 1966, 367 F.2d 980; *Montclair, Incorporated v. Commissioner,* supra; *Rowan v. United States,* supra; Bittker and Eustice, *Federal Income Taxation of Corporations & Shareholders* 123 (2nd ed.).

9 *Harlan v. United States,* supra; *Tomlinson v. The 1661 Corporation,* supra.

Exhibit 1. Analysis of Debt Versus Equity			
		Indicator	
	Factor	Debt	Equity
1	The names given to the certificates that evidence indebtedness	x	
2	The presence of a fixed maturity date	x	
3	The source of payments	x	
4	The right to enforce payment of principal and interest	x	
5	Participation in management flowing as a result	x	
6	The status of the contribution in relation to regular corporate creditors	x	
7	The intent of the parties		x
8	Thin or adequate capitalization		x
9	Identifying interest between creditor and stockholder		x
10	Source of interest payments		x
11	The ability of the business to obtain credit from outside lending institutions		x
12	The extent to which the advance was used to acquire capital assets		x
13	The failure to repay on the due date or to seek a postponement		x
	Total factors	6	7
	Percentage of factors	46.20%	53.80%
	Indication of Debt or Equity		Equity

The *Mixon* court goes on to state: "This stands only for the principle, well-recognized in all areas of the law, that a subjective intent on the part of an actor will not alter the relationship or duties created by an otherwise objectively indicated intent. See *Dillin v. United States,* 5th Cir.1970, 433 F.2d 1097-1100. Judge Goldberg states the proposition thusly: 'Tax law requires that creditorship have genuine existentiality. (citation omitted) This requires more than a declaration of intention to create an indebtedness and more than the existence of corporate paper encrusted with the appropriate nomenclature captions.' *Tyler v. Tomlinson,* supra, 414 F.2d at 850."

The court also pointed out that this is in no way contrary to the proposition that, in cases in which the objective facts of the case are ambiguous as to objective intent, then subjective intent is relevant on the issue. Judge Goldberg, in *Tyler v. Tomlinson,* supra, pointed out: "If appellants mean to say that a mere showing of an intent to create an indebtedness and the existence of something called 'notes' is sufficient to take their case to the jury, we must disagree. If that were true, every debt-equity case would require a jury verdict no matter how transparent the attempt at tax avoidance. We therefore look not to mere labels or to the self-serving declarations of the parties, but to the more reliable criteria of the circumstances surrounding the transaction. If none of these circumstances are in dispute, there is no jury question. As this court recently observed: 'It is not the jury's function to determine whether the undisputed operative facts add up to debt or equity. This is question of law.' 414 F.2d 850"

The *Mixon* court concluded: "Within the confines of this case, wherein the objective signs point in all directions, there is no doubt that the district court was correct in looking to the subjective intent of the parties to ascertain the correct direction to follow." Both sides in the case agreed that the directors subjectively intended the advances to be loans.

Thin or adequate capitalization. Thin capitalization is "very strong evidence of a capital contribution where (1) the debt to equity ratio was initially high, (2) the parties realized the likelihood

Exhibit 2. Debt Versus Equity in a Divorce Context

BVU subscribers have access to a massive library of articles, many of which are written by guest contributors. Doing a search of "debt vs. equity" at BVLibrary (www.bvlibrary.com) brings up a number of articles and court case digests, including a series of articles by Christine Baker, CPA/ABV/CFF, of Charter Capital Partners (Grand Rapids, Mich.) that examine debt versus equity in a divorce context.

Baker points out that the sum of the guidance for legal and valuation experts boils down to this: The resolution of a debt-versus-equity issue is like searching for a result along a continuum, which has at one end debt and at the other end equity. In the absence of a bright-line test, "economic reality" may prove to be the basis on which decision-makers consider what constitutes an equitable conclusion.

Practical idea. Baker suggests that, in some cases, a practical step for the valuation expert may be to present counsel with two valuation scenarios. One scenario could offer a valuation conclusion assuming the loan is not a bona fide debt of the company. The other scenario could offer a valuation conclusion assuming the loan is legitimate and is to be included (at its fair market value) in the overall determination of the parties' net worth. This approach may provide enough information for the parties and their respective counsel to negotiate an equitable settlement.

The three-part series of articles, titled "Shareholder Loans in Divorce," focuses on loans a shareholder makes to a business entity and options for dealing with such loans when doing a valuation in divorce. The articles also examine the factors that some courts have weighed when deciding whether an advance of funds from an owner should be treated as a bona fide debt or as contributed capital.

that it would go higher, and (3) substantial portions of these funds were used for the purchase of capital assets and for meeting expenses needed to commence operations." The subject firm fell into this category.

Identity of interest between creditor and stockholder. The court noted that advances made by stockholders in proportion to their respective stock ownership are indicative of an equity capital contribution. On the other hand, a sharply disproportionate ratio between a stockholder's percentage interest in stock and debt strongly indicates a bona fide debt. In this case, the funds advanced were not in proportion to the directors' risk capital.

Payment of interest only out of dividend income. There was no provision for the payment of interest on the advance, and the government argued that this fact alone militates strongly against a finding that the advance was a loan. "It is true, as this court stated in *Curry v. United States*, 5th Cir.1968, 396 F.2d 630, that 'a true lender is concerned with interest.'[10] The failure to insist on interest payments ordinarily indicates that the payors are not seriously expecting any substantial interest income, but are interested in the future earnings of the corporation or the increased market value of their interest."[11]

10 See also *National Carbide Corporation v. Commissioner of Internal Revenue*, 336 U.S. 422, 435 n.16, 69 S.Ct. 726, 93 L.Ed. 779 (1949).

11 *Curry v. United States*, 396 F.2d at 634.

Ability to obtain loans from outside lending institutions. If a business is able to borrow funds from outside sources at the time an advance is made, the transaction has the appearance of a bona fide debt. "The purpose of this inquiry is obviously to test whether the shareholder contributors acted in the same manner toward their corporation as ordinary reasonable creditors would have acted," the court wrote. "If no reasonable creditor would have loaned funds to the corporation at the time of the advance, an inference arises that a reasonable shareholder would likewise not so act."

The extent to which the advance was used to acquire capital assets. The lower court examined whether there were existing sources for repayment of the loan, such as an income-producing asset. "Further, the court considers whether the funds are temporary advances to provide working capital that can be repaid in the near term or whether the funds are used to acquire capital assets (i.e., capital asset financing which is longer term)," the appellate court noted. "A determination needs to be made as to whether the funds were used for working capital or used for the acquisition of assets."

The failure of the corporation to repay on the due date. This factor and the previous factor supports the district court's characterization of the advance as a bona fide debt. "The advance was without question utilized to provide working capital for the day-to-day operations of the bank and was in no way connected to any acquisition of capital assets. Moreover, it is clear that the bank repaid the advance as soon as the conditions previously discussed were met."

Conclusion. Sometimes it is not obvious as to the appropriate classification of a "loan" on the balance sheet. The analysis from the *Mixon* case can be useful in making that determination. An analysis of each factor with supporting documents, where available, will assist in supporting the professional judgment exercised to provide an opinion as to the appropriate classification. The accompanying sample analysis in Exhibit 1 can help the analyst make an informed decision as to the classification of debt versus equity—and it can be used for all types of transactions where the issue arises.

J. Richard Claywell, *CPA, ABV, ASA, CBA, CVA, ICVS, CM&AA, MAFF, CFD, ABAR, is the co-author of* Capitalization and Discount Rates: The Value of Risk *and is contributing author of the NACVA Fundamentals Theory & Techniques training materials. He is also the director of education for the International Association of Consultants, Valuators and Analysts (IACVA). He can be reached at 281-488-7531 or richard@biz-valuation.com.*

A Quantitative Model Evolves for Determining Passive Appreciation

A vexing problem for business valuators is determining the allocation between active and passive appreciation of a closely held business caught up in divorce. Due to societal and demographic trends, this is an issue of growing concern. Also, the courts are becoming more demanding in terms of proof. Gone are the days when you could demonstrate passive appreciation by saying the business owner was always on the golf course. Therefore, a more quantitative method is necessary.

Empirical approach. There are various methods for doing this allocation, including one developed by Dr. Ashok Abbott (West Virginia University). He uses an empirical estimation method for identifying significant economic environmental factors and their relative contribution to growth in business revenues. These factors, such as population growth, level of inflation, and changes in disposable personal income, represent market forces that are outside the control of a company's management. The results of the analysis form the basis for a percentage allocation of the growth in value that can be attributed to passive (economic environment) components. In previous articles in *Business Valuation Update*, Abbott has explained the background and earlier thinking behind his method.[1]

Since first developing the method, Abbott has had the opportunity to refine it based on feedback from the BV community and also from his experience using it in a litigation setting. A central question that needs to be answered is the progression from observing correlation to establishing causation. Therefore, he has refined the model to include more rigorous causality testing. He presented this enhanced version of the model during a recent BVR webinar.[2]

Testing the factors. To demonstrate the model, Abbott has conducted an empirical analysis of the revenue impact of economic environmental changes on product sales over the period 1992 to 2014. Using publicly available quarterly economic data, he applies a multistep approach:

1 "Identifying Active and Passive Appreciation Using Econometric Analysis" (*BVU*, December 2005); "Demographic Trends: Apportioning the Active and Passive Components" (*BVU*, December 2011).

2 Passive Appreciation in Divorce (BVR webinar, March 8, 2016).

1. Identify the theoretical nexus for causal relationships between economic variables and product sales (e.g., through industry studies, management interviews, etc.).

2. Confirm that a significant relationship exists between the level of reported quarterly sales of the product and the economic variables being investigated, using Pearson correlation coefficients.

3. Empirically test theoretically valid causal relationships, with confirmed correlations, for causality using a series of Granger-Causality Wald Tests to verify a cause-and-effect relationship between the revenues and economic variables.

4. Test and rank the identified causal factors for economic significance. Since the impact of economic changes can occur over longer periods of time, an autoregressive model is employed to correct the observed elasticities for such delayed reaction.

5. Test the economically significant factors for multicollinearity to identify and avoid any double counting of impact for the economic variables.

6. Estimate partial elasticities for the confirmed causal factors to determine the incremental impact of each variable on the revenues of the business.

7. Compare the aggregate change in the value of the revenues over the period of the analysis with the indicated change attributable to the changes in the causal factors over the same period.

For this last step, the changes in individual causal factor values over the period are tabulated. Then, each factor change is multiplied by the estimated partial elasticity for the factor to get the individual impact of each of the factors. The sum of these impacts represents the overall change in revenues attributable to the changes in the causal factors. The proportion of the total change in revenues attributable to the changes in causal economic factors, which are outside the control of the managers of the business, represents the passive component of the change in revenues.

Example. One of the product categories Abbott has examined is groceries, a staple necessity. You would expect that the passive component is high for this type of product. That is, a substantial part of the change in grocery revenues would come from environmental factors beyond management's control. Indeed, Abbott finds that a very significant relationship exists between two economic environment factors (the level of growth in population and the level of inflation) and sales of groceries. He finds that other factors, namely, income, interest, and debt service levels, do not appear to have a significant impact on the consumption of groceries.

The regression parameters show a strong relationship. Elasticities are positive and significant, indicating that a 1% change in population leads to a 1.2477% change in grocery sales (see Exhibit 1). Similarly, a 1% change in the level of inflation leads to a change of 0.5533% in grocery sales. For

Exhibit 1. Grocery Sales Elasticity Estimates					
Variable	DF	Estimate	Standard	t Value	Approx. Pr > |t|
Intercept	1	-6.9517	4.0627	-1.71	0.0906
% change total population	1	1.2477	0.3743	3.33	0.0013
% change CPI	1	0.5533	0.1409	3.93	0.0002

Exhibit 2. Passive Component in Grocery Sales				
Total Change in Grocery Sales				80.04%
Factor	Elasticity Estimate	Factor Change	Factor Impact	% of Total Change Due to Factor (Passive Component)
% change total population	1.2477	25.27%	31.53%	39.39%
% change CPI	0.5533	70.87%	39.21%	48.99%
Total			70.74%	88.38%

the period 1992 to 2014, we know that the population growth was 25.27% and the level of inflation grew by 70.87%. Multiplying each growth level by the corresponding elasticity, the aggregate impact of changes in population and inflation level is 70.74%, which accounts for 88.38% of the change in grocery sales (see Exhibit 2).

It should be noted that this analysis is based on aggregate national data. Additional, business-specific factors should be identified and an analysis performed using national, regional, and local data to get results specific to the subject business.

Hypothetical illustration. A local grocery store chain was established in 1982 with an initial investment of $100,000. The business grew, and, in 1987, the founder's son joined the business and was given a 5% share of the equity. Over the next five years, the son was given additional annual gifts of 10% of the equity. By 1992, the son owned 55% of the business. In 1993, the son got married. The business was valued at $500,000 at the time of the marriage. The son continued to manage the business, and the value of the business grew to $5,000,000 by the end of 2014. The couple filed for divorce in 2015.

The issue of equitable distribution of the marital estate including growth in value of the business during the marriage is one of the central issues in this divorce. The business appreciated in value by $4,500,000 during the marriage overall, so 55% of that, or $2,475,000, is the amount of appreciation that needs to be apportioned. The wife claims that the entire amount of the growth in value is part of the marital estate subject to distribution as the hard work the husband performed is the primary driver of the increase in value of the business and that $1,237,500 should be her share of this appreciation. This claim can be substantially refuted, as shown below, in jurisdictions that recognize the issue of active and passive appreciation.

The analysis done on a national level reveals that the aggregate impact of changes in certain economic factors accounts for 88% of the change in grocery sales. Similar analysis using publicly traded grocery retailers shows that the market value/revenue multiple increased from 0.41 to 0.59 over the same period.[3] The revenues of the grocery store chain grew from $1.5 million to $12 million over the period of the marriage. When the analysis is localized for this particular chain, 80% of the increase in revenues can be explained by external economic factors and the market value/revenue multiple is found to have changed from 0.33 to 0.42 over the same period as a result of the changes in cost of capital due to the decrease in interest rates.

The analysis can be made in two steps. First, undo the change in revenue multiple as the change in interest rates impacting cost of capital is outside the control of the management. Applying the revenue multiple of 0.33 to the increased sales of $12 million, the business value would be $4 million. The appreciation in value exclusive of the change in revenue multiple is now $3.5 million. Further, if 80% of the change in revenues is attributable to external passive factors, the potential active appreciation in value is 0.20 × $3.5 million, or $700,000. Therefore, if this entire remaining appreciation of $700,000 is active appreciation, the proportional share of the husband to be included in the marital estate, subject to distribution, is 0.55 × $700,000, or $385,000. The 50% share for the wife in this distribution becomes $192,500. The difference in value of the required distribution between these two alternatives is $1,045,000 (0.50* ($2,475,000 - $385,000)).

When external economic factors are identified and accounted for, the husband retains almost $1 million more of the business value.

How to get it. During the webinar, an attendee asked: "Are there any published sources of causal factors and elasticities by industry?" Abbott replied "no," but he offered to provide some of this analysis in future issues of *Business Valuation Update.*

3 This market multiple factor was very kindly suggested by Chris Mercer while reviewing this presentation, based on his rate and flow paper.

A Low-Risk, Low-Cost Option to Enhance a Damages Claim

Editor's note: A fascinating new chapter in the fourth edition of The Comprehensive Guide to Economic Damages *deals with the wrongdoings of corporate outlaws. The chapter, "Compensation Forfeiture: Stacking Remedies Against Disloyal Agents and Employees," is written by George P. Roach, J.D., who practices almost strictly in damages and remedy law. Very little has been written on this topic, so* BVU *had the pleasure of speaking with the author.*

BVU: *As a damages analyst, how will your chapter on compensation forfeiture help me?*

George P. Roach: For the client of the damages expert, compensation forfeiture is a low-risk option that plaintiffs can seek that does not preclude other remedies nor is it difficult or expensive to prove. Compensation forfeiture represents an enhancement or supplement to the damages or remedies that may be assessed against the defendant individual or company. The widespread applicability to various claims is not generally appreciated by either lawyers or damages analysts. Therefore compensation forfeiture represents an opportunity for a damages analyst sometimes to suggest an enhancement to the client's claims that can be made at a small increase in professional fees.

In some cases, compensation forfeiture may prove to be the only form of damages that can be proven with reasonable certainty. In the areas of disloyal competition or abuse of an employer's intellectual property, it can be difficult to prove damages with sufficient precision.

BVU: *In a nutshell, what is compensation forfeiture?*

GR: Compensation forfeiture is based on the doctrine that faithless agents or disloyal employees should not be compensated for any service after the disloyalty or faithlessness first occurs. As such, compensation received after that date is similar to unjust enrichment and the compensation to be disgorged is generally not offset by the benefits that the principal otherwise enjoyed from the defendant's service.

It is controversial for at least three reasons: few employees (hourly or salaried) are aware of their potential liability for compensation forfeiture, the typical case facts against a faithless corporate executive may be so inflammatory that forfeiture as a remedy can be excessively punitive, and some cases have revealed an employer who employed the claim of disloyalty and forfeiture to chill the First Amendment rights of hourly employees.

BVU: *Can you provide some examples of behavior that might warrant compensation forfeiture?*

GR: Typically, it would require repeated actions to embezzle from or defraud one's employer (unless the amount of the first embezzlement is sizable). It can include any form of compensation or profit that a fiduciary gains from his fiduciary position that the principal has not specifically approved. Areas such as abuse of confidential information, trade secrets, or other forms of intellectual property are also included.

Some employers have been accused of abusing compensation forfeiture by threatening to seek forfeiture for an employee's "disloyalty" in word or speech in public forums or websites. Various state legislatures have responded with statutes intended to protect employees' first amendment rights from such overreach.

BVU: *Who is a fiduciary? Can it include the rank and file?*

GR: The hallmark of a fiduciary is someone who is hired with a reasonable expectation of trust. The exact definition of "fiduciary" has been subject to extensive litigation. Typically, fiduciaries include lawyers, real estate brokers, and trustees but not lenders or insurance agents. It can include family members and spouses. The majority position in state law is to include rank-and-file employees, but some courts condition that holding on the exact nature of the disloyalty.

BVU: *What is the valuator's role in the issue of compensation forfeiture?*

GR: Many studies suggest that employee fraud and embezzlement is widespread. When a damages expert or fraud auditor reviews the evidence and determines the dates and amounts of theft, he or she can now also determine the dates, amounts, and bases for compensation that the perpetrator of the fraud was compensated.

Alternatively, a damages/valuation expert may be needed to determine whether an agent's or employee's conflicted transactions with the principal were priced on a fair market basis.

A fraud audit of a corporate officer's corporate dealings should include a preliminary review of whether each form of the officer's compensation was authorized and disclosed beforehand. If the CEO was paid some form of profit sharing or contingent bonus, did the relevant business operation actually meet or exceed the standard provided for such a bonus?

One tool in the valuation expert's bag is the ability to assess a reasonable level of executive compensation. Without first complying with the necessary safeguards, the payment of excessive compensation to oneself can be a breach of loyalty and warrant full disgorgement (not just the amount in excess of reasonable compensation).

BVU: *How is the amount determined? Can it get complicated?*

GR: Retirement compensation can be complicated as forfeiture in this area depends on ERISA statutes and possibly even the employee's employment contract. The applicable dates for bonus plan payments and profit sharing have at times been litigated (whether the relevant date is the date of payment or the period of service for which the payment is made.) Remember, in most states, the compensation to be forfeited does not have to relate to the disloyal actions.

BVU: *What about retirement benefits that are required to be nonforfeitable?*

GR: The forfeiture nature of retirement benefits can be tricky. In a couple of cases, regular retirements were found nonforfeitable but "top-hat" plans were found to be forfeitable. However, it has also been suggested that the forfeiture nature of "top-hat" plans and other forms of compensation may be controlled by the terms of the compensation agreement. That point has yet to be litigated.

BVU: *Does all of the compensation get forfeited? Does the wrongdoer get any credit for any good deeds?*

GR: Generally, the trial judge decides how much forfeiture is appropriate. There have been enough cases that you can find any one holding for most variations: bonuses only, bonus plus salary but not retirement benefits, and all compensation not protected by ERISA. In a minority of states, compensation forfeiture also qualifies for prejudgment interest. The biggest issue is whether compensation is going to be allocated by time (typical) or transaction or customer (generally for commission compensation).

A minority of states do effectively give credit for good deeds or at least for showing up at work for the prescribed hours. It's also not unreasonable to expect courts to be tougher on agents/employees with higher compensations and corporate titles.

BVU: *The title of your chapter refers to "stacking." What does this mean and why is it emphasized?*

GR: Most state and federal courts have some formula or process for determining when punitive damages are excessive in relation to actual damages to avoid violating the constitution. For such purposes, compensation forfeiture is not included as an exemplary or punitive remedy, so in some cases the ratio of punitive damages plus compensation forfeiture can exceed such limits. In some states, compensation forfeiture is included as actual damages such that it would by itself permit a greater amount of punitive damages. In many of the cases described in the article, compensation forfeiture exceeded actual damages. Thus, the executive who embezzles $200,000 a year may be in jeopardy of disgorging his annual compensation of $1,000,000.

So it is possible that, if the defendant is found liable for stealing $100,000, he or she can be found liable also for punitive damages, compensation forfeiture, and prejudgment interest.

BVU: *You say that compensation forfeiture is a remedy in equity versus a remedy at law. What's the difference and why is this important?*

GR: In most states, in an action in equity, the trial judge determines on his or her own whether to award and how much compensation should be forfeited. Second, there are a number of eclectic and counterintuitive options for measuring remedies in equity that do not apply to remedies at law: Ex post evidence is generally admissible, and causation is somewhat relaxed.

Third, it's always useful to remember that an order from a court in equity to pay the equivalent of damages can be enforced with the full power of the court in equity. While rare, a court in equity can order the defendant to jail for failure to pay the required sums.

***BVU:** You mention that when compensation forfeiture is stacked onto other remedies, it typically results in financial ruin even to the well-heeled defendant. Does this mean that courts are reluctant to apply it, especially to lower-level employees?*

GR: Generally, most any kind of remedy will financially ruin an hourly employee because he or she generally enjoys few financial reserves. The trend that I have noticed is that some plaintiffs elect not to sue hourly or junior executions for compensation forfeiture for fear of appearing too tough or ruthless.

***BVU:** Do you see the increased use of nonforfeiture arrangements to fend off this remedy?*

GR: That question should be referred to executive compensation experts. It is probably too early to tell, but it seems reasonable to expect in senior executive agreements. One key issue will be whether such exemptions comply with a court's public policy sensitivities.

***BVU:** How can the valuation expert optimize the working relationship with the attorney in this type of matter?*

GR: The damages analyst can add value to his or her assignment by suggesting compensation forfeiture as an additional remedy for the client that can realize a sizable award for not much additional cost in professional fees.

The Comprehensive Guide to Economic Damages, 4th edition, is edited by Nancy J. Fannon, CPA, ABV, ASA, MCBA (Meyers, Harrison & Pia), and Jonathan M. Dunitz, Esq. (Verrill Dana). It is available at www.bvresources.com/publications.

Valuation and Forensics Expert Provides Tips on Damages Engagements

Lee D. Sanderson, CPA, ABV, CFF, CVA, MST, is the founder of Valuation Forensics LLC, a firm with offices in Boston, New York, and Florida. As its name implies, the firm integrates business valuation with forensic accounting in order to respond to the increased demand for accuracy and credibility in litigation. It began as a typical business valuation firm but evolved into some specialized areas, including damages. BVR interviewed Sanderson for his insights into damages engagements.

BVU: *How did you get into valuation?*

Lee Sanderson: I got into valuation about 20 years ago when I was on the venture capital team at PwC (when it was Price Waterhouse), and it sparked a curiosity, so I decided to build a career out of it. After doing some valuation work, I discovered an aptitude for forensics engagements. In my opinion, the two have to go hand in hand. The mistake a lot of practitioners make is doing valuations without merging in forensics. This is especially true in a contested litigation where someone's trying to hide something and the lawyers hire us to get to the bottom of it.

In contentious litigation, such as divorce, one party will have something to gain by having a business appraised at a lower value. People will use smart advisers who know valuation formulas, and they may employ techniques to accomplish this. Sometimes these techniques can rise to the level of fraud. We see this every day in our practice dealing with matters such as shareholder disputes and divorce, so we need to know how to detect these things because it could have a tremendous impact on the outcome of the case.

BVU: *Outside of contentious litigation, where can forensics come into play?*

LS: When looking at historical financial information, such as tax returns, you need to verify whether that information is accurate. There's an illusion out there that a tax return prepared by a CPA has some type of assurance element to it. But the reality is that tax engagements by CPAs do not include an audit, unless there's a separate auditing engagement. CPAs are completely within their professional standards to prepare returns with information given to them by their client without delving into the accuracy of the information, unless something really jumps out at them. There's a disclaimer in the engagement letter that says they are relying on the accuracy of the information provided and that they are not responsible if that information is wrong. For years, valuation practitioners have relied on tax returns as being accurate, and we believe that's a critical mistake.

BVU: *Why did you start your own firm?*

LS: I founded Valuation Forensics about 16-plus years ago out of my passion for those two areas: valuation and forensics. My belief was that those areas had to be merged in order to provide a better product in the marketplace.

BVU: *Were you doing damages cases at the beginning?*

LS: No. We started out doing business valuations for divorce or shareholder disputes and when we got into forensics it was a natural transition to branch out into damages cases. As we got better at uncovering schemes, we got more calls from attorneys asking us to dig into a damages or lost profits case on a granular level. Of course, they wanted us to determine just how much damage an action or a wrongful act caused in terms of a monetary loss, but more often it was in terms of how the wrongful act impacted the value of the business. When you do that, you have to merge forensics and business valuation and connect it to those wrongful acts.

BVU: *What is the toughest aspect of a damages case?*

LS: The toughest aspect is avoiding the high level of speculation that clients and quite often the attorneys always want to insert into the analysis. They have a certain theory of a case, and the attorneys have identified what they determine to be a wrongful act. That's a legal determination that they have to make—we can't make that determination. Clients will also have a theory that, if the act didn't occur, revenue would have grown by a certain percentage, certain customers wouldn't have left, and so on. Sometimes there's a big disconnect between what they feel the future would have held and practical reality. So the toughest part is bringing them down to reality and not being influenced by their particular theory of the case.

BVU: *How do you deal with that?*

LS: Don't be afraid to tell the client "no." You point out that your name is associated with the analysis and the report and there's no one client worth risking your credibility on. So don't hesitate to tell the client that "this is my professional opinion of what I believe the damages are." Naturally, they will want the damages to be high, but you can't be swayed by that.

I had a recent case where the client was convinced that, were it not for the wrongful act, revenues would have increased for the next 10 years at 30%. They were irate at the notion that I would not opine in the same way.

BVU: *What did you do in that case?*

LS: An approach we used in that case—and other cases—is to create a range of damages. For example, start at a 3% or 5% growth rate and then go up to 20% in increments of 5%. In court, we would testify that the highest end of the curve is "highly unlikely" and show where the "likely" analysis would be with regard to a growth rate. This "likely" analysis would be based on actual data—something other than what the litigants said.

The "but for" world must be based on solid empirical data and solid evidence, such as reports of economic growth of that particular industry, direct conversations with clients of the company, and so on. That information is far more solid than the statements by the damaged parties as to what they think would have happened. The minute you rely on the statements of one of the litigants, you have created a speculative analysis. An analysis that's speculative and not rooted in empirical data is an analysis that will lose.

BVU: *Some companies will have good projections. How do they figure into your analysis?*

LS: Some have very good projections, and others may have best-case projections, so it's difficult to determine which is which. We would certainly consider their projections and the assumptions they believe to be true and which ones are realistic and which ones are not. But, for those that are potentially realistic, we need to verify them in some way other than through the litigants.

My advice to anyone doing damages calculations is to take every assumption and raise the questions: How do you know? Can you prove it? What is your backup for that assumption? If you say the backup is that "the client said that the growth rate is such-and-such" or "the client says that those customers would have stayed," then your analysis will be subject to great challenge in court. If the judge believes that your analysis is speculative, I think there's sufficient case law out there that says the court can give very little weight to your analysis.

BVU: *What about when you're analyzing the loss in value of a company?*

LS: If the issue is the loss in value of the company, you have to look to state law because the issue will be what standard of value to use, fair market value or fair value. Fair market value requires an analysis of comparable transactions, while fair value is more company specific and focuses on the economic benefits that the company has lost because of the transactions as opposed to the decrease in value in the marketplace.

When looking at comparable companies, you have to be very careful that you have a good match. It's mind-boggling how many valuation analyses are based on companies that are not good matches. A common mistake is to do a search by SIC or NAICS code and do an aggregate analysis based on the companies in that code. The trouble is, the overall companies in that code might not be a great match for the subject company, and there may be no way to know whether they are or not.

BVU: *Are there more damages cases out there than before?*

LS: I see a huge increase in the number of damages cases, both lost profits and lost business value cases. One reason is that we have the highest number of attorneys now than ever in history. I think there's a statistic that something like 90% of attorneys are either sole practitioners or they work for small firms, and they are the ones likely to take contingency cases, which is quite often where these damages and lost profits cases fall. So you have a huge number of attorneys wanting to take on these cases hoping they will hit or that the other side will agree to a settlement.

BVU: *Any particular types of cases increasing?*

LS: Yes, cases that require computer forensics have increased. We incorporated computer forensics into our practice a number of years ago. In this day and age, it is the fastest and most efficient way to get to the bottom of what's going on inside a company. The fraud detection techniques that can be used with the use of computer forensics and the efficiency by which they can be used keeps growing every year.

BVU: *Have you seen any changes in the courts with respect to damages cases?*

LS: Courts have become much more savvy on the issue of whether an analysis is speculative or not—and to what degree it is speculative. The more conservative and realistic the analysis, the better.

BVU: *Have you seen or do you use any new methods or techniques for damages calculations?*

LS: The biggest one is computer forensics. But we are always updating and modifying our methods and techniques by learning from the disciplines of forensic accounting and business valuation to enhance what we do. We also read case law and observe what others are doing in this area.

BVU: *I see you do training sessions for attorneys.*

LS: Yes, sometimes law firms will call us to do a training session on whatever topic they need—it could be business valuation or damages calculations. We also do a lot of teaching for the American Academy for Certified Financial Litigators (AACFL), and we provide training to attorneys nationwide on the financial aspects of litigation. We're not teaching litigation, but we show them what they didn't learn in law school about business valuation, forensics, and how tax returns or financial statements can be misleading. That helps them in their cases, it helps the clients, and also helps the courts.

BVU: *What kinds of things do you do to optimize the working relationship between you and the attorneys on a case?*

LS: There are two main ways. First, the management of expectations, that is, having a clear understanding right from the beginning of what's expected from the engagement. Second, you need to approach every engagement in phases. For example, the first phase might be meeting with the attorneys and client, gathering all data that are available, and then presenting to them what can be done with the data. At every step of the way, you should get their authorization to make sure everyone is on the same page. There's nothing worse for a relationship with an attorney than to take on an engagement and go in the wrong direction with it.

As I mentioned before, you almost always have to tell them that what their initial hope for what the damages will be are unrealistic. The biggest mistake you can make is to agree with the attorney in the initial interview that the client has been damaged at the dollar amount they believe. That's what attorneys want to hear, but no credible expert will do that. You say, "Yes, I see your position, but I can't opine on it without doing an analysis." If you give the impression that you agree with the attorney's position, then you're in a very awkward position if you later have to backtrack.

BVU: *You gave a testimonial for the new 4th edition of the book,* The Comprehensive Guide to Economic Damages.[1] *How does a resource like that help you in your practice?*

LS: The book is a wonderful sanity check throughout the course of an engagement as far as methodology and what others are doing out there. It's also a great resource for case law examples, which alert us to what to be cautious of when putting a report together. We will refer to the book throughout the course of an engagement and also at the end of an engagement to see whether there's anything in there that relates to our case. More often than not, the book will have something right on point with respect to our particular case that we can use to reinforce the opinion of damages and strengthen the integrity of our analysis.

The authors did a spectacular job in hitting on the key elements and challenges practitioners face in damages cases. It's clear that the authors have broad experience in these matters. We can all learn from others—it's a good community when we can learn from each other.

BVU: *Any other advice you'd like to give to practitioners doing damages engagements?*

LS: Once you develop your opinion, stick by it and maintain your integrity. Don't be swayed by the attorneys or the litigants.

1 Nancy Fannon, Jonathan Dunitz (eds.), *The Comprehensive Guide to Economic Damages,* 4th edition, BVR, www.bvresources.com/publications.

DLOMs in N.Y. Fair Value Cases:
Private Company Discounts Are Not Caused by Lack of Marketability

By Gilbert E. Matthews, CFA

Are private companies worth less than public companies solely because they are not publicly traded or because of other identifiable factors (some of which would apply to various public companies as well)? A school of thought consisting of experienced and thoughtful experts believes they are. Shannon Pratt and Roger Grabowski set forth this view:

> Discounting the expected net cash flows for a closely held business using an "as if public" cost of capital does not provide an estimate of the value of 100% of the closely held business. Even 100% of a closely held business suffers from a lack of liquidity.[1]

The equally thoughtful Chris Mercer represents a different school of thought. Although agreeing that private companies often sell for less than public-company multiples in their industry, he states, "Fundamental adjustments account for observed differences in size, risk profile, or growth expectations between subject private companies and the [public] guideline company group."[2] He says:

> [Value] is a function of expected cash flow, risk, and expected growth. If an appraiser adequately measures expected cash flow and the risks and growth of those cash flows, the result is enterprise value.... If enterprise value is determined based on expected cash flows, expected growth of those cash flows, and the riskiness of these cash flows, then what additional factors would support a discount from this value?[3]

Bill Quackenbush has posed the same question and notes the continuing debate:

> Is a 100% equity ownership interest in a privately held company less liquid than the underlying publicly traded stock data upon which the value is calculated in an income approach (discount rates) or market approach (market multiples) that must be addressed through some sort of valuation adjustment?[4]

1 Shannon P. Pratt and Roger J. Grabowski, *Cost of Capital*, 5th ed., Wiley, 2014, p. 654 ("Pratt and Grabowski").

2 Z. Christopher Mercer and Travis W. Harms, *Business Valuation: An Integrated Theory*, 2nd ed., Wiley, 2007, p. 151 ("Mercer and Harms").

3 Mercer and Harms, pp. 94-95.

4 William C. Quackenbush, "DLOMs in N.Y. Statutory Fair Value Cases—A Follow-Up to Matthews," *Business Valuation Update*, March 2016, pp. 2-3 ("March *BVU*"). The article is reprinted on page 45.

The discussions regarding private-company enterprise value, however, do not always employ the same conceptual frameworks, terminology, nor even center on the same level of valuation, e.g., enterprise value versus the discount for lack of marketability on controlling shares.

The author believes no private-company discount (PCD) is attributable to closely held or private-company status as such, and I will present my thinking below. First, however, the following questions are an attempt to center the discussion on the same issues and to stimulate a clearer or more cogent presentation of them:

1. If a private-company discount is compelled on the basis of the company's closely held structure, how would we isolate any factors that are due solely or primarily to the private versus public status of the company?

2. Have many factors of value been "lumped" into a liquidity discount when they are better understood as components to be applied in fundamental adjustments to risk, cash flows, and expected growth?

3. If valuators do incorporate into their fundamental analysis of the specific company's value factors better analyzed as essential components of risk, cash flows, and expected growth, then should a marketability discount, as a separate discount, be placed on the enterprise-level value of private companies at all? How would the valuator avoid double counting in those cases?

4. Are there other factors that might conceivably lead to marketability discounts after the steps above are taken without double counting for the same factors?

The discount for lack of marketability. Chris Mercer has long written on the misplacement of many factors such as holding period, readiness for sale, risk of nonconsummation, quality of earnings, etc., into the discount for lack of marketability for minority interests. For controlling interests, which trade in a different market with different buyers, his position is that factors that directly affect entity value are appropriately treated as fundamental adjustments in the valuation process rather than as factors to be reflected in a DLOM (which he argues seldom exists). He writes:

> There is almost unanimous agreement in the valuation profession that ... the value of a business depends on the expected cash flows of the business (including their expected future growth), and the risk of generating those cash flows (manifested in a discount rate).[5]

This understanding leads to the recognition that a DCF valuation should account for issues that affect entity value in the DCF calculation, not through a DLOM. For a valuation using the market approach, appropriate fundamental adjustments must be made in the multiples.

5 Mercer and Harms, p. 89.

Chris Best states cogently:

> If an appraiser's job is to mimic the thought process of buyers and sellers in the marketplace and interpret the market data in the valuation process, then separately considering marketability *as a stand-alone risk factor* violates this concept. [emphasis added] Buyers and sellers do not think this way; they generally consider marketability in their pricing decision and not as a separate adjustment.[6]

Factors that directly affect entity value. A basic misconception regarding private-company valuations must be addressed. To the extent that there is a private-company discount, it derives not from the fact that its shares are not traded in a public market but, in fact, from the characteristics of the company. The value of a company to an acquirer does not increase by virtue of having publicly traded shares. A well-run private company may be as marketable as a similar public company. In fact, in the author's experience, sale of a private company can occasionally be negotiated and consummated in a shorter period. Transactions for public companies may be subject to delays in clearing a proxy statement with the SEC and to the risks of shareholder opposition and class actions.

Nonetheless, there are factors that affect private companies much more often than public companies, causing private companies generally to be valued at lower multiples. Differentials in value between companies stem from specific identifiable factors, e.g.:

- Size;
- Diversification—geographic and/or product line;
- Dependence of key supplier and/or customer;
- Dependence on key man;
- Quality of earnings;
- Quality of financial reporting;
- Quality of management; and
- Lesser name recognition.

The factors discussed above directly impact the valuation of a business as a going concern. A DLOM for these items would be double counting. There are other factors that affect enterprise value, such as built-in gains and contingent liabilities (environmental, litigation, etc.), but these are also separate from a DLOM. Rather, these factors should be risk-adjusted, presented-valued, and deducted from enterprise value.

6 Letter to editor by Chris E. Best, *Business Valuation Update*, June 2016, p. 12. This article is reprinted on page 86.

Can a DLOM be applicable to entity value without double counting? After the above factors are taken into account, some factors might conceivably lead to marketability discounts without double counting. Impediments to the sale of a company as a whole that could impact the decision of a prospective buyer, but do not affect its going-concern value, could justify a DLOM. For example, a restriction on the sale of a business, such as a third-party's right of first refusal, could justify a DLOM because it has an adverse effect on the willingness of a potential acquirer to consider bidding.[7]

Another factor that New York has accepted as a basis for an entity-level DLOM is selling expenses, i.e., the hypothetical costs that would reduce the proceeds received if a company were sold at its going-concern value.[8] This is not double counting—costs of executing a transaction affect the proceeds from a transaction but not the going-concern value of a company.[9] When there is an intent to sell the business, an adjustment for selling costs is equitable.

Adjustments to entity-level valuations in appraisals using the market approach. As discussed above, companies valued using the income approach generally do not require a DLOM when the relevant factors are included in the DCF valuation. Similarly, when the market approach is applied and the relevant company-specific factors are reflected in adjustments to multiples, a discount for lack of marketability would be redundant. The multiples should reflect the impact of size, future growth prospects, quality of earnings, contingent liabilities, etc., i.e., the same factors that are applicable in a DCF analysis.[10]

It is clearly inappropriate to adjust for a DLOM based on premiums paid in other transactions (a statistically invalid sample of transactions that often includes synergistic benefits for the acquirer), discounts in private placements (based on sales of minority interests, not of control), or IPO studies (studies that exclude failed IPOs and are based on transactions separated by several months). Quackenbush points out:

> [S]ome business appraisers and accountants who have provided expert witness work for statutory fair value in New York have applied DLOMs based on their analysis of restricted stock studies and pre-IPO studies, both of which generate evidence for DLOMs for *noncontrol* interests [italics in original].... These flawed reports typically derive DLOMs of 30% to 50% based solely on the evidence of discounts attributable to noncontrol, minority interests with no discussion or empirical evidence connecting the studies referenced to the subject at hand: the pro rata share of the whole.[11]

7 A franchisor's right of first refusal was considered in a recent decision but was rejected because the respondent's expert did not quantify it. (*La Verghetta v. Lawlor*, 2016 N.Y. Misc. LEXIS 845 (N.Y. Supr., Mar. 9, 2016) at *60 and *62.) However, restrictions pursuant to shareholder agreements cannot be considered in determining fair value in New York. (*Friedman v. Beway Realty Corp.*, 661 N.E.2d 972, 977 (N.Y.1995) at 977, citing *Pace Photographers Matter of Pace Photographers, Ltd.*, 525 N.E.2d 713,719 (N.Y. 1988)).

8 *See, e.g., Adelstein v. Finest Food Distrib. Co., N.Y., Inc.*, 2011 N.Y. Misc. LEXIS 5956 (N.Y. Sup., Nov. 3, 2011) at *12, *21; *aff'd*, 116 A.D.3d 850 (N.Y. App. 2014) (5% discount for selling costs).

9 Mercer and Harms, p. 96.

10 Mercer proposes a methodology for adjusting multiples of private companies. Mercer and Harms, pp. 135-141.

11 See page 48. For example, New York courts have expressly accepted entity-level DLOMs based on discounts in private placements of minority interests in several cases. *See, e.g., Friedman v. Beway* at 65; *Hall v. King*, 675 N.Y.S.2d 810, 814 (N.Y. Supr. 1988; *aff'd*, 265 A.D.2d 244 (N.Y App. 1999)).

Studies of private-company multiples. Several studies have examined the differences between prices paid in acquisitions of private companies compared to acquisitions of public companies.[12] Various studies of "matched pairs" of acquisitions reached varying conclusions.

A study published in 2000 concluded that multiples of acquired private companies were 18% lower based on EBITDA and 30% lower based on EBIT but that the difference in multiples of sales was not statistically significant.[13] A 2003 study showed PCDs of 34% based on earnings, 20% based on cash flow, and 17% based on sales.[14] A 2007 study showed PCDs of about 24% based on EBITDA, EBIT, and sales.[15]

A 2007 study of acquisition transactions (not matched pairs) from 1979 through 2003 compared multiples paid in approximately 4,000 acquisitions of public companies (median size of $293 million) with multiples in approximately 400 acquisitions of private companies (median size of $53 million) and 400 acquisitions of unlisted subsidiaries of public companies (median size of $255 million). It looked at the average difference in the arithmetic mean[16] of multiples of revenues, EBITDA, net income, and book value. The study concluded that, compared to public companies that were acquired, private companies sold at average discounts of 17% but that subsidiaries sold at average discounts of 28%.[17] The subsidiaries were on average far larger than the private companies in the sample, and it is reasonable to assume that subsidiaries of public companies are likely to have good quality financial statements. Why would subsidiaries sell at smaller multiples? This question calls for further empirical research. One plausible explanation is that the discount was unrelated to size but instead due to the likelihood that companies that sell subsidiaries tend to sell off their underperforming businesses that command lower multiples.

A 2009 study used public filings of acquirers to obtain information on acquisitions of 947 private companies (those with average sales of $16 million) and 2,249 public companies (those with average sales of $130 million). After adjusting for differences in size, growth rates, R&D expense, and profit margins, the PCD was 20% based on sales and 39% based on EBITDA. The study reviewed the impact of auditors on transaction multiples and concluded that, if a private company's financials are not audited by a Big Four accounting firm, it sells at a multiple 11% to 24% lower.[18] The study also examined differences in the quality of financial data, finding that the differences between cash earnings and accrual earnings were larger for private companies. Shannon Pratt and Roger

12 Pratt and Grabowski, Chapter 24.

13 John Koeplin, Atulya Sarin, and Alan C. Shapiro, "The Private Company Discount," 12 *J. of Applied Corp. Fin.* 94 (2000) (84 transactions from 1984 to 1988).

14 Maher Kooli, Mohamed Kortas, and Jean-François L'Her, "A New Examination of the Private Company Discount: The Acquisition Approach," 6 *J. of Pvt. Equity* 48 (2003) (331 transactions from 1995 through 2002).

15 Stanley Block, "The Liquidity Discount in Valuing Privately Owned Companies," 17 *J. of Applied Fin.* 33 (2007) (91 transactions from 1999 through 2006).

16 The arithmetic mean gives greater weight to high multiples than to low multiples.

17 Micah S. Officer, "The Liquidity Discount in Valuing Privately Owned Companies," 83 *J. of Finl. Econ.* 571 (2007).

18 Gus De Franco, Ilanit Gavious, Justin Y. Jin, and Gordon D. Richardson, "Do Private Company Targets That Hire Big 4 Auditors Receive Higher Proceeds?" 28 *Contemporary Acctg. Research* 215 (2011).

Grabowski comment, "This [difference] is consistent with the theory that acquirers are more suspect of the earnings quality of the closely held firm."[19]

In contrast, two studies published in 2012 conclude that private companies do not necessarily sell at lower multiples than public companies. One study found that, although the private companies it reviewed that were acquired for more than $100 million sold at lower multiples, on average, than public companies, it arrived at a contrary result for firms selling from $20 million to $100 million. In fact, it found "a public ownership discount that is pronounced and statistically significant for smaller firms ($20-$100 million selling price)[,] opposite of the traditional view of a discount for the privately held firms."[20]

Another matched-pair study of private-company transactions in 11 Common Market countries found that the PCD was about 5% but noted that this amount was less than the cost of going public and concluded that, "when using the acquisition approach, size and profitability have no significant influence on the private company discount."[21]

Why do many studies show that private companies are acquired at materially lower multiples? One plausible reason is that, although the studies did consider size, they did not reflect the other factors enumerated above (in the section with the subhead "Factors that directly affect entity value"). It would be informative if a future study could attempt to measure the impact of these factors on PCDs. Proxy statements issued when public companies use shares to acquire a private company are a potential source of useful publicly available data over and above the information available from the databases, such as SDC, that are used in the various studies.[22] Summaries of the investment bankers' fairness opinions in the proxy statements and disclosures by acquirers of information regarding the acquired entities provide significant analytical data (over and above data available in databases) that can be helpful to researchers.

Regarding another factor, sales process, Pratt and Grabowski comment:

> Other reasons for the private company discount may hinge in part on the very sales process used in the sale of a private company. Often the entrepreneur restricts the sales process to be followed by the business broker engaged to sell the business.[23]

They appropriately explain why some private sellers may not obtain an optimum price. However, although the quality of the sales process may adversely impact the selling price, it does not change the value of the company itself. Instead, it results in the seller receiving *less than full value.* To the

19 Pratt and Grabowski, p. 660.

20 Anthony J. Anderson and Michael S. Long, "Evidence on Lack of Liquidity for Small Public Firms," 7 *J. of Bus. Val. and Economic Loss Analysis* 1, 2012.

21 Christian Klein and Marcus Scheibel, "The Private Company Discount From a European Perspective: An Analysis Based on the Acquisition Approach for Comparable Transactions of European Target Companies," 16 *J. of Pvt. Equity* 72 (2012).

22 Generally, a shareholder vote is required if a company issues 20% of its shares or more in the transaction. The sample is small—there were only about a dozen stock-for-stock acquisitions of private companies in 2009-14 that were large enough to require shareholder votes.

23 Pratt and Grabowski, p. 681.

extent that the studies discussed above included companies that sold for less than full value, they overstate the differences between *values* of public and private companies.

The discounts found in the various studies appear to the author not to reflect the difference in value deriving from whether or not a company's shares are publicly traded. Instead, I believe that they reflect differences that result from company-specific identifiable factors as well as the inefficiency of some sales processes that result in suboptimum selling prices.

In any event, a private-company discount includes company-specific factors and may in a few cases also include a DLOM. New York courts have sometimes imposed a "DLOM" that they attributed to the fact that the company is private. When the valuation has already accounted for the company-specific factors that engender a PCD, the resulting double counting has penalized dissenters.[24]

DLOMs in New York courts. Ongoing commentary agrees that when DLOMs are automatically applied at the enterprise level, the effect is to penalize the value of the minority or oppressed shareholder's shares, as Quackenbush and others experienced in New York statutory fair value practice attest. He believes that it would be helpful for experts to employ a "valuation-speak" in appraising a minority interest under New York statutory fair value:

> To determine the value of a non-control interest *not burdened with the penalties*, if any, regarding the subject interest's lack of control vis-à-vis a control level value, including any illiquidity or lack of marketability attributable to the lack of control nature of the oppressed interest—essentially the value of a pro-rata share of the whole. [emphasis added][25]

Quackenbush's attempt to arrive at a private-company enterprise value not encumbered with penalties that fall solely upon the minority or dissenting shareholder appears to correspond to statutory fair value in Delaware and almost all other states. This fair value principle posits that no DLOM should be applied to dissenters in fair value cases merely because their equity interests may not have liquidity. This principle underlies what he believes that the New York statute itself aims for: "an 'either-or' option: liquidate and pay out pro rata or buy out pro rata."[26] If the company had marketability or other issues that had already been reflected in the calculation of its entity value and the controller was forced to liquidate or sell the company, then all shareholders would receive their pro rata share of this "discounted" value and the principle of equal treatment for all shareholders would not be violated.

It should be noted that some New York trial court judges have recently taken the position that a DLOM is inapplicable when the control shareholder has expressed an intent not to sell the business, reasoning that the continuing shares would not bear the burden of illiquidity.[27]

24 *See, e.g., Ferolito v. AriZona Beverages USA, LLC*, 2014 N.Y. Misc. LEXIS 4709 (N.Y. Supr., Oct. 14, 2014) (valuation based on projected cash flows, discount rate included key man discount, 25% DLOM applied to 50% interest).

25 See page 45.

26 See page 47.

27 *Zelouf Intl. Corp. v. Zelouf*, 2014 N.Y. Misc. LEXIS 4341 (N.Y. Sup., Oct. 6, 2014) at *23; *La Verghetta v. Lawlor* at *63-*64.

Looking ahead. In the wake of recent New York fair value cases, Peter Mahler wrote in January 2016:

> As the debate evolves, personally I'd like to see more attention paid to appraisal doctrine, methodology, and data supporting or undermining the existence and quantification of DLOM at the enterprise level, *i.e.*, the "good" DLOM in fair value cases. It would be nice if the business valuation community could speak with one, clear voice on the issue, which would then facilitate consideration by legislators or, should they defer to the courts, appellate judges, of any needed changes to New York's policy toward DLOM in fair value proceedings.[28]

If the valuation community could coalesce over the reconceptualization of the PCD and its components, as well as the role, if any, of a DLOM, and then articulate clearly what the factors in that discount is, that common understanding could then be conveyed to the courts.

A good start for Mercer's view on the nonexistence or very small marketability discount for private enterprises is his *Business Valuation: An Integrated Theory* and his current series of blogs titled "Statutory Fair Value and Business Valuation."[29] To consider the countertheory that PCDs do exist because of a company's private or closely held structure, a reading of Pratt's and Grabowski's chapter on valuing controlling interests is recommended.[30]

Mercer's conclusions proceed from the conceptual framework in his book. His objective is to "create a theoretical framework and vocabulary with which we can talk about the valuation concepts that arise in statutory fair value determinations."[31] We think that, for valuators to reach agreement on private-company liquidity discounts and DLOMs, Mercer's framework presents a place to begin.

Other valuators might have criticisms or refinements to Mercer's approach or offer a better alternative. Our goal here is to support the heightened call from the valuation community to at least be able to speak with the same language to the courts and to each other. It is no longer helpful to ponder which differences are "semantic" and which substantive because of the absence of a shared professional language.[32] When a profession shares a common vocabulary, the disagreements can meet head on and not collide in a cloud of confusion. On the positive side, when a common foundation is shared, new contributions can be recognized as such.

28 Peter Mahler, "The DLOM Debate Heats Up," Jan. 25, 2016, available at www.nybusinessdivorce.com/2016/01/articles/valuation/the-dlom-debate-heats-up/.

29 Available at chrismercer.net/category/statutory-fair-value/.

30 Pratt and Grabowski, Chapter 24.

31 *BVWire*, #162-1, March 2, 2016.

32 Pratt commented that some factors that Mercer includes in his entity valuations could be included in a DLOM and called the differences "semantic." He said that you could "choose to call them by another name rather than lumping them under the marketability discount, but that is just a semantic argument." (Pratt, as quoted in Mercer and Harms, p. 148.)

Mercer and the author both believe that is not a "semantic difference" when a DLOM lumps in company-oriented factors that should be specifically considered in a valuation. These factors can be identified and their economic impact can be estimated in determining going-concern value. A DLOM, if and when it exists, is an adjustment to going-concern value.

Gilbert E. Matthews, *CFA, is chairman of the board and a senior managing director of Sutter Securities Inc. (San Francisco) and can be reached at gil@suttersf.com. He has more than 50 years of experience in investment banking and has spoken and written extensively on fairness opinions, corporate valuations, and litigation relating to valuations.*

The author would like to acknowledge the considerable assistance of Michelle Patterson, Ph.D., JD, in the preparation of this article.

Letter to the Editor:

Definitional Problem Underlies N.Y. Courts' Unfair DLOM Stance

Dear Editor:

Thanks for highlighting the article "NY's Unfair Application of Shareholder-Level Marketability Discounts" (page 21). I believe the problem with the case law is definitional. Whenever parties discuss DLOMs or any valuation discounts, the most important question that needs to be answered is: "Discount from what?" What "value" are you ultimately trying to determine?

Conceptually, the correct answer to the question is a pro rata share of the equity value of the company *as a closely held or non-publicly traded company.* The italicized part of the preceding definition, while implied in some decisions, is never explicitly discussed in any of the court cases I have reviewed and therein lies the confusion of the courts (and, it appears, of many business appraisers). The MBCA and ALI definitions of fair value do nothing to clarify the issue but rather obfuscate it because they do not define explicitly that the value that should be determined is that of a closely held or non-publicly traded company.

Clearly if an appraiser is using pricing data from the public marketplace in determining the value of the business without making some adjustment for differences in marketability of the public company and the closely held business, then the conclusion of value will reflect the marketability of a public company, not that of a closely held business. Therefore, not applying a marketability adjustment to this preliminary estimate of value may unduly enrich the dissenting shareholder. Applying a marketability adjustment, while proper, seems to violate the prohibition against applying a DLOM. To get around this issue, the author suggests that appraisers are considering the difference in marketability by adjusting the pricing multiples or cost of capital or some other area in the valuation process. Conceptually, this is the proper way to consider marketability in a valuation anyway. If an appraiser's job is to mimic the thought process of buyers and sellers in the marketplace and interpret the market data in the valuation process, then separately considering marketability as a stand-alone risk factor violates this concept because buyers and sellers do not think this way; they generally consider marketability in their pricing decision and not as a separate adjustment. I have never had a buyer or seller calculate a preliminary estimate of value and then apply valuation discounts; they just don't do that. They consider issues of control and marketability in determining their cost of capital.

Judges are not appraisers and may not understand the nuances of the valuation process. When they see a DLOM in a valuation, they tend to immediately disregard it based on the MBCA and ALI definitions without understanding the need for the DLOM in the valuation in order for it to reflect the proper value that is fair and equitable to all parties. In states that have adopted the MBCA definition, my concern is that ownership interests of dissenting shareholders are being overvalued because of this lack of understanding of basic valuation principles by the courts (and some business appraisers). Therefore, it is critically important for the appraiser that acts as the testifying expert to educate the court on the concept and clearly explain what value we are attempting to determine and why this is the appropriate definition of "fair value." Explaining this concept to the judge and educating him or her on how this affects the valuation process should account for a significant portion of and should be the centerpiece of the expert's testimony.

The authors are correct that the profession should take a stance on this issue. But, if we do so, we should define fair value without using the term "discount for lack of marketability" in the definition and do a better job of clearly explaining conceptually what value we are attempting to determine—the pro rata value of the business *as a closely held or non-publicly traded company*—and why. If we do so, we will provide the courts with a conceptual framework that judges can understand, which should result in more consistent, and equitable, decisions.

Chris E. Best, CPA/ABV, ASA, MCBA, ABAR
Managing Director
Acclaro Valuation Advisers
Kissimmee, Fla.
(www.AcclaroValuation.com)

ESOP Valuations in the Wake of 'Final' DOL Rule

The valuation community breathed a sigh of relief when the Department of Labor removed appraisals entirely—not just ESOP appraisals—from fiduciary treatment in its final rules[1] designed to strengthen retirement security. But the appraiser-as-fiduciary issue is not completely put to rest.

Strong signal. In the final rules, the DOL makes it a point to say that it is very concerned about this matter and will take it up again in separate rulemaking. "I think the DOL is sending a signal … actually a fairly strong one," says attorney Bruce Ashton (Drinker Biddle Reath LLP). Ashton's firm was involved in drafting the DOL/GreatBanc Fiduciary Process Agreement, an important settlement agreement that covers ESOP transactions and valuation issues.

"The good news for appraisers and valuation professionals, of course, is that they were dropped from the final rule," says Ashton. "The bad news is that the DOL goes out of its way to say—a number of times in one page—that this is an area that it is concerned about—especially in the ESOP context—and strongly suggests that it will take up this issue later on in a 'separate project.' So the issue is not dead, just on hold—though perhaps an extended hold."

He points out that this extended hold also represents good news and bad news. "On the good news side, the 'separate project' is unlikely to happen during the remainder of the Obama Administration, and whether it comes to pass under a future administration is anyone's guess," he says. "I suspect that if a Republican is in the White House, it will not, but—and here is the bad news part—if the next president is a Democrat, there is a fair chance that it will. Probably not right away, because they will have their hands full dealing with issues related to the just-released regulation. But I don't think the appraisal issue will go away."

Good outcome—so far. Valuation experts have reason to be happy with the outcome so far. "Stern Brothers Valuation Advisors is pleased to see that ESOP valuation experts are exempted from being named as a fiduciary to the ESOP," says Steven York, the firm's senior vice president. *BVU* attended a session on ESOPs York presented at the AICPA Forensic and Valuation Services Conference 2015 in Las Vegas. "The concerns expressed by various practitioners in the valuation industry about the

1 www.dol.gov/ebsa/regs/conflictsofinterest.html.

increased costs of liability insurance, increased time to prepare the annual valuation reports and related burdens were all addressed appropriately by the valuation industry," he says.

But York notes that it would have been helpful if the DOL had given more guidance since the appraiser-as-fiduciary issue is still open. "What was not discussed was the issue that if the valuation expert were to be the fiduciary for valuation issues for the ESOP trust, what role does the trustee play?" He also hopes that the DOL would issue a regulation defining the "adequate consideration" regulation that limits the value at which an ESOP can conduct a transaction. "Since a proposed definition[2] of adequate consideration was published in May of 1988 no regulations have been published or proposed by the DOL," he says.

Different animal. York explains that the valuation of an ESOP is very different from other valuation engagements. "The conclusion of value for ESOP purposes can cause a run of employee terminations if the value is set too high," he says "It can cause the ESOP participants to call for DOL review if the value is set too low, and it can facilitate an unfair transaction."

York feels that the best training for ESOP valuation work is to value the same interests in an ESOP trust for a 25-to-30-year period. "Only then can valuation experts understand their role with ESOP transactions, ESOP benefit payments to participants, the effect of debt structures used in stock purchases and the impact of the repurchase obligation on the future cash flows of the sponsoring company," he says. "In addition, if a valuation expert is to prepare any conclusion of value for ESOP purposes, they must read and understand the ESOP Trust and Plan documents, any Stock Purchase agreement, any Debt agreement, the benefit payment policy of the sponsoring company and all the related documents that support the ESOP documents."

Crackdown continues. The DOL continues to take action against valuations it perceives as faulty. "I've seen it in lots of DOL investigations of ESOPs where they frequently question the valuations used," says Ashton. For example, the agency recently obtained a judgment[3] against fiduciaries of a California ESOP in a lawsuit alleging the fiduciaries paid inflated prices for company stock. Also, the DOL recently filed a complaint[4] against owners of a Florida company for selling their stock to their ESOP for almost double the alleged fair market value. "I think it is an ongoing issue that probably is going to continue regardless of whether the DOL takes regulatory action," he says.

Ashton advises that practitioners should proactively think about how to strengthen ESOP valuation practices and procedures in the future. "Put effort into thinking about a worst-case scenario in terms of a DOL regulatory regime. That's not an over-the-top suggestion because something's going to happen." He also suggests that a self-regulation approach—a renewed effort on the setting of standards and practices—may make some sense for the valuation profession.

2 FR Doc. 88-10934 Filed 5-16-88; 8:45 a.m.; David Walker (assistant secretary, Pension and Welfare Benefits Administration, U.S. Department of Labor).

3 www.dol.gov/ebsa/newsroom/2016/16-224-SAN.html.

4 www.dol.gov/ebsa/newsroom/2016/16-127-ATL.html.

What to do. Use the recommendations contained in the GreatBanc settlement agreement when doing an ESOP valuation. The agreement includes a set of policies and procedures that GreatBanc must follow in the future when it is engaged to purchase or sell employer securities that are not publicly traded. The DOL has made past remarks that everyone will "do well to take notice of" the agreement, even though it formally applies only to GreatBanc. For example, it contains rules on independence and stresses the importance of documenting the reasonableness of management projections. A few of the other guidelines it recommends are:

- The trustee is required to request five years of audited, unqualified financial statements. If the trustee relies on a lower level of financial statements (i.e., qualified or unaudited financial statements), the trustee must document the reason that it is prudent to rely on such financial statements in order to proceed with the transaction.
- A "Trustee Report" that constitutes an analysis of the valuation report must be created. According to the settlement, 16 specific items (which relate to methodologies, accepted practices, documentation, and analytical measures) must be documented.
- Documentation of the trustee's evaluation of the valuation report must include disclosure of material points on which personnel disagreed.

After the GreatBanc agreement was issued, valuation analysts began to incorporate relevant parts of it into their reports, such as additional boilerplate language and more explanation and documentation.

"Stern Brothers Valuation Advisors treats the settlement agreement as guidelines for a good ESOP valuation," says York. "The rules on independence we follow, but we always have for more than 30 years. The other topics in the settlement agreement are being reviewed for all DOL valuation 'enforcement actions' as the DOL calls them now, so we include a statement that we have prepared the report in compliance with the guidelines from the settlement report. Then we back up that compliance in the text of the report by addressing all the items in the settlement agreement, to the extent they are applicable in each report."

You can get a copy of the actual GreatBanc agreement from the DOL's website[5] or you can purchase a version with excellent commentary from the attorneys who negotiated the agreement. That version is *The DOL Fiduciary Process Agreement for ESOP Transactions,* and it's available from the National Center for Employee Ownership (www.nceo.org).

5 www.dol.gov/ebsa/pdf/esopagreement.pdf.

Government Crackdowns, M&A, S Corps in Spotlight at NYSSCPA BV Conference

Some of the profession's hottest topics were covered at the annual business valuation conference of the New York State Society of CPAs (NYSSCPA) in New York City. Interestingly, representatives of both the Public Company Accounting Oversight Board (PCAOB) and the Department of Labor (DOL) were there giving presentations, which is uncommon for an event such as this one. Here are a few of the key takeaways from those sessions—as well as the others.

Fair value audits. George Wilfert of the PCAOB gave an update on audit deficiencies for 2015. While the agency found that the overall number of audit deficiencies decreased compared to 2014, preliminary results indicate an increase in the number of audit deficiencies regarding auditors' testing of fair value measurements associated with business combinations. In addition, there were frequent deficiencies in evaluating impairment analyses for goodwill and other long-lived assets. Auditing internal control over financial reporting and assessing and responding to risks of material misstatement were also areas where the PCAOB found frequent audit deficiencies.

He also mentioned that the standards for auditors' use of specialists will be changing. Last year, the PCAOB issued for public comment a staff consultation paper on potential standard-setting activities related to the auditor using the work of specialists, including valuation professionals. The University of Wisconsin-Madison is conducting a survey[1] on the role of specialists in developing and evaluating the fair value estimates used in audited financial statements. This research may help in the PCAOB's standard setting in this regard. If you complete the survey, you will receive a $10 Starbucks gift card. The data collected will be confidential, and a second phase of the study will involve optional interviews of survey respondents.

DOL vs. ESOPs. The DOL continues its crackdown on ESOP valuations it perceives as faulty, according to Thomas Leroe-Munoz and Daniel Schiffer, both part of the DOL's ESOP enforcement efforts. The agency recently obtained a judgment against fiduciaries of a California ESOP in a lawsuit alleging the fiduciaries paid inflated prices for company stock. The DOL also filed a complaint

1 Access the survey at uwmadison.co1.qualtrics.com/SE/?SID=SV_bKQl541Kd4WeCAR.

against owners of a Florida company for selling their stock to their ESOP for almost double the alleged fair market value.

Leroe-Munoz points out that the agency frequently questions the projections used in the valuations. True, the valuation analysts can include a disclaimer that the projections came from management, but the fiduciary needs to question this. Often, the individuals selling shares to the ESOP are the same ones who provide the projections. Responding to a question from the audience, Schiffer confirmed that auditors have been held criminally liable.

Recently, the DOL removed ESOP appraisals from fiduciary treatment in its final rules designed to strengthen retirement security. But this issue was not completely put to rest. There will be separate future rule making on the issue of appraisals and fairness opinions in the context of investment advice subject to the fiduciary requirements. In the meantime, the DOL has made past remarks that everyone will "do well to take notice of" the DOL/GreatBanc Fiduciary Process Agreement[2] that covers ESOP transactions and valuation issues. Although the agreement formally applies only to GreatBanc, it serves as overall guidelines. However, Leroe-Munoz told the audience that the GreatBanc agreement is "not a totality of all the requirements."

S corp model in Tax Court. A much-debated issue in the valuation community is tax affecting the earnings of a pass-through entity (PTE), and there is no definitive answer. The tax-affecting issue has been argued in a number of Tax Court cases (most notably the *Gross* case). In all of these cases, the IRS and the Tax Court have refuted the notion that shareholder-level taxes affect a firm's value, so the valuation conclusions in these cases were based on earnings not being tax affected. The valuation community disagrees, so a number of models were developed that are designed to reflect the impact of shareholder taxes on value.

Daniel Van Vleet (Stout Risius Ross) revealed that the Van Vleet model (S corporation economic adjustment model) is being used for the first time in a U.S. Tax Court case. What's more, both the IRS and the taxpayer are using it in this case, says Van Vleet.

The case is *Cecil et al. v. Commissioner of Internal Revenue,* and it involves a gift of shares in the Biltmore Co., which operates the famous Biltmore estate, a Gilded Age mansion built by the Vanderbilts that is now a tourist attraction. The Cecils (descendants of the Vanderbilts) valued the stock gift at $20.88 million, but the IRS said those shares are actually worth $95.29 million. The valuation difference is due to the Cecils' use of going-concern value while the IRS says a liquidation value makes more sense. Details of the case and specifics on the valuations have not been disclosed because the case is ongoing.

Industry-specific analyses. Years ago, some valuation reports had very minimal industry information, but those days are gone. There is a great deal more industry-specific information at your

2 www.dol.gov/ebsa/pdf/esopagreement.pdf.

fingertips than years ago, which means that a better assessment of industry-specific risk can be done, according to Mark S. Gottlieb (Mark S. Gottlieb, CPA, PC). His firm spends a good deal of time on an industry-specific review that can be very meaningful in terms of drawing conclusions of value. But he notes that a proper industry-specific analysis and presentation in a report can be expensive—especially when you're doing an industry for the first time. Fortunately, a great deal of research online and some third-party vendors provide industry-specific information. He mentioned that BVR is a good portal for some of this information (e.g., BVR offers First Research industry profiles).

Preclose M&A engagements. More companies are performing preacquisition valuations, and valuators are being called in earlier in the process, according to Raymond Weisner *(Valuation Research Corp.—VRC)*. Large and multinational companies are bringing in their valuation firms one to three months in advance of any deal announcement. Valuators are being asked to assist with due diligence support, working alongside of the quality of earnings, tax, and technical due diligence teams. In particular, this is done for the purpose of valuing intangibles and to conduct an analysis of any contingent consideration.

Weisner pointed out that 50% of clients' acquisition models have material errors. So VRC reviews the model prior to a deal closing. In one case, a U.S.-based pharmaceutical company was considering the acquisition of a company in the U.K. The buyer's internal models included tax amortization of goodwill. But, in the U.K., purchased goodwill can be recognized for tax purposes in an asset acquisition but not in an acquisition of shares. This change impacted the buyer's forecasts to the degree that the buyer withdrew from the deal.

Cost of capital. James Harrington (Duff & Phelps) gave an overview of the *Valuation Handbook* series his firm publishes (all available from BVR). There are four separate volumes, all published annually with updated data and optional updates. There are two "U.S.-centric" D&P handbooks: (1) the *Valuation Handbook - Guide to Cost of Capital,* which provides size premia, equity risk premia, industry risk premia, and other critical valuation inputs; and (2) the *Valuation Handbook - Industry Cost of Capital,* which provides industry-level cost of capital statistics for around 180 U.S. industries.

Then there are two international volumes: (1) the *International Valuation Handbook - Guide to Cost of Capital,* which provides country-level base cost of equity and other information for around 180 countries, from the perspective of investors in up to 56 different countries; and (2) the *Valuation Handbook - Industry Cost of Capital,* which provides the same type of rigorous industry-level analysis published in the U.S.-centric *Valuation Handbook - Industry Cost of Capital,* on a global scale.

An audience member asked: "When valuing an international firm, do you do it from the perspective of the home country or from the perspective of the U.S.?" Harrington says D&P does it both ways, in the home currency and then using local inputs and then converting to home currency. Of course, he points out that local inputs are not always available.

As for other data resources, D&P recently acquired the rights to the *SBBI Classic Yearbook* from Morningstar, which will be published by John Wiley & Sons. This resource provides a history of the returns on the capital markets (i.e., "Stocks, Bonds, Bills, and Inflation") in the United States from 1926 to the present.

Stock tip. When determining a discount rate when valuing redeemable preferred stock, consider the current market yield, advises Jaime d'Almeida (Duff & Phelps). If the dividend is at or close to the current market rate for preferred stock with comparable features and risks, the stated rate can be a proxy for market yield. If the dividend is not close to a current market yield rate, you need to estimate a current market yield rate. But how? Consider S&P Preferred Stock Ratings Criteria and "notching," the use of spreads, and preferred stock comparables (publicly traded and new issues). *Important point:* Consider adjusting for any differences in key features, such as special voting rights, liquidation rights, and callability.

Domain name/trademark combo. In his session on branding, trademarks, and domain names, Craig Jacobson (GlassRatner) advised that, when a domain name is part of a trademark, it's not possible to separate out the value of the two. When a domain name is not part of the trademark, the valuation is based on the traffic generated to the website. He also mentioned that there is "very little written" on the valuation of domain names.[3]

He also mentioned an Internet phenomenon known as "cyberstuffing." Under this scheme, a competitor's trademark is encrypted into a domain name to redirect the competitor's customers to the perpetrator. This, of course, can trigger a claim for damages.

Jacobson also pointed out that the new federal law, the Defend Trade Secrets Act (DTSA), will change the protections for trade secrets. In the past, trade secrets were protected only at the state level, with most states (other than New York and Massachusetts) adopting their own version of the Uniform Trade Secrets Act (UTSA). The DTSA creates a trade secret action under federal law that is intended to supplement, rather than preempt, state laws.

Personal injury. Personal injury and wrongful death damages is an area of increasing interest to valuation experts, so a session by attorney Paul Cohen (Gialleonardo, McDonald & Turchetti) was met with a great deal of enthusiasm. Speaking specifically about the jurisdiction of New York, Cohen mentioned that New York courts do not use a *Daubert* standard (a federal standard), but rather the *Frye* standard (which is tougher than *Daubert*). Also, a very negative aspect to practice in New York is that the experts are not generally deposed, so the first time an expert appears is in court. And the trial often hinges on the experts—medical, valuation (economic), and vocational experts—who all work hand-in-hand to determine damages.

3 A new article on valuing domain names, "Internet Domain Valuation: Not Just Economic Theory," by Jim Horvath and Jeff Horvath, appears in this issue.

Cohen also pointed out that experts in New York cannot consider issues that the court feels are too speculative in determining damages. These include medical advances, cyclical layoffs, and industry conditions. You can, however, consider matters if there is enough support for your position. For example, if a worker is at risk of losing his or her job due to bad performance reviews, that can be taken into account when projecting out lost earnings. He also noted that selecting the discount rate for future losses is simple—it's automatically set by New York statute to the 10-year Treasury rate.

BVU congratulates the NYSSCPA for a very fine conference, and we look forward to attending next year!

Debate Rekindles Over Private Company Cost of Capital Model

A recent issue of *The Value Examiner*[1] devotes a good deal of space to the implied private company pricing line (IPCPL), a model designed to better estimate the cost of capital for small private companies (those with revenues below $150 million). The model has been "gaining traction" since it was first introduced in 2012 and after a series of articles that appeared in *Business Valuation Update* starting in 2013.

In *The Value Examiner* issue, an article by Richard Conn (Conn Valuation Services Ltd.) calls into question whether IPCPL is "well-founded on empirical evidence as its proponents claim." To its credit, *The Value Examiner* had the IPCPL developers respond in the same issue. This is a practice *BVU* applauds because, otherwise, criticism can take root for months while a response is bogged down due to publishing time frames. Rod Burkert (Burkert Valuation), Pete Butler (Valtrend), and Bob Dohmeyer (Dohmeyer Valuation Corp.), who are on the IPCPL development team, wrote the rebuttal. There is also a Letter to the Editor written by Igor Gorshunov, a business valuation and private equity professional, that addresses some of Conn's concerns.

The IPCPL model aggregates 500 *Pratt's Stats* private-company transactions and directly estimates the aggregate internal rate of return (IRR) on free cash flows. By using the prices paid for small privately held companies, there is no need to extrapolate returns of public equity securities, which is something that makes many valuation professionals uncomfortable. By looking to private-company transactions, the effects of liquidity, unsystematic risk, taxes, and so on are "baked-into" the clearing prices paid (fair market value) for the businesses. This ex ante approach is fundamentally the same as the implied equity risk premium approach used by Professor Aswath Damodaran (New York University Stern School of Business).

Two problems. In his article,[2] Conn points up two issues he feels are problematic. The first is that the IPCPL model is based on the belief that there is a reliable correlation between cost of equity

1 *The Value Examiner,* National Association of Certified Valuators and Analysts (NACVA), January-February 2016 (www.nacva.com/valueexaminer).

2 A full version is available at www.connvaluation.com/caseStudies/Conn_Does_IPCPL_Make_Sense.pdf.

and company revenues. Conn believes that this is not logical, and he conducted some tests on his own that found that, "at best, revenues are only very poorly correlated to cost of equity."

His second issue has to do with the use of the double-Lehman curve. A "double Lehman" is a variation of the Lehman scale, which is a formula used to compute the commission paid to an intermediary in the sale of a business. In the IPCPL context, it's used to adjust for transaction costs. The "assertion of the double-Lehman curve appears to be entirely artificial," according to Conn, who says there is no empirical evidence to support its use in this context, which undermines the utility of IPCPL.

Rebuttal. In their rebuttal, the IPCPL developers address Conn's contention that it doesn't make sense to expect revenues to be a reliable predictor or determinant of cost of equity. "In our IPCPL presentations, we note that appraisers agree, on average: very small privately held companies have higher total risk, lower debt capacity, and are less liquid than much larger companies and as a consequence, have a relatively higher cost of capital." They also point to analysis by Duff & Phelps that shows an inverse relationship between the historical equity risk premium and sales.

As for the issue of the double-Lehman curve, the IPCPL developers respond by saying that its use is not "based on faith (alone), but on well-accepted theory." They point to an independent review of IPCPL[3] that confirms that the use of the double-Lehman formula is consistent with asset pricing theory.

The IPCPL developers specifically rebut other points in Conn's article. For example, he indicates throughout his article that IPCPL is capturing a cost of equity. "This is not true. The IPCPL calculates a weighted average cost of capital (WACC), not a cost of equity."

Independent validation. In a Letter to the Editor, Gorshunov says that Conn, while concentrating on the relationship of company size to cost of equity, "unfortunately skips a major part of the model, called 'Point 1' in IPCPL terminology." In Gorshunov's view, this is the main point of the model "because it addresses the cost of capital on private market directly, avoiding reliance on public market cost of capital.... And to do this, the IPCPL relies on a very appealing assumption—that the private market as a whole is always in a steady state, and thus, can be described by a Gordon formula."

In a 2015 article,[4] Gorshunov describes an empirical test of the IPCPL cost of capital and the concept of margin reversion. He describes the test: "By arranging companies in the market by their operating profit margin we could observe the market valuation line (based on the market data) and steady-state valuation line, which represents the hypothetical valuation of the company based on

3 David H. Goodman and Malcolm McLelland, "The Implied Private Company Pricing Line (IPCPL): On the Nature, Scope, and Assumptions of IPCPL Theory," June 19, 2015. Available at SSRN: ssrn.com/abstract=2609159.

4 Igor Gorshunov, "IPCPL and Margin Reversion: Implications for the Valuation of Small Privately Held Companies," *Business Valuation Review*, Summer 2015 (reprinted in *Business Valuation Update*, September 2015).

Available Resources on the IPCPL Model

Bob Dohmeyer and Peter Butler, "The Implied Private Company Pricing Line: Empirically Observing the Cost of Capital," *Business Valuation Review*, Spring 2012.

Special feature (complimentary) on the implied private company pricing line/the implied private company pricing model, available in BVR's Cost of Capital Resource Center,[1] contains the following articles from *Business Valuation Update:*

- "The Implied Private Company Pricing Line 2.0 $K_0 = (FCFF_1/P) + g$";
- "The Implied Private Company Pricing Model (IPCPM) $K_0 = (FCFF_1/P) + g$";
- "BV Community Reacts to New Cost of Capital Tool";
- "IPCPL Developers Field Queries on the New Model's Underlying Data";
- "The Implied Private Company Pricing Line";
- "Utilizing the Implied Private Company Pricing Model: The Cost of Capital Wizard"; and
- "Frequently Asked Questions."

David H. Goodman and Malcolm McLelland, "The Implied Private Company Pricing Line (IPCPL): On the Nature, Scope, and Assumptions of IPCPL Theory," June 19, 2015. Available at SSRN: ssrn.com/abstract=2609159.

Igor Gorshunov, "IPCPL and Margin Reversion: Implications for the Valuation of Small Privately Held Companies," *Business Valuation Review*, Summer 2015 (reprinted in *Business Valuation Update*, September 2015).

Richard R. Conn, "Does the Implied Private Company Pricing Line Make Sense?" *The Value Examiner*, January-February 2016, www.nacva.com/valueexaminer.

Rod Burkert, Pete Butler, and Bob Dohmeyer, "Rebuttal: The IPCPL DOES Make Sense," *The Value Examiner*, January-February 2016, www.nacva.com/valueexaminer.

Igor Gorshunov, "Letter to the Editor Re: 'Does the Implied Private Company Pricing Line Make Sense?'" *The Value Examiner*, January-February 2016, www.nacva.com/valueexaminer.

Webinar: The Implied Private Company Pricing Line, with Bob Dohmeyer and Rod Burkert, Business Valuation Resources, Nov. 7, 2013 (www.bvresources.com/pastevents.asp).

Webinar: Utilizing the Implied Private Company Pricing Model: The Cost of Capital Wizard, with Bob Dohmeyer, Peter Butler, and Rod Burkert, Business Valuation Resources, March 5, 2014 (www.bvresources.com/pastevents.asp).

Data: *Business Valuation Update* includes a Private Company Cost of Capital Index (updated monthly) based on *Pratt's Stats* data and IPCPL.

1 www.bvmarketdata.com/defaulttextonly.asp?f=IPCPL.

the IPCPL cost of capital and constant growth rate. If both IPCPL cost of capital and the margin reversion concept are correct, these two lines should intersect at the point of average margin." For the test, the author used 840 data points on private-company transactions sourced from *Pratt's Stats*. Based on the test results, the author states: "This independent test indicates that IPCPL is a reliable source for small private companies' cost of capital."

This article, the IPCPL developers say, clears up many of Conn's concerns, and it will be reprinted in an upcoming issue of *The Value Examiner* (but it is available now to *Business Valuation Update* subscribers—see Footnote 4). Also, Conn will provide a Part 2 of his questioning of IPCPL.

Available readings. The IPCPL developers note that Conn says he has followed the literature on IPCPL, but they point out the difficulty of that because articles and research have appeared in various places. They also say it is unclear whether he is aware of the implied private company pricing model (IPCPM), which is used to fine-tune private-company cost of capital for factors other than just revenue.

In the accompanying sidebar is a list all of the literature available to date on IPCPL and IPCPM. *BVU* urges readers to look at all of this material to develop their own conclusions and to continue this discussion. Your feedback is welcome!

Internet Domain Valuation: Not Just Economic Theory

By Jim Horvath and Jeff Horvath

For many people, establishing the value of an Internet domain name appears to be a well-defined black-and-white process that considers a variety of economic variables and formulae to obtain a satisfactory conclusion. But, ultimately, determining that amount is much more an art than a science. Domain names are one of the few items whose value is truly specific, based primarily on the price a buyer is willing to pay and the seller to accept.

Background. There are two categories of domain names. Those created by industry users such as "hiltonhotels.com," which usually have also been trademarked, and those speculatively initiated as inventory to be sold or monetized in some fashion; most transactions fall into the latter group. Both are traded in one of the two types of active markets for domain names. The first is for and between "domainers" (Domainer2Domainer transactions) who hold portfolios of domain names as investors seeking returns; the other is with "trade" buyers (Domainer2B transactions) who want the name as part of their marketing program.

Trademarked-related domains referred to above include those protected as a registered or an unregistered trademark or an unregistered trademark that is also a pending application, and/or a trademark for which a registration certificate has been issued. If so, and with respect to any of the above, where? The value of a mark increases with actual use and is affected by: (i) inherent distinctiveness; and (ii) the surrounding landscape (such as cluttered with similar marks).

Prices differ greatly between the two. In a 2011 business-to-business (B2B) transaction, Apple bought "icloud.com" for $4.5 million as the "i" prefix had become its corporate symbol. To a domainer, it would have a value based only on possible revenues. Assuming those were $9,500 a month (the average for comparable websites), the bid prices (minimum) would be $115,000 based on a 12-month payback. His offer price (maximum) would be $370,000 reflecting a 20% discount rate over a five-year life. Each of those is only a small fraction of what Apple was willing to pay as part of its branding process.

However, most transactions are in neither league. During the last working week of March 2016 (ending April 3), the highest price reported by *Domain News Journal* was $176,000 for "debit.com" and the smallest of the 500 listed "top" transactions was only $1,155 for "world-schizophrenia.org"; the median sale price was $3,000. Based on those, a domainer offering the minimum amount for iCloud would be paying significantly over the odds while a trade buyer would settle for many times more. Realistically, unless the domainer already has a potential buyer in mind and was buying purely for the purposes of flipping, he or she would only be willing to pay a speculative amount.

Many methods and models have been suggested for valuing domain names. The most commonly used is the real estate model that suggests that values should be based on prices paid for comparable properties in a neighborhood. This is a fair analogy considering domain names are a form of online real estate (effectively a Web address) and that some neighborhoods are more desirable than others. As with real estate, the extent to which the property has been developed affects a domain's value; a name of a site that is generating significant revenue is worth more than one that is not in use. There are always examples that don't fit the model, although, as markets become more efficient, real anomalies are becoming scarcer. Ultimately most deals reflect a buyer with a unique requirement that can't be satisfied in any other way and a seller who is patient enough to not settle for the first offer that comes along.

Real transactions. For example, consider the sale of "eBet.com" in September 2013 by Rick Schwartz (known as the "Domain King") to Network Solutions LLC. Allegedly the latter started on Aug. 29, 2013, with a lowball opening bid of $50,000, which was countered by an offer of $1.8 million. A few days later, Network's bid was increased to $1 million. The next round was a response of $1.6 million, being countered with a $1.1 million bid, resulting in a $500,000 spread. At this point, Schwartz reduced his asking price by $250,000 (splitting the difference), to $1.35 million, which, on September 16 (18 days after the initial bid), Network accepted.

What was the fair market value of that domain? Schwartz's original cost in 1996 was $100; 18 years later, he sold for $1.35 million. During this long period, he had the vision that one day the name might have a significant perceived value to someone and that if he held out he could obtain a substantial premium price. In such a sales process, the owner and the brokers or agents involved have to convince the buyer of the benefits of the acquisition.

That is not great news for an executor who needs a value for the purposes of dividing a set of assets owned by an estate among the heirs in a time-limited tax filing window, nor for an owner/operator seeking an exit by the sale of a business. There simply isn't enough time to find the right premium buyer. In our example, the waiting game paid off. Schwartz knew full well that, for select domains, within reason, of course, there is at least one corresponding prospective premium buyer with deep pockets that fully understands the value of the name for its own use.

The key for a domainer (who has the supply) is to find or wait for a suitable end user, which, as Schwartz says, has the "need, want, and desire" (the demand). In many cases, there may only be a single suitable prospective buyer, so, to generate a transaction at a premium price, the seller has to play hardball and clearly demonstrate the benefits of the name to the specific buyer. Often the domainer/investor/broker will only be able to suggest likely benefits and will not be in a position to quantify all of them to the particular purchaser.

Major trends. Pockets are not as deep today as they were in years gone by; there are still some significant sales, although they are few and far between. Since the late 1990s (about 18 years), Schwartz has recorded about 20 "many zeros" transactions (often contain a lucky number "8") from a portfolio of about 6,000 domains.

We have reviewed the 128 reported transactions in domain names for over $1 million each. Only eight (6.2%) were not ".com," the major top-level domain (TLD) for the United States. Based on a limited search of (same first name) comparable sales, a ".com" is worth at least four times as much as the one with the second-ranked U.S. TLD, ".net". The other non ".com" TLDs in the over-$1 million class are: "Inn.im" (Isle of Mann offshore U.K. tax haven, $1,800,000 in 2009); "bank.ht" (Haiti, $6,400,000 in 2010); "kredit.de" (Germany, $1,169,000 in 2008); "motorcycle.se" (Sweden, $1,100,000 in 2000); "cruise.co.uk" (United Kingdom, $1,100,000 in 2008); "poker.org" (U.S. not for profit, $1,000,000 in 2010); and "beauty.cc" (Cocos Islands in the Indian Ocean, $1,000,000 in 1999).

Exhibit 1 lists the 22 reported sales for $7,000,000 or more. Of those, six included some content or other business assets, meaning that a portion of the price was likely non-domain-name related.

Exhibit 1. Top Domain Name Sales

Rank	Name	Price (US$)	Year
1	CarInsurance.com	49,700,000	2010 + Content
2	Insurance.com	35,600,000	2010 + Content
3	VacationRentals.com	35,000,000	2007 + Content
4	PrivateJet.com	30,180,000	2012 + Content
5	LasVegas.com	24,264,000	2005 $90M aggregate to 2040
6	Internet.com	18,000,000	2009
7	360.com	17,000,000	2015
8	Insure.com	16,000,000	2009 + Content
9	Bankaholic.com	15,000,000	2008
10	Sex.com	13,000,000	2010
11	IRS.com	12,500,000	2007
12	Hotels.com	11,000,000	2001
13	CardRatings.com	10,200,000	2008
14	Fund.com	9,999,950	2008
15	Porn.com	9,500,000	2007
16	Prono.com	8,888,888	2015
17	Fb.com	8,500,000	2010
18	RealEstate.com	8,250,000	2011
19	We.com	8,000,000	2015-2016
20	Business.com	7,500,000	1999
21	Diamond.com	7,500,000	2006
22	Beer.com	7,000,000	2004 + Content

As might be expected, such high value sales started in 1998 with the Internet stock market bubble, disappeared in 2002, and hit a peak in 2008 just before the financial crisis as shown in Exhibit 2. However, the exhibit also shows that, after 2008, this top end of the market revitalized itself, with 53% of the value of such transactions being obtained from 2009 to 2015 with a significantly higher (35%) average sale.

Name benefit. Our first insight from the high value sales listing is that, excluding four numbers, 12 abbreviations, and 18 compound phrases ("carinsurance"), a large majority (74%) are common generic, single,

Exhibit 2. Summary Top Domain Names

Year	Total > US$ million	Number	Average (US$)
1998	3,300,000	1	3,300,000
1999	17,300,000	7	2,471,429
2000	26,840,000	12	2,236,667
2001	11,000,000	1	11,000,000
2002	–	–	–
2003	16,545,000	10	1,654,500
2004	13,850,000	4	3,462,500
2005	29,994,000	4	7,498,500
2006	20,100,000	6	3,350,000
2007	75,830,000	11	6,893,636
2008	69,321,895	14	4,951,564
2009	53,905,000	12	4,492,083
2010	118,608,830	10	11,860,883
2011	24,050,000	7	3,435,714
2012	43,630,000	6	7,271,667
2013	12,565,000	5	2,513,000
2014	32,385,800	13	2,491,215
2015	38,988,888	6	6,498,148
	608,214,413	129	4,714,840

Period	Total > US$ million		Number		Average Sale	
1998-2008	284,080,895	46.7%	70	54.3%	4,058,299	86.1%
2009-2015	324,133,518	53.3%	59	45.7%	5,493,788	116.5%
	608,214,413		129			

pronounceable words, spelled correctly with no hyphenation, mixed characters, or numbers. Such common words are more likely to appear as search terms, and therefore probably websites using such names will receive more traffic (especially type-in traffic), although that too is changing as Web surfers are becoming more reliant on search engines and apps.

Our second insight is that more than half of the names on this list have six characters or less. That is not to say the shortest names are the most valuable; the top four all have eight characters or more. However, a shorter name is likely more memorable and therefore has a higher value. In the *DNJournal* list of "2014 Top 100 Domain Sales," 15 of the first 17 listed transactions reflect names with five characters or less (the two longer ones were "whisky .com"—six characters—and "teamwork.com," with eight). The DNpric.es top 1,000 also reflects a short name bias as more than half on the list have six characters or less.

For 2015, DNJournal.com reported that the aggregate selling price of the top 10 domain sales (all extensions) was $23.4 million, with the largest amounts being $8,888,888 on the sale of "porno .com" by Schwartz, followed by the private sale of "we.com" for $8 million. In that year, Schwartz realized an aggregate $10.5 million from the first, fifth, and seventh highest prices. After No. 10, the prices dropped significantly, with the next 90 ranging downwards from $555,050 to $80,000 with a median of only $140,000. However, unreported by DNJournal.com was the February 2015 sale by Vodafone Group to Chinese Internet security company, Qihoo 360 Technology Co. Ltd. of "360.com" for $17 million (USD). Qihoo's chairman and CEO, Zhou Hongyi, is sometimes referred to as "domain gangster" by Chinese media.

A notable example is "marijuana.com" (No. 38 in the over-$1 million list), which was sold in 2011 for $4.2 million by WeedMaps, a subsidiary of General Cannabis Inc. As worldwide acceptance for medical and recreational marijuana increases, the value of this domain undoubtedly will also rise.

This provides our third insight: Value is in some way dependent on social conditions and current events. For example, "elections2016.com" has significant value up to and perhaps a little after the U.S. federal elections in November 2016 but likely not much after that date. In fact, this domain has been registered and is currently for sale.

Longer names are also differentiated by their full meaning; websites such as insurance.com, privatejet.com, or crosswordpuzzles.com are unambiguous as to their likely subject matter (nearly half of all ".com" registrations are English keywords), which encourage consumers to click through search results, giving the owner access to better qualified online traffic—hence, a higher value.

Other TLDs. In the past, there was no question that ".com" domains have garnered the highest values. It remains to be seen whether this trend will continue. The laws of economic supply and demand are very effective for ".com" names. With more than 100 million registered, it is becoming increasingly difficult to find one that matches a user's unique requirements and is still available. This issue is further exacerbated by the fact that the Internet landscape recently changed dramatically with the 2015 introduction of nearly 400 new English TLDs ranging from "academy" to "zone" plus similar ones in Arabic, Chinese (traditional and simplified), Cyrillic, Devanagari, Greek, Hangul, Hebrew, Japanese (Kanji + Kana), Persian, and Tamil. Those are in addition to the seven original U.S. TLDs (".com," ".org," ".net," ".info," ".edu," ".gov," and ".mil") and 253 country TLDs. Buyers now have a choice of over 1,650 types of domain names, giving consumers a wealth of options beyond the traditional ".com." For example, recently "ottawapizza.com" was registered, while "ottawa.pizza" was still available. How the numerous new TLDs will affect the value of ".com" domain names is subject to ongoing debates with proponents both for increases and decreases. In our view, it is hard to imagine that the impact of more choice, better availability, and greater relevance will not drive down the values of all domain names, not just ".coms."

Currently, the awareness of the range of new TLDs is low, but we believe that will soon change particularly as brands adopt them (Barclays, the international bank, operates ".barclays" as a secure platform for customers). It is also debatable to what extent search engines may favor TLDs that add relevance to a result. For example, in a search for "mycity ski club," which domain might generate a higher favored result: "mycityski.club" or "mycityskiclub.com"? Google says its search algorithm would rank both sites the same, meaning that now it is the content that drives results. However, whether this situation will persist is not clear. It is reasonable that in the future a search for some kind of "club" would rank ".club" domain names more highly.

Plurals. Names that are plurals tend to have a higher value than the singular version of the same word. For example "hotels.com" sold for $11 million in 2001. Today "hotel.com" simply redirects a visitor to the plural version of the site, which is part of a network of 85 locations in 24 languages. This particular domain also provides our fourth insight about the relationship of a domain name with the business itself. In 2003, *Forbes* magazine reported that USA Interactive acquired the "business" of "hotels.com" LP for $1.1 billion (at the time, that firm was quoted as planning to merge with Expedia Inc.). This indicates the value of a business is much greater than that of the specific domain name from which it is inseparable. Another example, "toys.com," was sold by Toys R US, by auction in 2009, when in Chapter 11 for $5.1 million. Currently, it is a vibrant website offering an online retail platform for a variety of children's toys providers, while "toy.com" is simply a parked page.

DomainNameWire recently posted an interesting article about the value of ".com" domains as compared to the new TLDs. They compare, for example ElectionSoftware.com, which has an asking price on open market of $3,477, to the availability of Election.Software, retailing at $25. A more extreme example is SoftwareStudio.com, listed at $44,888 when Software.Studio can be acquired at retail as a premium name for $1,250. Similar to the notion behind ".club" domains, the question remains: For how long will consumers or indeed Web surfers the world over have this predetermined notion that a domain name must end in ".com"? Only time will tell for sure, but, clearly, with these kinds of massive difference in cost, buyers are going to be a little more careful.

Generic words. Domain names are governed by a Uniform Domain-Name Dispute-Resolution Policy (UDRP). If a trademark holder wants to claim the rights to a domain name using its trademark, it must prove, among other things, that the current registrant obtained the name in bad faith and has no entitlement to it. If the domain was registered before the trademark, it is difficult if not impossible to prove bad faith. Trademarks, usage, and domain names are very complex; however, pre-existing domain registrations that reflect a subsequently established trademark would likely not be considered an infringement on the trademark owner's rights. The domain name may even have a higher value due to subsequent trademark issues. Beauty is in the eyes of the beholder, and the main premise of this article is that every domain has an optimal buyer willing to invest heavily to ensure its online presence is maximized.

Generic words are less likely to be trademarked and are viewed by dispute resolution panels as eligible for registration by just about anyone. The fact that a domain holder (registrant) is not also the owner of a related trademark does not necessarily mean the domain has a lesser value. This is based on the assumption the trademark holder can take it away. An investor holding a domain for which a trademark exists may be perfectly within its rights to retain the registration of the domain under challenge.

Millard Brown's BrandZ™ study in 2015 ranked Apple as the most valuable global brand, estimated to be worth $247 billion. Despite the high brand value, its "apple.com" and "itunes.com" domains were only valued at about $6.4 million and $700,000, respectively, by leading domain valuation programs. Such differences are similar for many of the 100 most valuable global brands. The reasons for the seemingly low values include:

- Trademark protection under UDRP;
- A single potential owner/buyer;

- Not major drivers of traffic and revenue; and
- Domain names are sold in an inefficient, circumstance-specific market, where the most talented sellers hold out to get the buyer's estimate of perceived value.

Previous offerings and usage. Some current registrants are fortunate enough to have a history of purchase offers from which much can be learned. Was the interested party a domainer looking to resell the name or a business owner looking to establish a unique online presence? Regardless of the source, previous offers and rejections often provide good insight into current values. The objective then becomes how best to sell the asset (a subject for another discussion) with a number of options including online sales portals, auction platforms, and brokers.

In addition to purchase history, a domain's usage can positively contribute to its value. Has it been a live site for a long period? How well does it rank in search engines? A domain that has been used for a number of years and ranks well will have higher value than one that does not.

Other considerations. As well as the market approach, various income methods are used for domain name valuations. They are based on forecasts of potential advertising revenue. In addition to considering the nature of the TLD involved, the following factors (many of which have already been discussed) are important.

- *Length.* The shorter the better. Domain names of up to six letters are excellent; if they are four or more, they must be pronounceable even if they are not a real word. More than six should be in a dictionary, or the domain has little value. (On March 3, 2016, "tp.com" sold for $929,000.)
- *Number of words.* When a domain name combines words, two are acceptable. Values normally plunge when three or more are linked. For example, "exporters.com" sold for $60,000 in October 2012, while two-word versions such as "rugexporters.com" were available for about $7,000 each. Three-word versions such as "exportersinindia.com" trade for around $2,000.
- *Inclusion of numbers.* Including a mix of numbers and words in domain names lowers values by 50% or more due to difficulty in "branding."
- *Hyphens.* Hyphens are difficult for a user to remember and therefore reduce value.
- *Spelling.* Names deliberately misspelled, like "dribble," or with double letters, such as "alternativeenterprise," that must be memorized, sell for significantly less than the conventional versions.
- *Pronounceability.* Names that are hard to spell, pronounce, or remember have lower values. The industry routinely uses the "radio test," suggesting that if you were to hear the domain

name spoken on the radio would you be able to unambiguously browse to that Web address.

- *The registry.* The registry in which it is recorded (".com/" one or more local registries).
- *Registered trademark.* A related trademark substantially increases the value of the name provided the domain registration precedes that of the trademark, although, as mentioned previously, valuing domain names that reflect trademarks can be tricky.
- *Operating freedom.* The freedom to operate in social media, without boundaries.
- *Memorable term.* Any term that has the advantage of being memorable increases value, for example, "exporter.com".
- *Search engine page rank.* Names achieving a top result on searches based on Google algorithms that appear to stress keywords and branding are more valuable.
- *Age.* The longer a domain name has been in use, the better.
- *Site activity.* Figures for global and local (U.S.) monthly searches, which are a good proxy for recent traffic, are available from "Google AdWords Keyword Tool" (GAKT).
- *Source of traffic.* The more inward and outward links, the better the name's value; every outward link from an external site is a validation.
- *Current revenue.* Websites with significant traffic have more value than those with few or no visitors. Ones with substantial revenue are often rated by potential cash flow. Estimates of "click-through rates" are available (the default is about 18%), while "callrail.com" offers price-per-click rates; those have been increasing, rising on average 55% from $1.02 in 2014 to $1.58 in 2015; for 2016, they are up about 5%. Valuators should be aware that certain keywords may carry very high click-through premiums based on the value of the product to which the visitor is being referred.
- *Marketability.* A large number of potential customers contribute significantly to a name's value. For example, "pizza.com" rates relatively high because of the dish's popularity.
- *Development potential.* A domain name that is relevant to the product has more value than one with little or no immediate connection because it is self-explanatory. The website "dietbooks.com" will likely draw some of the large number of individuals who are interested in books and other material on various weight loss methods.
- *Market bubbles.* Recently, the industry has experienced remarkable growth driven almost entirely from transactions based in China. Domain names, typically transacted in U.S.

dollars, are attractive shelters for Chinese investors seeking to shore up the weakness in their own currency.

Online automatic appraisal sources. None of the criteria discussed provide a solid base on which to establish fair market values. So where does one start? There are a number of free automatic domain appraisal services. Most buyers will say they consistently overestimate values, while sellers will suggest their figures are on the low side. They all use their own proprietary appraisal algorithms that may incorporate a number of parameters that are easily quantified such as: keyword analysis, Google ranking, Alexa rank, DNS report analysis, traffic, recent sales of similar names, domain length, type in ranking, etc. Nonetheless, different sites usually offer wildly different assessments.

In preparing this article, in April 2016, we looked at 27 sites that referenced domain name appraisal services. Of those, eight offered free automated appraisals; we used them to provide value estimates for five existing site domains with interesting results as shown in Exhibit 3.

The Web software stats in Exhibit 3 are extremely interesting—as well as inconsistent in the analysis of value. This is likely due to the value drivers on which they rely. One, "urlappraisal.net," is obviously unreliable for general business valuation purposes; a "google.com" value of $10,580 doesn't pass our possible value test nor does a $60 value for "pepsi.com." Of the above, "estibot.com" is the leading online domain valuation tool and is the one most relied on by leading domainers. About 75% of the time that we've used estibot, we also employed three other online domain valuation programs or more and gave a higher weighting to estibot.

Clearly, automated tools cannot provide a clear and accurate prediction of what a domain might sell for. But they can reliably position one domain versus another in terms of relative value, which serves as a very good starting point, especially if one of the values has already been proven in a real market transaction.

Exhibit 3. Value Estimates Provided by Online Domain Apraisal Software April 2016

	pepsi.com	google.com	bvexpert.com	888.com	888.cn
cubestat.com	$77,248	$3,992,509,954	N/A	$734,189	$2,428
domainindex.com	$142,000	$375,000,000	$-	$728,625	N/A
estibot.com	see Note 1	see Note 1	$-	$727,000	$380
freevaluator.com	$134,097,582	$146,421,330	$84	$83,848	$212
siteprice.org	$91,851	$2,343,985,921	$787	N/A	$3,526
valbot.com	$2,521,508	$10,560,122,612	$241	$69,711	$10
websiteoutlook.com	$34,240	$2,410,000,000	N/A	$219,970	$1,800
urlappraisal.net	$60	$10,580	$57	$58	$54

Note 1: Pepsi and Google are trademarks. As with many strong trademarks, it is impossible to separate the value of these domains from the trademark itself. Furthermore, it would not be possible to sell such a domain in the marketplace due to intellectual property law guidelines. Thus, estibot does not place a value on such domains.
N/A: Not available or not enough data available to provicde a value estimate.

Lessons learned. In our experience valuing domains, one key lesson is to know the value of what you are fighting for. In one case in the U.S., two parties spent an aggregate of over $250,000 on legal fees in a battle over the ownership of a domain that had a real value of less than $20,000. After two years of litigation, the registered owner gave it up as part of a negotiated settlement after finding out how little the existing business relied on the domain. The cost of transitioning to a new name was immaterial, with essentially no customer loss. The seeker (the plaintiff) of the domain had obtained a trademark on his family business's name about 15 years after the defendant had acquired the domain; now he owns both.

The other important lesson is to perform due diligence. In one case, our client purchased the domain name of a bankrupt company for $10,000. Had the trustee performed some due diligence or engaged a valuation specialist, he should have easily discovered that there would have been many potential buyers, and the fair market value likely exceeded $250,000.

Conclusion. For a domain seller, patience is a virtue—even a necessity. Considering lackluster returns available on cash (less than 1%), the opportunity cost for a seller to hold a domain awaiting a better offer down the road is not high. Combined with an ongoing annual cost of less than $10 to maintain registration, waiting around for just the right offer is the easy choice. In valuing domains, the valuator and potential buyer/seller should consider a host of factors such as the most suitable industry for the domain, who are the prospective buyers, keyword analysis to identify similar names, the income and other benefits the name offers, the authoritative sounding value of the domain in a particular market space, the supply of equally good names (the supply of domain names is more than 10 times larger than demand), the value estimates provided by online appraisal services, the nature and comparability of quasi-comparable domains that sold, select aftermarket trading prices, and other criteria previously discussed.

Jim Horvath, *FCBV, ASA, ICVS, CPA, MBA, and* ***Jeff Horvath,*** *CBV, ICVS, CPA, CA, HBBA, are managing directors with ValuQuest Limited in Canada. Jim is also chairman of The International Association of Consultants, Valuators and Analysts (IACVA).*

Debunking the Myth That Business Appraisers Lowball Brand Values

By Christof Binder, Ph.D., MBA

How does something as emotional and intangible as brands and someone as fact-based and conservative as an accountant fit together? Not particularly well, according to marketers and brand valuation specialists. When they say "accountant," they're talking about valuation professionals outside the world of marketing.

"Most accountants are very conservative and habitually underestimate the level of income attributable to brands they value. They also tend to assume very short useful economic lives, low growth rates and high discount rates. It is therefore no surprise that an analysis of brand values calculated for balance sheet purposes tends to undervalue brands,"[1] says David Haigh, CEO of Brand Finance plc, a world-leading independent brand valuation and strategy consultancy.

Reasons for the mistrust. There are three major reasons for marketers mistrusting and disqualifying business valuation professionals in relation to valuing brands. First, CMOs and marketers want to stay in control of measuring and valuing their most important assets, instead of leaving it to the finance and accounting folks. Second, specialized brand advisory and valuation firms want to sell their own services and grow their business. And, third, the mistrust is a long and profound belief based on flawed facts.

Fifteen years ago, the major intention of the implementation of FAS 141 and IFRS 3 was to reduce the portion of goodwill reported in acquisitions. Some commentators—as well as marketers—were surprised to see that 45% of the enterprise value of acquired businesses on average remained allocated to goodwill. They had expected to see larger amounts being allocated to identifiable intangible assets, including brands, and amounts allocated to goodwill to disappear. Realistically, 45% of enterprise value on goodwill is certainly not too much, considering the synergies expected from a business combination, the value of the assembled workforce, and all of the future value from human and organizational assets, including the ability to improve, innovate, adapt, and change

1 brandfinance.com/news/press-releases/why-variation-supports-the-need-for-brand-valuation/.

over the long term. Even with a sympathetic understanding for the role of marketing, brands have nothing to do with these components of goodwill.

Follow the money. From the countless brand value rankings they produced, brand valuation specialists concluded that the adequate average portion of brand value is 18% of enterprise value. Various studies on the results of purchase price allocations (PPAs) from Houlihan Lokey, PwC, EY, and others, show an average portion of brand of only around 10%, thus far less than the brand valuation specialists. The myth of the conservative accountant was born. But which party is right? Actually both, provided that we do not compare apples and oranges.

In all PPA studies, 40% of the cases observed do not report a brand value for three reasons. The brand is unimportant and will be replaced after the acquisition or because the acquisition was an asset deal that did not include a brand or trade name. In contrast, all cases sitting on brand rankings show a brand value. Furthermore, enterprise value in PPAs is different from nontransactional enterprise value for the control premium paid. This premium accounts for an average 35% on top of the share price prior to the announcement of the transaction. And, thirdly, there is an effect of sample composition. Adjusting for these effects, brand values found by "accountants" are in fact not lower but most comparable to those found by brand valuation specialists.

But that is not all. According to MARKABLES, the 100 most expensive brands acquired in business combinations since 2010 account for an average 34% of enterprise value.[2] Adjusting for the purchase premium, this percentage would amount to 46% to be fully comparable with the brand value rankings. Moreover, a comparative study[3] of 162 brand valuations reveals that accountants reported even higher brand values than brand valuation specialists in one-third of the cases.

As a matter of fact, accountants and business valuation professionals are neither more nor less conservative to value brands than brand consultants or marketers. There is no reason at all for accountants and business appraisers to stand in the shadow of specialized brand valuation firms. And marketers should finally begin to accept business appraisers, corporate finance advisors, and accountants as unbiased and experienced partners to value their most important assets: brands and customer relations. They have one important advantage over specialist brand valuators: They understand the value of all different assets of an enterprise and not only that of brands.

***Christof Binder**, Ph.D., MBA, is the managing partner of Trademark Comparables AG, the Swiss-based company operating the MARKABLES database of trademark valuation comparables. Christof has extensive experience in the valuation of trademarks for transactional, licensing, and litigation purposes.*

2 www.markables.net/files/Top-2014-Brand-Ranking.pdf.

3 www.markables.net/brand_value_rankings_are_they_blessing_or_curse.

Wrestling Match Over Valuation of Hulk Hogan Sex Tape

During the very public trial (it's on YouTube) in which Terry Bollea (Hulk Hogan) sued the website Gawker over the now infamous sex tape, a valuation expert testified about the amount of damages. His approach was not based on lost profits or damages related to right of publicity but rather one of unjust enrichment. Therefore, the expert's method was to calculate the gain in value of the Gawker website due to its misuse of Hogan's assets (his brand and other intellectual property). During the trial, the opposition attacked the specifics of the methodology and tried to have the expert thrown out of the ring.

Methodology. Content-driven websites such as Gawker generate revenue primarily from advertising, which is directly tied to the website's user base and its corresponding number of monthly unique users. These websites are often valued based on a multiple of monthly unique users, according to Jeff Anderson (CONSOR), who was the testifying expert in the *Hogan* case. "We calculated the benefit to the website by analyzing the change in value from before the video was posted (pre-damages period) to after the video was removed (post-damages period)."

The website's value was determined using a monthly unique user multiple, which was developed based on transactions for comparable websites, Anderson explains. A monthly unique user is a single user that visits a website one or more times in a one-month period. Unique monthly user data were analyzed for the 12-month period before the video was posted and the trailing 12-month period from the date it was removed.

Finding comparables. Traffic data were also analyzed using transaction data for six comparable websites that had been publicly acquired. To get those six comparables, they looked at hundreds (maybe thousands) of websites and based the search on four criteria: (1) free to use and content-driven (not an e-commerce site or fee-based membership site); (2) majority of revenue from advertising; (3) availability of a verifiable transaction amount (e.g., from M&A data); and (4) accurate data on unique monthly users. For the data, it was preferable that the comparable website used Quantcast, which was what Gawker used to measure its traffic. That's because different measurement services will gauge traffic differently, which could skew the data.

How were these four criteria determined? "They are the key drivers of value for a site such as Gawker," says Anderson. For example, an e-commerce site, such as eBay, has a totally different business model, monetization strategy, and value per user. So a site like that would not be comparable to Gawker.

"We determined a market multiple by using the purchase price for these comparable websites and their monthly unique user data," he says. The analysis revealed an average multiple of $19.34x, which it considered an upper bound (see Exhibit 1).

Using this upper-bound multiple applied to the website's traffic before and after the video, the Gawker website increased in value by $54.1 million (Exhibit 2).

Based on traffic the sex tape specifically triggered, it was then determined that 28.5% of the overall traffic was attributable to the video. That percentage was applied to the $54 million overall increase in value to get $15.4 million—the increase in website value attributed to the sex tape (Exhibit 3).

Going through this same calculation using the lower bound of $6.25, the value attributable to the video was $5 million. Anderson presented both the upper and lower bounds in his testimony

Exhibit 1. Valuation Multiple Per Monthly Unique User

Comparable Website	Monthly Unique Users	Company Value	Valuation Date	Monthly Unique User Multiple
Website 1	25,599,849	$170,000,000	2012	$6.64x
Website 2	135,925,889	$850,000,000	2014	$6.25x
Website 3	25,000,000	$295,900,000	2011	$11.84x
Website 4	5,130,718	$120,000,000	2014	$23.39x
Website 5	754,832	$31,280,800	2014	$41.44x
Website 6	136,283,099	$3,604,851,060	2014	$26.45x
			Minimum	$6.25x
			Average	$19.34x
			Maximum	$41.44x

Exhibit 2. Change in Website Value—Upper Bound

Month Ended	Trailing 12-Month Average Monthly Updates	Valuation Multiple	Value of Website
Sept. 30, 2012	11,989,092	$19.34x	$231,810,148
April 30, 2013	14,788,578	$19.34x	$285,938,464
Change	**2,799,486**		**$54,128,315**

Exhibit 3. Value Attributed to the Video (Upper Bound)

Change in website value	$54,128,315
Change attributable to video	28.53%
Change attributable to video	**$15,445,000**

Exhibit 4. Summary of Findings

	(Lower Bound)	(Upper Bound)
Value attributable to the video*	$4,995,000	$15,445,000

*Numbers rounded to the nearest thousand.

(Exhibit 4), arguing that the Hogan material had increased the value of Gawker.com by a minimum of $5 million, but the true likely value was $15.4 million, due to the traffic it generated to the site.

***Daubert* tussle.** The opposition attacked Anderson on several points in an attempt to have him excluded. Gawker contended that using monthly unique visitors to value a website leads to an inflated valuation and is rarely used in commercial deals. Under the Federal Rule of Evidence 702, expert testimony must be based on reliable principles and methods. Gawker's motion to exclude[1] states: "Hogan still has not pointed to a single instance in which anyone outside of Anderson's consulting firm has used the method Anderson employed to value a website. And, more problematically, Hogan has not pointed to any time that anyone has used Anderson's methodology to value a single web posting."

"The opposition kept trying to get me to admit that no one had ever valued a website based on monthly unique users," says Anderson. That's not exactly true, Anderson points out, but there was nothing in the literature nor in court precedent about it. He argued that the core value driver of a content-driven website such as Gawker is the traffic from unique monthly users.

The opposition also criticized the choice of some of the sites Anderson had deemed comparable to Gawker, such as Grandparents.com and BuzzFeed. Anderson argued that his comparables were valid because they are all content-driven and earn revenue primarily from advertising as opposed to e-commerce sites.

Anderson successfully fended off the *Daubert* challenge. One lesson learned: "Stick to your guns," he advises.

In the end, the jury felt that all of the $54 million increase in website value was due to the sex tape—it did not apportion any of the increase as Anderson had done. The jury awarded Hogan an amount for economic damages that matched that dollar figure. The remainder of the total award of $140 million included amounts for emotional distress and punitive damages. This points up another lesson for valuation experts in this type of case. That is, always present the higher amount and then show how you whittle it down because the jury may want to fall back on that higher amount. That's exactly what happened in this case.

More details: Anderson, Wes Anson, and David Noble (all with CONSOR) recently presented a BVR webinar, Litigation Dynamics and *Daubert* Challenges: Excelling as an Expert. In addition to the *Hulk Hogan* case, they discussed other cases, including *StoneEagle,* which illustrates that the *Georgia-Pacific* factors are no longer the ultimate standard in determining damages awards.

1 Gawker's motion to exclude the expert testimony is excerpted at cagesideseats.com; *Hulk Hogan vs. Gawker* Trial (Day 5): Sexed up figures? (March 12, 2016).

A Dozen Action Ideas From NACVA's 25th Anniversary Conference

One of the great benefits of attending conferences is the ability to gather all kinds of interesting and useful tips and advice from leading valuation practitioners. Here is just a sampling of what we picked up at the 25th anniversary conference of the National Association of Certified Valuators and Analysts (NACVA) in San Diego. This was a very strong conference in terms of speakers and content, so we congratulate NACVA for putting together this excellent event. The following ideas are in no particular order, and some are qualitative as opposed to technical, but they all can be acted on right away to help improve your valuation practice.

1. Learn to read faces. In management interviews, you may not always get straight answers. How can you tell whether they're hiding something—or just outright lying? By observing facial expressions, advises Darrell Dorrell (financialforensics), co-author of the book *Financial Forensics Body of Knowledge.* Reading faces is a skill that many valuators simply do not have.

For example, in an interview with a female employee at an architectural/engineering firm, Dorrell noticed that with certain questions blood would rush to her throat. To him, this was a red flag that triggered more probing. What he found out was that the woman was having an affair with the manager of one of the firm's offices and was also embezzling. She was later prosecuted.

Dorrell advises that you go to the website of Dr. Paul Ekman, a noted psychologist known as the "human lie detector" (www.paulekman.com). You'll find some basic tools for reading facial expressions. Ekman was technical adviser on the crime drama "Lie to Me," which ran for several years on the Fox Network.

All valuators have to deal with management forecasts at some point, so here are a few pointers from veteran practitioner Chris Best, a leading authority on the valuation of businesses that sponsor employee stock ownership plans, prospective financial information, and business valuation reviews.

2. Do a separate engagement letter for a forecast. "Our basic engagement letter allows for four hours for us to prepare a forecast," says Best. "If it takes us longer, we'll do a separate engagement letter." An audience member asked whether he ever goes back and compares actual results to forecast. Best pointed out that he does a lot of valuations for ESOPs regularly, so he has the opportunity to do variance analyses of actual to forecast. "Some of our clients are extremely accurate, even two-three years out," he says. The longer you work with them, the better they get (assuming they take it seriously and devote the necessary time to it).

3. Reject an unreasonable forecast. What if you don't agree with the forecast provided by management and management won't change it? "We reject it until management works on it and makes it reasonable," says Best. "If you're going to use it, you have to believe it's reasonable." An audience member asked whether Best ever adjusts the discount rate to reflect an unreasonable forecast. "I haven't done that," he says.

4. Use a disclaimer. The audience wanted to know whether doing a comprehensive forecast and then relying on that forecast to also do the valuation was in conflict with professional standards. Best pointed out that he uses a disclaimer saying that he is not expressing an opinion on the forecast—just assisting management in preparing it. An attendee from Deloitte in Ghana told the audience that his firm uses a "Chinese wall" strategy. The forecast is sent to Deloitte accounting, where it would get worked on and then sent back to the valuation folks.

One topic that doesn't get the attention it deserves is that of engagement letters. Maybe that's because they appear to be straightforward. But there's more to them than meets the eye, as Martin Abo (Abo and Co. LLC) illustrated during his session.

5. Include a provision for presigning time. Include language in your engagement letter that any professional time spent prior to the signing of the engagement letter is the responsibility of the client.

6. Don't use the term 'interest.' If you charge for overdue bills, call it a "late charge" rather than "interest." That way, you avoid any claim of being usurious (1.5% per month equals 18% annual—compared to a 3% prime rate).

7. Consider a 'disengagement' letter. If a successor replaced a client, have a disengagement letter that paves the way for cooperation with that new client. This can also act as an insurance policy for collecting any outstanding fees from the client who was replaced.

Abo also referred the audience to the 11th edition of the *CPA's Guide to Effective Engagement Letters,* which has over 100 sample engagement letters. The book is from CAMICO (www.camico.com), a CPA-owned provider of professional liability and risk management services for accountants.

Some people cringe when you bring up the subject of statistics, but they have a definite place in valuation. Several sessions gave attendees some food for thought.

8. Use regression in the market approach. Using the median and harmonic mean multiples from transaction databases, such as *Pratt's Stats,* is a common practice in the BV community. But C. Fred Hall III cautioned attendees to be careful because of the inherent shortfalls in these measures. So what's the harm? Using median and mean multiples only applies to average performing companies, says Hall. Median and mean revenue multiples will be too low for high-performing companies, and the cash flow multiple will be too high. Inversely, median and mean revenue multiples will be too high for low-performing companies, and the cash flow multiple will be too low. So what's the answer? Use regression, says Hall, because regression properly identifies where the market is, something the median and mean cannot do.

Hall showed the audience how to run regression in Excel, using the revenue multiple as the dependent variable and cash flow (as measured by SDE/revenue) as the independent multiple. Here, Hall demonstrated how the more profitable a business is, the higher its revenue multiplier should be. Attendees also saw the inverted relationship between profitability and the cash flow multiple (as measured by SDE): The more profitable a company is, the lower its cash flow multiplier is. Next, Hall showed how to eliminate outliers in the regression by removing observations that were outside the standard error in their regression output. Doing so yields a higher R-squared (a statistical measure of how close the data are to the fitted regression line) and provides a regression formula you can easily and accurately use to price your subject company.

9. Consider an empirical approach to passive appreciation. In the divorce arena, a vexing problem for business valuators is determining the allocation between active and passive appreciation of a closely held business caught up in a marital dissolution. Due to societal and demographic trends, this is an issue of growing concern. Also, the courts are becoming more demanding in terms of proof. During his session, Dr. Ashok Abbott (West Virginia University) presented his method, which uses an empirical estimation method for identifying significant economic environmental factors and their relative contribution to growth in business revenues. These factors, such as population growth, level of inflation, and changes in disposable personal income, represent market forces that are outside the control of a company's management. The results of the analysis form the basis for a percentage allocation of the growth in value that can be attributed to passive (economic environment) components.

Since first developing the method, Abbott has had the opportunity to refine it based on feedback from the valuation community and also from his experience using it in a litigation setting. He has refined the model to include more rigorous causality testing. He presented this enhanced version of the model during his session, and it's also explained in a recent article in *Business Valuation Update.*[1]

Communication skills are crucial for a valuation expert. We liked a session that gives a fresh look at strengthening the bond between numbers and narrative.

10. Learn to paint with numbers. Randell Bolten, the author of *Painting With Numbers: Presenting Finances and Other Numbers So People Will Understand You,* began his presentation with a disclaimer:

1 "A Quantitative Model Evolves for Determining Passive Appreciation," *Business Valuation Update,* May 2016.

"Everything in this workshop is obvious." Was that true? Sure, but sometimes things have a tendency to hide in plain sight, not fully revealing themselves as obvious until they are pointed out.

"Quantation," Bolten's portmanteau of quantative and communication, is the act of presenting numbers, such as financial results, electronically or in written form for the purpose of informing an audience. At its base, quantation is a not math skill or a computation skill. Rather, it's a communication skill that has rules, a narrative flow, and sends a message to your audience. Why is this important? Because, as an appraiser or other presenter, you want your audience to spend more time absorbing the information in your reports and less time trying to figure out how to read your reports. Graphs work best when you're trying to demonstrate a trend or a pattern (or the absence thereof) and when there are too many numbers to show. If neither of those cases hold true, Bolten suggested the audience consider whether a graph will be useful. Graphs should clearly and concisely communicate your message—avoid using visual effects for any reason other than clarifying, distinguishing, or adding meaning to information. Just make your most important, specific points.

Data presentation should be honest, so don't try to pull the wool over your audience's eyes by being misleading or adjusting the scale of your graph unnecessarily. Bolten warns, "If your audience is aware that a presentation tactic could be sleazy, they will conclude that it is sleazy. This perception applies to the presenter as well as his or her content." He also cautions against catering to people asking for a graph, who tell you that they are a "visual person." Your choice should be driven by your desired message, *not* your audience's alleged cognitive preferences!

Bolten also provided attendees with what he calls "deadly sins" of quantation. Included on the list: "Using a *pie chart*. Period." So stop doing that, he advises.

Building a valuation practice is a top concern for many attendees, so it's no surprise that a big crowd turned out for a session on practice development conducted by Mel Abraham (Mel Abraham Inc.) and Rod Burkert (Burkert Valuation Advisors), who are co-founders of the Practice Builder Academy.

11. Become an authority. One of the biggest obstacles to BV practice growth today is that too many generalist appraisers are trying to get work by competing on price, according to Burkert. Instead, you should be competing on the basis of your expertise and authority. "Think different, be different, stand out and make a difference with your knowledge," says Abraham. "Every industry stalwart we admire competes via authority, not price," says Burkert. Good ways to position yourself as an authority is through speaking and writing.

12. Use a 'strategy canvas.' To jump-start growth in your BV firm, you need to differentiate yourself and identify untapped opportunities. One way to help with this is to use the "strategy canvas," a tool developed by Blue Ocean Strategy. During Abraham and Burkert's session, they illustrated the use of this tool to assess a BV firm/practitioner by graphing competitive factors in the market and then plotting the firm versus competitors. This reveals gaps that may represent a "blue ocean" where the practitioner will find less competition and where the competition would not be as well educated in that niche. (A "blue ocean" is one with no red blood from a shark feeding frenzy.) Abraham and Burkert offer a free download of a strategy canvas template at www.pbadownload.com.

Adjustment Mapping and the Public-vs.-Private-Company Discount Debate

By Mike Smith

Editor's note: This article advances the discussion in the article "Private Company Discounts Are Not Caused by Lack of Marketability" that Gilbert Matthews wrote for the June 2016 issue of Business Valuation Update *(reprinted on page 77). The author of this article joins the call for action over the profession to speak with one voice and eliminate the confusion over the use of discounts. We welcome your feedback to continue this important discussion (send to andyd@bvresources.com).*[1]

Much has been written about how to adjust for the differences between public and private companies in the context of business valuation. The accepted valuation industry catchall for many adjustments is the beloved "discount." This seems to stem partly from the confusion and lack of understanding from valuation practitioners, existing case law, and the difficulty in producing reliable empirical measures regarding discounted public relative to private equity. Discounts have a warm place in the hearts of many practitioners, but I would submit that the valuation community is doing a disservice allowing such a wide diversity of practice regarding documentation of discounts and adjustments in general. Business valuation is a complex endeavor indeed, but a little transparency regarding all adjustments would go a long way toward educating each other, our clients, and the courts.

In the article "Private Company Discounts Are Not Caused by Lack of Marketability," published in the June 2016 issue of *Business Valuation Update* (reprinted on page 77), Gilbert Matthews recommends that the valuation community come together and develop a common language to dispel confusion and inspire unity among practitioners. I completely agree, so my goal with this article is to advance his call to action by introducing some nomenclature and more importantly a framework, which hopefully will help in developing a common language that could be applied to valuation reports.

1 The author would like to give special thanks to Gilbert Matthews for his comments and Lara Burita for her proofing.

Reasoning lost. In many valuation reports, lost is the discussion of the adjustment comparative, basically the reason for the adjustment. Note that valuation standards specify a "base value" or base of comparison that should be considered. BV standards also address disclosures. For example, ASA Business Valuation Standards, BVS-VII Valuation Discounts and Premiums, state in II (B):

> The base value to which the discount or premium is applied must be specified and defined.

Unfortunately, not all business valuation practitioners take heed. In fact, many omit this important definition from their report altogether. Paragraph 40 of the AICPA Valuation Standard Statement on Standards for Valuation Services, No. 1 states:

> During the course of a valuation engagement, the valuation analyst should consider whether valuation adjustments (discounts or premiums) should be made to a pre-adjustment value.

SSVS No. 1 goes on to say in paragraph 63 (c) that a detailed report should "describe the pre-adjustment value to which the adjustment was applied." However, it appears that, in a "summary report," a preadjustment value disclosure is not required.

Base of comparison. The first aspect of any discount is identifying the relative base value from which the discount applies. When applying an income approach, typically the base value is the universe of public stocks used to derive the cost of equity. This provides a point of departure and comparison relative to the subject interest. The "base value" may in fact change, depending on the valuation methods used. When the "base value," or better yet base of comparison, differs from the subject interest being valued, consideration of adjustments is appropriate. I prefer the term "base of comparison" because in my opinion it begs the question, "Compared to what?" When performing a market-based approach, the base of comparison is the transactions or companies used in the analysis. This may or may not be the same base of comparison that was used in the income approach, which is often derived from a universe of public companies (see Exhibit 1).

Business valuation reports should prominently state the base of comparison when making adjustments for each valuation method. Once we know the base of comparison, linking any subject interest adjustments is much easier and clearer through a mapping process.

Adjustment mapping. The base of comparison provides a point of departure for many of the adjustments made. The most prevalent income-based models in use provide three variables for adjustments: cash flow, growth, and risk. When all three variables are correctly and completely developed for the subject interest, no other adjustments are required. However, completely developed variables independent from a base of comparison elude many practitioners, which is why, when benchmarking to a base of comparison is used (primarily the public cost of equity), valuation analysts' models often add other valuation adjustment "knobs" called discounts and premiums.

Exhibit 1. Base of Comparison

Income Approach	Market Approach
100% Controlling Subject Interest vs. Universe of Public Equity Deriving Risk	100% Controlling Subject Interest vs. Comparable Private Transactions

Exhibit 2. Adjustment Factors

	Income-Based Valuation Adjustment Mapping					Market-Based Valuation Adjustment Mapping		
Adjustment Factor	Cash Flow	Risk	Growth	DLOM	DLOC	Multiple Adjustment	DLOM	DLOC
External Forces Impacting Value								

Note: DLOM: Discount for lack of marketability; DLOC: Discount for lack of control; csrp: Company-specific risk premium

While many discount/premium schemas exist, discounts commonly take the form of discounts for lack of marketability (DLOM) and discounts for lack of control (DLOC). One of the complaints of using discounts, which is pointed out in Matthews' article, is that many factors presumably represented in the "discount" are already accounted for in the risk, cash flow, or growth assumptions. Adjusting the three income approach model variables is likely the purest form of adjustment and should be the first place to turn when addressing an adjustment. But we still need a way to understand how all adjustments are knotted together. To complicate things further, market approach adjustments are slightly different.

Market-based approaches embed income approach valuation assumptions into a single number known as a multiple. Market-based expectations are generally reflected in security prices according to market efficiency. Most income-based approaches using cost of equity are based on historical averages or are smoothed. As a result, changes in market expectations often lag or are muted due to averaging or the historical nature of the transactions.

Since appraisers have free will to adjust and tweak DCF inputs, multiples, and discounts in the valuation process, one way to make sense of the adjustments is to provide a road map describing the adjustment process/method used. This mapping of the adjustment process would clearly show others where the valuation practitioner made the adjustments and the extent of each adjustment. Any factor the analyst feels requires an appropriate adjustment should be listed as one of the forces impacting value. Exhibit 2 shows how this technique could show the appraiser's intent with a model allowing universal application. Now we can use a cause-and-effect framework to characterize any potential adjustment factors.

Cause-and-effect model. Factors requiring adjustments can broadly be defined as either external forces on the subject interest or internal forces from the subject entity. External forces relate to factors that are outside the company's control, while internal forces are best described by the policies, actions, inactions, or decisions made by the owner(s) or management. Separating the factors into two distinct classifications helps appraisers decide where and how best to make valuation adjustments, being mindful of the base of comparison. Internal factors are best adjusted in the valuation model where a discrete adjustment is made to either cash flow, risk, growth, or the multiple. Some practitioners will continue choosing discounts to adjust internal factors, so disclosing it is important.

Primarily a function of the transaction market, external forces seek to adjust for an impact in demand and liquidity for the security from factors outside the organization. We can use an Ishikawa diagram, often called a fishbone diagram, to illustrate the cause-and-effect relationship between external and internal forces (see Exhibit 3).

Exhibit 3. Adjustment Causes and Effects

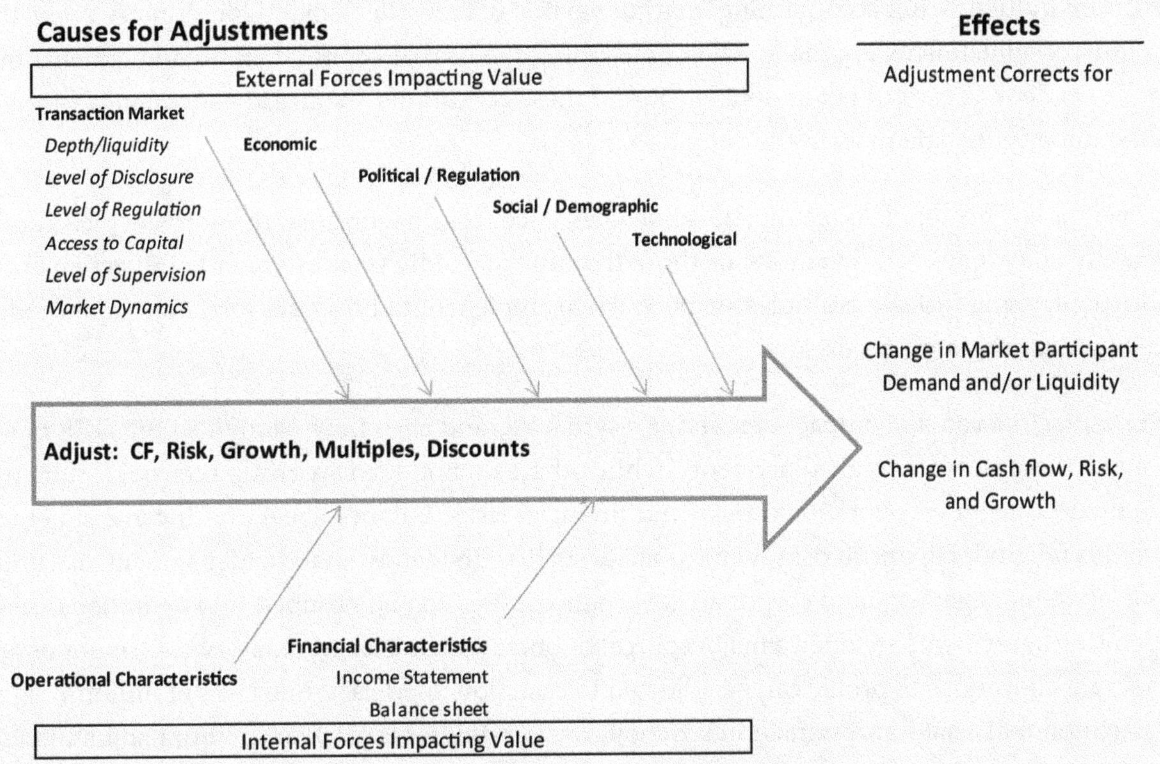

One of the concerns Matthews and others have pointed out is a lack of a common language used in discussing valuation adjustments. To address this concern, I submit a way to categorize the external and internal forces impacting value.

Transaction market. Transaction market defines the characteristics (discussed in depth later) of the market in which interests are bought and sold. Both the base of comparison and the subject interest will have a transaction market. The depth (liquidity) of the transaction market and other characteristics determine risks/costs associated with entities that are bought and sold in that market.

Economic. Economic conditions can temporarily impact prices in markets. Adjustments may arise when distortions exist in the base of comparison market. Examples include: currency crisis, economic-based market crisis, etc. Any economic condition distorting price discovery under one valuation method that is contrary to market expectations at the valuation date in another valuation method should be addressed. If the condition impacts all securities, including the subject equally, then perhaps no adjustment is needed.

Political/regulatory. Political or regulatory instabilities can disrupt or distort normal price discovery, adversely impacting market efficiencies. Examples may include pending industry regulation, crucial election, or temporary disruptions caused by leaving an economic union or new regulations recently enacted that are not reflected at the valuation date in the base of comparison.

Social/demographic. Dramatic temporal changes impacting demand, such as pandemics, natural disasters, or wars that interfere with orderly market activity. Also included is the social avoidance of certain industries (tobacco, gaming, marijuana) that narrow the demand for industry securities. If industry adjustments are made when developing the cost of capital, further adjustments may not be needed. Be careful not to double count if these conditions are already adequately reflected in the underlying data used in the valuation.

Technological. This refers to technological obsolescence from major breakthroughs, which fundamentally change market dynamics, or those that unexpectedly or subsequently impact an entire industry, leaving historic multiples suspect. An example would be a cure for cancer that renders existing drugs/treatments useless.

Internal factors can also impact demand, growth, risk, and cash flow. Many use the DCF model to make these fundamental adjustments, while others do not. We can group internal factors into two broad categories: operational risks and financial risks. Balance sheet and income statement accounts fall under financial risks, while policies such as dividends, shareholder agreements, litigation, labor, management, and corporate governance issues can be grouped into operational risks. Operating agreements are often a major source for operational risks. Mandatory contributions and disparate allocations of profits can be adjusted in cash flow models, while risks of dilution, rights to partition real estate, and transfer restrictions are candidates for risk or discount adjustments.

Appraisers would be well served to communicate where any adjustments were made, listing them under one of these two categories (external or internal). Describe each force impacting value, grouping them in terms of their impacts (cash flow, risk, or growth). Some external forces may in fact be addressed with cash flow adjustments. The important concept here is to identify and disclose how the factor is addressed, rather than getting the classification right.

Define the transaction market. One way investors are rewarded for taking risk is through the sale of their investment. Depending on the subject interest, various alternatives exist for putting together a transaction. The expected selling market of the interest is an important aspect in determining the risk and opportunity costs of holding the interest. Certain markets offer more liquidity, transparency, and access to a wide range of suitable buyers, allowing efficient price discovery. Generally, the more liquid a market becomes, the less "price risk" an equity holder incurs.

Does the transaction market even matter? Ask yourself why companies choose to go public. Considering the costs with going public, the perceived benefits must sometimes outweigh the cost, otherwise public filings would diminish to zero. When using a cost of public equity in the cost of capital estimate, we assume the benefits of the transaction market. Unless adjusted out, the transaction market risks and benefits are embedded or impounded in security prices through the cost of.... In addition, since equity returns are based on price, the collective market assumptions about equity cash flow, growth, and risk are also forever embedded in the cost of equity used.

Typically, the largest component of the external forces is due to the transaction market differential. Each valuation method may have a unique transaction market. Comparable transactions using the market approach may be from one market, while the universe of public companies reflects another market altogether. Each market has unique characteristics and may require separate analysis and adjustments. A selected list of transaction markets may include:

- Primary or secondary public markets (syndicates, NYSE, Nasdaq, AMEX);
- Electronic exchanges or e-markets;
- Auction markets (absolute, "forced under the hammer," Dutch, Vickrey, etc.);
- Third-party intermediary markets (business brokers, investment bankers);
- Individual private placements (accredited investor);
- Employee or direct purchase plans (ESOP);
- Entity market (redemption or buy-sell agreement programs);
- Wholesale markets (for assets); and
- Retail markets (for assets).

One definition of the transaction market for the subject interest is the most likely (or most advantageous under certain standards of value) market in which a transaction involving the subject will occur. Since the most likely or advantageous market can change with the standard of value, take care to document and disclose the transaction market for the subject interest.

The transaction market essentially defines the how the subject interest is bought and sold. In doing so, it also loosely defines the pool of "willing buyers" or "market participants" for the subject interest. The transaction market differential is an estimated relative marketability/liquidity adjustment between the base of comparison market used in the valuation methods employed and the transaction market anticipated for the sale of the subject interest.

For example, the transaction market for a transaction involving 100% of the subject interest may be business brokers. If an entity transferring in a third-party market is valued using a market approach based on third-party sales, the transaction market is likely business brokers and the transaction market differential may be zero. In this case, a lack of marketability discount may not be appropriate, assuming the subject interest value is similar from a transaction perspective to the average transaction used in the market method. In contrast, regulation requirements often drive the timing, cost, and complexities associated with the sale of a public company using investment bankers. To the extent the two comparison transaction markets are different, an adjustment may

Exhibit 4. Defining the Transaction Market

Subject Interest	100% Controlling **Income Approach**	100% Controlling **Market Approach**
Subject Interest Transaction Market	Business Brokers	Business Brokers
Basis of Comparison Transaction Market	Investment Bankers	Business Brokers

be appropriate. Exhibit 4 contains an example of defining the transaction market and valuation approaches.

Since each transaction market has its own characteristics, a general classification of the transaction market characteristics is needed. This will help with comparisons and establish a common language across the profession. Transaction market characteristics highlight and define the reason(s) for making valuation adjustments. Exhibit 5 categorizes market characteristics (differences) when comparing public transaction markets with private markets. These general characteristics can be used to describe many transaction markets.

A minority interest transaction of a subject may include the company itself as the most likely transaction market. Quite often the transaction market of the subject interest is defined in an operating agreement, with its own market depth. The implied holding period is part of market depth as a function of the transaction market. The triggering events, settlement terms, and the defined right of refusal process all define market depth in a hypothetical transaction. To complicate matters, while the agreement specifies one viable transaction market for the subject interest, management could sell the company as a whole under an alternate scenario. Now the valuation process becomes more nuanced as multiple liquidity paths exist. Status quo as a going concern may be the most probable path, but death, disability, and dissociation may have unique transaction market characteristics. To the

Exhibit 5. Market Characteristics (Public vs. Private)

Transaction Market Characteristics	Public Entity	Common Private Entity
Market Depth	Market makers	M&A firms
Liquidity	Hedgers/speculators	Brokers
Efficient price discovery	Pensions/mutual funds	Company agreements
Holding period	T+3	Undefined
Settlement	Cash	Cash, % financed
Hedging	Hedging/shorting/options	None provided
Level of Disclosure	GAAP, 10-K's 10-Q's, etc.	Unaudited statements
	Insider transactions	Tax returns
	Material events	
Level of Regulation	Fed/state law	Fed/state law
	SEC, exchanges, agencies	Agencies
	Investor suitability	None provided
Access to Capital	Bond markets	Small banks
	Equity markets	Angel, crowd, PE groups
	Large banks	Owners, relatives
	Accepted as collateral	May be accepted
Level of Supervision	Independent boards	Nonindependent boards
(provides management function)	Institutional investors	Small investors
	Analysts, investing public	PE group
	Mutual/hedge funds	Other owners
	Pension institutions	Controlling owner
	Management	Owner management
Market Dynamics	Sector rotation	PE demand
	Market contagion	Liquidity events
	High market correlations	Low correlations
	Acquisition cycles	Acquisitions

Exhibit 6. Other Transaction Market Differentials

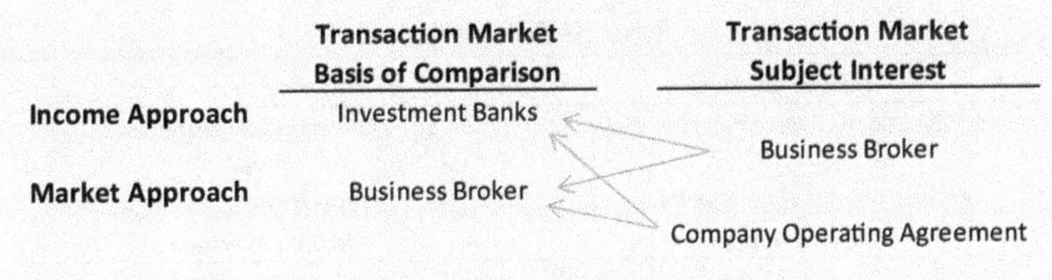

extent the original valuation approaches are used in determining price, the base of comparison may now have other transaction market differentials to consider (see Exhibit 6).

Exhibit 7. Event Weighted Average Holding Period

Liquidity Paths	Probability Estimate	Event Implicit Holding Period Estimate in Years	Event Weighted Average
Death	2%	0.3	0.01
Insolvency, Bankruptcy	2%	5.0	0.10
Status quo	91%	5.0	4.55
Disassociation	5%	2.5	0.13
Sum	100%	12.8 Years	4.78

For simplicity, it is common to estimate a probability weighted implicit event holding period based on operating agreement liquidity paths. This can simplify the analysis by essentially defining one transaction market based on the operating agreement. If the agreement also specifies the transaction price (the valuation method), then the transaction market base of comparison and the transaction market for the subject interest are identical, given the specified value used. Exhibit 7 presents an example of determining an event weighted average holding period.

An example of an adjustment for market dynamics would occur when the base of comparison market (public equity market) was highly volatile during the trailing 12 months prior to the valuation date. Market contagion was influencing prices, and hence market comps were suspect. The analyst perceived these to be an anomaly, requiring an adjustment to reflect normal ongoing expectations. In this case, the factor would be disclosed in the adjustment mapping table, which would clarify how the analyst accounted for the adjustment.

Each valuation analyst has his or her own take and methods to support the discount adjustment. A common language around the characteristics of the transaction market would allow analysts to communicate to clients, courts, and others reviewing the work the factors that were considered and what adjustments were made.

Exhibit 8 presents an example of the framework discussed here in a presentation format. The concepts are disclosed, and relevant factors mapped. From the presentation, we can see how the income approach, market approach, base of comparison, transaction market, and adjustments are related and the extent of any valuation adjustments made. I believe the presentation serves a useful function in a valuation report. The framework provides a common language and can be applied to various valuation engagements, including controlling and noncontrolling subject interests.

Conclusion. Discounts have long been a source of confusion for the users of valuation reports. Reports are typically unclear about what is being adjusted by the discount and whether adjustments overlap with other discounts or model variables including income, growth, or risk. One

Exhibit 8. Adjustment Mapping Framework

Adjustment Mapping	Base of Comparison: Income Approach	Base of Comparison: Market Approach
Subject Interest	100% Controlling Subject Interest	100% Controlling Subject Interest
	vs.	vs.
Base of Comparison	Universe of Public Equity Deriving Risk	Comparable Private Transactions
	Income Approach	**Market Approach**
Subject Interest Transaction Market	Business Brokers	Business Brokers
Basis of Comparison Transaction Market	Investment Bankers	Business Brokers

Adjustment Factor	Income-Based Valuation Adjustment Mapping: Cash Flow	Risk	Growth	DLOM	DLOC	Market-Based Valuation Adjustment Mapping: Multiple Adjustment	DLOM	DLOC
External Forces Impacting Value								
Transaction Market Differences								
Market Depth (holding period, liquidity)				3.00%			0%	
Level of Disclosure				0.50%			0%	
Financial Transparency and Periodic Reporting								
Level of Regulation				1.00%			0%	
Fed/State Law/SEC/Exchanges/Agencies								
Access to Capital		1				1		
Level of Supervision (boards/analysts/funds)				0.50%			0%	
Market Dynamics				0.00%				
Economic Risk Factors								
Dominant Economic Perspective	4					4		
Political/Regulatory Environment	4					4		
Social, Demographic Issues	2					2		
Technology								
Technological Obsolescence Expectations	2					2		
Internal Forces Impacting Value								
Operational Risks								
Dividends & Other Policies	3					3		
Financial Risks: Balance Sheet								
Company Size	1	7.20%				3		
Off Balance Sheet or Type of Assets Held	2					2		
Tax Factors, or Built-In Gain Risks	1							
Inventory Valuation Risks	2							
Other Off Balance Sheet Contingencies	2							
Financial Risks: Income Statement								
Revenue Makeup (customer concentration)	5	0.50%				5%		
Operating Leverage	1					3		

[1] Embedded in estimates and assumptions used, including: WACC, growth rate, cash flow or the multiple
[2] Not required by subject or not applicable to subject given the fact pattern
[3] No material difference from the base of comparison
[4] Systemic, faced equally by nearly all market participants
[5] Considered in a separate adjustment and added or subtracted from value

reason is a lack of empirical data breaking down the constituents of the discount data used. But that doesn't stop the widespread use of discounts; it simply obscures the appraiser's decisions and intent. Even if the industry had accurate discount data, the lack of consensus on methodology (where to make the adjustment) and language would still confuse users and continue to plague the valuation industry.

If the valuation industry is to achieve greater consistency among practitioners, the first step is laying a foundation to a fundamentally sound framework and lexicon. I offer a basic framework and nomenclature around valuation adjustments as a first step. If a common language and foundation are as important as I believe they are, perhaps the professional organizations should hear and recognize the heightened call from the valuation community. The valuation industry organizations have the means to gather consensus and adopt concepts that can be integrated into the valuation training and accreditation course work. Then the valuation leaders must decide the best method to disseminate the information to all practitioners. If appropriate, they can even facilitate changing the valuation development and reporting standards. Those organizations with the vision can make a meaningful contribution to the valuation industry by promoting a common language and requiring disclosure and transparency from practitioners making valuation adjustments.

Mike Smith, *ASA, CFA, CVA, is a senior manager in the valuation department of Baden, Gage & Schroeder LLC, a public accounting firm located in Fort Wayne, Ind. He has 15 years of experience in the area of valuations and focuses his practice on business valuation and litigation support services. Mike can be contacted via email at Msmith@badencpa.com.*

Changes in Regs and Standards Take Center Stage at ASA Fair Value Event

A slew of new and proposed changes to government standards, accounting rules, and valuation profession matters took the spotlight at the 11th Annual Fair Value Conference in Los Angeles. The American Society of Appraisers and the University of Southern California Leventhal School of Accounting host the conference.

Raymond Rath (Globalview Advisors) and Thomas Ryan (USC Leventhal School of Accounting), co-organizers of the event, greeted the audience—the largest ever so far. One of the reasons for the record attendance is that many changes related to fair value are going on from government regulators and from within the valuation profession itself.

FVQI update. The audience had a great deal of interest in the update of the initiative involving fair value for financial reporting valuations for U.S. publicly traded companies, which includes the development of a new credential. This project is a collaborative one that involves a number of organizations, including the ASA, AICPA, and RICS. It is in response partly to regulators' concerns over the fragmented nature of the profession and the inconsistent quality of the work being performed in terms of fair value for financial reporting.

Tony Aaron (Ernst & Young), who is the chair of the performance requirements workstream group for the initiative, gave an update on its progress. The credentialing process will be subject to ongoing quality oversight and compliance with a "mandatory performance framework." Importantly, a two-part exposure draft has been issued that is now out for public comment. It specifically deals with the mandatory performance framework, and the two parts are: Proposed Mandatory Performance Framework for the Fair Value Quality Initiative and Proposed Application of the Mandatory Performance Framework for the Fair Value Quality Initiative. They are available on the websites of the AICPA, ASA, and RICS.

The deadline for comment is Aug. 24, 2016, and Aaron urged the audience to review the drafts and make comments.

Important points about the initiative and the mandatory performance framework include:

- The focus of the exposure drafts is not on "how to" but "how much" work and documentation should be done in a fair value engagement subject to audit;
- The acronym for the credential (not yet determined) will be layered onto existing credentials, and it will be the same across any of the organizations that offer it;
- You don't need to have a valuation credential to get the new fair value credential; there will be a "path" for those with other designations (e.g., CFAs) to get the credential;
- A unified test will cover the mandatory performance framework as part of its scope; and

Once the initiative is up and running, a quality review mechanism will be put in place that will be "proactive in its nature," Aaron says.

Business Valuation Update applauds this global coordinated effort that will help enhance the valuation profession and improve the public's trust.

SEC concerns. Fair value estimates have been receiving significant attention from the SEC, says Kristopher Shirley, a professional accounting fellow at the SEC who focuses on fair value issues. After giving the audience the standard disclaimer that his remarks were his own and not that of the SEC, he explained that the commission is seeing several problems. One problem is not considering the principal market for the financial instrument being valued. He says that, if you identify a market but can't access it, you can't rely on it for the valuation, but you can use it as an input.

Another problem relates to management's responsibility for internal controls over financial reporting. Often, management does not understand everything that goes into the valuation, such as critical assumptions and how dependent the valuation is on these assumptions. He advises valuation practitioners to make sure management has a full understanding of these matters.

In terms of problematic industries, he singled out oil and gas firms, particularly with respect to bargain purchases. He also pointed to overly aggressive forecasts and goodwill impairments. Another area of concern is control premiums, and he mentioned that the SEC is seeing big premiums on entities with "razor-thin margins." He urges practitioners to make sure they are about to provide support in these cases.

FASB activity. The FASB will soon issue an "Invitation to Comment" about internally generated intangible assets, says Adam Kamhi, a valuation fellow at the FASB. The FASB wants to determine whether this should be added to the rule-making agenda and, if so, to then determine the project's scope. Current rules don't allow recognition of internally generated intangibles on the balance sheet. He pointed out that the IFRS has a model for capitalizing development costs, but the model has its critics.

Late last year, the FASB issued a proposed Accounting Standards Update designed to explain the definition of a business to assist organizations evaluating whether transactions should be accounted for as acquisitions (or disposals) of assets or businesses. This is important, says Kamhi, because the accounting treatment is different and, sometimes, fair value is not required. The project is still in its first phase (comments were due at the end of this past January). Kamhi mentioned that the feedback has been generally favorable in terms of, for example, consistency in practice and a framework for defining a business. He also noted that the IFRS will soon issue a similar exposure draft.

The FASB is considering allowing public companies and nonprofits to use the easier alternative for goodwill impairment. Out for exposure now, this simpler alternative was put forth by the Private Company Council (PCC), and it allows private firms to apply a simplified impairment model to goodwill. Step 2 of the impairment test would be eliminated and replaced with a simpler calculation. Companies will have to test for impairment only when a triggering event occurs that would indicate that the fair value of an entity may be below its carrying amount.

A new standard (ASU 2016-01) that takes effect in 2018 requires public companies to measure equity investments at fair value through net income, with certain exceptions. Kamhi points out that the standard also allows a fair value option for financial liabilities.

Fair value disclosures are addressed in an exposure draft that requires companies to disclose about the estimates and assumptions used to determine the fair values of assets and liabilities. While the new proposed disclosures may produce information investors will find valuable, some industries, such as banking and insurance, have some concerns. In comments (that were due February 2016), bankers say they will have to make sweeping changes to how they track certain assets that would be subject to the new rules. Insurers say it's not possible to comply with the proposed rules for some of their offerings.

PCAOB developments. Overall, the number of audit deficiencies decreased in 2015 compared to 2014, according to the Public Company Accounting Oversight Board. However, the news is not so good with respect to fair value audits. Preliminary results indicate an increase in the number of audit deficiencies regarding auditors' testing of fair value measurements associated with business combinations, according to George Wilfert, deputy director at the PCAOB. Plus, there were frequent deficiencies in evaluating impairment analyses for goodwill and other long-lived assets. The agency is also finding frequent deficiencies in the auditing of internal control over financial reporting and assessing and responding to risks of material misstatement.

Of particular note to valuation practitioners is that the standards for auditors' use of specialists will be changing. Last year, the PCAOB issued for public comment a staff consultation paper on potential standard-setting activities related to the auditor using the work of specialists, including valuation professionals. Kris Shirley of the SEC mentioned that his agency submitted comments on the standards, and he urged all stakeholders to review the standard and submit comments.

Related to this development, Stephani A. Mason (DePaul University) made an announcement to the audience about research being conducted on the role of specialists in developing and evaluating fair value estimates used in audited financial statements. The University of Wisconsin-Madison is conducting a survey on this issue, which was handed out to the audience.

Contingent consideration. A discussion draft of a proposed guide on valuing contingent consideration will be out shortly, according to Alok Mahajan (KPMG), chair of the working group under The Appraisal Foundation. Contingencies valuation is one of the most challenging areas of valuation with limited guidance. Although the task force is focused on contingent consideration, valuation insights should be helpful for many additional valuations. Mahajan told the audience that a few matters were still being ironed out: One is alternate techniques for estimating the market price of risk; the other has to do with subtleties related to the EBIT discount rate vs. WACC (tax adjustment).

Other takeaways. Here are some main points from several of the other sessions:

- "Uncertainty matters," stresses Amanda Miller (Ernst & Young), talking about volatility estimation and measurement. Valuation models are increasingly moving from single scenario to multiple scenario and other complex models. Therefore, volatility estimates are a critical component of an increasing number of fair value measurements. So far, however, there is limited guidance on the determination of volatility estimates.

- The three "pillars" of focus for transaction due diligence are: (1) the quality of earnings; (2) net working capital; and (3) debt (or debt-like) items, says Mike Kim (Ernst & Young). Think of net working capital as the gas that fuels a car—it really makes a difference how much gas is in the tank, adds Razmik Libarian (Ernst & Young).

- The average risk-free rate being used is 2.99% and the market (equity) risk premium being used is 6.35%, according to the recently released 2016 Private Capital Markets Report[1] from Pepperdine University Graziadio School of Business and Management. Craig Everett, director of the project, also pointed out that the average long-term terminal growth is estimated at 3.11%. The survey also reveals cost of capital data for each major capital type and its segments.

Business Valuation Update congratulates Ray Rath and Tom Ryan for an excellent conference.

1 Available at bschool.pepperdine.edu.

Economic Damages Experts Offer Top Advice at NACVA Confab

A hot topic at NACVA's annual conference in San Diego was lost profits and economic damages—four sessions were devoted to this growing area of practice. Here are some of the main points and key pieces of advice from these sessions.

Biggest mistakes. One of the main issues that causes problems with a damages analysis is that experts often do not understand the appropriate remedy for a particular action, according to Nancy Fannon (Meyers, Harrison & Pia), co-editor with Jonathan Dunitz, Esq. (Verrill Dana) of a new edition of the *Comprehensive Guide to Economic Damages.*[1] If you select the wrong remedy, your calculation of damages will be inadmissible. For example, in the 2014 *Winn-Dixie* case[2] that involved protective covenants, the damages expert was excluded under *Daubert* because she was "analyzing the wrong problem."

Another common mistake is applying the correct remedy the wrong way. For example, an expert was excluded for using the wrong date when calculating damages.[3] Fannon suggests that a reference to the date should be included in your engagement letter.

Talking about remedies, Fannon and Dunitz say that unjust enrichment is clearly the most troublesome to understand. The concept appears to be simple, but analysts frequently get fouled up over it. The concept of unjust enrichment is difficult, in part, because it is both a cause of action and a remedy, so that creates confusion and it affects how analysts calculate it, according to Dunitz. Also, there are significant differences in how it's calculated from one jurisdiction to another. Experts tend to get it mixed up with lost profits, and often it's double counted. They referred the audience to their book, which has extensive material on this topic.

In terms of growth areas for damages, they see intellectual property claims and cybersecurity issues triggering an increase in litigation. But they warn that you have to watch your remedy in these cases, as they are not always the same as in regular lost profits cases.

1 Nancy Fannon and Jonathan Dunitz (eds.), *The Comprehensive Guide to Economic Damages,* 4th edition, BVR, www.bvresources.com/publications.

2 *Winn-Dixie Stores, Inc. v. Dolgencorp, LLC,* 746 F.3d 1008, 1027-28 (11th Cir. 2014).

3 *Avocent Huntsville Corp. v. ClearCube Technology, Inc.,* 2006 WL 2109503 (N.D. Ala. July 28, 2006) (amend. Aug. 21, 2006).

More pitfalls. Lari Masten (Masten Valuation) presented a session in which she gave an excellent roundup of what she has seen to be the 11 most common failures in estimating lost profits and damages:

1. *Failure to analyze relevant economy and industry for damages model input.* For example, taking sales during a boom period and projecting them into a weak period will result in an exaggerated projection.

2. *Failure to use an industry expert when necessary.* Some industries are unique and require someone with specialized knowledge to help you understand the damages environment.

3. *Failures related to forecasts, management, and growth.* Examples: The use of an unusual or abnormal base or a revenue forecast. Also, using management's assumptions without verification or independent testing. Growth rate problems occur when the rate used is too high or speculative.

4. *Failure to conduct a reasonability test/sanity check.* Example: After projecting "but-for" revenues, step back and see whether it makes sense. What market share does the forecast imply? Is that share reasonable?

5. *Failure to identify and adjust for all/appropriate avoided costs.* These costs are incremental in nature, and, typically, fixed costs are excluded (but it's not always clear when step-fixed or variable costs are involved).

6. *Failure to properly account for mitigation.* Plaintiffs have the obligation to at least try to mitigate damages. It's up to the expert to determine whether or not to include other business activity in determining a reasonable estimate of damages.

7. *Failure to properly account for risk.* The correct way is to either capture the risk inherent in the business or product line in the discount rate or adjust the benefit stream to reflect the variability of the projected lost profits—but not both.

8. *Failures related to benchmarks and startups.* This includes not addressing the probability of success with a startup (which is especially difficult to do), failure to document the proof of loss with a startup, using estimates of sales/expenses of seller to project lost profits and the unsupported use of benchmarks (e.g., rules of thumb).

9. *Failure to prove reasonable certainty.* Proof of lost profits damages by a reasonable basis or a rational standard is all that's required. Masten referred the audience to the AICPA's practice aid[4] on this issue.

4 *Attaining Reasonable Certainty in Economics Damages Calculations*, AICPA Practice Aid, July 2015.

10. *Failure to use facts properly.* This includes assuming facts that are contrary to the evidence and inaccurate or inadmissible data.

11. *Failure to properly account for owner's compensation.* The deductibility of owner's compensation can make a big difference in damages calculation. Some states allow it, but others don't, so check the jurisdiction.

In conclusion, she posed these questions to ponder: Is the expert qualified for *this particular* analysis? How reliable are the underlying data? Are the expert's findings supported by the record (facts and/or other testimony)? Does the expert adequately deal with facts that are inconsistent with the expert's theory? Has the expert considered alternative scenarios?

IP misuse over the web. A very interesting session was conducted by Brian Buss and Doug Bania (both with Nevium), who talked about calculating damages from the misuse of intellectual property and defamation over the internet. For example, trademarks can be hidden in metadata to misdirect a competitor's customers. Also, social media can be a breeding ground for potentially libelous statements.

They presented a method they call "relief from pay per click." Some companies pay search engines (e.g., Google, Bing, Yahoo) so that their companies show up on the first page of an internet search ("paid search"). Other companies don't do this—they engineer their websites themselves so that they achieve the same results ("organic search"). But let's say Company A improperly uses Company B's trademark in its metadata so that, if someone searches for Company B, Company A shows up on the first page of the results. Under the relief from pay per click approach, the amount of the damage can be measured by what Company A would have had to pay the search engine to achieve those search results.

Social media data can also be used as a basis for calculating damages in the relief from pay per click method. For example, if a celebrity's image is used without permission to generate interest in a product via social media, the amount of damages could be based on the costs the infringer avoids by not having to use the celebrity as an endorser.

Bania and Buss point out that the tools for this analysis, such as Google Analytics, do not replace, but rather supplement, existing valuation and damages methodologies. They also say that many clients and judges are unfamiliar with the online world, so it's important to educate them before you explain how you estimated the damages. They wrote a chapter on this in the new Fannon and Dunitz book.

Tell the story. Calculating damages is fairly mechanical—the important thing is to tell the story, advised Chris Hamilton (Arxis Financial) during his session on explaining damages to juries and others. In terms of storytelling, he observes that there are three types of experts: (1) those who can do the work but who can't tell the story (very common); (2) those who can tell a good story but who cannot (or did not) do the work (these types are very dangerous); and (3) those who can do the work and tell a great story. He points out that becoming the third type is the goal, and he offers these tips:

- Catch your mistakes before someone else does;
- A picture is worth a thousand words;
- Short is sweet, and long is almost always deadly;
- Practice makes perfect;
- Your first effort probably isn't your best effort;
- Academic jargon is not your friend;
- Know the difference between direct and cross-examination;
- Arrogance smells from a mile away; and
- Everyone is a work in progress—including the opposing expert.

He also advises that you learn how to communicate because that is crucial. In another session during the conference, Tax Court judge David Laro said that your report is your testimony. Hamilton likes that idea and hopes the notion will spread.

How to Help Ensure a Valid Survey for a Damages Analysis

Surveys have been used for over 50 years to provide strong evidence in intellectual property matters and for an economic damages analysis. The use of surveys is not typically part of the damages expert's area of specialty, so it's left up to the survey expert. However, the damages expert should be involved in this process—up to a point.

The damages expert should be involved only to the point where the survey is ready to be piloted or pretested, according to Dr. Leon Kaplan (Princeton Research and Consulting Center), who spoke during a recent webinar.[1] Co-presenter Dr. Larry Chiagouris (Brand Marketing Services and Pace University) added that the survey expert will consult with both the damages expert and technical subject expert to make sure that the survey is properly constructed in a way that produces valid results.

Kaplan and Chiagouris are co-authors of a chapter on the use of survey research and damages estimation in the recently published fourth edition of *The Comprehensive Guide to Economic Damages.* In their chapter, they present a hypothetical example of how a properly constructed survey can help accurately estimate a loss in a dispute, which, in this case, concerns a patent infringement.[2]

Facts of the case. Company A and Company B each produce automotive paints. Both have comparable products that compete in all segments of the $12 billion automotive paint industry, including both the OEM and the aftermarket. After considerable R&D money and effort, Company A introduced a nonstick additive to its paints that allowed the painted surface to shed dirt, grime, and stains to an unprecedented degree. Being driven in the rain was all that was needed to return the car's exterior to its original new-looking finish. It also improved mileage by reducing the car's coefficient of drag.

Not surprisingly, this property was very desirable and sales of Company A's automotive paints with the additive rose dramatically. In a remarkably short time, Company B announced that it

1 Damages Estimation and Valuation: How to Use Survey Research, BVR webinar, June 29, 2016 (www.bvresources.com/pastevents.asp)

2 Larry Chiagouris and Leon Kaplan, Uses of Survey Research in Damages Estimation, Chapter 28 of *The Comprehensive Guide to Economic Damages,* 4th edition (www.bvresources.com/publications).

had developed an additive with similar properties. Company A subsequently filed suit against Company B for patent infringement. It asked for $1 billion, which equaled the sum of the profits Company A claims it lost from Company B's infringement of its patent.[3]

Company B hired a damages expert to review the basis for the $1 billion claim. Company B provided the damages expert with information on the amount of automotive paint with the additive sold in the relevant period. Among the things the damages expert did was to discuss the matter with a survey expert to see what kinds of relevant information a survey might provide. Here is what they discussed.

Survey design. A survey could be conducted among buyers of automotive paints for automotive companies and companies that did automotive body work and repainting of cars. A study could be conducted among a sample of consumers who purchased a new vehicle painted with Company B's new paint and a sample of consumers who had their vehicles painted with Company B's paint with the new additive. After some discussion of the merits of the two approaches, it was decided to study the consumers because the marketing strategy suggested that consumers "pulled" the paint through the market as opposed to car manufacturers and auto body painters "pushing" it through to consumers.

Among the questions that such a survey of people who had their cars painted with Company B's paint with the new additive could address are:

1. Did the consumer specify or participate in the decision to select the paint used?
2. Was the consumer aware of the brand of paint his or her car was painted with?
3. Was the consumer aware of the nonstick property of the paint? If so, was this property of the paint a factor in selecting the paint to be used on the car? If so, how important to the selection was this property (that is, was the nonstick property the reason the paint was selected or, if not, how important was it to the selection of the paint)?
4. Was the consumer aware of any other paints with that property? If so, what brands?
5. Did the consumer consider of any other paints with that property? If so, what brands?
6. What would the consumer have done if Company B's paint did not come with the property?

How can the answers to these questions help evaluate the validity of the $1 billion damages claim?

3 This hypothetical claim uses the unjust enrichment remedy, which is discussed in Chapters 30-32 of *The Comprehensive Guide to Economic Damages*, 4th edition.

- Question 1 both qualifies the respondent to complete the remainder of the interview and helps quantify the percentage of the automotive paint aftermarket that the consumer influences.

- Question 2 is very important because, if the consumer was not aware of the paint's benefits, it could not have been material in the selection of the paint and arguably the alleged infringing capability did not influence sales to consumers like that.

- Question 3 is a natural extension of Question 2 for those who were aware of the benefits of the paint. Being aware of the capability does not mean that it was the critical consideration in the selection of the paint or even that it was of any importance. Were there any other points of differentiation between Company B's new paint and other brands of automotive paint that favored Company B's paint and were any of them more important than the nonstick property? If so, Company B's paint would have been preferred anyway. This also can have a significant effect on the magnitude of the damages claim.

- Questions 4 and 5 can assess whether any of Company A's paint were or could have been among those the consumer considered. If the consumer was not aware of Company A's paints, with or without this nonstick property, then Company A's claim for damages is weakened.

- Question 6 addresses the "but for" issue. If the paint used did not come with the nonstick property, would the consumer still have chosen Company B's paint or selected Company A's paint or would they have chosen a third brand of paint? The percentage that would have switched to Company A's paint represents the actual profits lost by Company A because of Company B's alleged patent infringement. Other choices would not have affected Company A's sales.

These questions can have a very big impact on the damage estimate by reducing the aftermarket paint sales and ultimately the amount of Company B's sales that represent lost profits for Company A.

Watch out. Damages experts are not supposed to be involved in the execution of the survey, Kaplan and Chiagouris say. The attorney may hypothetically discuss some things with the expert, but the expert needs to be able to state that he or she was not at all involved in the actual implementation of the survey.

Top BV Experts Field Tough Questions at NACVA 'Hardball' Session

Most conference sessions are scripted affairs, but not "Hardball With Hitchner," one of the most popular sessions at the recent NACVA annual conference in San Diego. This session has become a tradition over the years, and it's where you get to hear unfettered answers to tough questions from the profession's top luminaries. This time, it was a double feature—two of these sessions were held on two different days. They covered such critical topics as the market approach, discounts, cost of capital, and valuation reports.

The panels included Shannon Pratt (Shannon Pratt Valuations), Roger Grabowski (Duff & Phelps), Nancy Fannon (Meyers, Harrison & Pia Valuation and Litigation Support LLC), and Z. Christopher Mercer (Mercer Capital). Not every individual was on both panels, so the responses below may not include remarks from everyone.

Moderator Jim Hitchner (Financial Valuation Advisors) has one long-standing rule with these panels: If someone answers "it depends," the audience gets to boo. We didn't hear any boos at this session (although there were some close calls).

What do you think is the most useful and important valuation method?

Fannon says it's the one for which you can get the best information to support it. She points out that, for a large firm, you may be able to find some good similar guideline public companies that closely compare. But you sometimes don't have the data, so you are precluded from using a method you may really want to use. She reminded the audience that the income approach is a hypothetical approach—you must estimate the cash flow and discount rate. On the other hand, market transactions are the "real world" so use the market approach if you can.

But, with the market approach, one of the most frustrating things is the lack of "pure play" public companies, added Grabowski, who thinks the market approach is much harder to apply than the income approach. True, the income approach involves a lot of assumptions, but he observes that it is sometimes a lot easier to apply than extracting the "potpourri of multiples" from larger conglomerates where the real key business that you're trying to compare is just one business among many inside these large companies.

How do you define a "similar" company?

Fannon starts out with a four-digit SIC code but then segregates S corps from C corps, or she will use three- or two-digit SIC codes. Hitchner says he's seen situations where there are no comparable companies using SIC codes but there are similar financial statistics, such as return on equity and growth rates and other investment fundamentals.

Pratt recalled that he valued the Gallo Wine Co. when there weren't comparable public companies, so he stretched out the definition of comparable companies to include distilleries, beer companies, and even soft drink companies. He points to the *Hallmark* case, where one side used only one public company, American Greetings (a card company). The other side stretched out and used Parker Pens and other consumer staples. The judge rejected the side that used American Greetings and said that "one company does not a market make."

Grabowski advised that you can also look at suppliers and customers. He was involved in a litigation with a mineral company where there was only one guideline company, but they used other mineral companies where the underlying minerals were highly correlated. By expanding the scope, they were able to come up with six to eight guideline companies.

Do you use calculation reports in either litigation or nonlitigation settings?

Hitchner points out that the AICPA neither prohibits nor endorses the use of calculation reports for litigation—you must use your own common sense. In Pennsylvania, a calculation report recently survived a *Daubert* challenge. While Fannon says she never uses them in litigation, she occasionally uses them in nonlitigation settings. She feels that the big problem with calculation reports is a general misunderstanding of what they are. To her, a calculation report is an "agreed upon procedure" report, not a valuation "lite," as too many analysts treat it. The engagement letter should be very specific as to what the analyst will do and what the report will contain.

Do you issue summary reports or just detailed reports? If you do issue summary reports, what information is OK to exclude?

Fannon almost always uses detailed reports because almost all of her work is for litigation. A detailed report helps the analyst think through what the conclusions are going to be. Hitchner points out that none of the valuation standards tell you how much you have to write. They tell you what you have to include, but there's nothing about how much detail to use—it's up to you. Like Fannon, he mainly does litigation, so he mostly does a detailed report. When he does a summary report, it's "pretty lengthy."

Do you apply a DLOM to a controlling interest?

This is one area where Hitchner, Fishman, and Pratt disagree.[1] Hitchner and Fishman do not do it. But Pratt says it's OK—he takes marketability discounts on controlling interests, including 100% ownership. He points out that you can't convert a company into cash in a couple of days, as you can with a liquid investment. Hitchner chimed in, saying that it's really a discount for lack of liquidity.

In *Cost of Capital*, 5th edition[2] (co-written by Pratt and Grabowski), a chapter on lack of marketability of operating companies presents five studies, according to Pratt. They all concur that private companies have multiples that are significantly less than comparable public companies. Grabowski notes that some people adjust the multiples to take into account the fact that the private company would sell at a lower multiple than a public company. In effect, you are applying some adjustment for that difference.

Do you use pre-IPO studies to support a DLOM?

Pratt believes that the pre-IPO studies have gotten a "bad rap" recently. He says that, if you adjust the data properly for differences in timing between the study and subject company, they can be used to substantiate discounts.

Which option models do you favor?

Grabowski revealed that Duff & Phelps often uses John Finnerty's model, but it never relies on a single methodology. Also, there's a great deal of uncertainty as to whether the option models actually mimic the market. For instance, studies show that actual market behavior is different than what the Black-Scholes option model theory suggests. Until the uncertainty is resolved, option models will have limited use, he feels.

Do transaction databases reflect synergies thereby moving it away from fair market value and toward investment value?

Pratt, the developer of the *Pratt's Stats* database of private company transactions, says there are probably synergies in the transactions. But, he notes, that doesn't mean it's not fair market value. If synergies are common in an industry, then they are included in fair market value.

What is your stance on tax affecting S Corps and other pass-through entities?

For operating companies, Hitchner says he tax affects and is fond of the Delaware MRI method[3] because it's easy to use and explain and "gets you in line" with the other models. If the distributions

1 Jim Hitchner, Shannon Pratt, and Jay Fishman are co-authors of *A Consensus View Q&A Guide to Business Valuation* (www.bvresources.com).

2 Shannon Pratt and Roger Grabowski, *Cost of Capital, Application and Examples* (5th edition), (www.bvresources.com).

3 In addition to the Delaware MRI model, there are others: the Van Vleet model, Mercer's quantitative marketability discount model (QMDM), the Grabowski model, the Christopher Treharne model, and a new approach explained in the book, *Taxes and Value: The Ongoing Research and Analysis Relating to the S Corporation Valuation Puzzle*, by Fannon and Keith Sellers (University of Denver).

are equal to the tax liability, then he's finished. If the distributions exceed the liability, then there may be a so-called S corp premium. If there are no distributions, then there's actually a disadvantage. Holding companies are a whole different ball game, he notes.

Mercer explained that, when he values an S corp, the earnings are tax affected at the enterprise level using a blended federal and state rate. If you're valuing a minority interest, the only reason that a minority interest in an S corp will have a higher value than a minority interest in a C corp is because of tax-advantaged dividends, which are available only for the expected holding period. So he calculates the benefit based on the expected dividend policy. If the S corp pays no dividends, then there is no advantage. He mentions that some of the models will create an S corp benefit into perpetuity. But, he points out, if you buy a minority interest, you don't buy it into perpetuity—you buy it for an expected holding period. That benefit is the present value of the differential between a C corp dividend and an S corp dividend, discounted to the present at a risk adjusted rate. A distribution over and above a distribution for taxes is where the "juice" is for S corp minority interests.

Where do you get your risk premium data? Duff & Phelps CRSP (Old Ibbotson)? Duff & Phelps Risk Premium Study? Both? Neither?

Mercer uses what he refers to as adjusted CAPM to build discount rates. He looks at the components including the ERP, the size premium and specific company risk. He uses the CRSP data, but, regardless of what data you use, his message has always been try to be right on the individual components but don't be wrong on the conclusion. If you get a discount rate that gives you an implied EBITDA multiple of 13 in a "7 world," it's just wrong, regardless of how you would justify the individual components. So he thinks valuation experts are focusing entirely too much on the individual components of the cost of capital and not nearly enough on the reasonableness of their conclusions. If there's a guideline group of companies, you need to calculate equity discount rates and WACCs for each one of them and compare that to the build-up method.

Hitchner points out that Duff & Phelps periodically comes out with a recommended equity risk premium that it believes should be added to a normalized risk-free rate, which Duff & Phelps believes should be 4%. So, if the spot rate of 20-year securities is higher than 4%, then you use the spot rate. If it is lower, then you normalize it to 4%. Currently, the recommended equity risk premium is 5.5%, up from 5% a few months ago. Duff & Phelps believes that it should only be applied to a normalized risk-free rate. Currently, the risk-free rate is 2.6%.

Mercer "confesses" that, on two occasions when Treasury rates precipitously fell, he normalized it but then thought about it. He realized that this is a multi-trillion-dollar market speaking as to the rate. While you could make all kinds of justifications for why the Fed artificially pushed rates down, you can't get away from the fact that what you have is a 20-year rate. And so he uses it.

Hitchner typically calculates discount rates as many as 10 different ways, and the answer doesn't change by more than two percentage points. Discount rates compound very differently at single-digit discount rates and low teens for large-cap companies than they do high teens, low 20s. They discount very differently because of the compounding. Can anyone get much more accurate than 20% plus/minus 2%?

If you estimate the discount rates and WACCs for reasonably sized publicly traded companies, you'll find high single-digit or low double-digit rates, Mercer observes. If that's the case, what do you do with a 4% Treasury rate and a 5.5% ERP? Something's wrong.

In a previous session on the size premium, it was mentioned that studies show that the difference in rates of return in the CRSP 10 deciles is largely due to liquidity differences. The implication of this is that when we are taking a DLOM that we are double counting our liquidity risk. Comment?

Liquidity is in the size deciles, particularly the smaller ones, Hitchner points out. Therefore, the 10a, 10b, 10y, and 10z include companies that don't trade as often as companies in the first decile. He believes that a component of that size premium is lack of liquidity. The fear is when you use restricted stock studies that you're double counting. If the lack of liquidity discount is embedded in the size premium of smaller companies, and you apply a 35% to 40% DLOM, is that a double count? He says the answer is no because, if you take a look at restricted stock studies, most of the companies are inactively traded, so they already have a liquidity discount in them. The restricted stock studies show that, off of that base, you have a restricted stock that is further discounted. When using restricted stock studies, he does not think it's a double count.

Do attorneys and the courts really care about BV standards and credentials?

Mercer finds that opposing attorneys care about credentials and standards particularly when they want to downgrade or criticize an opposing expert. If you're testifying and you have credentials, then it's very important to display them to the court. He also says it's important to be able to say that your testimony has never been disallowed.

Most of Hitchner's engagements require that he determine whether the other side's expert is in compliance with whatever organization it belongs to. He goes through the other side's report and (hopefully) its work papers to see whether it is in compliance—and a lot of the time, it is not. But here's the worst part: The other side is out of compliance but doesn't know it. In terms of whether the kind of credential matters, Hitchner observes that there's no such thing as one designation being better than the other. It's noticeable if you don't have a designation, but he doesn't think it matters which one you have.

Where do you see the BV profession going?

Hitchner thinks the overall business is peaking and observes that a lot of people are very busy. If you're in a traditional valuation practice and you're doing 100 valuations a year, "you're going nuts." The fair value world is on its way to being its own specialty, with the AICPA and the ASA putting out new designations. If you're doing fair value, then you have to do a lot of it to keep up. The growth area in business valuation is litigation. But estate and gift tax is very competitive, he says. He asked the young practitioners in attendance to look around the room and see a great number of older members of the profession. The next generation has a "tremendous opportunity to move in" because the veterans will not work forever. He says that some of his best friends in BV have retired.

Expanding the Cost of Capital Horizon Beyond CAPM

By Adam Manson

We will see many advances in estimating the cost of capital in future years, as it is still relatively unknown how risk is priced. That was one of the messages of two sessions on cost of capital at the recent NACVA annual conference in San Diego. In addition, insights were offered on such topics as normalizing the risk-free rate, the ERP, the size premium, and liquidity.

More than beta. Estimating the cost of equity has evolved from pre-CAPM ("chaos") to CAPM (introduction of beta) and then from modified CAPM (introduction of the size premium) to more factors (Fama-French multifactor models). In his session, Roger Grabowski (Duff & Phelps) cites Fama and French and other researchers who find that market returns are a function of other factors and not simply market betas. He also cites Pablo Fernandez (University of Navarre), who finds pure CAPM to be an "absurd" model with assumptions and conclusions that have no basis in the real world. James Harrington (Duff and Phelps), who presented a separate session, reiterated that pure CAPM is an imperfect indicator of expected returns. Until better models become more accepted and easier for the valuation profession to use, Harrington believes that the BV community will likely continue to widely use the modified CAPM. Grabowski pointed out that there are some new methods for estimating beta in D&P's *Valuation Handbook*.[1]

Ultimately, while pure CAPM is the most widely used asset pricing model, risk pricing has moved beyond considering CAPM beta as the sole measure of risk. Research seems to point toward the fact the market is pricing more systematic factors than just CAPM beta, including size risk (a systematic risk factor that proxies for characteristics of small-company size), information uncertainty (large beta estimation errors are correlated with low quality of earnings, low persistence of earnings, and high volatility of returns), and distress risk (a systematic risk factor that varies depending on recession or expansion). Going beyond modified CAPM, Grabowski points to Fama and French's five-factor asset pricing model, Zhang's investment CAPM, and Dohmeyer and Butler's implied private company pricing line.[2]

1 Duff & Phelps, *Valuation Handbook - Guide to Cost of Capital* (www.bvresources.com/publications).

2 More information on IPCPL can be found at www.bvresources.com under Valuation Topics: Cost of Capital.

Grabowski also discussed the recommendation by Duff & Phelps to normalize risk-free rates when they appear to be abnormally low due to flight to quality or other issues (e.g., massive monetary interventions). He also mentioned how ERP is expectational (forward-looking) over the expected duration of the net cash flows and that realized long-term average ERPs may contain nonrecurring factors in prior periods or changing economic conditions. One piece of research found that the artificially low U.S. Treasury rates between 1942 and 1951 created an upward bias in realized risk premium data from 1926 to 2015 of about 1.1%.

Size premium. In his session, Harrington presented empirical evidence that supported that returns for smaller companies, as measured by market capitalization, are greater for smaller companies than they are for larger companies. This size premium, however, is concentrated in the smallest-cap companies (or those based in the 10th decile in the *Valuation Handbook - Guide to Cost of Capital*). While returns on any given year can be higher for larger companies or for smaller companies, over a longer period, smaller stock returns greatly outperform that of larger companies. In other words, the longer the "race," the more small stocks tend to win. For instance, when reviewing the 1,069 one-year possible periods between 1926 and 2015, small stocks outperformed large stocks 53% of the time while large stocks "won" 47% of the time. When looking at the 901 15-year periods during 1926 to 2015, small stocks won 77% of the time. Finally, when examining the 721 30-year periods between 1926 and 2015, small stocks won 91% of the time, and large stocks saw greater returns a mere 9% of the time.

When the modified CAPM is used, size premia provide the BV community with an empirically based correction to the pure CAPM for the risks of smaller companies not captured by beta. Citing an article[3] by Ted Israel (Israel Frey Group LLP), Harrington also notes that many of the characteristics that are often cited as reasons for the additional of a company-specific risk adjustment are "the very attributes that generally define small companies," and adding a company-specific risk may be double-counting risks already embodied in the size premium adjustment.

Liquidity and size. An intriguing topic of discussion is liquidity and how it relates to the size effect. Harrington provided a nonexhaustive list of a dozen research papers covering the topic, as well as Dr. Ashok Abbott's findings that the observed level of liquidity is a superior predictor of future performance as compared to the market value of equity and that the liquidity impact may be a substantial part of the explanation for the size premium. Abbott's thoughts? "It appears that 75% of the size effect is liquidity." Next, research from Dr. Roger Ibbotson was presented that leads to a similar, but more dramatic, conclusion: "The small stock premium is completely explained by liquidity." Basically, if one controls for liquidity (as measured by the Amihud measure of liquidity), there appears to be no size premium.

In the end, the evidence does suggest that the size effect can be explained by liquidity. But does this mean that appraisers should stop using an adjustment for size? In short, the answer is: "No, it does not." In quoting Grabowski:

3 "Risky Business: A Generous Helping of Company-Specific Risk," *Business Valuation Update*, Vol. 14, No. 6, June 2011.

> The size effect and illiquidity are intermingled and the relative impact of each varies over time. But for non-public stocks, the distinction may not be very important. In valuing non-public stocks we typically assume that the non-public stock has characteristics like a typical publicly traded stock of a company of comparable size. The size effect remains a good proxy for the overall impact.

When the size premium was developed, research may not have known whether size was responsible for the effect or whether size was just a proxy for other factors correlated with size, but the presentation demonstrated the profession continues to make progress in this area.

Harrington provided a look into the next potential breakthrough area of research that may predict returns: popularity, where the asset with more desirable characteristics should have lower expected relative returns and the asset with less desirable characteristics should have higher expected relative returns. And this isn't only referring to risk, which is obviously unpopular. Popularity can include all types of other characteristics that do not fit well into the risk and return model.

In the end, attendees were reminded to use their own professional judgement and avoid using a cost of equity estimate just because it was computed by a formula. One final word of advice—use multiple methods when computing your cost of equity!

Adam Manson, *manager of financial analysis at Business Valuation Resources, can be reached at adamm@bvresources.com or 503-291-7963, ext. 105.*

Economic Obsolescence: An Adjustment That Is Often Overlooked

By Gary R. Trugman CPA/ABV, MCBA, ASA, MVS

When we perform a business valuation, the valuation analyst is constantly faced with addressing the highest and best use of a property, as well as different premises of value that can impact the conclusions. This article is intended to discuss an issue that arises regularly but is not necessarily addressed by the valuation analyst, namely economic obsolescence.

One factor that has to be considered in any business valuation is the highest and best use of the subject business. Assume that liquidation ended up being the premise of value that would return the greatest amount to the hypothetical willing buyer. During the course of this assignment, assume that a machinery and equipment appraisal[1] was performed and the valuation analyst requested that the machinery and equipment appraiser provide a "market value in-place" and "orderly liquidation value" for each of the assets. The "market value in-place" concept was defined as follows:

> The estimated gross amount expressed in terms of money that the subject property would most likely realize in its most common market. The transaction must be between a willing buyer and willing seller with neither party being under any compulsion to buy or sell and with both parties in full knowledge of all relevant facts. Consideration is given to costs of moving and installation in order to arrive at an "In-Place" value.

This definition did not consider the economic obsolescence that was specific to the subject company's use of these assets. However, the machinery and equipment appraisal defined economic obsolescence as follows:

> A form of depreciation, or loss in value, caused by unfavorable external conditions. These can include such things as the economics of the industry, availability of financing, loss of material and labor sources, passage of new legislation, and changes in ordinance. *(Economic Obsolescence, as it pertains directly to the current financial condition of the subject company, has not been considered in the valuation of the subject assets).* (emphasis added)

1 Economic obsolescence may be applicable to various types of fixed assets, inventory, etc., including certain types of real estate.

In this hypothetical example, assume that the valuation analyst consulted with the machinery appraiser who confirmed that the *underlying assumption* behind the machinery and equipment appraisal is that the economics of the subject company would support the values as they have determined them. However, based on the undercapacity and continued losses of the subject company, the valuation analyst knew that this could not be the case. As a result, the valuation analyst was required to make a further adjustment to support the economic obsolescence built into the balance sheet of the subject company.

A fundamental requirement of fair market value is the assumption of a willing buyer and a willing seller. However, according to the American Society of Appraisers (ASA), the term "fair market value" needs to be refined with respect to machinery and equipment appraisals to fit the purpose and the function of the particular appraisal. As a result, it is necessary to recognize different premises of value that are distinguished based on the anticipated use of the particular asset. These premises of value can be broadly classified into the following categories:

1. Sale or removal for a similar or alternate use;
2. Continued (or installed) use of the asset for the purpose for which it was designed and acquired; and
3. Liquidation.[2]

As a result, the term "fair market value" as it pertains to machinery and equipment appraisal is modified to create special definitions to fit the needs of a particular appraisal. These same definitions can be applied to many business assets, not merely the machinery and equipment. Course materials offered by the ASA contain the following definitions of fair market value:

> *Fair Market Value* is the amount expressed in terms of money that may reasonably be expected for property in exchange between a willing buyer and a willing seller with equity to both, neither under any compulsion to buy or sell and both fully aware of all relevant facts. (In the valuation of installed personal property with the intent for it to remain installed, this definition must be further defined based on the function and purpose of the appraisal.)
>
> *Fair Market Value in Continued Use* is the estimated amount expressed in terms of money that may reasonably be expected for a property in exchange between a willing buyer and a willing seller with equity to both, neither under any compulsion to buy or sell and both fully aware of all relevant facts and including installation and *assuming that the earnings support the value reported.*
>
> *Fair Market Value—Installed* is the estimated amount of an installed property expressed in terms of money that may reasonably be expected in exchange between a willing buyer and a willing seller with equity to both, neither under any compulsion to buy or sell and both fully aware of all the relevant facts.
>
> *Fair Market Value—Removal* is the estimated amount expressed in terms of money that may

2 American Society of Appraisers, *Valuing Machinery and Equipment: The Fundamentals of Appraising Machinery and Technical Assets*, 2nd edition (Washington, D.C., 2000, 2005): 2.

> reasonably be expected for an item of property between a willing buyer and a willing seller with equity to both, neither under any compulsion to buy or sell and both fully aware of all relevant facts, considering removal of the property to another location.[3] (emphasis added)

The definitions of fair market value are refined to reflect the intended use of the assets. The concept of value can assume removal, installation, or continued use of the assets. The removal concept considers the removal of the particular assets to a new location. However, certain assets require large installation costs and any removal concept tends to incur large discounts for all items that are not economical to remove. According to the ASA, the difference between the installed concept and the continued use concept is the application of what is referred to as "economic obsolescence."

Economic obsolescence is defined as the "loss in value of a property caused by factors external to the property." These factors can include the economics of the industry; availability of financing; loss of material and/or labor sources; passage of new legislation; changes in ordinances; increased cost of raw materials, labor, or utilities; reduced demand for the product; increased competition; inflation or high interest rates; or other similar factors.[4] One author suggests "to determine if economic obsolescence is present, a review must be made of the economics of the subject property and the industry in which it competes, as of the valuation date. The review can be made by examining the earnings history of the subject property and any local or other influences that may affect the economic performance of the subject and its assets." This author goes on to state:

> Economic obsolescence may exist in any industry or property where the following attributes are found:
>
> - Reduced demand for the company's products;
> - Overcapacity in the industry;
> - Dislocation of raw material supplies;
> - Increasing cost of raw materials, labor, utilities, or transportation, while the selling price of the product remains fixed or increases at a much lower rate;
> - Government regulations that require capital expenditures to be made with little or no return on the new investment; and
> - Environmental considerations that require capital expenditures to be made with little or no return on investment.[5]

The ASA teaches "words of art" to assist practitioners in distinguishing between different types of economic obsolescence. These are referred to as "item-specific," "industry-specific," and

3 American Society of Appraisers, Course Materials for ME207: The Advanced Cost Approach.

4 *Valuing Machinery and Equipment*: 67.

5 Michael J. Remsha, P.E., ASA, CMI, *Identifying and Quantifying Economic Obsolescence* (2010):1-2.

"business-specific" economic obsolescence. These terms are intended to provide assistance in eliminating confusion as it relates to economic obsolescence. ASA's course materials discuss the definitions of the three types of economic obsolescence as follows:

> *Item-specific* economic obsolescence is defined as the reactions of purchasers after the deduction of physical and functional depreciation factors. It is measured from the market as items similar to the subject that are sold.
>
> *Industry-specific* economic obsolescence is related to the industry in which the equipment works. If a machine were operating in the textile industry and the economics of that industry are good, the appraiser could possibly conclude that the industry is standard and has no economic obsolescence factor. On the other hand, if the textile industry was considered as less than standard, there may be an economic penalty that may be assessed that relates to other companies that must compete for like products or operations.
>
> *Business-specific* economic obsolescence is usually provided by the valuation analyst. It is that factor for which the subject is measured, as a business, in order to demonstrate whether the earnings can support the values provided by the personal property appraiser and any other capital asset appraisers. In referencing the definition of fair market value in continued use, there is a statement of an assumption that the earnings can support the values reported. If the business indicates that the earnings do not support the values reported, that economic obsolescence factor as a percentage of that difference is the business-specific economic obsolescence. Business-specific economic obsolescence is only important as it relates to Fair Market Value in Continued Use as applied to the current business.[6] (underlined for emphasis)

Item-specific and industry-specific economic obsolescence are typically accounted for by machinery and equipment appraisers through use of a cost approach or a sales comparison approach. However, the values derived by machinery and equipment appraisers assume that the earnings of the business are sufficient enough to support the values derived. It is up to the valuation analyst to determine whether this assumption is applicable to the valuation subject. This business-specific economic obsolescence is the primary factor that distinguishes the installed concept versus the continued-use concept. According to ASA course materials:

> The difference between Fair Market Value—Installed and Fair Market Value in Continued Use is the application of economic obsolescence as explained earlier.
>
> For Fair Market Value—Installed, the concept considers that the buyer is not concerned with the business and its management but rather what new management could create or accomplish with the subject equipment. The new management would consider each machine as a stand-alone piece with some credit for installation. For Fair Market Value in Continued Use, the concept considers that the buyer appreciates the business for what it can accomplish with the combination of *all* equipment. *The Fair Market Value in Continued Use is normally applied to a profitable business and substantiated through a business value appraisal in order to determine if there is any business-specific economic penalty. When a business value is accomplished, it is many times stated as an "overlay" that indicates whether the subject business can support the values indicated. The machinery and technical specialties appraiser must understand that the business valuer could discover an additional economic penalty for the subject over and above any that might be determined for the industry.* If the business value appraiser finds additional economic penalty, it may be necessary for the machinery and equipment appraiser to be consulted. Under the internal revenue tax code, an allocation of purchase price

6 Course Materials for ME207.

> applied to the equipment should not have a value lower than that for which the equipment can be liquidated. *It is always possible that prorating the equipment values downward in order to meet this allocation requirement could bring them below a number in which they could sell in the marketplace. If this were true for all equipment, the recommendation would be to liquidate the company rather than continue the operation.*[7] (emphasis added)

So what are we supposed to do as valuation analysts? The analyst must deal with the economic realities of the subject company. In the hypothetical business valuation discussed at the beginning of this article, the valuation subject was a company that had not generated a profit for the past decade. A financial analysis of the subject company's historic financial statements revealed that, combined, the company was legally insolvent (more liabilities than assets), had underutilized assets, and had a high likelihood of going bankrupt in the near future. All of the subject company's facilities were operating well below capacity, and no individual facility had been operating at capacity for the past decade. An analysis of the subject company's forecasts indicated that the company was expected to continue to lose money in each of the next five years. All of these factors suggested that there was a significant amount of business-specific economic obsolescence related to the subject company's assets as the business enterprise was not generating any profits to support the fair market values of the equipment, real estate, or any of the other assets that had been valued.

To quantify economic obsolescence, the valuation analyst used the five-year forecast to perform a discounted cash flow analysis taking the subject's projected losses over the next five years into consideration. The fair market value balance sheet reflected the values of the subject company's assets as of the valuation date. However, if the company were to continue to operate as a going concern, it will continue to incur losses that would further deplete its cash reserves, resulting in diminishing shareholder's equity over the next several years. Therefore, to value the subject company's assets as a going concern as of the valuation date, the valuation analyst must consider the impact that these continued losses will have on the company's balance sheet going forward. This is the economic obsolescence that relates specifically to the company. In reality, the subject company cannot survive for the five-year period being forecast without exhausting all of its reserves.

The valuation analyst performed a discounted net earnings analysis over a five-year period. Since the going-concern concept is perpetual in nature, a five-year period was determined to be conservative. To discount these losses to present value, the analyst must determine an appropriate discount rate. In this instance, the analyst determined that the subject company's total combined cost of debt was the appropriate rate to use in the analysis.

Based on the average cost of debt of 6.93%, economic obsolescence was calculated as shown in the exhibit.

Although economic obsolescence had been calculated to be $34,106,182, it must be noted that this amount can only pertain to the tangible business assets owned by the company, namely inventory

7 Id.

Calculation of Economic Obsolescence

		20X1	20X2	20X3	20X4	20X5
Forecasted losses		($9,269,579)	($8,263,054)	($7,434,658)	($7,434,658)	($7,434,658)
Discount rate	6.93%					
PV factors		0.9671	0.9044	0.8458	0.791	0.7397
PV of losses		($8,964,610)	($7,437,106)	($6,288,234)	($5,880,815)	($5,499,417)
Total present value of losses		($34,106,182)				

Note: Figures may not add due to rounding.

and fixed assets. There would be no depreciation relating to the financial assets of the company. Therefore, the amount of economic depreciation allocated to the tangible business assets was as follows:

Inventory	$10,722,898
Fixed assets	15,880,000
Economic Obsolescence	$26,602,898

The $26,602,898 would be recorded on the fair market value balance sheet as a going-concern adjustment to reduce the value of the assets. This results in bringing the asset-based approach back to a more realistic level if the business is valued as a going concern. No economic obsolescence adjustment would be required under a liquidation scenario.

This is an important adjustment that is needed to reconcile values and make the going-concern valuation more realistic. While this is not the only manner in which economic obsolescence could be calculated, it seemed logical when it was done. This topic deserves more consideration in the future.

Gary Trugman, *CPA/ABV, MCBA, ASA, MVS, is president of Trugman Valuation Associates Inc., a valuation firm with offices in Plantation, Fla., and Parsippany, N.J. He is also an editorial advisor of* Business Valuation Update.

Experts Size Up Controversial IRS Estate Valuation Regs

Valuation experts were anxiously awaiting the proposed IRC Section 2704 regulations designed to crack down on estate valuation discounts. Now that they have been released, they have triggered strong reactions from the valuation community, the legal profession, and others.

The IRS wants to eliminate the technique of putting valuable property into entities such as family-owned partnerships or corporations just to reduce the value in the property to avoid estate and gift tax. To do this, the proposed regs[1] address the treatment of some lapsing rights and restrictions on liquidation in determining the value of transferred interests in corporations and partnerships. Liquidation restrictions would be disregarded for valuation purposes. Overall, it appears that the proposed regulations eliminate almost all minority discounts for closely held entity interests, including operating businesses owned by a family.

Redefining FMV. "The recently released IRC Section 2704 family limited partnership (FLP) discounts proposed regulations include much of what appraisers had been dreading for the past year," says Carol Carden (PYA PC), chair of the AICPA FVS executive committee. "The proposed regulations provide new rules and limits that (if included in the final version) will impact estate planning with FLPs," she says. "This is indeed a very significant issue for business appraisers, notwithstanding the impact the higher exemption limits have had on the number of taxpayers exposed to estate taxes," says Ronald Seigneur (Seigneur Gustafson LLP), a veteran valuation practitioner. "In my opinion, this is a legislative attempt to redefine the fundamental premise of fair market value."

Michelle Gallagher (Gallagher Valuation & Forensics PLC) agrees. "They are changing the definition of fair market value," she says, pointing to the Federal Gift Tax Regulations (Treas. Reg. Sec. 25.2512-1), which define fair market value as:

> [T]he price at which property would change hands between a willing buyer and a willing seller, when the former is not under any compulsion to buy and the latter is not under any compulsion to sell, both parties having reasonable knowledge of the relevant facts.

1 The proposed regs (REG-163113-02) are available at sub.bvresources.com/defaulttextonly.asp?f=downloads.

"Seems to me, the proposed regs carve certain types of transfers completely out of the FMV definition," she says, referring to transfers:

- Within three years of death;
- Between family members;
- Resulting in the lapse of liquidation rights; and
- Eliminating comparison to the liquidation rights of state laws.

The proposed regs are typically complex and difficult to understand, but Gallagher says there are some good examples at the end of the document that help sort them out.

"I view it as a full frontal assault on economic reality, but that really isn't anything new for the current Administration," says Donald DeGrazia (Gold Gerstein Group LLC). "The IRS has long been hostile to the concept of discounts for lack of marketability and control despite losses in court and their own previous rulings. These discounts merely recognize that an interest in an entity, active or passive that doesn't enjoy the prerogatives of control is not proportionately equal in value to an interest that does enjoy control. That hostility is manifested in these proposed regs."

"The regs seem to be an attempt to ignore economic reality through use of attribution rules (despite IRS Revenue Ruling 93-12) and nonrecognition of succession planning restrictions on transfer of ownership interests in entities," observes DeGrazia. "It is an attempt to invalidate discounts that reflect the economic impact on value of minority ownership interests in entities." Legal observers feel that this is an attempt by the IRS to overturn many years of settled law. Richard Dees, an attorney and partner at McDermott Will & Emery LLP in Chicago, who last year sent a 29-page letter[2] to the government critiquing the proposal as beyond the scope of its powers, says the proposed regs appear to eliminate all valuation discounts. "Liquidation restrictions and minority and marketability discounts are flip sides of the same coin; you can't separate the two," he says.[3]

Other stakeholders are also weighing in, such as the Family Business Coalition, which issued a document[4] explaining the proposed regs and warning that they would pose a big problem for family firms. Also, estate planners have been advising clients to complete transfers before the new rules take effect, so those efforts will now likely gain steam.

"Hopefully the valuation, accounting, legal and business communities will come together to challenge these proposed regs before they are made final," says DeGrazia. Those efforts are now underway.

2 sites-mwe.vuturevx.com/27/1960/uploads/tax-notes---dees-valuation.pdf.

3 "Proposed Regs Seek to Close Estate and Gift Tax Preference," *Tax Notes Today*, Aug. 3, 2016.

4 familybusinesscoalition.org/wp-content/uploads/2016/08/FBC2704Regs.pdf.

Taking action. Shortly after the proposed regs were issued, the AICPA, ASA, and NACVA told *BVU* that they are forming task forces to study the regs and submit comments. "The AICPA plans to draft and submit comments to the IRS prior to the December 1 hearing," Carden says. Both Seigneur and Gallagher are part of the AICPA task force set up to study the regs and prepare formal comments. William Johnston (Empire Valuation Consultants LLC), chair of the BV committee of the American Society of Appraisers (ASA), says that the ASA is also forming a task force and preparing an action plan. Brien K. Jones, chief operations officer and executive vice president of NACVA, says that it is also taking action and asks members to join in the effort. "NACVA is convening a task force of board members, instructors, and members to address this issue as it has significant impact to the membership and profession at large," he says. "I invite interested members to contact me if they are interested in supporting this initiative."

What to do. The proposed regulations are subject to a 90-day public comment period in advance of a scheduled December 1 public hearing. *BVU* urges readers to read the proposed regs and submit comments to the IRS by the due date (November 2). "Luckily, the new rules are not effective until the final regs are published, but we think appraisers should start considering the proposed regs for their clients' prior and new estate plans," says Carden. Seigneur agrees, adding: "It is not unusual for this process to take years to get to a stage of final implementation, but the proposed regs often act as *de facto* regulations for purposes of enforcement and planning."

The proposed regs are very detailed and are still being studied. Further insights and developments will be covered in *BVWire* and *Business Valuation Update.*

BVR offered a webinar on this topic on September 29 featuring Curtis Kimball. To learn more, visit www.bvresources.com/TrainingEvent.asp?WebinarID=537.

Proposed Sec. 2704 Regs Fly in the Face of BV Theory and Tax Law

By Ronald D. Rudich, CPA/ABV/CFF, MS, MCBA, CVA/ABAR/MAFF, CM&AA, CMEA, BCA

For many years, the Internal Revenue Service has argued that business valuation adjustments when applied to family-controlled entities are utilized merely to reduce the gifted or inherited asset. Valuation experts, accountants, and attorneys contend that this is not true: The adjustments recognize that the change in ownership is primarily market-based and such adjustments are practical and cogent under the specific circumstances.

The proposed regulations under IRC Section 2704 seek to accomplish the IRS's goal of curtailing valuation discounts for transfers of interests in family-controlled entities.[1] The trouble is, the proposed regs go against Chapter 14 of the tax law and its interpreted meaning by the courts—as well as IRS Revenue Ruling 93-12. Plus, they are in direct opposition to accepted business valuation theory that goes back at least 35 years.

IRC Chapter 14. Congress passed Chapter 14 of the Internal Revenue Code, which covers Sections 2701 through 2704, in 1990. Its sole purpose was to prevent perceived abuses of the tax system. The sections are: Section 2701, *Special Valuation Rules in Case of Transfer of Certain Interests in Corporations or Partnerships*; Section 2703, *Certain Rights and Restrictions Disregarded*; and Section 2704, *Treatment of Certain Lapsing Rights and Restrictions*, which is on point with respect to transfers of equity interests in family limited partnerships (FLPs). Section 2702 does not pertain to FLPs.

The following points are germane to the three sections of Chapter 14:

1. The sections apply to all transfer restrictions in the partnership agreement;
2. They are designed to prevent the use of buy-sell agreements, options, calls, puts, and/or other transfer restrictions to distort the value of the assets for transfer tax purposes; and

1 For background information, see "Experts Size Up Controversial IRS Estate Valuation Regs," *Business Valuation Update* (Sept. 2016).

3. The sections provide a safe harbor for transfer restrictions, when they are: (a) a bona fide business arrangement; (b) not a device to transfer property to family members for less than full and adequate consideration; and (c) comparable to similar arrangements entered into in an arm's-length transaction.

It has long been practiced that, as long as an agreement has been prepared that hasn't exceeded any restriction that is governed by state law, it would be acceptable to the IRS and not be deemed abusive.

Chapter 14 safe harbor disregarded. The proposed three-year rule with regard to the loss of the donor's voting and/or liquidation rights, which now occurs immediately, will cause the donor to include the asset in his or her gross estate if the gift happens within three years of his or her date of death.

This is by no means a future "safe harbor," since currently the "add-back" is not a forced situation. Notwithstanding the three-year rule, no one can predict when he or she is going to expire, so the proposed rule artfully grabs back assets to be taxed and essentially reverses the donor's gift and nullifies the intent that the donor had while still alive.

Impact of Rev. Rul. 93-12 ignored. The headnote of this ruling states: "Valuation; stock; intrafamily transfers; minority discounts. In determining the value of a gift of a minority block of stock in a closely held corporation, the block should be valued for gift tax purposes without regard to the family relationship of the donor to other shareholders. Rev. Rul. 81-253 revoked."

The above refers to family aggregation, which this revenue ruling has revoked. Thus, when a donor control owner gifts to minority interests to the family members, the specific minority interests are not added together to give the appearance of a "control" gift.

Rev. Rul. 93-12 further states that "Rev. Rul. 81-253, 1981-1 C.B. 187, holds that, ordinarily, no minority shareholder discount is allowed with respect to transfers of shares of stock between family members if, based upon a composite of the family members' interests at the time of the transfer, control (either majority voting control or de facto control through family relationships) of the corporation exists in the family unit. The ruling also states that the Service will not follow the decision of the 5th Circuit in *Estate of Bright v. United States*, 658 F.2d 999 (5th Cir. 1981)."

Therefore, it specifically states that the valuation process should consider a discount for lack of control.

Much to consider. Many issues need to be resolved before the regs can be enacted. Your comments now and through the hearing process[2] are most important. It is the only time and way for

2 Comments are due to the IRS on Nov. 2, 2016. A public hearing is scheduled for Dec. 1, 2016, in Washington, D.C.

us to express our professional opinions. Many issues will have to be extensively discussed and researched before the proposed regulations can be enacted. They are:

- *A transfer document will only become effective upon an individual's demise.* Therefore, the gray area in which the IRS wants to govern is the particular control ownership at the specific period (moment) *before* death. This is a distinct difference from actual death, which will begin the transfer process and *not before.*
- The marketplace does not support undiscounted values of limited partnership interests and corporate interests.
- Family members do not always get along. Sometimes, arguments force the family to expunge themselves of particular assets.
- Sometimes a "control" owner doesn't have any prerogatives of control—for instance, a parent who has a control interest but is retired, but his children are legally running the business with the prerogatives of control.
- Sometimes the board of directors is the one in control.
- The reality of published closed-end funds are reported at their net asset value. The difference of the traded value to the NAV is usually described as the indicated lack of control discount.
- Since 2002, this author has written and lectured about "limited marketing costs" that are inherent in any valuation whether they are between control and minority interests within the same company or an external arm's-length transaction. They are: (1) the time value of money; (2) accounting costs; (3) tax structuring fees; (4) broker fees; (5) legal fees; (6) transaction costs; (7) announcement costs; (8) settlement/closing costs; (9) advertising costs; (10) built-in capital gains; (11) fix-up costs; and (12) miscellaneous costs. Depending upon the specific transaction, one or more of the above costs would form the "floor" of marketability adjustments.
- Further marketability issues, the first of which is U.S. Tax Court Judge Laro's decision in the *Mandelbaum v. Commissioner* case, are:

    1. Financial statement analysis;
    2. Dividend history and policy;
    3. Nature of the business, its history, its position in the industry, and its economic outlook;
    4. Management;

5. Amount of control in the transferred shares;
6. Restrictions on transferability;
7. Holding period for the stock;
8. The company's redemption policy; and
9. Costs associated with an initial public offering.

- The author believes the following additional marketability factors need attention:

1. Number of shareholders and multiple classes of common stock;
2. Concentration of a control owner;
3. Desirability of the business;
4. Number of potential buyers;
5. Access to capital markets;
6. Size of the business;
7. Existence of noncompete agreements;
8. Divergence of owners' business philosophy;
9. Business yield;
10. Volatility of the business assets;
11. Liquidity of control owners;
12. Size of the block of stock;
13. Existence and impact of pending litigation; and
14. Secondary market liquidity.

What to do. It is our responsibility as a profession to not just sit back and accept the inevitable. Contact every association that you belong to, and make sure that a consensus letter is drafted so that our thoughts and concerns may be heard.

If the proposed regulations are accepted as law, there will be more work for us in the short-term to prepare gift valuations before the enactment date. However, in the big picture, the action by the IRS does not bode well for the profession as a whole because the federal government will try to do more of the same to reduce adjustments applied to business valuations.

The Tax Court, particularly with Section 2704, has had a long history and understanding when making judicial decisions. The proposed regulations literally "fly in the face" of Chapter 14 and its interpreted meaning by the courts, Revenue Ruling 93-12, and more than three decades of business valuation theory. Much discussion needs to take place before sweeping changes are enacted into law.

Ronald D. Rudich, *CPA/ABV/CFF, MS, MCBA, CVA/ABAR/MAFF, CM&AA, CMEA, BCA, is the senior director of the business valuation, machinery and equipment valuation, and litigation support services of the accounting and business consulting firm of Gorfine, Schiller & Gardyn, PA, Owings Mills, Md. In practice since 1966, Rudich is a frequent speaker, writer, teacher, mentor, and was recently named as a "Business Valuation and Financial Forensic Master" by the National Association of Certified Valuators and Analysts (NACVA) as part of its "Industry Titans—The Financial Consulting Profession's Most Influential" awards at its 2016 annual conference.*

PPA-Style Method Helps Fine-Tune Estimate of Personal Goodwill

A twist on traditional methods for carving out personal from enterprise goodwill can be used to determine the goodwill attributed to an individual. The technique boils personal goodwill down to its essence: the difference between enterprise value and the sum of all the identifiable tangible—and intangible—assets.

How it works. "The method is basically analogous to a purchase price allocation that you would do for financial reporting purposes," says Harold Martin (Keiter, Stephens, Hurst, Gary & Shreaves PC), who spoke during a webinar.[1] After determining enterprise value, you assign value to the various tangible assets and then to the specifically identifiable intangibles. These intangibles can include customer relationships, location, assembled workforce, trade name/company reputation, contracts, business processes, and know-how. Of course, some of these intangibles are difficult to value, such as location and reputation, but it can be done. For example, you could gather any available data and make an estimate of a portion of sales related to a favorable location. For a trade name and reputation, you could use a royalty rate using the relief-from-royalty method.

"This is one method that we consider for determining the allocation of goodwill in divorce cases," says Martin. "We have actually used this methodology for purposes of valuing identifiable intangibles in order to allocate total goodwill into its personal and entity components." He noted that he has not yet had a case where there is a published court opinion. "It is certainly a better way to estimate personal goodwill and one that is more explainable to a judge," says Jim Alerding (Alerding Consulting LLC), who was a co-presenter on the webinar. He points out, however, that you need the time and budget to do it. Martin agreed and acknowledged that it may be a costly process depending on the number and complexity of the intangible assets to be valued.

Caution. Alerding raised the issue that some part of the value of an intangible could be attributed to personal goodwill, such as for a client list. "It would seem to me that, if you take that approach, you would have to look at your values that you determine on each of the intangible assets and further bifurcate them into their personal and enterprise components," he points out.

1 Goodwill: Let's Get Personal, BVR Webinar, Aug. 9, 2016; R. James Alerding (Alerding Consulting LLC) and Harold G. Martin Jr. (Keiter, Stephens, Hurst, Gary & Shreaves PC). An archived version is available at bvresources.com/pastevents.asp.

"You are exactly right," says Martin. "There could potentially be overlap in certain of the specifically identifiable intangibles, and you hit on the one that I would consider the most relevant, which is customer relationships. So if you are going to apply this approach, be careful and make sure you have considered this issue."

Alerding points out one further issue in light of the *McReath*[2] decision. In that case, the Supreme Court of Wisconsin upheld decisions by the lower courts to include salable personal goodwill as part of the marital estate. Prior to this, the state excluded personal goodwill from the marital estate, but this case splits goodwill into three pieces: enterprise, salable (or transferable) personal goodwill, and "pure" personal goodwill). Therefore, the valuation analyst might be in a position where he or she must look at each intangible asset and the residual goodwill value and determine each of the three pieces pointed out above.

2 *McReath v. McReath*, 2011 WL 2706249 (July 12, 2011).

The Valuation of Restricted Stock Grants Based on Total Shareholder Return

By Robert Barnett, CFA, FRM

Share-based payment awards have been a subject of formal valuation for financial reporting and tax purposes since the Financial Accounting Standards Board adopted FAS 123R for US GAAP in 2004. This significant step immediately made the previously less familiar use of option-pricing theory a regular mainstay of audited financial statements. For the first time, the concepts around the use of numerical-based valuation models, including lattice and Monte Carlo simulation, were now front and center. While the attention was focused on stock option awards because of their prevalence and popularity, other forms of awards and their variants proliferated. At the root of this valuation evolution are the companies that choose to adopt equity incentive plans with the intent of aligning management and shareholders' interests. Employee stock options have long been the best-known form of share-based payment granted to senior executives, management, and other stakeholders.

Restricted stock grants. For purposes of this discussion, we will turn our attention to the increasingly popular *restricted stock* grant. Restricted stock and stock options share in their intent to benefit the recipient in the event the underlying common stock appreciates in price. Each form of award is available to and granted by both public and private companies. Public companies have the obvious advantage of an observable stock price. This enables vesting requirements that are not applicable to a private-company share with an unobservable stock price. This article focuses on a specific form or market condition that is only available to a public company called total shareholder return (TSR) or relative total shareholder return (rTSR).

Restricted stock valuations come in a wide variety of forms and complexity. The form refers to the conditions that make the stock restricted, i.e., vesting terms. This is not about a lock-up or other non-vesting-related restriction. Rather, restricted stock awards require some measure of vesting, be it service-based or performance-based, before the recipient (grantee) has ownership of an unrestricted stock. TSR is a specific type of vesting condition that has become popular among public companies issuing restricted stock awards. The basic premise is a comparison of the company's stock performance over a defined measurement period to that of a selected group of other public companies, often referred to as a peer group since they will generally be companies in the same industry or sector. Thus, the vesting is based on a measure of *relative performance* with the idea being that an employee should benefit in a manner that is aligned with the company's performance versus its peers rather than its own stock exclusively (like an option) or to a less-descript, more-diffuse comparison such as a broad-market index (e.g., S&P 500).

Measuring TSR. TSR restricted stock vesting will award a percentage of the total grant to the recipient at the end of the performance period based on the performance of the stock. In the parlance of GAAP accounting, this is a *market condition*. Market conditions must be considered in the fair value of the award as of the date of grant. Thus, for a TSR award, the fair value must incorporate the measurement of TSR, the peer group, and the vesting percentages given the ranking of the company's TSR. All of these components would be explicitly defined in the award agreement.

The next consideration is how to do all of this. The quick answer is a simulation process that projects the stock performance for each peer company and the company itself. By simulating stock performance, the TSR calculation can be made as all the necessary ingredients will be in place, most importantly the starting (S0) and ending stock price (ST) over a defined period of time (T). Total shareholder return is most frequently defined as the percentage return on the stock in the form of:

$$[\frac{S_T}{S_0}]^{1/n} - 1$$

Thus, the percentage return on the stock is the relationship between the ending stock price and the beginning stock price solved for the return over the performance period. While variations on this theme exist, this is the basic form. In addition, dividends and their inclusion or exclusion should be stipulated by the award agreement and considered in the measure of TSR.

The simulation process gives us the needed inputs to compute TSR and make a comparison, but what is required to perform the simulation? The fundamental form is geometric Brownian motion (GBM), which is a stochastic (random, nonconstant) diffusion process that results in a distribution of future prices consistent with a lognormal curve and generally accepted as a reasonable proxy for the behavior of a random variable such as a stock price. The form of this equation is readily available and presented here:

$$S_i = S_0 * exp\left(\left(r_f - \frac{\sigma^2}{2}\right)\Delta t + \sigma\sqrt{\Delta t}\varepsilon_i\right)$$

Overall, the stock price evolves according to a constant underlying drift rate (rf), a volatility estimate that speaks to the dispersion of prices around the drift rate, and a random variable (εi) selected from a standard normal distribution. The stock process could be adjusted for dividends as needed. The result is an ending stock process consistent with the stock's own volatility and the time period.

A logical choice for drift rate would seem to be the required return on the stock, meaning the estimate of the company's cost of equity. After all, we are projecting the company's stock price to the end of the performance period to measure the return realized on the stock. But we would be wrong. This is the "ah-ha" moment of the article! Rather than using a cost of equity drift rate for each company, we will instead use a single risk-free rate consistent with the remaining time between the grant date (t0) and the end of the performance period (T). Fortunately, identifying the appropriate risk-free rate is a much simpler and more objective task than a cost of equity.

Applying an option pricing framework. But why? Well the "ah-ha" moment is the realization that the performance-based restricted stock award is a closet option—or at least close enough that we will value the TSR market condition award in an option-pricing framework. This is a big concept that deserves to be considered carefully. Why option pricing? There is no strike price. Furthermore, the actual award when settled will be based on the ending stock prices for all of the peer companies, which grow in the real world at a risk-adjusted rate. Instead we're going to work with a risk-free rate that, when swallowed up by volatility, has a negative expected ending stock price in the simulation process. Given the nature of the award, this seems to be a strange outcome.

The key in this conclusion set is the payoff diagram or profile associated with holding a share of restricted stock subject to a market condition such as TSR. The payoff diagram has a "kink," meaning it is not linearly associated with all ending stock prices. Rather, there is a "zero value" for otherwise nonzero stock prices that don't satisfy the TSR condition. If the stock price does not attain a certain level of performance, then the share will be forfeited at zero value to the holder, despite the stock itself having a value. This is the analog to principles associated with option-pricing valuation.

In option pricing, the cost of equity turns out not to matter based on the notion that the current stock price fully reflects its expected return. In this context, the correct drift rate becomes the risk-free rate. This insight and outcome is a big advantage to the valuation process because it alleviates the need to estimate all the individual costs of equity. We can observe the risk-free rate and be done!

Consideration of correlation. With the stock price process settled, we turn our attention to the consideration of correlation. Given that the market condition is designed to consider relative performance across a peer set of companies, it is likely that these stock prices will evolve in a generally connected way reflecting similar influences to movements in both industry-specific and broader economic conditions. Thus, we measure the TSR using correlated stock prices based on measures from historical stock prices.

Arriving at a fair value conclusion. With all the pieces in place, the simulation is set to measure the dollar value of a single restricted share based on the ending stock price for each individual trial of the simulation. The ending stock price enables the calculation of the TSR and the rank of the company's stock in the peer set, which determines the percentage of a share received. This vesting percentage is defined by the award agreement based on the TSR rank and will range from zero to 100% or more. The dollar value is then the vested percentage of a single share multiplied by the ending stock price and converted to a present value. The present value factor is consistent with the risk-free drift rate, again avoiding the potentially challenging question of applying the correct discount factor.

The restricted stock fair value is the mean of all the simulation results. The result should not be a complete mystery. The fair value must be less than the grant date stock price if the maximum vesting provides for 100%. If the award allows vesting in excess of 100%, then the award could have a fair value in excess of the current stock price. Even with the possibility of excess vesting, the fair value is generally at a discount to the observable stock price on the grant date.

Incorporation of the TSR market condition into a fair value measurement introduces some interesting inputs that may not have been immediately intuitive, as well as a surprise realization that the restricted share is more like an option than a share of stock.

Robert Barnett, *CFA, FRM, is senior vice president at Valuation Research Corp., specializing in the valuation of financial instruments for financial reporting, portfolio valuation, and general planning needs. Barnett's experience frequently involves complex or highly developed equity structures, stock-based compensation, convertible securities, and derivatives. Many valuations are performed in the context of a transformative financing such as initial public offerings, large private placements, and conversions from an LLC to a corporate entity. He can be reached at RBarnett@ValuationResearch.com.*

Groundswell Builds as IRC Sec. 2704 Regs Sink In

A great deal has been written and said about the proposed IRC Section 2704 regulations that attack estate valuation discounts. This article distills some of the interpretations down into several main points. A caveat, however, is that these regs are utterly incomprehensible and continue to be studied. Therefore, there are no definitive answers. But it's clear what the IRS is up to, so it has sparked a firestorm of protest with the hope of derailing the proposal.

Likely impact. At the ASA Advanced Business Valuation Conference in Florida, William Frazier (Stout Risius Ross) presented an example showing that, under the new rules, the tax bill for estate and gift taxes might rise by up to 50% (Exhibit 1). The example assumes no prior gifting of any interests. He pointed out, however, that even the top tax lawyers in the country "can't agree on what these regs really mean," so we can't be 100% sure of their impact.

During a presentation at the Family Business Coalition, a group of trade associations that supports the repeal of the estate tax, Frazier showed an example of the tax impact on companies of varying sizes depending upon a 0% combined discount or a 20% combined discount (Exhibit 2). "We aren't sure if any discounts would be allowable under the proposed regs but my best assessment is that the ability to discount would be cut by at least half," he tells *BVU*. "The IRS' rationale for this is unrealistic and unworkable. Either way, it demonstrates the use of a large 'stealth' tax increase."

"The regulations would create a two-tiered tax system where a family-owned business would pay higher taxes on transfers than a 3rd-party owned business," said Bruce Johnson (Munroe, Park & Johnson) at the ASA event. "As a result, family businesses might be forced to sell or take on debt to pay the additional tax burden." Johnson is on an ASA task force studying the regs and preparing official comments.

This two-tiered phenomenon is one of the main objections to the proposed regs. The IRS using the notion of "family attribution," which the Supreme Court rejected in the *Bright*[1] case, triggers this unfair approach. In that case, the court dismissed the IRS's position that families will always work

1 *Estate of Bright v. U.S.*, 658 F.2d 999 (5th Cir. 1981).

in perfect harmony over business and financial matters. Later on, the IRS itself dismissed family attribution in Revenue Ruling 93-12, which makes it clear that discounts for lack of control cannot be denied merely because the interests are passed between family members.

Exhibit 1. Estate Valuation Impact of Proposed IRC Sec. 2704 Regs Assume Estate Owns 30% of a Family-Owned Business With an Equity Enterprise (Sale) Value of $50 Million

Preproposed regs				
		Gift Tax	**Estate Tax**	
Shareholder's fair market value		$9,750,000	$9,750,000	(a)
Prior gift		$–		
Tax rate		40%	40%	
Tax		$–	$3,900,000	(b)
Net estate value		$9,750,000		
Net family value			$5,850,000	(c)
Total taxes paid		$–	$3,900,000	(d)
as a percentage of gross assets		0%	40%	
as a percentage of net transfer			67%	
Effective tax rate (disregarding exemption amounts)				
Enterprise equity value		$50,000,000		
Discount	35%	$(17,500,000)		
FMV of the aggregated shares (discounted)		$32,500,000		
Increase of IRS "minimum value"		$17,500,000		
Percentage increase in FMV to MV		54%		
Post-proposed regs				
		Gift Tax	**Estate Tax**	
Revalued estate		$15,000,000	$15,000,000	(a)
Prior gift		$–		
Tax rate		40%	40%	
Tax		$–	$6,000,000	(b)
Net estate value		$15,000,000		
Net family value			$9,000,000	
Taxes paid		$–	$6,000,000	(c)
Additional taxes paid v. preproposed regs			$2,100,000	(d)
as a percentage of gross assets		40%	40%	
as a percentage of net transfer			67%	
as a percentage of "true" fair market value			103%	(e)

(a) Net estate plus prior gift
(b) At 40% but with credit for gift taxes paid
(c) Estate value and donee(s) gift value
(d) Includes gift taxes
(e) Net family value preregs/taxes paid post-regs
Source: William Frazier (Stout Risius Ross)

Exhibit 2. How Proposed Regulations to IRC Section 2704 Appear to Affect Valuation and Taxes ($000)

Scenario 1 (no adjustments)					
EBITDA (range in $millions)	**1-5**	**6-10**	**11-20**	**21-40**	**41-100**
Midpoint of EBITDA range	$2,500	$7,500	$15,000	$30,000	$70,000
EBITDA multiple	5	6	7	8	9
Enterprise equity value (a)	$12,500	$45,000	$105,000	$240,000	$630,000
Proposed Reg 2704 available adjustment for lack of control and lack of marketability	**0%**	**0%**	**0%**	**0%**	**0%**
Proposed Reg 2704 adjusted fair market value	$12,500	$45,000	$105,000	$240,000	$630,000
Proposed Reg 2704 taxable value (b)	$2,500	$35,000	$95,000	$230,000	$620,000
Pre-Reg 2704 adjustment for lack of control and lack of marketability	**35%**	**35%**	**35%**	**35%**	**35%**
Current regs—fair market value	$8,125	$29,250	$68,250	$156,000	$409,500
Current regs taxable value*	$—	$19,250	$58,250	$146,000	$399,500
Estate or Gift Taxes					
Proposed regs	$1,000	$14,000	$38,000	$92,000	$248,000
Current regs	$—	$7,700	$23,300	$58,400	$159,800
Percentage increase	0%	82%	63%	58%	55%
Actual estate tax rate (on true FMV)	40%	73%	65%	63%	62%
Additional taxes paid	$1,000	$6,300	$14,700	$33,600	$88,200
Scenario 2 (some adjustments)					
EBITDA (range in $millions)	**1-5**	**6-10**	**11-20**	**21-40**	**41-100**
Midpoint of EBITDA range	$2,500	$7,500	$15,000	$30,000	$70,000
EBITDA multiple	5	6	7	8	9
Enterprise equity value (a)	$12,500	$45,000	$105,000	$240,000	$630,000
Proposed Reg 2704 available adjustment for lack of control and lack of marketability	**20%**	**20%**	**20%**	**20%**	**20%**
Proposed Reg 2704 adjusted fair market value	$10,000	$36,000	$84,000	$192,000	$504,000
Proposed Reg 2704 taxable value (b)	$—	$26,000	$74,000	$182,000	$494,000
Pre-Reg 2704 adjustment for lack of control and lack of marketability	**35%**	**35%**	**35%**	**35%**	**35%**
Current regs—fair market value	$8,125	$29,250	$68,250	$156,000	$409,500
Current regs taxable value*	$—	$19,250	$58,250	$146,000	$399,500
Estate or Gift Taxes					
Proposed regs	$—	$10,400	$29,600	$72,800	$197,600
Current regs	$—	$7,700	$23,300	$58,400	$159,800
Percentage increase	0%	35%	27%	25%	24%
Actual estate tax rate (on true FMV)	40%	54%	51%	50%	49%
Additional taxes paid	$—	$2,700	$6,300	$14,400	$37,800

Notes:
(a) Assume company has no debt
(b) Assume family owns 100% of company, founder is second to die and has $10 million in lifetime exemption left

La-la land. During a BVR webinar,[2] Chris Mercer (Mercer Capital) put it best when he said that the proposed regs "create a world in which families are assumed to live in some la-la land and get together better than any sizable family that I have ever seen."

Another point here is that there is disparate treatment of transfers between family members and transfers involving nonfamily third parties. Under the proposed regs, nonfamily third parties would still be able to claim the discounts. Why does this disparate treatment exist? The IRS provides no reasoning. This is just one aspect of the proposed regs that prompted Mercer to call them "an outright attack on family operating businesses."

More fantasy. During the BVR webinar, Mercer and Curtis Kimball (Willamette Management Associates) made the point that the proposed regs are introducing a new standard of value with an unknown definition that goes against years of accepted valuation theory and Tax Court precedent.

For example, there is the introduction of a hypothetical "put right," which disregards restrictions in a shareholder or LLC agreement to liquidate interests. This put right would give each member of the entity the ability to force the company to buy back his or her interest for cash equal to a "minimum value" within six months of exercising the right. The minimum value is defined as a pro rata portion of the fair market value of the entire entity. Of course, no such right exists in the real world. "That is not a realistic or commercially reasonable provision," says Mercer. "These limitations are placed in operating agreements of family and non-family businesses in order to allow the business to stay in business to achieve its business purpose."

For many years, the deciding point for every business valuation has been Revenue Ruling 59-60, which is very clear on what standard of value to use. We all know it: The price at which a hypothetical willing buyer and seller at arm's length would agree to buy or sell an interest. In the economic real world, the fair market value of a minority interest is not worth as much as its pro rata share of the entire entity. We all know the reasons why. Minority interests do not have control, and they're harder to sell, so discounts are applied. The new valuation theory the IRS put forth in the proposed regs has the seller and buyer as known to each other. This, of course, is opposite of what the IRS says in its own standard.

This proposed provision throws a valuation into a hypothetical world. During the BVR webinar, an audience member asked: "Aren't we already rendering hypothetical appraisals because they're based on hypothetical transactions?" No, the speakers said, pointing out that a valuation of an entity is not hypothetical because the appraiser does not assume hypothetical or untrue facts and circumstances.

Another audience member asked an interesting question: "How do you handle hypotheticals in a valuation report under the standards? Am I as a valuator exposed to any liability?" The speakers

2 The IRS' Proposed Section 2704 Regulations: The Impact on and the Future of Estate and Gift Valuation, Curtis Kimball (Willamette Management Associates) and Z. Christopher Mercer (Mercer Capital), BVR webinar, Sept. 29, 2016.

agreed that there would be no additional exposure as long as you specify what the hypothetical conditions are and state clearly that they could affect value.

Comments flow. As of this writing, the IRS has received over 80 written comments,[3] many from family business owners. This is important because it should not just be the valuation community or wealth planners making comments. Observers agree that the impact to family businesses could be devastating, forcing them to take on debt or delay capital investments or hiring in order to pay the increased tax bill. Some business owners may decide to sell or liquidate the business rather than continue on as a family-owned going concern. The owner of a recreational park writes to the IRS:

> Our business is a family run business. This park has been up and running for 40 years. I would like to pass it on to my sons. Your proposed rules would make it burdensome to transfer the business and cause serious financial hardships for a small businessman working around the clock. I am speaking for all small businesses. Please do NOT pass these rules. Thank you.

Support is growing in Congress to quash the proposed regs. In the House, Republicans have introduced two bills, H.R. 6042 and H.R. 6100, to nullify the proposed regs. The latter bill, the Protect Family Farms and Businesses Act, adds an "or else" aspect if the proposed regs are finalized as is. The bill would not allow any federal funds from being used to finalize, implement, or administer the regs. In the Senate, members of the Senate Finance Committee (which has oversight authority over the Treasury and IRS) are among those who have sent a letter to Treasury Secretary Jacob Lew requesting that the proposed regs be withdrawn. There is also a Senate companion bill (S. 3436).

The Family Business Coalition supports the efforts by Congress and has launched a lobbying campaign of its own to build opposition to the proposed regulations. "I think the goal of the legislation is to put as much pressure as possible on the Treasury Department to withdraw the regulation or to delay enactment until the next Treasury secretary can review the regulation," said Palmer Schoening, the coalition's chairman.

More to come. The IRS hopes to implement new rules as soon as possible, preferably before a new administration takes effect. Of course, all of the valuation professional organizations want to stop the regs from being finalized as proposed. Also, if practitioners can successfully argue that changes the IRS has made in its rules don't make sense in real-life scenarios, a court could strike them down.[4]

3 www.regulations.gov/docket?D=IRS-2016-0022.

4 In *Altera Corp. v. Commissioner,* the court struck down 2003 IRS regulations because the Treasury ignored comments from practitioners who said the scenarios simply did not happen in real life. The court concluded that the rules were invalid because the government couldn't explain why it didn't consider the comments, which is in violation of the Administrative Procedure Act (APA).

Transaction Valuation Tips From an Investment Banker

An interesting perspective on valuation for mergers and acquisitions comes when you talk with an investment banker. At the 2016 ASA Advanced Business Valuation Conference, Michael Poole (PCE Investment Bankers Inc.) gave some valuation insights from his viewpoint. By the way, PCE is a finalist in the 2016 Valuation Firm of the Year category for the 15th Annual M&A Advisory Awards.

Fast facts. Poole presented some recent M&A statistics, and the implications this information has on valuations. The source of the data is five years of historical information primarily from CapIQ, but other databases were also used.

1. Eighty percent to 90% of mergers and acquisitions are strategic;
2. Private equity makes up 35% to 40% of deals;
3. Platform companies make up 10% to 15% of deals;
4. An investment banker does not represent most transactions; and
5. Transactions that are represented receive a premium.

The strategic nature of the vast majority of transactions is expected, and so is the level of private equity involvement. Platform companies are those initial companies that a PE firm buys with the idea that they will buy add-on companies to grow it. From a value perspective, there is a different sense of value when looking at a platform versus an add-on company. "Traditionally, add-ons have lower multiples than platform companies," Poole says. These differences may not be large, but it's something to consider when looking at comparables. And you'll see that add-ons make up the most of these deals.

Also keep in mind that only about 25% of transactions are reported, so most of them are not on the radar. Is there a selection bias in the transactions that gets reported? Yes, says Poole. The "bragging rights" phenomenon results in the better deals getting reported.

Another factor that will affect multiples is whether an investment banker represents a company on the block. An investment banker represents only about 25% of transactions, but this affects the price. A transaction represented by an investment banker generally commands at least a 20% premium when sold (based on 10 years of data), so take that into account when looking at multiples in transaction data, Poole advises. CapIQ data show what deals were represented.

Friction points. One of the friction points between M&A experts and valuation experts is the issue of value transfer, Poole says. A question the valuation should be asking is: Can value be transferred from the seller to the buyer? Often, the expert assumes the answer is yes, but this is not always the case, so it has to be examined. For example, the seller may have a large valuable contract with a big client. The valuation expert figures this contract into the valuation, assuming the buyer will take it over. But the buyer may not be able to do this if the contract is not assignable. The fact that this large piece of revenue may not materialize would affect the valuation analysis.

Another major issue in whether value can transfer is the strength of the seller's management team. Private equity buyers view this as absolutely essential and will point to this issue as the reason why acquisitions go bad. That is, the strength of the management team was overestimated. Therefore, this aspect of a valuation analysis takes on heightened importance in this context.

Another friction point involves the impact that deal terms have on value. It's improperly assumed that deal terms have no impact on value. "Terms have a huge impact on the value transfer," says Poole. This often comes up when doing fairness opinions, and there may be a tendency to not take the terms into account. The trouble is, when valuation experts look at market multiples, you often have no idea as to the terms. Did the seller take some financing back? Did the buyer get stock that was deeply subordinated? You can't simply assume the multiple is based on an all-cash deal. Yes, some of the reported transactions will disclose terms—there are always exceptions—but most will not.

The session highlighted the parallel universe in which valuators and transaction advisors often find themselves in terms of looking at value. Views do converge over certain matters, such as developing discount rates. Poole says they follow a traditional build-up method. The risk-free rate is from 20-year Treasury bonds, then added to that is an equity risk premium and size premium (both from Duff & Phelps data), and then a company-specific risk premium. If there are big gaps between the DCF and market methods, they will dig down into the various elements to reconcile them, just as a valuator would do.

Social Media, Sec. 2704 Regs, New Fair Value Credential Highlight IACVA/SECBA Conference

The Southeast Chapter of Business Appraisers (SECBA) and the International Association of Consultants, Valuators and Analysts (IACVA) co-sponsored Business Valuation in an Upside Down World recently in Atlanta. Bill Hanlin (Hanlin Moss Yi, PS) and Bob Brackett (Crandall & Brackett), IACVA's president and secretary general, respectively, acted as hosts of the event.

IACVA focuses its efforts outside of North America to promote the uniform application of valuation theories, approaches, methods, and models throughout the world. Hanlin pointed out that this effort is especially important in emerging economies where money is starting to move in and out in terms of business transactions. The governments are starting to take notice of this and want to make sure there is discipline where there is uniformity in the application of valuation theory and models. Hanlin said that much work needs to be done in this area all over the globe.

Economic update. In an economic update, John Robertson of the Atlanta Federal Reserve Bank noted that the U.S. has had strong employment growth but this has not generated faster real GDP growth. Real GDP growth is a function of growth in the overall workforce and the productivity of that workforce. Why have we had solid growth in the workforce but not a corresponding growth in labor productivity? In fact, labor productivity has been declining over the past year. One possible reason is a weak pace of capital spending by firms due to an uncertain demand for output, lack of good investment opportunities, or limited access to financing. Another possible reason for weak productivity growth is that the new hires are simply less productive. Also, there could be a "statistical mirage," meaning the output is increasingly hard to measure.

Fair value credential. Bob Morrison (Morrison Valuation & Forensic Services LLC) and Bill Johnston (Empire Valuation Consultants), who is head of the ASA BV committee, gave an update on the Fair Value Quality Initiative designed to improve financial reporting valuations for U.S. publicly traded companies. A new credential, Certified in Entity and Intangible Valuations™ (CEIV™) will be available soon through the ASA, AICPA, and RICS. Morrison made the point that this is not an additional credential but an add-on to existing credentials. Individuals must attain the credential through one of the approved valuation professional organizations (VPOs) and adhere to the ethical and membership requirements of that VPO. There are other requirements for attaining the credential, including experience, education, submitting to an ongoing engagement-level quality review process, and complying with a new performance framework to ensure confidence in the consistency and transparency in the credential holder's work, all to the benefit of the public interest.

The credentialing process will be subject to ongoing quality oversight and compliance with a "mandatory performance framework," which is the subject of two exposure drafts, Proposed Mandatory Performance Framework for the Fair Value Quality Initiative and Proposed Application of the Mandatory Performance Framework for the Fair Value Quality Initiative. Written comments were due in August 2016. Johnson noted that some of the commenters are concerned about the 3,000 hours of fair value work experience needed to qualify for the new credential. He pointed out that this amount of time can represent any type of work on fair value, not just billable hours, over a five-year period.

Once the Mandatory Performance Framework is finalized for the fair value quality initiative, the new credential will be rolled out. A special website (ceiv-credential.org) has been set up, and there is also information on the websites of the ASA, AICPA, and RICS. The AICPA has a "pathway" tool to help individuals with different credentials and experience levels choose the best way to attain the new credential.

Peer review. An exposure draft on a peer review process for valuation firms is in the works by IACVA, according to Bill Hanlin, the organization's president. This process will be designed for firms and will address how they control the quality of valuation work. He stressed that the focus of peer review will not concern itself with whether a valuation is being calculated correctly or whether the mathematics are accurate. Rather, it will focus on whether the amount of work done and the related disclosures and support are sufficient. One of the reasons for this is to fend off international government regulation.

Social media. Mark Zyla (Acuitas) gave a fascinating presentation on social media valuation and noted the lofty prices in transactions involving social media companies. For example, there's the Microsoft Corp. acquisition of LinkedIn for $26.6 billion (expects to close by end of this year) and Facebook's purchase of Whatsapp for $19 billion.

Are we in another "internet bubble" that may burst? Zyla remembers back in 1999 doing valuations for internet firms with no revenue, but he says it's a different situation today because they're banking on advertisers. "The one difference today is that the new technology allows for target marketing and advertisers are willing to pay for that," he says. You can measure the value of a "like" or a "share," and the technological atmosphere is much different than it was back then. Zyla also notes that a lot of smart people are in this arena—but he also points out that there were smart people back in 1999, too.

Zyla also referred the audience to some articles and tools to help understand valuation in a social media context. One is a *Harvard Business Review*[1] article that presented the Zerrella model for valuing a "like." There's also an article from Appraisal Economics on social media valuation.[2] Plus, there's a website that allows you to calculate the value of a "like" by plugging in a few metrics (valueofalike.com).

Sec. 2704 regs. Curtis Kimball (Willamette Management Associates) gave the audience an update on the controversial proposed IRC Section 2704 regulations designed to rein in valuation discounts for transfer tax purposes. Recently, he and Chris Mercer (Mercer Capital) conducted a BVR webinar[3] that sorted out the issues in the proposed regs that have caused a firestorm of protest. One of the issues is the disparate treatment of transfers between family members and transfers involving nonfamily third parties. Under the proposed regs, nonfamily third parties would still be able to claim the discounts. Why does this disparate treatment exist? The IRS provides no reasoning, prompting observers to call the proposed regs an outright attack on family operating businesses.

Also, the proposed regs seek to introduce a new standard of value with an unknown definition that goes against years of accepted valuation theory and Tax Court precedent. For example, the introduction of a hypothetical "put right" disregards restrictions in a shareholder or LLC agreement to liquidate interests. This put right would give each member of the entity the ability to force the company to buy back his or her interest for cash equal to a "minimum value" within six months of exercising the right. The minimum value is defined as a pro rata portion of the fair market value of the entire entity. Of course, no such right exists in the real world.

These are just a few of the problematic issues with the proposed regs. Kimball urged attendees to submit comments to the IRS in advance of the public hearing scheduled for Dec. 1, 2016.

1 "How to Calculate the Value of a Like" by Dan Zerrella, Hubspot Marketing Analytics. *Harvard Business Review*, Nov. 26, 2012.

2 "Social Media Valuation," Appraisal Economics (www.appraisaleconomics.com).

3 The IRS' Proposed Section 2704 Regulations: The Impact on and the Future of Estate and Gift Valuation, Curtis Kimball (Willamette Management Associates) and Z. Christopher Mercer (Mercer Capital), BVR webinar, Sept. 29, 2016.

Cultures and Continents Clash in High-Stakes Divorce Valuation

By Andrew Strickland

Valuation experts who find themselves involved in a divorce engagement with globe-trotting spouses can glean some valuable insights from a recent United Kingdom case.[1] The judge in the English Family Court found herself bemused by wholly different approaches to expert evidence in divorce litigation.

There were three expert witnesses: one for the wife and two for the husband. On the wife's side was an expert valuer in the U.K. He had significant experience in high-profile divorce work in the English courts; he was steeped in the approaches of family courts in the U.K. and the requirements of Part 25 of the Family Procedure Rules 2010, which govern the conduct of experts in this jurisdiction. The two experts for the husband were partners in Big Four firms in the U.S. with a combined 60 years of experience of business valuation. It was evident that they had encyclopedic knowledge of academic research into discounts relating to the absence of liquidity and the lack of control.

The divorced couple were U.S. nationals and had an international lifestyle but had been based in London in recent years. Their combined wealth was approximately $245 million, made up of $180 million in property or cash and the balance in a range of investments, including private equity, hedge funds, and venture capital trusts. The judge described the breadth of these instruments as ranging from Brazilian private equity to London commercial property investments. The valuation date was the end of December 2014.

Relationships had clearly broken down between the former husband and wife. The judge, Justice Roberts, felt that it was telling that at one point the husband described his former wife as his "counterparty." The judge clearly found the wife to be an attractive witness: "She sought with grace and elegance (if I am permitted to say so) to convey to me the strength of her feelings and the importance which she attached to the principle that the assets should be split in a fair way."

1 *William Work v. Mandy Gray* [2016] EWHC 562 (Fam) (United Kingdom).

The view of the judge with regard to the evidence from the husband (H) had a subtly different flavor: "Having heard H at some length in the witness box, I do not consider it entirely fair to cast him in the mould of a husband who has left no stone unturned in order to reduce his financial obligations to W. He gave his evidence in a calm and measured way but, perhaps not surprisingly, his evidence was shaped and honed by his experience as a very sophisticated financial investor of many years' standing."

What is fairness? There were various arguments about the comparability of the certainties and immediacy of cash with illiquid and risky assets. Did the differentials in market pricing provide adequate compensation for the risks and illiquidity of the various investments or were further discounts required to provide true comparability between the two asset classes?

On behalf of the husband, the position of the wife was challenged: "If discounts are ignored, as she contends they should be, she will have received as her share of these investments a substantial cash payment which, in relation to the illiquid assets left in H's hands, ignores the facts of deferred receipt, illiquidity, uncertainty and H's lack of control."

Discounts: specific or generic evidence? Investment banking specialists had valued the private equity and other specialist funds in 2013 on behalf of the husband for the purposes of his statement of assets and liabilities, the Form E. This form has to be completed by each of the parties to a divorce in the U.K. and exchanged long before any court proceedings take place.

The investment bank had used a report by Cogent Partners, "Secondary Pricing Trends & Analysis Report" (January 2013) (the Cogent Report) and the "ELM Capital Report" (2012). These dealt with statistically collated information relating to the secondary market—the acquisition of existing investors' interests in private equity and related funds.

The U.K. expert instructed by the wife had placed himself on what might be considered to be the firmest and most secure of foundations: He used the above information but updated the figures by reference to market movements between early 2013 and January 2015. Cogent Partners had issued a 2015 report, and he understandably considered this as the more relevant evidence when considering values in late 2014. He had shown in graphical form the reductions in discounts that were evident in the secondary markets during 2014.

He had undertaken his own valuations of the investments. Based on this work, he concluded that, at Dec. 31, 2014, the discounts the husband applied were too high, to the extent of $15 million.

A large part of the arguments about discounts related to the husband's investment in the Lone Star Fund. By the close of 2014, this fund was in final run-off and sizable cash payments had already been made. It was the view of the U.K. expert that the discounts that were justifiable in early 2013 could no longer be supported due to this materially changed position. He felt that no discount at all was warranted and certainly not the husband's discount of 39.5%. The maximum discount that he considered could be warranted was 10%.

One of the U.S. experts for the husband had looked at such financial data as were available, including what he described as "research reports, third party discount studies and other documentation." Significantly, he did not look at, or rely on, the Cogent Report. The expert concluded that the original discounts as applied in 2013 appeared to be "within a reasonable range."

In relation to funds to which discounts had been applied because of a perceived lack of control (i.e., minority or limited partnership interests), the expert's report described the underlying methodology that had been used to consider values and discounts. These involved an analysis of closed-end funds and a transaction review of acquisition premiums. Several industry studies were identified with brief descriptions of their pedigree and conclusions.

The second U.S. expert said that, from what he had seen, nothing had come to his firm's attention that would cause it or him to believe: (i) that H's general approach to valuation and discounts as of May 2013 (the valuation date for his Form E exercise) was inconsistent with commonly accepted valuation practice; and/or (ii) that H's approach and the methods used were improperly applied; and/or (iii) that his estimates of discounted value were unreasonable.

Appended to the report were extracts of various industry standard tables based on empirical data showing how discounts for lack of control and marketability had been tracked over a number of years by date, volume of transactions, and price in order to ascertain the implied discount in any one year in accordance with whatever formula the particular study deployed.

This expert's review of the publicly available data relating to discounts for lack of control revealed an overall average of 26%. In relation to the restricted stock, the range of discounts was fairly wide (between 13% and 45%) with an overall average of 29% (or 13% in relation to the more recent transactions). The discounts applicable to secondary markets were between 20% and 37%. These ranges were used by this expert as a cross-check against H's own figures and formed the basis for the view that his figures were "not unreasonable."

Divided by a common language? The two experts from Texas had doubtless spent many years engaged in contentious valuation work in the U.S. The legal systems in the U.K. and the U.S. share the same rootstock of common law; the U.S. legal framework has grown into a judicial system that imposes increasingly stern tests on the expert witness. The risk of having expert testimony rejected under a *Daubert* challenge is seemingly ever present. It is sufficient to strike fear into the hearts of the stoutest. As a consequence, a widely used method with a substantial pedigree of case precedent may well be preferred to a previously untried innovative and novel source.

Many considered this to be a good discipline: It is designed to ensure that the half-baked and scarcely formed random ideas from those who are poorly taught in their area of knowledge do not make their way into court decisions.

In the U.K., the regime for expert witnesses is markedly different: Great store is laid on the importance of the expert being objective and dispassionate. One of the worst offenses that an expert can commit is becoming an advocate on behalf of his or her client. Judges have given excoriating, career-ending judgments in some cases in which experts have been seen to be too enthusiastically partisan. The expert who develops a reputation as a hired gun will be likely to come to a sticky end.

In the U.K., there is no real equivalent of the *Daubert* challenge; it is the judge who uses his or her experience to determine the relative weight to attach to the evidence before him or her. This has meant that those with only a poor grasp of business valuation have on occasion wandered naively and innocently into court as so-called experts. It is for the opposing expert to demonstrate the relevance and strength of his greater skill and knowledge; it is the job of opposing counsel to lay bare the frailties in the expert evidence of the untutored novice; it is then the task of the judge to recognize the gold of sound evidence from base metal.

This legal approach is set within an environment in which the parties are forced together to try to settle their differences through mediation and exchanges of information. These stages are meant to happen long before the parties see the outline of the courtroom steps.

Wrong kind of experience? With the background of the U.S. legal system, and with all of the years of the constraining discipline of the Big Four in a highly combative North America, it is as if the Texan experts were not prepared to stray away from tried and proven evidence, tempered in the crucible of U.S. litigation, with very carefully crafted conclusions. As noted above, this evidence derived from various restricted stock studies, academic studies of closed-end funds, acquisition premiums, and other research into the impact of illiquidity and lack of control on value.

The experts from the U.S. therefore appeared to view the question of discounts for lack of control and less than full liquidity as being separable from the relevant investments and capable of independent measurement. More importantly, they appeared to share a desire to remain within those evidence sources that they considered were unimpeachable.

What was considerably more surprising was the absence of knowledge of the applicable procedures of the English courts. It is difficult to speculate on the nature of the communications between the two U.S. experts and their U.K. instructing solicitors. It was the U.K.-based lawyers who had the responsibility for schooling the experts in procedure.

The Texan experts did not see it as part of their role to "trade information" with their opposite number. Furthermore the judge referred to one of these experts' "lack of familiarity with Part 25 of [the Family Procedure Rules] 2010 (and he told me during the course of his evidence that he had not read it and knew nothing of its contents)."

The cultural differences were also given an added focus by the updating of the reports by the experts. The U.K. expert had produced a report that reviewed the position and the evolving circumstances to the end of 2014.

The two U.S. experts reissued their original 2013 reports with virtually no changes other than the dates. For whatever reason, they were not prepared to amend their original conclusions for a different valuation point.

Court's findings. The judge had no difficulty in concluding that the evidence the U.K. expert provided was relevant in respect of the reduced discounts that were applicable. She stated: "I collect no assistance from the written reports prepared by H's experts nor from their oral evidence as to what they consider to be an appropriate range or where within that range H's assets fall. In particular, I find no commentary on how the discounts which applied in 2013 are still appropriate in December 2014 when it appears to be accepted that there was a considerable downturn in the level of discounts applied to these types of investments over that period, as evidenced by the 2015 Cogent report."

The judge made the point that one of the experts from the USA appeared to rely on his 32 years' experience. On this basis, he considered that he was entitled to ignore the 2015 Cogent Report because he had access to superior information that enabled him to take a more informed view, but "I was left at the conclusion of his evidence not knowing what that superior information was."

Andrew Strickland, *for many years a corporate partner at Scrutton Bland, is now a consultant to the firm. He is a member of the valuation committee of the Institute of Chartered Accountants in England and Wales (ICAEW) and is on the board of the International Institute of Business Valuers.*

Section II.
Industry-Specific Valuation

AICPA Conference Covers Healthcare Valuation Challenges and Opportunities

The ever-changing landscape of the healthcare sector was examined at the AICPA's 2015 Healthcare Industry Conference in Las Vegas, where 375 attendees were treated to some very informative sessions, including a learning path devoted to valuation. *BVU* was there, and we provide this recap.

Big picture. The big challenges in the industry continue to center on health reform and changes to reimbursement models for healthcare providers. These have become more complex than ever, due in part to the move toward value-based payments. Keynote speaker Bill Rutherford, CFO and executive vice president of HCA, said that a "lot of changes" are still going on that will affect the revenue model. For example, right before the conference, the federal budget bill was passed with a provision whereby hospitals will see lower revenue from new off-campus outpatient departments. These facilities will get lower reimbursements under Medicare, but existing facilities are grandfathered, so they are not affected. The provision caught many people off guard.

Rutherford also noted that the next presidential election may spark a "repeal and replace" situation that could affect healthcare delivery and the revenue model. However, he pointed out, "historically, changes in healthcare delivery happen very slowly."

There's also a trend of patients becoming price-shopping consumers. There was a lot of discussion about "retail" health—Walmart, CVS, and other big retailers opening health clinics. In addition, hospitals are paying serious attention to the rise of urgent care centers, and they are now getting into the business, even creating joint ventures with retailers. Speaking of joint ventures, many nonprofit hospitals are teaming up with for-profit hospitals, which are now more receptive to arrangements with the tax-exempt sector.

As if this weren't enough, substantial risks have emerged over hospitals acquiring medical practices, which continues at a fast clip. The government has been suing hospitals, challenging the fair market value of these transactions—and it has been winning. In four recent cases, *Tuomey*, *Halifax*, *Citizens*, and *North Broward*, the hospitals paid $300 million in fines to settle charges of fraud under the Stark Law. The thrust of the cases is the measurement of the fair market value of physician compensation. This, of course, raises the bar for appraisers, and it also presents some practice opportunities in terms of assessing commercial reasonableness of these deals. The government's position in many compensation cases is that, if the arrangement generates losses, it may fail the commercial reasonableness test. However, valuation experts point to many flaws in the government's arguments and methodology, including the use of faulty survey data.

Flawed thinking. In their session that examined the *Tuomey* and *Halifax* cases, Richard Romero (CBIZ Valuation Group) and Timothy Smith (Ankura Consulting Group) said the key quantitative analysis the government uses is "significant losses" on an acquired practice. However, some have misread the cases to read that, if compensation is greater than collections, there's a potential problem. But this is not what was said in the cases, they point out. Romero's firm was an expert for the government in *Tuomey*, but he himself did not work on the case. Smith is the co-editor of the *BVR/AHLA Guide to Healthcare Industry Compensation and Valuation*, available at bvresources .com/publications.

They also mentioned one claim the government made concerning the mobility of the doctors in which it uses a "highest and best use" concept for determining FMV of doctor compensation. That is, if a doctor's compensation falls below the median, he or she will relocate to where earnings are higher. But Smith points to extensive research by Mark O. Dietrich on physician mobility that refutes the government's position on this.

There is virtually no official guidance to help valuation experts in this area. The OIS/CMS says that the issue of FMV of compensation under the Stark Law and anti-kickback statutes is unique and requires a departure from standard appraisal methodologies—but there is no guidance as to what that is. As to the hot-potato concept of commercial reasonableness, there is no standard methodology, body of knowledge, standards, nor authoritative literature on this key concept.

What is clear, the speakers say, is that the sole reliance on survey data is inconsistent with standard appraisal methodology—you need to do all three approaches (market, cost, and income).

Breakthrough method. Dietrich presented a breakthrough new valuation method for determining the FMV of physician compensation in his session in which he challenged the conventional model for physician compensation in valuation. He explains that most practitioners focus on survey data, especially MGMA, in establishing reasonable or fair market compensation. Many hospitals and practices use relative value units (RVUs) as a means of measuring productivity, but the compensation data and RVU rates in the surveys are a seriously flawed means of setting compensation.

Dietrich explains that the present use of physician compensation surveys to establish fair market value is based on several false premises, including: (1) that the surveys have statistical significance for the 90% or so of physicians not included in the surveys; (2) that survey compensation per work RVU is always fair market value and commercially reasonable—the common work RVU technique utilized virtually assures that the employing institution will lose money on the practice, something that appears to be commercially *unreasonable* based on the recent court cases; (3) that physicians will relocate to earn the median and therefore everyone should earn the median—an idea that is both statistically incoherent and not born out by academic research; and (4) that the 75th percentile of compensation per work RVU or compensation-to-collections ratio is a mythical ceiling on fair market value.

Local-market conditions not measurable in the surveys may necessitate losses on physician practices due to supply and demand, payer contract rates, local-market competition, and national shortages of high-demand specialties, among other factors, he says. The commercial reasonableness of these losses should be documented in advance and can, in fact, be documented through use of a new method he developed, the RBRVS fair market value method, as well as other techniques.

The RBRVS method is a significant development in this area, and it is fully described in the upcoming new fourth edition of the *BVR/AHLA Guide to Healthcare Finance and Valuation*, edited by Dietrich.[1]

New practice op. Hospitals and other healthcare organizations are entering into affiliation arrangements at a "torrid" pace, with 2015 shaping up to be a record year in healthcare M&A activity, reports Jim Lloyd (Pershing Yoakley & Associates PC) in his session on healthcare affiliations. "Everybody wants to affiliate with everybody else in some contractual arrangement," he says. However, the recent court cases demonstrate the risk associated with these transactions, especially in competitive markets, he notes. For example, if two hospitals are vying to acquire a practice and they want to sweeten the deal, "we remind them of these cases and the risks that can be associated with these deals."

Under OIG regs, the focus is on "commercial reasonableness" of the transaction. A by-product from all of these court cases is a brand new healthcare valuation practice area that is emerging: conducting an independent analysis of commercial reasonableness for healthcare acquisitions, he says. This is done after a regular valuation of the proposed deal is completed including a post-transaction compensation valuation. An independent firm is called in to answer the question: "Is this deal commercially reasonable?" This is important because, if it does not satisfy the requirements, then the fair market valuation of the arrangement is moot.

Lloyd described one such engagement that involved a hospital looking to buy a large orthopedic group, which was to be a $20 million transaction. An independent analysis of commercial reasonableness was done, which resulted in an opinion that the deal had a "high probability of failing the test for commercial reasonableness if looked at by the OIG." The hospital scrapped the deal.

It seems to us that the commercial reasonableness test is nothing more than doing a business plan of a potential venture to decide whether it's a good deal. It looks as though hospitals sometimes put the cart before the horse and decide on a deal and then are going back to see whether it makes

1 Also discussed in a recent webinar, Why You Need to Use Local Market Rates for FMV in Physician Compensation and How to Calculate Them, Mark O. Dietrich and Tim Smith, BVR webinar, October 2015.

good business sense. Weren't they supposed to do that up front? Be that as it may, it's going on and creating an opportunity for valuation experts to come in and do the assessment.

CFO panel. Several hospital CFOs participated in a panel Britt Tabor (Erlanger Health System) moderated. The panelists were Geoff Gardner (Novant Health), Lori Ritchey-Baldwin (St. Elizabeth Healthcare), and Steven R. Blake (Paladin Healthcare Management LLC and Avanti Hospitals). They pointed out that many healthcare valuators are surprised to learn that retail healthcare is a huge financial concern—second only to changing reimbursement models. Retail healthcare are the urgent care centers, Wal-Mart and CVS clinics, and the like springing up as patients become price-shopping consumers also looking for convenience. It's a trend that's growing, and it's here to stay, the panel says.

In response, some hospitals are entering the retail sector. "We invested in it," reports Ritchey-Baldwin, indicating that her organization is a participant in retail health. Gardner says that Novant Health has moved into urgent care centers by opening up its own (Novant Health Express), partnering with some existing urgent care centers, or investing in others. Urgent care is "great for kids and millennials," so it's attractive to Novant—and many other hospitals. Blake's hospitals are not-for-profit, so he says they are not looking to get into retail healthcare.

In terms of the new insurance exchanges, Gardner reports that patient volumes have increased even though the exchanges offer high-deductible plans. Possibly, people had been putting off healthcare until they got any kind of insurance. Has this increase in volume of these types of patients increased bad debt? No, says Ritchey-Baldwin, and the other panelists agreed.

NP-FP joint ventures. For-profit healthcare entities have had a change of mind about joint venturing with nonprofits—they are now more receptive to these deals. In the past, traditional transactions involved outright sales or acquisitions, but now the parties are willing to share in equity or governance. So look for more joint ventures between for-profits and nonprofits in healthcare, according to attorney James Pinna (Hunton & Williams LLP), but there are valuation wrinkles due to the federal tax laws governing charities.

There are two types of joint ventures you'll see: (1) ventures involving ancillary service lines, such as ambulatory surgical centers, rehab facilities, urgent care centers, and the like; and (2) whole hospital ventures involving one or more acute care hospitals. Typically, the nonprofit is the minority owner in the venture, Pinna says.

The federal tax laws governing nonprofits include prohibitions against the use of charitable assets for private gain, known as private inurement. Egregious violations of the private inurement rules can cost the hospital its tax-exempt status. There's also the rules concerning unrelated business income, which is income from an activity that is not substantially related to a nonprofit's charitable mission. Too much of this can also cost the nonprofit its tax exemption, but it's more of a risk with whole hospital joint ventures as opposed to those involving ancillary service lines.

In a joint venture, a nonprofit's contribution of assets must be done at fair market value. This would also include intangibles, such as a valuable brand name. Also, the remuneration the nonprofit pays to get into the venture (purchase price, management fee, etc.) must also be at fair market value.

Key governance considerations for these types of ventures can be found in two cases: *Redlands*[2] and *St. David's.*[3] In Redlands, a nonprofit lost its 501(c)(3) tax-exempt status after it entered into a partnership with a for-profit as its sole activity. In *St. David's,* the nonprofit retained its tax-exempt status after a battle with the IRS over its involvement in a joint venture with a for-profit. There are also two IRS Revenue Rulings: 98-15 and 2004-51. They discuss board control, reserved powers, the term of the management agreement, and charity care policies.

Final note. Healthcare will continue to be a growing and challenging area for valuation experts. It will be particularly interesting to see how the issues of compensation valuation and commercial reasonableness play out in light of the government's success in litigation on these matters.

2 *Redlands Surgical Services v. Commissioner,* 113 T.C. 47 (1999), affirmed, 242 F.3d 904 (9th Cir. 2001).

3 *St. David's Health Care System v. United States,* 349 F.3d 232 (5th Cir. 2003).

Valuation Multiples for Accounting Firms Per *Pratt's Stats*

By Adam Manson

Editor's note: It's merger mania time for accounting firms—and it won't let up anytime soon, according to the new 2015-2016 Rosenberg MAP Survey *of CPA firms. This article examines recent transaction data for sales of accounting firms to help valuation analysts assist their CPA firm clients that are the buyers—or targets—in this ongoing wave of M&A activity.*[1]

To determine the value of an accounting firm, it is important to know the price at which similar firms have been sold. Business appraisers often apply the selling price multiples from comparable companies that they find in transaction databases, such as *Pratt's Stats,*[2] to their subject company's underlying financial data to develop an indication of value. These data points are also helpful to the business owner when benchmarking the value of their businesses.

Here, we present data from the *Pratt's Stats* database on accounting firms that sold between January 1990 and June 2015. The analysis includes 172 accounting firm purchases from a population of 23,290 business purchases across all industries. The data presented include medians, the middle number in an ordered set, and averages. A selling price-to-revenue ratio (also known as a valuation multiple) of 0.30, for example, translates to a company that sold for 30% of its last 12 months of revenue.

Of the 172 transactions, 160 provide information on company type: 61.3% of accounting firms are S corporations, 15.6% are sole proprietorships, 10.0% are LLCs, and 8.8% are C corporations (see Exhibit 1).

Of the 172 accounting firm deals from the *Pratt's Stats* database, 151 are asset deals and 21 are stock deals (see Exhibit 2).

1 This material is part of a new report, *What It's Worth: Accounting Firm Value,* available from BVR (www.bvresources.com/publications).

2 *Pratt's Stats,* available at www.BVResources.com/PrattsStats, is a robust online database boasting the most complete financial details on thousands of acquired private companies, with up to 100 data points per sale. With six valuation multiples and 13 financial ratios, each transaction includes detailed data vital to applying the market approach, deriving a selling price, benchmarking performance, or performing a fairness opinion analysis.

Exhibit 3 presents the median and average selling price multiples of accounting firm transactions from the *Pratt's Stats* database. The multiples presented compare the selling price of the firm to the last 12 months of revenues, the selling price of the firm to the last 12 months of seller's discretionary earnings (SDE), and the selling price of the firm to the last 12 months of earnings before interest, taxes, depreciation, and amortization (EBITDA). *Pratt's Stats* computes SDE as EBITDA plus owner's salary.

Exhibit 1. Accounting Firms—Company Types

	Count	% of Total
S corporation	98	61.3%
Sole proprietorship	25	15.6%
LLC	16	10.0%
C corporation	14	8.8%
Other	7	4.4%

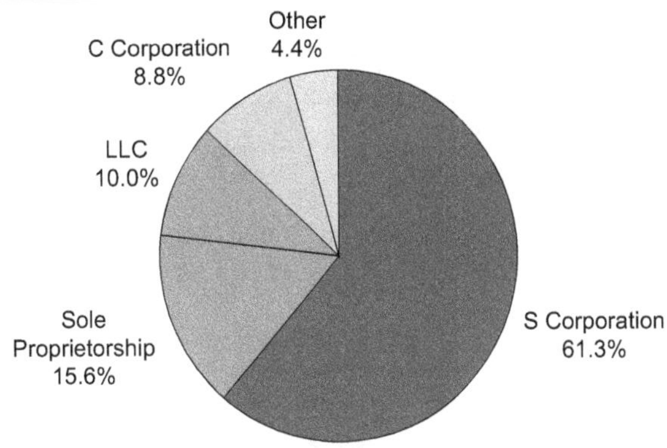

Exhibit 2. Accounting Firms—Sale Type

	Count	% of Total
Asset	151	87.8%
Stock	21	12.2%

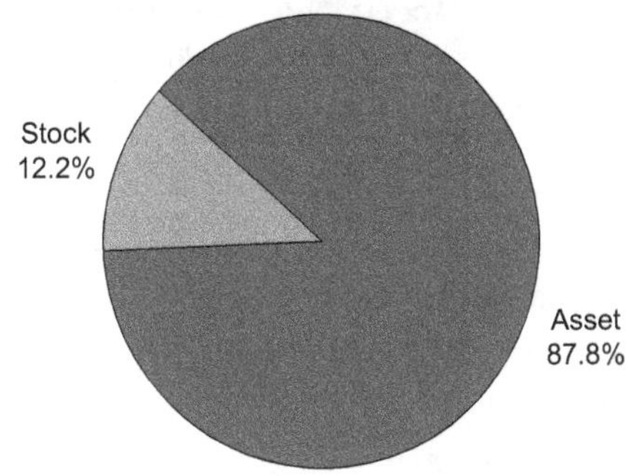

Exhibit 3. Accounting Firms Selling Price Multiples

	Median	Average
Selling Price/Revenue	1.0	1.1
Selling Price/SDE	2.3	2.6
Selling Price/EBITDA	4.2	7.3

SDE = seller's discretionary earnings (operating profit, plus owner's compensation, plus noncash charges)

EBITDA = earnings before interest, taxes, depreciation, and amortization (operating profit, plus noncash charges)

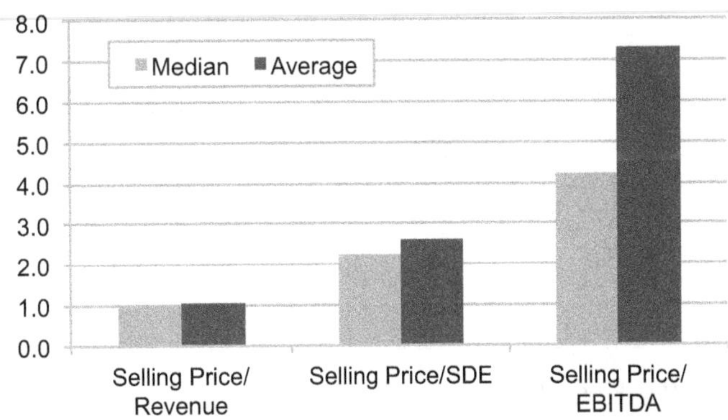

Accounting firms compared to all industries. Exhibit 4 compares the median selling price multiples of accounting firms to all other businesses in the *Pratt's Stats* database. The data indicate that the sample of accounting firms was sold on a median basis at higher multiples relative to revenue but at slightly lower multiples relative to EBITDA, compared to all other businesses. The selling price-to-SDE ratio was the same in both groups (see Exhibit 4).

Exhibit 4. Median Selling Price Multiples

	Accounting Firms	All Other Businesses
Selling Price/Revenue	1.0	0.6
Selling Price/SDE	2.3	2.3
Selling Price/EBITDA	4.2	4.4

SDE = seller's discretionary earnings

EBITDA = earnings before interest, taxes, depreciation, and amortization

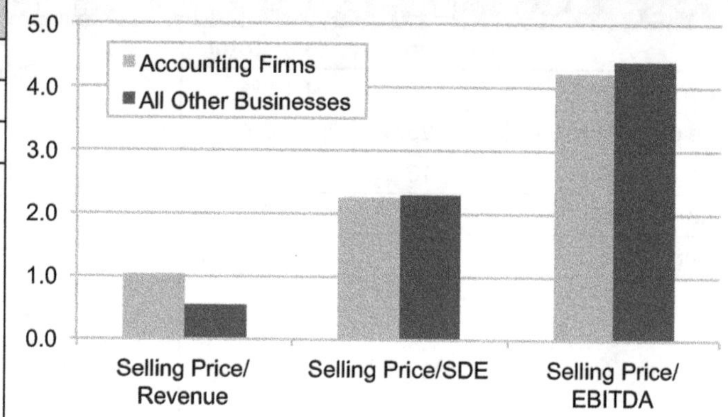

Exhibit 5. Average Selling Price Multiples*

	Accounting Firms	All Other Businesses
Selling Price/Revenue	1.1	1.5
Selling Price/SDE	2.6	3.5
Selling Price/EBITDA	7.3	8.6

SDE = seller's discretionary earnings

EBITDA = earnings before interest, taxes, depreciation, and amortization

*Values over 100 were determined to be outliers and thus have been eliminated.

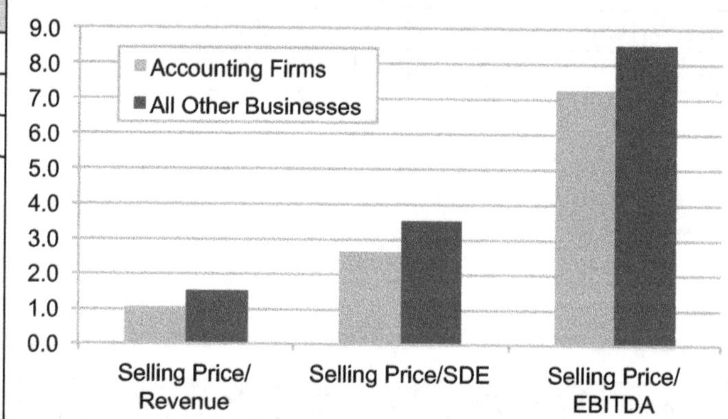

Exhibit 6. Median Profit Margins

	Accounting Firms	All Other Businesses
Gross Profit Margin	100.0%	59.5%
Operating Profit Margin	21.0%	8.4%
Net Profit Margin	20.5%	6.8%

Gross profit margin = gross profit/revenue

Operating profit margin = operating profit/revenue

Net profit margin = net income/revenue

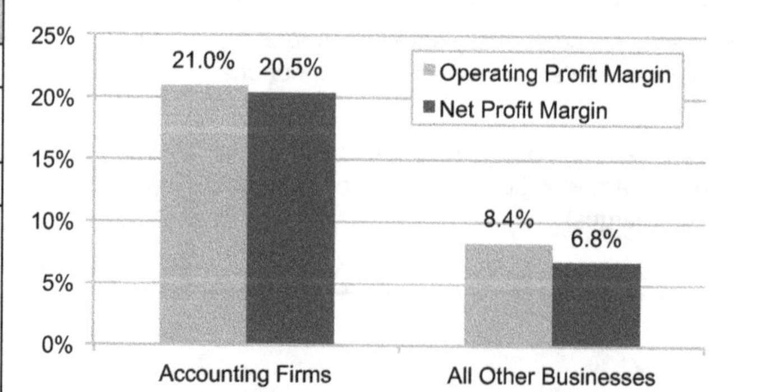

The data also indicate that accounting firms sold on an *average* basis at lower multiples relative to the three earnings measures when compared to the group of all other businesses (see Exhibit 5).

Based on the *Pratt's Stats* data, median profit margins of accounting firms are higher than the group of all other businesses (see Exhibit 6).

Exhibits 7 and 8 display the interquartile range of profit margins for accounting firms relative to all other businesses. The interquartile range provides a measure of dispersion. Interquartile range is the difference between the 25th and 75th percentiles (also called the first and third quartiles), so the interquartile range describes the middle 50% of observations. The top of the orange rectangle indicates the 75th percentile, the bottom of the blue rectangle indicates the 25th percentile, and the line where the two rectangles meet represents the median. If the interquartile range is large, it means that the middle 50% of observations are spaced wide apart, and, if the interquartile range is narrow, it means the middle 50% of observations are spaced close together.

Exhibit 7. Operating Profit Margin—Interquartile Range

	Accounting Firms	All Other Businesses
90th percentile	53.4%	34.0%
75th percentile	39.0%	19.8%
Median	21.0%	8.4%
25th percentile	7.0%	0.7%
10th percentile	-1.2%	-10.4%

The graph displays the interquartile range. The blue rectangle indicates the spread between the first quartile (or 25th percentile) and the median, and the gray rectangle indicates the spread between the median and the third quartile (or 75th percentile).

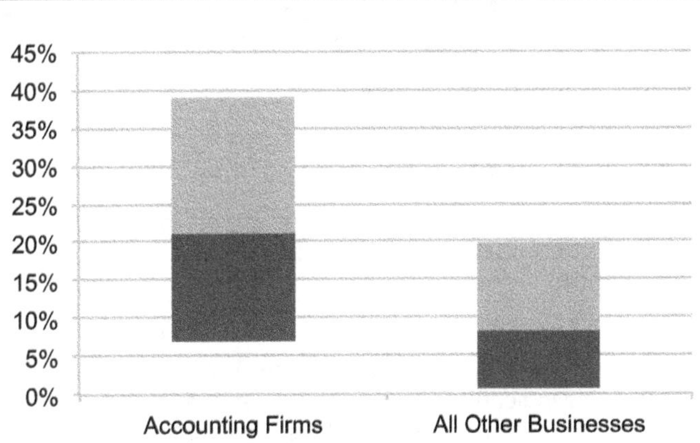

Exhibit 8. Net Profit Margin—Interquartile Range

	Accounting Firms	All Other Businesses
90th percentile	53.6%	32.9%
75th percentile	38.0%	18.5%
Median	20.5%	6.8%
25th percentile	5.0%	0.0%
10th percentile	-3.3%	-12.3%

The graph displays the interquartile range. The blue rectangle indicates the spread between the first quartile (or 25th percentile) and the median, and the gray rectangle indicates the spread between the median and the third quartile (or 75th percentile).

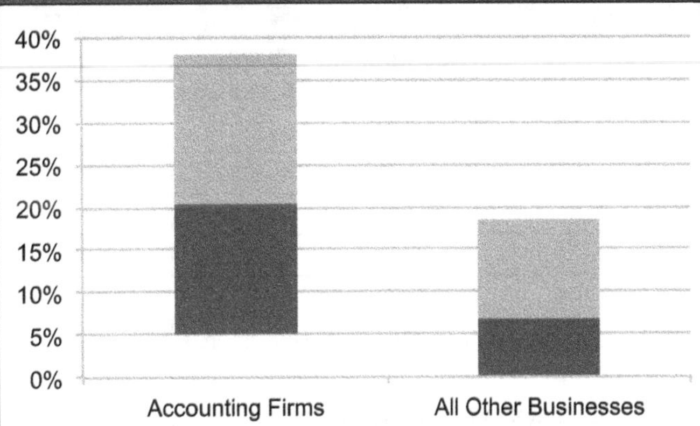

Exhibits 9, 10, and 11 display the interquartile range of the selling price multiples for accounting firms compared with all other businesses.

Exhibit 9. Selling Price/Revenue—Interquartile Range

	Accounting Firms	All Other Businesses
90th percentile	1.5	2.3
75th percentile	1.1	1.0
Median	1.0	0.6
25th percentile	0.7	0.3
10th percentile	0.5	0.2

The graph displays the interquartile range. The blue rectangle indicates the spread between the first quartile (or 25th percentile) and the median, and the gray rectangle indicates the spread between the median and the third quartile (or 75th percentile).

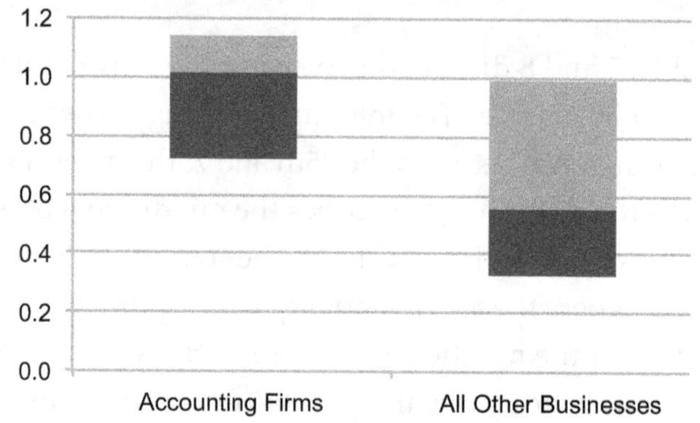

Exhibit 10. Selling Price/SDE—Interquartile Range

	Accounting Firms	All Other Businesses
90th percentile	4.7	5.8
75th percentile	3.0	3.6
Median	2.3	2.3
25th percentile	1.5	1.5
10th percentile	1.1	1.0

SDE = seller's discretionary earnings

The graph displays the interquartile range. The blue rectangle indicates the spread between the first quartile (or 25th percentile) and the median, and the gray rectangle indicates the spread between the median and the third quartile (or 75th percentile).

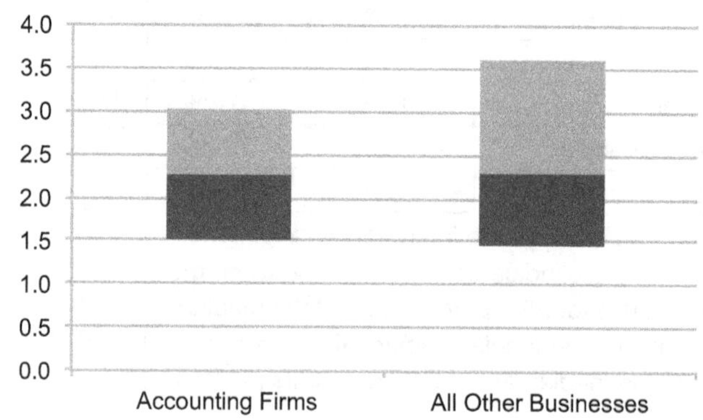

Exhibit 11. Selling Price/EBITDA—Interquartile Range

	Accounting Firms	All Other Businesses
90th percentile	13.3	18.7
75th percentile	7.4	9.3
Median	4.2	4.4
25th percentile	2.5	2.2
10th percentile	1.3	1.3

EBITDA = earnings before interest, taxes, depreciation, and amortization

The graph displays the interquartile range. The blue rectangle indicates the spread between the first quartile (or 25th percentile) and the median, and the gray rectangle indicates the spread between the median and the third quartile (or 75th percentile).

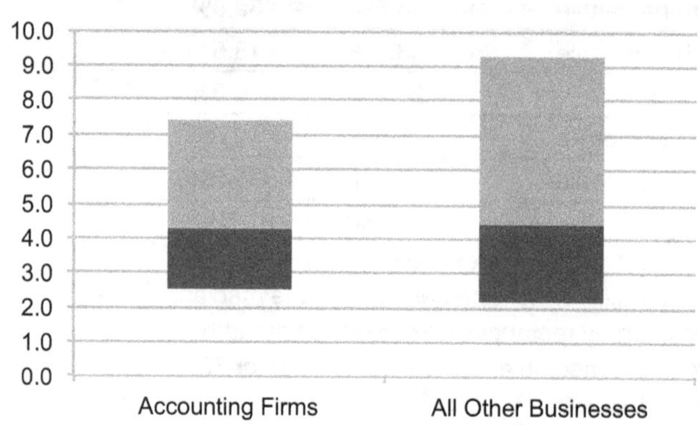

Median ratios are provided in Exhibit 12. The quick ratio measures a company's ability to meet its short-term obligations with its most liquid assets. The data indicate that the accounting firms had a higher quick ratio than the other sold businesses in *Pratt's Stats* and therefore stronger liquidity. The return on equity ratio measures a firm's profitability by displaying how much profit a company generates with the money shareholders have invested. The data indicate that accounting firms generated higher profits from equity investments than the other businesses. The fixed-asset turnover ratio measures a firm's ability to generate net sales from fixed-asset investments (specifically property, plant, and equipment, net of depreciation). Accounting firms generated significantly greater sales relative to fixed assets when compared to the other businesses, but the difference may be explained by accounting firms utilizing fewer fixed assets than the other businesses.

***Adam Manson,** manager of financial analysis at Business Valuation Resources, can be reached at* adamm@bvresources.com *or 503-291-7963, ext. 105. For more information regarding the* Pratt's Stats *database, view www.bvmarketdata.com.*

Exhibit 12. Median Ratios

	Accounting Firms	All Other Businesses
Liquidity		
Current ratio	1.9	1.3
Quick ratio	2.5	1.0
Profitability		
Return on assets	0.2	0.1
Return on equity	0.6	0.2
Activity		
Total asset turnover	1.6	2.4
Fixed asset turnover	18.9	10.3

Median Liquidity Ratios

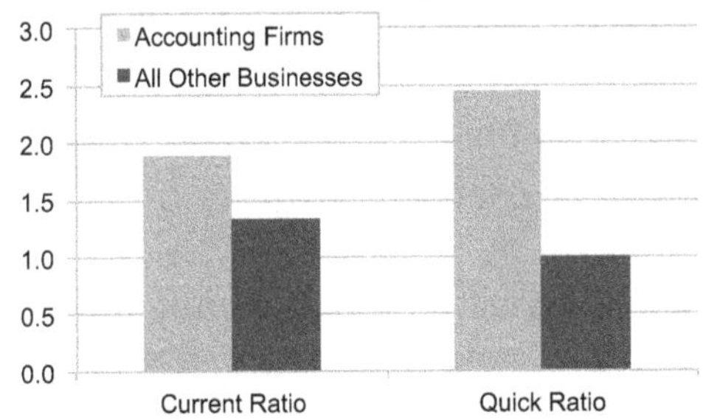

Median Profitability Ratios

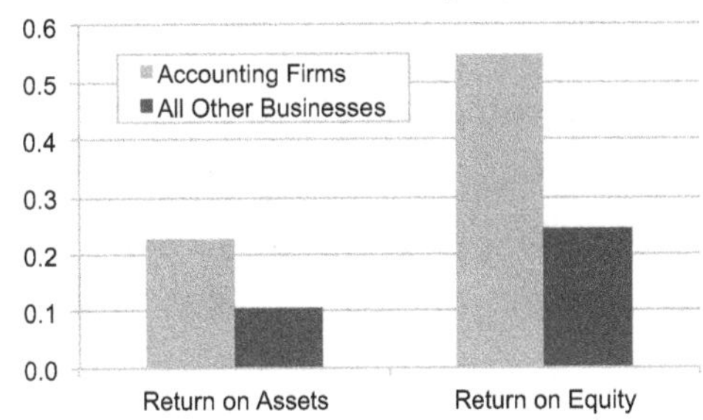

Median Activity Ratios

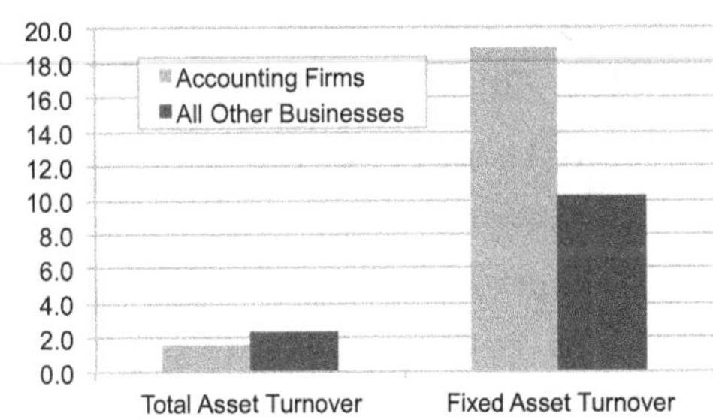

Current ratio = current assets/current liabilities
Quick ratio = [current assets - inventory]/current liabilities
Total asset turnover = revenue/total assets
Fixed asset turnover = revenue/total assets
Return on assets = net income/total assets
Return on equity = net income/equity

9 Pitfalls of Valuing OTC Derivatives in the Oil and Gas Industry

Oil and gas firms are in an industry that is highly sensitive and subject to volatility in returns, so these firms use derivatives regularly to manage their risks. Many other companies, including private firms, now use derivatives. For example, a U.S. manufacturer that buys parts from overseas may use forward contracts to hedge currency risk. A trucking company might use energy futures to stabilize profit margins. Some derivatives are traded on an exchange, but most derivatives are traded over the counter (OTC).

The types of derivatives most common to the oil and gas industry are: futures/forwards, options, swaps, costless collars, three-way collars, swaptions, and differentials (or basis) swaps, according to Ernest De Lachica, a director at BDO. De Lachica explains the most common pitfalls he sees in valuing OTC derivatives.

Derivative instruments not identified as such (validating the population). At first glance, an OTC instrument sounds pretty straightforward. There are just a few basic types of instruments, and they are usually valued with a variety of closed-form models. "Well, it is a little bit more complicated than that," he says. With oil and gas firms, you will usually find a good number of these types of instruments. You won't typically see four or five different swaps—you could see 300 of them, so the sheer volume can create additional complexity.

Each instrument is unique—and time-consuming. The instruments that you find will be unique, and a model will have to be set up to pick up all the different variables and changes that may occur to individual contracts. "It becomes more a numbers and a management type of exercise, and it can sort of mushroom on you if you are not careful," he says. It's surprising to find that a lot of clients have issues with even identifying a lot of these instruments.

Lots of moving pieces. Often, the instruments will be restructured, which results in a maze of moving pieces that can be difficult to navigate. "If you are not really on top of it, you could potentially miss some of the pieces, which would translate into a significant value that is not being captured accurately," De Lachica says.

Valuation approaches sometimes vary. The valuation approaches with these instruments tend to vary quite a bit. For example, if you have 300 instruments, they are potentially using varying types of models. You could have 100 different types of collars, another 100 that are swaps, and another 100 that are different types of forwards or futures or different types of instruments themselves. "All of a sudden you realize that the level of effort is expanding and if you can't pull all those pieces together, it can be very, very difficult and take a great deal of time." In addition, adjustments can differ for each type of instrument, and you have to understand which adjustments are appropriate.

Derivative agreements are not explicit. Derivative agreements are not really standardized, so, if there is a similar instrument with three or four different counterparties, you will see three or four different types of agreements. Some of them are going to explain certain aspects of the instrument very well—but others will not. "You often have to take an educated guess about what the instrument is doing," he observes. Often, there is a great amount of nuance in the language of the agreements, which, depending on the user's familiarity, can make it difficult to determine the specific terms.

Data sources are expensive and not readily available. In terms of the energy industry, the various data sources include, but are not limited to, Opus, Argus, Bloomberg, and Platts, which are "extremely pricey," he notes. However, to be able to value these types of instruments, you must have the supporting structures, and a lot of it is the data sources. Subscriptions to these sources can start at $10,000, and that may only be a limited subscription.

Instruments extend further than market data. OTC instruments sometimes extend further out, so there is not going to be market data for some of these instruments. "When you start looking at a normal West Texas Intermediate forward curve, it is going to go out 10 years," he says. "But when you start talking about other locations, they may only go out two or three or four years." If an instrument that is priced off of one of these locations goes further out than the information you have, you have to use some form of curve development or bootstrapping to actually come up with a forward curve that you can apply to determine a reasonable forecast.

Adjustments are subjectively based. Numerous different types of credit adjustments can be applied to these instruments. The adjustments can be based on a bond rating or a credit default swap curve if one is available. There are a number of different types of accepted approaches in applying these adjustments, so understanding what is acceptable is critical. "If you are not familiar with them there are several white papers that you should read to make sure you understand them and use one that will not create problems with the auditors," he advises.

Available data may require adjustments. The available data are constantly changing, and it may need to be adjusted. "A very simple example is when they were developing the Eagle Ford in central Texas," he recalls. "You could go out and find an Eagle Ford forward curve very easily, but you learned from the people out in the field that there were so many different varieties of pricing for Eagle Ford crude that the curve really was not valid." If you used that curve, you would have come up with huge differences in valuation.

For more information. De Lachica, as well as Pablo Alfaro and Matthew Goldberg, also with BDO, participated in a webinar, Complex Financial Instruments in the Energy Sector. They have extensive experience valuing a wide range of complex derivatives and other hedging instruments. To acquire a recording of the webinar, go to www.bvresources.com/dlc.

Experts Answer Queries on Hot Topics Affecting Midstream Oil & Gas Firms

As consumers, we're happy to see prices fall at the gas pumps and smaller bills for home heating oil. But the oil and gas industry is reeling from the current economic environment. At today's prices (around $30 a barrel), it's almost impossible to be profitable, so firms are cutting back production and laying off workers. This means revenues drop and debt obligations become a problem—some bankruptcies have been triggered. There's also impairment of oil and gas reserves sitting on the financial statements. Bottom line: Classic supply and demand forces are at work in this industry—demand is not keeping up with supply increases, so prices fall.

Dan Visich and Tom Ramos, oil and gas valuation experts who are both with BDO Consulting, recently fielded questions on how some current issues are affecting oil and gas firms in the midstream sector.

There are four sectors of the oil and gas industry: upstream, midstream, downstream, and oilfield service companies. Upstream firms deal with exploration and production (E&P). The midstream sector handles the transportation, storage, and wholesale marketing. "A typical midstream transportation company is composed mainly of pipelines, rail, barges, oil tankers, and trucks," says Visich. "Some names there are Plains All American, Enbridge, ONEOK Partners, and Energy Transfer Partners, which are some of the bigger players in the midstream area." Most midstream companies are also in the downstream sector, which involves refining and distribution operations (including gas stations). The fourth sector, oilfield services, includes drilling equipment, manufacturing, production, and well services.

Q: *Because the impact on pricing and production is first felt in the E&P sector, does this sector suffer more volatility than the midstream or downstream sectors?*

"Yes, I would say that the E&P sector definitely feels it more than the midstream or the downstream sectors," says Ramos. "I would also say that the oilfield service sector almost feels it to the same degree as the E&P sector, mainly because these firms are fully supporting the E&P sector. Therefore, as production decreases in the face of lower prices of oil and gas, both of those sectors get hit because you will see less production, so less revenues on the E&P side which equates to less revenue on the oilfield service sector side as well."

The midstream sector moves the product from one place to another, so issues concerning the transportation industry need to be considered.

Q: *What are the implications for future rail shipments of oil taking into consideration local municipal concerns regarding the potential for rail accidents?*

This is a valid concern of local municipalities, notes Visich. "Exploration has expanded, but there is not enough pipeline near where all the exploration is taking place, so there is definitely a need for more rail and truck transportation," he says. "I assume this issue will probably get a lot more attention down the road as the amount of transport via rail increases. No one has an answer to this issue—we'll have to see how it plays out. The pipeline infrastructure is not in place to handle the increased need for transport."

In the oil and gas industry, fracing (pronounced the same as "fracking," an alternate spelling) is a controversial but important process that has increased production. Fracing is a hydraulic process that uses a high-pressure mixture of water, sand, and chemicals to fracture shale formations to extract more oil and gas. Visich and Ramos note that the spelling of the word with a "k" has a negative connotation, i.e., those against the process spell it "fracking."

Q: *What is the future potential of fracing taking into consideration the need for water?*

"I don't know if everyone has seen it, but the water crisis for utilities has increased over the years," says Ramos. "The reason is that fracing requires a great deal of water. Then, of course, once the frac water is used, it has to be disposed somewhere because it contains chemicals—it can't go back into the drinking system." Ramos notes that there has been an increase in salt water disposal wells, which is where the used water is being disposed. The salt water disposal well generally is just a dried up oil well, so companies engaged in that activity have started to pop up over the last few years. "I think fracing will continue, but, of course, water has become more of a need in certain locations, such as in the shale formations at Eagle Ford or Bakken, where water is particularly a hot commodity."

Q: *Are there any regions in the world (such as Venezuela or Colombia) that have the potential to increase oil and gas production by embracing fracing?*

"Yes, definitely," says Ramos. "The United States is the frontrunner in fracing and has started to become very efficient and knowledgeable about the process. There are countries that are starting to do a little more fracing, but they are looking to the U.S. for help with the knowledge and technology. You might see these countries enter into joint venture agreements with some U.S. companies for purposes of knowledge sharing."

Because of the recent economic pressures on the industry, the issue of impairments naturally become a concern.

Q: *What are the most notable examples of impairment write-offs that you've seen in E&P, midstream, or downstream public companies?*

"Most of the impairments I've seen are in the oilfield service sector because they will have goodwill as a result of acquisitions," says Ramos. "A firm in this sector has the typical intangible assets that you would find in most any other type of industry, such as customer relationships, trade name, and technology. What results from that is usually some amount of goodwill. As the revenues and the value of the business is decreasing, you will see a direct impact in the form of goodwill impairment write-downs. In the E&P sector, the impairment analysis is different because there are different methods of accounting that these companies can use. One is full cost accounting, and the other is based on successful efforts, and the impairments are very much different between those two accounting methods. I would say that you are definitely seeing impairments in E&P companies as well as oil field service firms."

For more information. Visich is a director in the New York office of BDO Consulting, supporting the firm's valuation and business analytics practice. Ramos is in BDO's Houston office and is a director with the firm's valuation services practice. They recently conducted a webinar, Valuing Midstream Oil and Gas Companies. To access a recording, go to www.bvresources.com/dlc.

New Approach to FMV of Physician Pay Could End Hospital Woes

Unless there's a change of mindset over the fair market value of physician compensation, hospitals will stay on the government's radar for fraud and abuse claims. At the recent AICPA Healthcare Industry Conference, speakers at several sessions refuted conventional wisdom regarding compensation hospitals pay to employ physicians. Two issues are at the heart of this matter were: physician relocation and the use of compensation survey data.

What's at stake. The government has been winning False Claims Act (FCA) lawsuits against a number of hospitals, reaping hundreds of millions of dollars in fines. The lawsuits have emerged out of the trend of hospitals acquiring medical practices. In four recent cases, *Tuomey, Halifax, Citizens,* and *North Broward,* the hospitals paid $300 million in fines to settle charges of fraud. Many more of these cases are most likely under seal, and the recent successes could spark more complaints. The thrust of the cases is the measurement of the fair market value of physician compensation. This, of course, raises the bar for appraisers, and it also presents some practice opportunities in terms of assessing commercial reasonableness of these deals.

In their conference session that examined the *Tuomey* and *Halifax* cases, Richard Romero (CBIZ Valuation Group) and Timothy Smith (Ankura Consulting Group) say the key quantitative analysis the government uses for commercial reasonableness is "significant losses" on physician practices. If the arrangement appears to fail this commercial reasonableness test, the government may suspect a Stark law violation (e.g., payments for referrals). Romero's firm was an expert for the government in *Tuomey,* but he himself did not work on the case. Smith is the co-editor of the *BVR/AHLA Guide to Healthcare Industry Compensation and Valuation.* This session identified many flaws in the arguments and methodology used by the experts for both the government and *Tuomey,* including the misuse of survey data which frequently leads to losses in physician practices.

Relocation myth. Hospitals feel that median pay is the "magic number," and, if they don't pay their physicians at least the median compensation for their specialty, they will relocate to earn more. Smith and Romero point out that the government's expert follows this thinking and uses a "highest and best use" concept for determining FMV of doctor compensation. But Smith points to extensive research done by Mark O. Dietrich, CPA, PC, on physician mobility that refutes the government's position on this. Dietrich is the editor of the fourth edition of the *BVR/AHLA Guide to Healthcare Finance and Valuation.*

Physicians are less likely to relocate than other occupations, based on significant research that has been done on physicians' mobility, according to Dietrich. For example, 10 years after being trained, two-thirds of physicians are still in the same state, according to the Association of American Medical Colleges, which tracks physician training and practice patterns. When a physician does move, it's most likely after residency is completed. There are exceptions, such as neurosurgeons, who are heavily recruited due to demand for that specialty. But, overall, Dietrich contends that the notion that a physician will relocate if he or she doesn't get the median compensation does not hold up to scrutiny. However, this is the current mindset among hospitals and appraisers—a mindset that needs to change. In addition, Smith has completed studies using placement survey data to show experienced physicians usually get paid around 85% of the median for starting compensation.

Faulty use of survey data. In establishing reasonable or fair market compensation, Dietrich explains that most practitioners focus on survey data, especially from the Medical Group Management Association (MGMA) but also from the American Medical Group Association (AMGA). The problems with the surveys are that they are not based on random samples and the same organizations are reporting to at least two different surveys, according to Smith. Also, survey data don't always jibe with information on collections in the same surveys. Dietrich points out that, in the 2014 MGMA survey, the median compensation paid per work relative value units (wRVU) for internal medicine physicians was $50.74, while median professional collections was $37.09 for each type of wRVU. Based on this, if hospitals ignore collections in favor of survey data, losses will result (unless other forms of compensation are involved).

Many hospitals and practices use wRVUs as a means of measuring productivity, but the compensation data and wRVU rates in the surveys are a seriously flawed means of setting compensation, Dietrich says. He explains that the present use of physician compensation surveys to establish fair market value is based on several false premises, including: (1) that the surveys have statistical significance for the 90% or so of physicians not included in the surveys; (2) that survey compensation per wRVU is always fair market value and commercially reasonable—the common wRVU technique utilized virtually assures that the employing institution will lose money on the practice, something that appears to be commercially *unreasonable* based on the recent court cases; (3) that physicians will relocate to earn the median and therefore everyone should earn the median—an idea that is both statistically incoherent and not borne out by academic research; and (4) that the 75th percentile of compensation per wRVU or compensation-to-collections ratio is a mythical ceiling on fair market value.

Local-market conditions not measurable in the surveys may necessitate losses on physician practices due to supply and demand, payer contract rates, local-market competition, and national shortages of high-demand specialties, among other factors, he says. The commercial reasonableness of these losses should be documented in advance and can, in fact, be documented through use of a different method as well as other techniques.

New approach. Dietrich and Smith are developing strategies hospitals can use to compensate physicians in a way that is consistent with their business goals without triggering government lawsuits. Instead of paying physicians the median compensation, hospitals could set fair market value compensation based on the resource-based relative value scale (RBRVS), they say. RBRVS is a fee schedule that uses a complex formula to determine the payment due a physician for patient services and takes into account such factors as the resources used, practice expenses, malpractice expenses, geographic location, and others. It measures direct compensation and benefits for physicians and excludes other costs or revenues unrelated to the physician's personally performed clinical services. RBRVS reveals how much of what is collected should go toward paying doctors instead of overhead, according to Smith. The amount of collections could be allocated to physicians based on compensation vis-à-vis overhead and insurance, which allows the hospital to set compensation based on conditions in the local market, he says.

Another way to avoid the rash of lawsuits and government attacks on practice losses is for hospitals to focus more on negotiating for better rates for physician practices, advises Dietrich. Hospitals typically don't think of this on the practice side—they normally focus on getting better commercial rates for hospital services in order to show profits in that area. But, if they put this same effort into the practice side, the physicians could be paid more with less exposure to compliance risk, observes Smith.

These strategies could help reduce or eliminate losses on physician practices, which would take hospitals out of the line of fire of FCA lawsuits, according to Smith and Dietrich. However, this will require a different mindset and a willingness to rethink compensation surveys, they say.

There is virtually no official guidance to help valuation experts in this area. What is clear, the speakers point out, is that the sole reliance on survey data is inconsistent with standard appraisal methodology—you need to do analyses under all three approaches (market, cost, and income).

Valuing a Franchise? Consider These Seven Specific Characteristics

A court case[1] involving the valuation of a chain of Planet Fitness operations underscores the challenge of valuing a franchise. True, many of the factors you consider will not be very different than those for any other type of company. But there are franchise-specific characteristics that can trigger a much greater degree of risk than an independent business.

First thing to do. Examine the franchise offering documents and the franchise license agreement (and any amendments). These documents control the investment and working relationship with the franchisor. There is a wide disparity of relationships between franchisees and franchisors that can drive the risk and the value of the business, so you need to thoroughly understand the provisions. Many of the following franchise-specific elements reflect what is contained in the franchise documents and the underlying nature of the relationship with the franchisor.

1. *Outside control.* The franchisor exercises significant control over the franchisee's operations. This control can extend to many details of the operation, including location, suppliers, hours of operation, signage, and so on. The franchisee must also make required payments during the year. There also may be a restricted ability to make business decisions, such as limits on expansion, product offerings, marketing costs, and many other aspects—all buried in the franchise agreement.

You can think of the franchisor's influences over growth or direction of the business as akin to key-customer risk. That is, someone can take actions outside of the control of the business that could affect brand value. What is the franchisor's plan to build up the brand? What about expansion plans? Of course, these plans can go awry, such as the overexpansion of Krispy Kreme. That franchise has rebounded, but there's a long list of defunct franchise brands. Has anybody eaten a hamburger lately at a Burger Chef?

2. *Local market.* In certain market areas, there are well-established franchises and franchisees who already have several locations, so there's a built-in ready market for a seller. For less-established

1 *La Verghetta v. Lawlor,* Index No. 5934/2014, N.Y. Sup. Ct. [County of Westchester] (March 9, 2016). See a detailed discussion later in this issue.

franchises, it will be tougher to sell, so marketability will be an issue. Also, because franchisors typically have the right of first refusal on the sale of any business, they are a potential bidder. The franchisor will always know more about the available franchises than any other potential bidder, so an outside bidder has to spend more money and effort to even approach the franchisor's knowledge of the available franchise.

3. *Required improvements.* One element that often pops up is in the area of improvements or maintenance of the location. The timing of this issue may not always be a good thing. For example, a franchise restaurant could make significant improvements to its dining area—and then the franchisor mandates a makeover of the restaurant design and layout. The franchisee will likely be required to make those changes despite the fact that it has just sunk a significant capital expenditure into the business. Therefore, ask the franchisee whether it is aware of any plan changes. If the franchisor has a tendency to make changes fairly often, or if it has not done so for a while, a change may be due.

4. *Franchise disputes.* Another significant risk in franchise businesses is franchise dispute risk. The potential outcome here is the loss of the ability to continue doing business. A good example of this is Quiznos, where franchisees filed lawsuits over disputes about food costs, marketing, royalties, and other matters. This went on for years, and, after a settlement was reached, Quiznos filed for bankruptcy. While the chain has rebounded, more than 2,000 locations were closed.

5. *Threats by franchisors.* Franchisors keep their franchisees in line with the threat of nonrenewal. But you should be able to see warning signs, such as below-average sales, skipped payments, lots of opting out of marketing campaigns, too many customer complaints, or legal troubles.

6. *Image problems.* While franchise owners enjoy whatever positive image there may be in the brand name, they also run the risk of negative effects, such as what happened with Subway or Chipotle. When bad news hits the media, sales for all locations can plummet. Sometimes, the franchisees have no recourse because they often waive their rights to sue the franchisor for any such incident in their franchise agreement.

7. *Escape hatch.* If a nonfranchised business opens and the owner sees that it's just not going to work out, he or she can simply get out. But it can be a lot tougher to get out of the business in a franchise because the owner may not have that option.

Once you consider these franchise-specific elements, how do you deal with their impact? You can adjust the discount rate or the cap rate to take into account the extra risks, or you could adjust the cash flows. For example, assume there's a serious dispute and you estimate that there is a 50% chance that the business will lose 50% of revenue this year, a 25% chance of growth, and a 25% chance of staying even. A probability-weighted cash flow that incorporates this risk can be developed.

Separate from this—and another challenge—is selecting the right data for market comparisons. The sidebar gives some advice for this.

Tips for Choosing Comparable Data for Franchise Valuations

There is a great deal of data available on franchises, but it's a challenge to select the data. For example, the franchise industry provides information on rules of thumb. The data misses certain elements, such as variations in franchise brand strength or weakness, location factors, or differences in the franchise relationship or agreement. Therefore, the data should only be used as a check to corroborate a value conclusion achieved via other methods.

If you examine overall transactions in the subject company's industry and market, be aware that franchises can have significantly different deal multiples from nonfranchise businesses that are otherwise similar. In some industries, the multiples are higher for franchises, but in some industries the multiples are lower. The best comparable transactions are sales of franchises with the same franchisor. Franchisors usually won't share this information, but you can find sales of franchise locations within a specific industry in the typical transaction databases. However, they may be subject to different franchise agreements.

Franchisees make royalty payments to franchisors according to the terms of the franchise agreement. Are these payments reasonable? To compare royalty rates paid to similar franchisors with similar agreements, you can get data from sources such as ktMINE or Royalty Source, which contain franchise agreements. With a little digging, you can see whether the franchise actually has a reasonable royalty rate for what is provided.

Latest Study Reveals Valuation Differences in the A/E Industry

New data seem to suggest that architectural practices are less valuable than engineering and environmental consulting firms. This is according to the *2016 A/E Business Valuation and Merger & Acquisition Transactions Study*. The study also shows a notable difference between valuation multiples (specifically earnings multiples) of architecture firms and those of engineering and environmental consulting firms.

The study includes valuation multiples for internal (minority interest) stock transactions, ESOP transactions, and mergers and acquisitions. The stock transaction data are in three distinct groups: (1) minority interests in privately held firms; (2) minority interests in publicly traded firms; and (3) controlling interests in privately held firms.

Minority interests. Most transitions of ownership in the A/E sector consist of transactions of minority interests (noncontrolling interests) of stock between multiple buyers and multiple sellers. Such stock is often governed by a shareholders' agreement that restricts the transfer of shares and allows for redemption only in cases such as retirement, termination of employment, death, and disability. Accordingly, the value of minority interests in privately held firms must reflect the lack of control and the limited liquidity of the stock.

Exhibit 1. Enterprise Value/ Preowners' Bonus EBIT

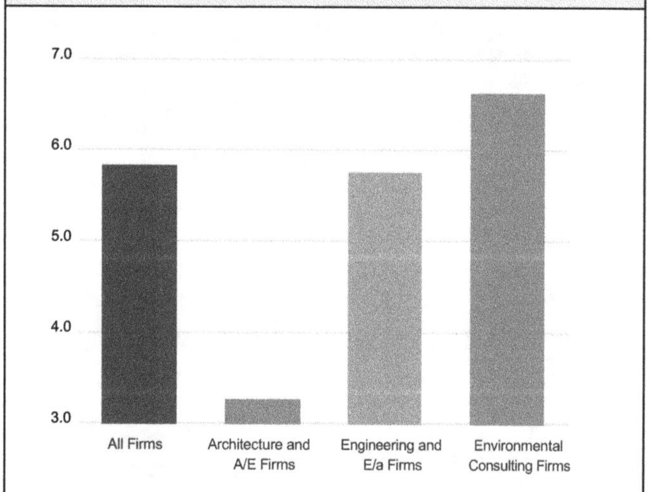

The study includes valuation multiples that represent transactions of minority interests in privately held stock over the last three years. The study reveals that there is a fair degree of consistency in valuation multiples between the various types of firms responding to the survey. For example, the median enterprise value as a multiple of earnings before interest, taxes, and owners' bonuses ranged from 3.32x for architecture and A/E

Exhibit 2. Enterprise Value/Preowners' Bonus EBIT				
	All Firms	Engineering & E/a	Architecture & A/e	Environmental Consulting
Median	5.88x	5.86x	3.32x	6.70x
Mean	8.45x	9.43x	6.64x	8.30x
Trimmed Mean	7.44x	7.84x	6.05x	7.92x
Upper Quartile	10.12x	10.37x	9.77x	9.50x
Lower Quartile	3.37x	3.97x	2.58x	4.62x

firms to 6.70x for environmental consulting firms, with a median for all firms surveyed of 5.35x (see Exhibit 1 and Exhibit 2).

Word of caution. Keep in mind that one or two valuation multiples don't always tell the whole story. You also have to consider financial performance metric data. For example, the study shows that the participating architecture firms have the highest pretax, prebonus profit margin and the highest predistribution return on average total assets.

The *2016 A/E Business Valuation and M&A Transaction Study* is from Rusk O'Brien Gido + Partners and is available at www.bvresources.com/publications.

Eleven Special CSR Factors That Can Affect the Value of a Veterinary Practice

The valuation of a veterinary practice presents a number of special considerations—unique issues—that ultimately affect the value or capitalization rate through the company-specific risk (CSR) premium if a build-up method is being used. The following are a few of the more important risk factors.

1. *Practice type.* There are many types of practices including: small- or companion-animal practice, large-animal practices (dairy, cow, mixed farm, equine, etc.), equine-specific practices, ambulatory or mobile practices that do not have a fixed facility, emergency practices, specialty practices that have one specialty or a collection of specialties, etc. Many unique differences should be recognized, and applying statistics from one type to another should be done carefully. For example:

- Some practices (equine, large animal, and those operating at a resort) have dramatic earning seasonality.
- Accounts receivable balances are very low in small-animal practices. Many large-animal practices can have significantly high client accounts receivable balances, and they are usually collectible. Emergency practices can have multiple shareholders that are also the referring doctors. Many emergency practices originated because the local veterinarians did not want to do their own emergencies anymore, so the local veterinary hospitals got together and built an emergency clinic. They are all shareholders of that, so that might be a little unique compared to other types of medical practices.
- Franchise practices, such as Banfield's Charter Practice program, had lower profit margins and less buyer demand in part due to the royalty fees paid to Banfield and in part due to the industry's resistance to corporate America entering the profession.

2. *Cash flow/profitability.* For most practices, the rate of growth of the historic revenue generation can be a predictor of the future. A history of consistent and substantial revenue growth over recent years reduces risk.

Transferring Goodwill	
Practice Type	**Transferability of Goodwill**
ER	High
Companion animal	
Mixed animal	
Food animal	
Mobile	
Equine	
Specialty (e.g., surgeon, cardiology, etc.)	
Subspecialty	Low

3. *Goodwill transferability.* Professional (personal) goodwill refers to the intangible attributes associated with an individual practitioner. To assess the magnitude of professional goodwill, one must consider whether there would be a major impact on income generation and practice operations if the practitioner suddenly left the practice. Unlike practice goodwill, professional goodwill often does not increase the value of the practice. This is because professional goodwill is personal in nature and difficult to transfer to the new owner. Because the professional or personal goodwill is more difficult to transfer to the buyer, the risk increases in practices where levels of professional goodwill are high. Conversely, risk decreases as practice goodwill increases.

The transferability of goodwill is species-specific. For example, horse owners do not hire the practice; they hire the doctor. When Dr. Jones leaves and Dr. Smith comes in, the transferability of goodwill is predicated on how long and how much they do together during that transition period. With an ambulatory equine practice, the seller will frequently ride in the truck with the buyer to make personal introductions to the main clients in order for that significant goodwill to transfer.

On the other hand, consider a three-doctor, small-companion-animal practice in a fixed facility in an area where people are moving in and out of the community frequently. There is a reasonable chance that a large portion of the client base may be either unaware who the owner is or does not interact with the owner regularly. These cases have a high degree of transferability of goodwill. It is relatively easy for the next veterinarian to take the owner's place, and the rest of the community does not pay attention.

The exhibit presents how the different types of practices can impact the transferability of the goodwill and some of the assumptions that will be expected in a transaction scenario.

4. *Income growth.* What a practice is expected to earn in the future depends on many factors such as the economic state of the region, the regional demographics, etc. The more uncertainty there is in these factors, the greater the risk.

5. *Location.* The location of a practice can significantly affect business risk. The visibility of the facility from primary traffic route, the client drive time or ease in getting to the facility, and the ease of ingress and egress to the facility are all important factors in the client's decision process to utilize or not utilize a particular practice's services. Risk decreases as location factors are more favorable.

6. *Staff quality.* Many factors in combination comprise a quality staff. Issues to consider include: adequacy of staff, training and cross-training of members, longevity, pride in practice, staff turnover rate, likelihood of the staff remaining with the practice after a sale transaction, etc.

7. *Facility.* Facility considerations include the contemporary nature of the overall facility floor plan and design, whether it is visually appealing, physical condition of building, apparent care and cleanliness, inherent environmental or zoning problems, and provisions for future expansion.

8. *Demographics.* Demographic factors such as trends in population numbers, growth rate and growth directions, income levels, the presence of a single-sector or diverse economy, unemployment trends, and other demographic parameters are predictors of the persistence of the practice's revenue stream. Less-than-favorable demographic trends increase risk and increase the capitalization rate.

9. *Management systems.* This risk factor examines the practice's compliance to various regulatory requirements including OSHA, MSDS, medical waste disposal, and controlled substance management. Also assessed is the degree of implementation and utilization of information management systems, in particular, veterinary practice management systems.

10. *Competition.* This factor examines the risks associated with the loss of clients and associated goodwill from current or potential competing veterinary practices. It is especially important to assess the impact of competition during the time of transition in a buy-in situation. Barrier of entry is an additional factor to consider since different types of practices are more or less resistant to new competition. The barrier of entry is low when considering a competing mobile ambulatory practice—a vehicle with some equipment and inventory and you are in business. Compare that with a brick-and-mortar facility built on a key corner in a great location.

11. *Practice stability.* The practice stability risk factor examines the consistency and likely persistence of the practice and its earnings. This assessment looks at the length of time the practice has existed in the community and at this location, employee stability, consistency of growth trends in gross revenues, and especially the constancy and adequacy of net income.

This is an excerpt from What It's Worth: Veterinary Practice Value, *available at www.bvresources.com/publications.*

How to Avoid Harsh HIPAA Penalties When Doing Healthcare Valuations

Changes in federal healthcare law have expanded the requirements for maintaining the security of patient data. What does this have to do with your valuation engagement? When doing a valuation of a healthcare entity, you may receive protected patient information. When that happens, you face exposure to the tough new rules under the Health Insurance Portability and Accountability Act of 1996 (HIPAA)—and the penalties for violations are severe.

What's at stake. The Health Information Technology for Economic and Clinical Health Act of 2009 (HITECH) significantly expanded the law to impose privacy rules beyond traditional entities such as healthcare providers and health plans ("covered entities"). Regulations under HITECH were published in January 2013, and certain provisions became effective late that year. The rules now apply to a healthcare entity's "business associates," which can include you as an appraiser, according to Mark Dietrich, editor and contributing author to *The BVR/AHLA Guide to Healthcare Industry Finance and Valuation,* 4th edition. Dietrich wrote a new chapter in the book devoted to HIPAA and medical records in the context of valuation and litigation.

HITECH provides four categories or tiers of violations that reflect increasing levels of culpability for the violation of HIPAA. The four corresponding tiers of penalty significantly increase the minimum penalty amount for each violation, and the maximum annual penalty is $1.5 million for all violations of an identical provision.

The four tiers of violations are: (1) the offender did not know (and by exercising reasonable diligence would not have known) that it violated the provision; (2) the violation was due to reasonable cause and not willful neglect; (3) the violation was due to willful neglect but was corrected within the required time period; and (4) the violation was due to willful neglect and was not corrected.

Anybody who knowingly violates the HIPAA rules can also be hit with criminal penalties. Also, Dietrich points out that HIPAA trumps state law unless there is greater privacy protection under state law.

Inadvertent exposure. No matter whether the valuation engagement involves a standard appraisal or is in the context of litigation support, divorce, damages claims, shareholder buyouts or other matters, you may fall under the HIPAA rules. For instance, you can come into contact with PHI in the conduct of a forensic investigation through testing of internal controls, while reviewing a healthcare provider's revenue cycle activities, or even in utilizing bookkeeping and accounting data. Something as simple as a client's patient refunds account in the general ledger can constitute PHI and trigger HIPAA exposure.

Also, you don't have to be providing appraisal services directly to a covered entity to come into contact with PHI. Under a downstream concept, if your client is a business associate of a covered entity, you can easily be deemed a business associate as well. For example, you may be valuing a firm that provides medical billing services and writes refund checks to its clients' patients. The possibilities of inadvertently falling under the HIPAA rules are "nearly endless" according to Dietrich.

What to do. When valuing a healthcare provider, you often have to get reports from the revenue cycle system that show the units, charges, payments, and adjustments by service and by insurer, as well as an aged accounts receivable. It is not necessary, however, for any of the data to contain confidential patient information. When no PHI is necessary in the engagement, you should carefully structure your data requests and be certain that the client understands that no PHI should be provided. You can also request that health information be redacted to remove identifiers.

Sample PHI Provision for Engagement Letters

Valuation practitioners with healthcare clients should consider adding a provision to their engagement letter that specifically deals with the improper provision of protected health information (PHI) by a client and the related costs of unauthorized transmission. Here is sample language that might form the basis for such a provision:

> Practice agrees not to provide me, directly or indirectly, any Protected Health Information ("PHI") without advance written notification including an explanation of the need to do so and a fully executed Business Associate Agreement which is acceptable to and has been signed by [Representative of Firm]. Any such data must be the minimum necessary for the purposes of this engagement. For this purpose, PHI and minimum necessary have the meaning set forth in the Health Insurance Portability and Accountability Act of 1996 ("HIPAA"), the American Recovery and Reinvestment Act of 2009 ("ARRA"), and their implementing regulations set forth at 45 C.F.R. Parts 160 and 164 (the "Privacy and Security Rules"). Additionally, if Practice provides me with PHI in violation of the Privacy and Security Rules, the Business Associate Agreement, and/or the terms specified above, then Practice agrees to indemnify and hold me harmless for any related damages or costs incurred by me or any other third party as a result of such unauthorized transmission.

Before using a provision such as this, consult your legal advisor first.

Source: Mark Dietrich, *The BVR/AHLA Guide to Healthcare Industry Finance and Valuation*, fourth edition, www.bvresources.com/publications

If you need direct access to the client's revenue cycle system containing PHI during the engagement, you should consider whether maintaining any written or electronic patient identifying information in workpapers is necessary. Although the appraiser is responsible for maintaining the confidentiality of all PHI encountered in accordance with HIPAA's privacy rules, you can avoid having to implement a costly physical and electronic security plan if you leave all physical and electronic PHI in the client's office. However, you will still be responsible for maintaining the confidentiality of any PHI that you've seen.

In his chapter on medical records, Dietrich also recommends including a provision in your engagement letter that causes the client to be liable for costs and damages for unwarranted disclosure of PHI to you or your firm (see the sidebar).

Your best protection is to have a full understanding of the HIPAA rules and regulations in the context of valuation, including the definition of PHI, the HIPAA Security Rule, and what triggers a business associate relationship.

Valuation Characteristics and Methodologies for Urgent Care Centers

By Aaron Murski, CVA and Elliott Jeter, CFA, CPA/ABV

Editor's note: Retail healthcare is a serious concern to healthcare entities. With the rise of urgent care centers, hospitals will become bigger players in this market, which is consolidating. This article is an excerpt of a chapter on valuing urgent care centers in the 4th edition of the BVR/AHLA Guide to Healthcare Industry Finance and Valuation, *available at www.bvresources.com/publications.*

Buyers of urgent care centers (UCC) most commonly analyze and price controlling equity interest transactions in a straight-forward manner, using a multiple of EBITDA less interest-bearing debt. UCC owner-operators often prefer to own a controlling equity interest in order to enhance the ability to achieve economies of scale and enhance negotiating influence and leverage across a platform.

Unlike UCC owner-operators who typically price controlling equity interest transactions using a range of multiples of EBITDA, most hospital systems rely on the fair market value opinion provided by an independent appraiser to ensure that they meet Stark and fraud and abuse statute requirements and private inurement concerns. Various professional standards require that business appraisers consider all relevant approaches and methods in developing an opinion of value. These other approaches and, in particular, the income approach or discounted cash flow method may provide a superior framework for measuring the impact of the individual facts and circumstances surrounding a subject UCC. Like all fair market value analysis, the cost approach, market approach, and income approach should be considered when valuing an urgent care center or chain under the fair market value standard. Important to understanding the value of UCCs is the size and scale of the operations, which have implications for the market and income approaches to value.

Cost approach. Many smaller urgent care chains or single-site operations owned by physician entrepreneurs are either breakeven or not expected to provide a return greater than the required return on the working capital and fixed assets employed in the operation of the UCC. These UCCs may be generating sufficient cash flow to pay physician compensation but generate no profit for the owners. In these cases, the asset approach provides a "floor," or lowest minimum value, related to a controlling interest in a UCC. This may be the appropriate approach when the market and income approaches produce lower values.

In a transaction for a controlling interest in the context of marginal or zero earnings, a UCC owner-operator is not likely to pay for all, or maybe even any, of the intangible value created through the ownership and management of a UCC. However, in the context of a make-or-buy decision typical of this type of transaction, the buyer may pay for the assembly of all tangible and some intangible assets under the premise of value in continued use, as part of a mass assemblage of assets.[1]

From the perspective of a single-site or small urgent care chain, UCCs can appear to be an asset-intensive business (e.g., to a physician starting a UCC). The average gross property and equipment plus working capital per location hovers around $750,000. The UCCs may be overbuilt relative to the realized average daily visit volume. This type of circumstance can lead to transaction and, often, the application of the cost approach.

Market approach. The two common market approach methodologies include the guideline public company method and the merger and acquisition method. The guideline public company method relies on valuation metrics from publicly traded companies, while the merger and acquisition method relies on valuation metrics from transactions involving comparable UCCs. Given the lack of publicly traded pure-play urgent care concerns and lack of comparability between other publicly traded healthcare services companies and UCCs, the guideline public company method is not typically considered applicable to derive a value indication for UCCs.

Given the number of transactions that occur in the UCC space, the merger and acquisition method is considered applicable. Virtually all buyers use a multiple of EBITDA less interest-bearing debt in pricing a controlling equity interest in a UCC. While UCC operators often reference and use these general-market-guideline multiples, many factors may lead to an adjustment of the historical EBITDA or an ultimate transaction price that resides outside of this typical range.

In the discussion of the primary UCC value drivers, we detailed the need to consider changes in Medicare and commercial payer reimbursement when analyzing historical information and developing future projections. Based on our experience, the acquisition multiple used to price the purchase of a controlling interest is often applied to prospective or adjusted, rather than historically reported, EBITDA. A UCC company may have one or more startup UCCs. In fact, an aggressive growth strategy could substantially depress reported EBITDA for a growing UCC platform. These startup losses from existing recently opened sites should be normalized before applying a multiple in order to understand a reasonable EBITDA run rate after operations stabilize. UCC developers and operators also often adjust for startup losses and changes in reimbursement, as well as service mix,

1 An in-depth discussion of premise of value and utilization of the cost or asset approach can be found in Chapters 4, 21, 22, and 23 in the *BVR/AHLA Guide to Healthcare Industry Finance and Valuation*, 4th edition.

TIC/EBITDA Multiple Ranges

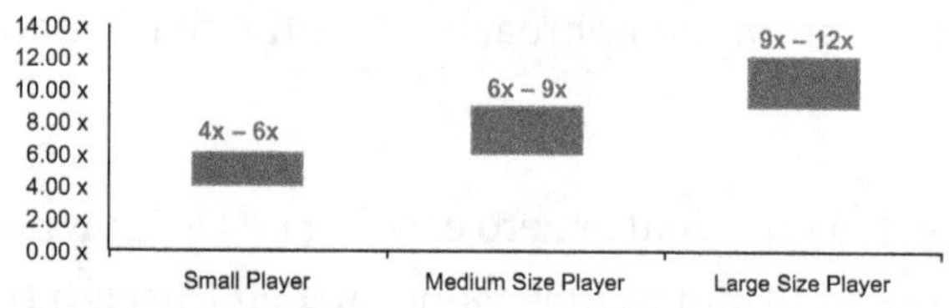

Source: VMG internal database

to estimate the EBITDA to which the multiple is applied. Typical UCC multiples, varying with the size of the platform, are displayed in the exhibit.

Income approach. Two general income approach methods may be utilized in the application of the income approach, which include capitalizing a single-period cash flow, as well as discounting multiperiod cash flows. Due to the ever-changing healthcare landscape, changes in local competition, and growth prospects, the single-period cash flow capitalization approach is not considered applicable. The multiperiod discounted cash flow is considered applicable, as many variables may be incorporated into the cash flow projections, which can affect value. In this method, the revenues, earnings, and resulting cash flows of the UCC are projected over typically five years. These cash flows are then discounted to present value utilizing an appropriate discount rate.

The terminal value is most often calculated using the Gordon growth model, which is then discounted to present value as well. In practice, certain types of buyers, primarily private equity buyers, may use an exit multiple approach to calculate a terminal value, as an exit is actually expected at some point at or near the end of their forecast period. The exit multiple approach may imply a cost of capital or growth rate that is inconsistent with the forecast period or may assume market conditions that are inconsistent with past or current conditions experienced. Considering these factors, the Gordon growth model is the preferred approach. The total enterprise value or equity value, depending on the benefit stream that was used in the forecast, may then be calculated as the sum of the discounted cash flows from both the discrete period and terminal period. For a growing UCC chain, UCC management may be very bullish on the prospects of the enterprise. Whether the appraiser projects a number of scenarios with a range of applicable discount rates or develops a single most likely case scenario with a single appropriate discount rate, the mechanics of the projections should be similar.

Patient volume is a primary determinant of financial performance for an urgent care center. Volume is typically analyzed and projected in terms of number of patient visits. Given the seasonality of urgent care businesses, average daily patient volume by month should be trended and considered when forecasting patient volume. Reimbursement levels are the second and equally as important determinant of financial performance. Shifts in payer mix and service mix can have a dramatic impact on overall average net revenue per visit, and trends should be analyzed and factored into the reimbursement forecast.

UCC cost structures are somewhat fixed in nature and can exhibit a high degree of operating leverage. Assuming an efficient staffing model given overall volume levels, incremental volumes over the break-even level create significantly higher margin. Physician and staff costs are the largest two expenses for the typical UCC, making the staffing model a primary area of scrutiny when forecasting expenses.

Capital expenditures (CapEx) are also significant to the discounted cash flow method for UCCs. A UCC is typically an asset-intensive business. While the dangers of following rules of thumb have been subject to lively debate throughout the history of the valuation profession, annual amounts ranging from $20,000 to $40,000 per year can be considered typical amounts. In addition to considering the age and condition of the existing furniture and equipment and the potential maintenance required, CapEx assumptions should also consider possible growth in volume.

For UCC chains and larger operators, the consolidated back-office and administrative functions are typically fixed for a given number of sites. As the platform grows, these expenses are a step function based on the number of sites. When forecasting the revenue and expenses of larger UCC chains, bifurcating the forecast between the "four-wall" revenue and expenses associated with the actual UCC sites and the back-office and shared administrative functions is crucial. For growing UCC chains, this enables the valuation professional to understand the ramp-up timeline for specific UCC sites.

Consistent with the tendencies of UCC owner-operators, we typically perform a discounted cash flow analysis whereby the market value of invested capital (MVIC) is calculated using debt-free cash flows and book value of debt is deducted from MVIC to arrive at a total equity value. While most UCCs typically use long-term debt to fund initial operations, many UCCs fund subsequent furniture and equipment purchases out of cash flows.

Prior to opening, the selection of the location of an urgent care center's facility is crucial to ensuring the success of the UCC. Virtually all UCCs lease their facilities. If not, the UCC's valuation may be impacted. If the UCC does own the real estate as well, the business appraiser should consider the potential difference in required returns on the real estate versus the UCC operations. The preferred solution is to engage a real estate appraiser to value the land and building separately and impute the implied market rental rate as an expense of the UCC. Then the values of the real estate and the UCC operations may be combined to arrive at an overall value.

If a separate real estate appraisal cannot be obtained, adjust the discount rate utilized in the discount cash flows to reflect the generally lower expected returns associated with the real estate. An adjustment to account for real estate may be considered when using the market approach (discussed earlier) and is applicable in the valuation of either a controlling interest or noncontrolling interest.

The valuation of a controlling equity interest approaching 100% requires an additional consideration. Under the income and market approaches, the pricing of most controlling interest transactions is for 51% to 60% interest. The same market multiples and rates of return may not apply to the incremental 40% to 49% interest of a 100% equity purchase.

Conclusion. The UCC industry has grown significantly because of its popularity with patients. To continue to grow, the industry must survive challenges to the business model. These include the proliferation of lower-cost access points such as telemedicine and retail health centers. Threats to growth will also occur from higher-cost, higher-service models such as freestanding emergency rooms. For now, UCCs are well positioned to become a key player in the changing healthcare landscape. To ensure viability, UCCs must understand their position in their local market and how they can be differentiated from a patient's other options in that market.

As health systems continue to pursue urgent care strategies through acquisition and development, the question remains as to where urgent care centers fit within alternative payment model methodologies. This is not likely to be answered anytime soon; however, until that time comes, urgent care centers are well positioned relative to the "triple aim," as UCCs provide low-cost, quality care in local communities they serve.

***Aaron Murski**, CVA, and **Elliott Jeter**, CFA, CPA/ABV, are managing directors at VMG Health, which focuses exclusively on healthcare fair market value services (www.vmghealth.com).*

Hotel Valuation: Breaking the Rules—But Getting It Right!

By Franz H. Ross, CBA, CVA, MRICS

This article explains why the dominant method for the appraisal of hotels is contrary to the main methods used for the appraisal of other real estate-centered enterprises (RECEs) and is therefore flawed. Furthermore, this method does not mimic the way hotels are typically sold, and the real estate appraisal profession's continuation of this method creates a void for other (business) appraisers to fill, simply by appraising hotels the same way as nursing homes, golf courses, and C-stores: as going concerns!

The dominant methodology for appraising hotels. Hotel appraisal specialist Stephen Rushmore, MAI, FRICS, CHA, was the originator of a method known as the Rushmore approach, in which he advocates for stripping out income attributed to the business value of a hotel in order to appraise just the tangible assets (real estate and personal property). In a 1993 article,[1] Rushmore advocates for deducting 8% to 15% of total revenue. In a 2004 article,[2] full revenues are used (with no subtractions made), and then all of the hotel's operating expenses are subtracted, including a reserve for capital replacements and a 4.9% revenues management fee. This management fee is said to remove the income to the business component.

Another way that intangible value is removed is by subtracting the franchise fees paid to the franchisor, including the royalty and reservation system fees. These expenses "also represent a portion of the income stream attributed to the business component."[3]

Concerns with the Rushmore approach. Franchise fees are paid to the franchisors, who own the brands we know so well: Comfort Inn, Hilton Hotel, Marriott, etc. The total amounts paid each year in the form of royalty, reservation system fee, IT charges, and other fees generally cost a hotel 7% to 11% of revenues. But paying obligatory franchise fees owed to the franchisor removes no more value of the franchise (to the franchisee) than paying any other obligatory expense. Franchise fees

1 Stephen Rushmore, "Time to Reduce Property Taxes," *Lodging Hospitality,* September 1993, p 17.

2 Stephen Rushmore, HVS.com, "In Defense of the 'Rushmore Approach' for Valuing the Real Property Component of a Hotel," April 13, 2004, pp 1-17.

3 Id., page 4.

create business value for the franchisor, but the franchisee is simply paying a required operating expense under the real estate concept of "highest and best use."

The Rushmore approach focuses on subtracting a management fee to remove business value so that the remaining capitalized income produces the value of the tangible assets only. This premise is logical for hotels that are operated by third-party management companies but is misleading for hotels that are unencumbered by management contracts. When appraising a hotel encumbered by a management contract, the terms of that contract, including the base management fee and incentive management fee, should be properly input into the income analysis to accurately value the property owner's interest (considering also the term of the management contract). But even this logical advice is at odds with Rushmore, as he suggests to not subtract the incentive fee in determining NOI but to instead make an upward adjust to the yield or equity dividend rate.[4] The incentive portion of the management fee is tied to profitability and therefore is the part of the fee that truly is indicative of excess earnings or business value. Amazingly, Rushmore violates the Rushmore approach by recommending against deducting the incentive management fee from cash flow.

For hotels that are unencumbered, use of the Rushmore approach is contrary to market behavior, as sellers do not withhold any intangible assets when they sell. They sell all of the assets, including goodwill (or business value). These intangibles also include the franchisee's interest in the franchise agreement (understanding that franchisors have to approve the buyer or can set financial requirements as a condition for approving a new franchisee).

The HotelManagement.net March 2016 survey[5] listed 168 firms that manage 4,680 U.S. hotels. While it is likely that a significant number of firms do not respond to the survey, it is likely that most of the major players want to be on the list. The American Hotel & Lodging Association's (AHLA) 2015 Lodging Industry Profile[6] indicates that there are 53,432 hotel properties in the U.S., including motels with 15 rooms or more. If a more restrictive definition of a hotel is used, interpolation of the AHLA data would suggest there are about 36,000 hotels with 50 rooms or more, and the 4,680 managed properties represent just 13% of this set. No data are perfect, but this information suggests that the vast majority of hotels are owner managed.

Some 17,888 U.S. hotels have 75 to 149 rooms.[7] The number of third-party management contracts at less-than-75-room properties has to be near zero (1% or 2% at most), and the number of management contracts for the 75-to-149-room group also has to be quite small. Just 6,141 U.S. hotels exceed 150 rooms, and public data suggest that perhaps about half or more of the larger properties are third-party managed. *The solution: Use the Rushmore approach when appraising a hotel encumbered by*

4 Stephen Rushmore, MAI, John O'Neill, MAI, and Stephen Rushmore Jr., MAI, *Hotel Market Analysis and Valuation: International Issues and Software Applications*, The Appraisal Institute, Chicago, 2012, p. 279. But there is lack of clarity on this, as the 2004 article referenced in the second footnote does deduct the incentive management fee in determining income to the tangible assets.

5 HotelManagement.net, Top Third Party Management Companies, March 2016. This listing is available upon logging on for a free subscription.

6 AHLA.com, "Lodging Industry Trends 2015." This four-page document can also be found for free on the Internet.

7 Id. All of the data in this paragraph are from the AHLA document.

a long-term management contract, and use the going concern/excess earnings method when valuing a hotel property that is not encumbered by a management contract.

Unsuccessful efforts to unify real estate appraisal theory. The appraisal profession is wrestling with the inconsistency between the appraisal methods for hotels versus other RECEs. The author was one of 10 invited to the Appraisal Practice Board's roundtable, Valuation Issues in Separating Tangible and Intangible Assets, in Washington, D.C., on Oct. 2, 2014.[8] Advocates of both going-concern and Rushmore approaches presented their positions, with only a few chairs flung across the room during the somewhat heated debate. (Pardon the slight exaggeration). The profession's lack of comfort with the dominant Rushmore approach is the likely explanation that The Appraisal Institute's 408-page text by primary author Stephen Rushmore, MAI, *Hotel Market Analysis and Valuation,*[9] essentially does not address the topic of intangible assets or business value in a hotel. While this is the most in-depth source for hotel appraisers (and is heartily recommended here), the over-400-listing index has no entries for intangible, or Rushmore approach, and has a single reference for business value, only mentioning that a market value appraisal may include business value among the component assets of a hotel.[10] That's the only mention or discussion in 400 pages.

How significant are intangible assets in hotels? Hotel development is costly, even for a midlevel limited-service property. Since most intangibles come from the value in excess of real estate costs, intangibles typically represent a small portion of value. Furthermore, the American consumer will not stay at a hotel not being maintained in virtually new condition—even if it's 30 years old. The market requires that carpeting, furnishings, etc. be replaced as they show signs of wear. Franchisors (Hilton Worldwide, Marriott International, etc.) require their franchisees to maintain corporate standards. Franchisees receive "property improvement plans," or "PIPs," when franchisors determine that standards are not being met. Failure to comply with the PIP generally results in the loss of the franchise (or flag). Accordingly, the depreciation that one might expect in a 30-year-old property does not typically occur. By contrast, nursing homes see such depreciation, and the loss in value of the improvements is often largely offset by an increase in business value.

The elimination of intangibles in most hotel appraisals by real estate hotel appraisal specialists is a flawed method, but these same appraisals are usually reasonably accurate, since the intangible asset values are typically small—except when they are not! For hotels, where there is substantial business value, the use of this flawed method can result in large valuation

8 The invitees were Brian Glanville, Bruce Kellogg, David Lennhoff, Daniel Lesser, Richard Marchitelli, Suzanne Mellen, Franz Ross, Carl Sheeler, James Tellatin, and Gordon Smith. The Appraisal Foundation members participating were Rich Baumgardner (APB chair), Jay Fishman (APB vice chair), Barry Shea (Appraisal Standards board chair), David Bunton (The Appraisal Foundation president), John Brenan (The Appraisal Foundation director of appraisal issues), and Adriana Berrocal-Gonzalez (member, APB). Other participants included Robert Parson, the Office of the Comptroller of the Currency's appraisal policy specialist.

9 Stephen Rushmore, MAI, John O'Neill, MAI, and Stephen Rushmore Jr., MAI, *Hotel Market Analysis and Valuation: International Issues and Software Applications*, The Appraisal Institute, Chicago, 2012.

10 Id., p 326.

errors. Appraisers tend to use one-size-fits-all metrics. They tend to use the current mean cap rate even though properties with greater upside potential and better condition deserve lower cap rates (and higher values), and properties with less upside potential and inferior condition warrant higher cap rates (and lower values). When valuing the going concern, hotels that have significant business value will also tend to have higher cap rates. The same one-size-fits-all approach tends to be used with management fees used to remove business value. Most hotel appraisals I have reviewed have imputed management fees of 3% to 4% of revenues. If the business value (BV) is nominal (which is often the case), the use of a 3.5% management fee truly removes profits attributed to the business component of perhaps just 1% to 1.5%, with at least half of the fee being payroll and overhead for the usually hypothetical third-party management company. Capitalization of 1% or 2% of revenues at a 15%-to-25% BV cap rate will yield only a small amount of business value, making the Rushmore Approach quite accurate in measuring tangible asset value in such cases.

Isn't more information better than less? For a high-performing hotel, use of a 3%-to-4% management fee is generally inadequate to remove BV, and yet it is likely that the appraiser will make this one-size-fits-all error. If the true BV is accurately removed, the remaining value will seem low. The appraiser will explain that the value is low because the BV was removed. But wouldn't the client prefer an appraisal that discloses the amount of BV rather than to state that the value is (relatively) low because the BV was removed?

Case study: a full-service hotel with significant business value. The example that follows is the appraisal of an imaginary hotel. The example shows the importance of appraising hotels as going concerns, including values for the intangible assets.

Jake Stewart operated a successful restaurant in the city for many years under the name Jake's Steaks. In 2009, there was a bad fire, but by 2011 the restaurant was rebuilt at a new location, with room to build an attached 100-room Best Western Hotel, named Jake's Best Western Hotel. The land cost $800,000, and the hotel and restaurant cost $10 million to build, including entrepreneurial incentive. The FF&E and other personal property cost another $1.2 million. The franchise agreement was for 20 years, and the capital cost of the franchise, including software, and required training for staff was $120,000. The 82,000-square-foot restaurant and hotel were both immediately successful. In addition to the main dining room, the banquet space could serve groups of up to 100. The synergy of Jake's Steaks' reputation and the hotel resulted in higher-than-market-average occupancy and higher dining revenues than is typical for a smaller full-service hotel. Tragically, in 2014, Jake suffered a heart attack and died, leaving his estate to his three adult children. Jake was a widow, and his son Steve had worked in the business for 15 years, assisting his father, but the siblings were not involved. It is now 2016, and it is our assignment to appraise the hotel, as Steve wants to purchase his siblings' interest. Business continues to be excellent, with earnings growth expected to continue at about 1% each year.

Exhibit 1. Historical and Estimated Hotel Statistics: Subject and Subject's Market

A) Occupancy				B) Average Daily Rate (ADR)				C) Revenue Per Available Room RevPAR = A x B			
Year	Subject	Set	Index	Year	Subject	Set	Index	Year	Subject	Set	Index
2013	87.1%	71.2%	122.3%	2013	$99.01	$98.44	100.6%	2013	$86.24	$70.09	123.0%
2014	86.8%	71.4%	121.6%	2014	$100.77	$99.86	100.9%	2014	$87.47	$71.30	122.7%
2015	87.0%	70.8%	122.9%	2015	$103.89	$103.78	100.1%	2015	$90.38	$73.48	123.0%
Pro Forma	**87.2%**	**71.5%**	**122.0%**	**Pro Forma**	**$106.00**	**$106.00**	**100.0%**	**Pro Forma**	**$92.46**	**$75.79**	**122.0%**

Exhibit 1 compares the subject to its competitive set, using data from STR.com.[11] Jake's has similar average daily rates (ADR) compared to the competition but has superior occupancy. Since the subject is outperforming its competition in terms of RevPAR while having similar location, quality, condition, and amenities, there is evidence of significant excess earnings or business value at Jake's Best Western. The market is considered stable, and our investigations indicate that no new hotels are planned in the immediate market area for the foreseeable future, making a detailed supply and demand analysis unnecessary.

Since the market is judged to be stable, it is not necessary to provide a discounted cash flow analysis. Instead, a single-period capitalization is performed (Exhibit 2), which is based mostly on historical performance, with some adjustments. To the right of each line item is a brief explanation of how it was derived.

Capitalization rate analysis. The comparison to STR data demonstrates that Jake's is achieving a substantial occupancy premium over its competitive set. Further, the ratio of food and beverage (F&B) to room revenues is typically in the range of 25% to 30% for smaller full-service properties, yet the subject is at 52%. Both factors indicate large business value. An analysis of *Pratt's Stats* data and other sources indicates that the cost of capital is significantly higher for BV, usually in a range of 15% to 30% (pretax). High BV cap rates are necessary due to the lesser certainty of their earnings. The BV component of a RECE tends to be reasonably durable compared to other types of BV, so cap rates of 15% to 20% are most often applicable. For this appraisal, a BV cap rate of 18% is selected. A much lower cap rate will be used for the Best Western franchise, as this asset is more durable than the goodwill, and the adopted cap rate is 10%. (Hotel and other real estate appraisals typically use pretax discount rates and cap rates).

The real estate cap rate is found relatively easily. Since most hotels have minimal BV, with the small BV typically stripped out by imputing a 3%-to-4% management fee, and with personal property

11 The property owner typically receives monthly reports comparing the subject's average daily rate (ADR), occupancy rate, and revenue per available room (RevPAR) to its primary competitors. STR requires a minimum of four hotels in the set to ensure confidentiality. It is the appraiser's responsibility that the proper competitive set is used. If the owner's report has data for a group of three-star hotels when the subject is a two-star property, or if nearby competitors are omitted, then the appraiser should select the competitive set and purchase his or her own report from STR (found at STR.com). STR reports currently cost $475 and should be ordered a week in advance, as STR charges a significant premium for expedited service. Many users of hotel appraisals require use of STR reports.

Exhibit 2. Pro Forma Analysis

		Jake's Best Western			
1	Rooms in service	100			
2	ADR	$106.00			
3	Occ. rate	87.2%			
4	Available rooms	36,500			
5		**$ Amount**	**Ratio**	**$/Room**	
	Revenue				**Derived**
6	Rooms	$3,374,929	63.9%	$33,749	31,839 rooms @ $106 ADR
7	Food & bev.	$1,754,963	33.2%	$17,550	Based on history: 52% of room revenues
8	Other income	$151,872	2.9%	$1,519	Based on history: 4.5% of room revenues
9	**Total revenue**	$5,281,763	100.0%	$52,818	
		$ Amount	**Ratio**	**$/Room**	
	Departmental Expenses				
10	Room supplies, cleaning & front desk	$636,779	12.1%	$6,368	Payroll & supplies @ $20 per occ. room
11	Restauant - F&B cost	$561,588	10.6%	$5,616	32% of F&B revenues
12	Restaurant - payroll	$508,939	9.6%	$5,089	29% of F&B revenues
13	Telephone & cable	$47,000	0.9%	$470	Historical cost inflated 3%
14	Total dept. expenses	$1,754,306	33.2%	$17,543	
	General exp. & reserves				
15	Payroll: Admin-GM (Steve)	$100,000	1.9%	$1,000	Payroll cost of Steve Stewart as GM
16	Asst. mgr & rest. mgr	$177,000	3.4%	$1,770	Allo payroll lines incl. taxes & benefits
17	Sales & office	$173,000	3.3%	$1,730	1 FT sales, 1 FT accting., 2 PT admin. asst.
18	Repairs & maint. - incl. payroll	$140,000	2.7%	$1,400	1 FT maint., 1 PT maint., & supplies/misc.
19	Laundry: Incl payroll	$48,000	0.9%	$480	Historical inflated 3%
20	Admin & gen. & Prof. fees	$51,000	1.0%	$510	Historical inflated 3%
21	Marketing & commissions	$52,818	1.0%	$528	1% of revenues
22	Franchise fees	$253,120	4.8%	$2,531	7.5% of room revenues
23	All utilities	$184,500	3.5%	$1,845	$2.25/SF for 82,00 SF
24	Management fee	$132,044	2.5%	$1,320	Asset mgmt. earned by Steve: 2.5% of rev.
25	Property taxes	$310,000	5.9%	$3,100	Historical inflated 3%, & similar to comps.
26	Insurance	$32,991	0.6%	$330	Historical inflated 3%
27	Reserves for replacement	$158,453	3.0%	$1,585	3% of revenue
28	**Total gen. exp & reserves**	$1,812,925	34.3%	$18,129	
29	**Total op. exp. & reserves**	$3,567,232	67.5%	$35,672	
30	**Net operating income**	$1,714,532	32.5%	$17,145	Note: 32.5% NOI margin is above average
31	Overall capitalization rate	9.91%			From Total excess earnings model (TEEM)
32	Capitalized value	$17,300,000			NOI/cap rate

values being just a small part of value (though at higher cap rates), the real estate cap rate is derived to be only 50 to 75 basis points lower than the overall rate. Sale comps and published surveys indicate that good quality properties such as the subject warrant overall rates of 8.0% to 8.25%, so let us say 8.125%. Accordingly, the adopted real estate cap rate here is about 60 basis points lower, at 7.5%.

The personal property cap rate needs to account for its lack of durability. While there is a reserve for replacement in the pro forma, its purpose is mostly to fund replacement of parking lots, carpeting, and other real estate improvements. A personal property cap rate sufficient to account for replacements and risk is estimated at 15%.

Estimating tangible asset values via the cost approach. The principal of substitution makes appraisers consider what it would cost to replace the property as a means of valuing the real estate. It cost $10,000,000 for just the building and site improvements in 2011 (including entrepreneurial incentive). The current cost[12] has increased to $160 per square foot for the 82,000-square-foot hotel and restaurant, and this amount of $13,120,000 will be depreciated by an estimated 8%, since the subject is no longer in new condition. Adding the $900,000 current value of the subject land (found via comparison to other recent land sales), the subject real estate value is found via the cost approach:

Apply depreciation to cost-new of improvements: $13,120,000 × 0.92 =	$12,070,000
Add current land value: 2.0 acres @ $450,000/acre or $9,000/room =	$900,000
Real estate value via cost approach	$12,970,000

The personal property had an original cost of $1,200,000. Allowing for 10% in cost increases, and then depreciating by 25% since it is not new, the personal property is valued at $990,000, which is rounded to $1,000,000.

The franchise agreement and highest and best use. Some appraisers argue that the value of a franchise agreement is the value difference between operating with the franchise and operating without a franchise. If true, the franchise value would be a large percentage of the going-concern value. What this premise ignores is that the appraisal must assume that the real estate will be used and improved at its "highest and best use." Highest and best use must meet these four tests: (a) physically possible; (b) legally permissible; (c) financially feasible; and (d) maximally productive. It is the use that will result in the highest possible value for the property. In following these requirements, the property cannot be rundown, but it also means that, if there is space for a parking

12 Marshall & Swift (marshallswift.com) is the recognized source for base cost estimates for various building types. A developer's fee, also known as entrepreneurial incentive, is added to the base cost, with the incentive typically around 10% to 20% of the base cost of the building and site improvements. Its data also offer geographic adjustments.

lot, it must be developed. And, if the highest and best use is as a hotel, analysis must be done to determine how many rooms should be developed. Highest and best use analysis will determine whether the hotel should be full service or limited service and at what quality level. For example, developing a luxury hotel in a location that cannot support high room rates represents a failure to achieve the highest and best use. Most hotels should have a brand or flag, though there are high-quality independents that are most profitably operated without a flag.

But, for most hotels, achieving the highest and best use necessitates having an appropriate flag. Our case study subject is a standard full-service hotel. The Best Western flag is just about right, while making it an EconoLodge (with too low a brand average daily rate) or a Hyatt Place (with too high a brand ADR) would probably be a mistake. There are a handful of flags that would be appropriate, such as Clarion, Holiday Inn, or Sheraton. They are virtual commodities, as each flag would accomplish more or less the same thing in getting the subject better recognized by travelers. Jake bought his franchise for $120,000. If Best Western International could have charged more, it would have. This cost approach data supports that the $120,000 cost was the original value. As a 20-year agreement, there has been some amortization, though not on a straight-line basis, since renewal agreements are less costly than the original agreement generally. The estimated remaining flag value is amortized to $100,000.

One last scenario regarding highest and best use may add clarity. If the hotel did not have TVs in each room, occupancy would plummet, and room revenues would fall by a million dollars or more. Yet this deficiency can be cured by purchasing 100 TVs for $500 each, or $50,000 for the hotel. Failure to have TVs in rooms is a violation of the principle of highest and best use just as is failure to have an appropriate flag.

Total excess earnings model (TEEM). We have now determined all of the inputs necessary to complete the TEEM[13] model. All that remains involves addition, subtraction, multiplication, and division. First, the model is shown before the math in Exhibit 3.

The final steps are as follows:

1. *Calculate the income of the asset.* Multiply the cap rate for each component asset by the appraised value for the real estate, the personal property, and the flag. (The incomes are respectively: $972,750, $150,000, and $10,000).

2. *Subtract each of the calculated income allocations (Step 1) from the pro forma NOI of $1,714,532.* The result of $581,782 is the excess earnings, or income to the BV.

13 Franz H. Ross, BVR webinar, Business Valuation for Banks, September 2014, slides 44-47. Also, "Sorting Out the Value of a Business that Owns its Real Estate," (interview of Franz Ross), *Valuing Companies with Real Estate: Appraisal Experts Untangle the Issues*, 2014, pp 16-19. And Franz H. Ross and Adam A. Alessi, "Using TEEM-Work to Extend Your Reach on the Real Estate/Business Value Continuum," *The Appraisal Journal*, Summer 2011, pp 229-239.

Exhibit 3. Total Excess Earnings Model (TEEM) Jake's Best Western Hotel

	Real Estate	FF&E/Personal Property	Intangibles: Best Western Flag	Intangibles: Business Value	Combined Going Concern
1. Appraised Value	**$12,970,000**	**$1,000,000**	**$100,000**		
1A Source	Cost Approach	Cost Approach	Cost Approach	V = I/R	Sum of Asset Values
2. NOI Allocation (Or Net EBITDAR)					**$1,714,532**
2A Source	I = V*R	I = V*R	I = V*R	Residual or "Excess" Earnings	Pro Forma NOI
3.Capitalization Rate	**7.50%**	**15.00%**	**10.00%**	**18.00%**	
3A Source	Typical Hotel Real Estate Cap Rate	Typical PP Cap Rate	Low Intangibles Cap Rate	Typical Hotel BV Cap Rate	R = I/V

3. *Calculate business value.* Divide the income to intangibles (or excess earnings) of $581,782 by the 18% BV cap rate. The result is $3,230,000 after rounding.

4. *Get the total value of the going concern.* This is found by adding the component assets together, and the result is $17,300,000. The cap rate for the going concern of 9.91% is calculated by dividing the NOI into the GC value.

The completed TEEM model is presented in Exhibit 4.

Reconciliation. Often it is best to use sale comps or surveys to peg average hotel cap rates. But when there is an indication of above-average business value, the likelihood is that such a hotel will have an above-average cap rate due to the BV, but how much higher? In our example, the TEEM model estimates a rate about 180 basis points above the typical hotel overall rate (9.91% compared to 8.125%).

What is the result via the Rushmore approach? Had almost any real estate hotel appraisal specialist performed thies assignment, the Rushmore approach would have been used, and the results would have been different. Following are the two most likely scenarios, assuming the only difference to the income analysis was relying on the Rushmore approach:

1. The analysis is unchanged except that the 2.5% management fee would be increased to the top of the narrow range usually adopted, at 4.0% of revenues. Total NOI would be reduced to $1,635,305, and the total value (of tangible assets) spikes from the excess earnings and cost approach method all the way to $20,125,000 when capitalizing the NOI by a typical hotel cap rate of 8.125%. Exhibit 5 shows how the Rushmore approach can substantially overvalue a hotel.

2. Somehow, the appraiser opines a management fee sufficient to truly remove the business and flag values, or perhaps the appraiser uses the cost approach. The management

Exhibit 4. Total Excess Earnings Model (TEEM) Jake's Best Western Hotel					
	Real Estate	FF&E/Personal Property	Intangibles: Best Western Flag	Intangibles: Business Value	Combined Going Concern
1. Appraised Value	**$12,970,000**	**$1,000,000**	**$100,000**	**$3,230,000**	**$17,300,000**
1A Source	Cost Approach	Cost Approach	Cost Approach	V = I/R	Sum of Asset Values
2. NOI Allocation (Or Net EBITDAR)	**$972,750**	**$150,000**	**$10,000**	**$581,782**	**$1,714,532**
2A Source	I = V*R	I = V*R	I = V*R	Residual or "Excess" Earnings	Pro Forma NOI
3. Capitalization Rate	**7.50%**	**15.00%**	**10.00%**	**18.00%**	**9.91%**
3A Source	Typical Hotel Real Estate Cap Rate	Typical PP Cap Rate	Low Intangibles Cap Rate	Typical Hotel BV Cap Rate	R = I/V

Exhibit 5. Total Excess Earnings Model (TEEM) Jake's Using 4% Management Fee and No Intangibles: Has the BV Been Removed?					
	Real Estate	FF&E/Personal Property	Intangibles: Best Western Flag	Intangibles: Business Value	Tangible Assets Only
1 Appraised Value	**$19,125,000**	**$1,000,000**			**$20,125,000**
1A Source	Residual value	Cost Approach			V = I/R
2 NOI Allocation	**$1,485,305**	**$150,000**			**$1,635,305**
2A Source	Residual Income	I = V*R			Pro Forma NOI: 4% Mgmt Fee
3 Cap Rate	**7.77%**	**15.00%**			**8.125%**
3A Source	R = I/V	Typical PP Cap Rate			Typical Hotel Cap Rate

fee necessary to remove intangible assets is the existing fee from the pro forma plus the income from BV and from the flag (as shown in the original analysis).

Management fee = $132,044 + $581,782 + $10,000 = $723,826

This revised management fee of $723,826 is 13.7% of pro forma revenues, and this fee removes all intangible income and all intangible assets, but the author is skeptical that an appraiser using the Rushmore approach would reach that conclusion.

Finally, even if the appraiser did use the cost approach and concluded the same tangible asset value of $13,970,000, that Rushmore approach appraisal is less useful because it stops there and does not conclude the value of the business, flag, or total going concern. This makes the Rushmore approach appraisal less useful than the excess earnings/going concern appraisal, whether the report is for an estate, financing, tax certiorari, marital, or other purpose.

Hotel appraisal nuggets. This article focuses on asset allocation—a complex topic. The following are some other concepts—some alluded to in this article—which are pointed out below:[14]

- *Business value or land value.* In some cases, it is the dirt (location) and not the hotel's business aspects that creates the value premium.
- *How to value land.* Land sales are public record, and sales of area land used to develop hotels are best (if at arm's length).
- *Look for business value drivers.* Properties with extensive restaurant, banquet, and meeting use can create substantial business value from synergies with the hotel rooms.
- *Location, location, location.* Not only a prominent physical location, but online location (e.g., on the first page of recognized travel sites' recommendations) is also an indicator of BV.
- *Are new hotels in the pipeline?* If so, occupancy rates and ADR can be negatively impacted. A single-period capitalization method isn't enough—a DCF may be necessary when changes are occurring in the market.
- *Room expense and franchise fees.* Include the payroll cost of housekeeping staff and front-desk staff along with room supplies in the room expense line, and separate all amounts paid to the franchisor as a general operating expense named "franchise fees."
- *Utility expense.* This expense varies considerably among properties, so consider using expense per square foot of building area as a unit of comparison.
- *Management fee.* As we've discussed throughout this article, most hotel appraisers use management fees of 3% to 4% of revenues and state that they have removed the intangibles with this fee. For the going-concern appraisal recommended here, reduce this fee to an asset management fee, as was done in the case study. Trustees of estates typically charge management fees in the range of 1% of assets managed, whether the assets are traded stocks or a hotel. The case study management fee at 2.5% of revenues is equivalent to 0.76% of the asset value, which is a reasonable asset management fee.[15]
- *Sales comparison approach.* Analysis of local sales of operating hotels similar to the subject that sold within the last year or two is an important way to test the value found via the income approach. The best unit of comparison is typically price per room. Adjustments

14 Expanded comments on these points can be found in the BVR special report, *What It's Worth: Hotel Business Value,* from which this article has been adapted (available at www.bvresources.com).

15 Another type of management fee exists for an owner-managed hotel, which is part of a small group owned by the same owner. It is likely that a number of functions such as accounting and marketing are performed at the headquarters level, with only a skeleton staff at the property level. Higher management fees are needed to cover these mostly payroll costs and are not indicative of business value.

will have to be made to the comparables for market conditions/time, location, quality and condition, functionality, amenities, and business components.

Conclusion. For hotel appraisals, one alternative that has been advocated is for a real estate appraiser to value the real estate and a business appraiser to value the business component. The U.S. Small Business Administration (SBA) no longer allows this, according to its latest SOP. In fact, SBA requires a real estate appraiser with experience in the property type for all appraisals of special purpose properties. That appraiser must allocate to land, building, equipment, and intangible assets.[16] Aside from SBA, using two appraisers is not recommended here for the following reasons:

- Coordination between the two appraisers is difficult and even unlikely. This creates a strong likelihood of cash flow double counts or omissions.[17] Regarding the personal property, which appraiser should value the swimming pool equipment (is it attached to the real estate or not?)

- It is more costly for the client to pay for two appraisals, and the added time coordinating with another appraiser may make the project more costly for each appraiser in terms of time.

The owner of hotel real estate that is third-party managed also owns the majority of the business value unless the third-party manager has a contract extending at least five years into the future. If the operator has a one-year contract, that operator has no assurance of being in place for more than a year, and therefore the property owner will own most of the business value, and asset allocations should be made accordingly.

Hotels are, in some ways, an easy-to-appraise property type thanks to the existence of STR market reports. It still takes skill to resolve whether above-average profitability is due to the excellent location (land) or business aspects. Estimating future occupancy rates takes due diligence.

The real estate appraisal community appraises nursing homes, C-stores, quarries, golf courses, and other businesses as going concerns, but almost all real estate appraisers will not appraise a hotel as a going concern. The Rushmore approach may be the best approach when the hotel is operated under a third-party management contract but can result in large valuation errors when there is no third-party management. This odd practice does create an opportunity for those willing to provide a more useful (and perhaps more accurate) appraisal by valuing the going concern for hotels unencumbered by management contracts, which are clearly the majority of hotels.

16 U.S. Small Business Administration, *SOP 50 10 5(H),* May 1, 2015, p. 172.

17 Franz H Ross, "How Too Many Cooks Can Spoil the Broth: A Case Study," *Valuing Companies With Real Estate: Appraisal Experts Untangle the Issues,* 2014, pp. 10-15.

Franz H. Ross, *CBA, CVA, MRICS, is a Certified General Real Estate Appraiser in New York and is complex asset specialist for First Niagara Bank (soon to be KeyBank) in Buffalo, N.Y. Ross can be reached at 716-843-1889 or at* franz.ross@fnfg.com. *The author reminds readers that the numbers and metrics used in the case study are not from a real property and should not be relied upon. Contact Ross if you would like a copy of the Excel file used in this article.*

IRS Reasonable Compensation Job Aid: Healthcare Perspective

By Mark O. Dietrich, CPA/ABV, MBA, MST

(Editor's note: This is an excerpt from the author's chapter, "Using Work RVUs and 'Particular Market' Rates to Establish Fair Market Value of Physician Compensation" (Chapter 15), in BVR's Guide to Physician Practice Valuation, *3rd edition.)*

Aside from examinations that result in court cases, this is the first significant, recently published view on the issue of reasonable compensation from the IRS. It specifically states it is for both not-for-profit and for-profit entities. The Aid suggests at the outset that courts favor the market approach, but much of the later text seemingly contradicts or at least weakens this statement, as does an understanding of the usual application of the market approach.

Consistent with a discussion of benefits in excess of the direct compensation typically utilized as the basis for opinions based on survey data, the Aid lists the following fringe benefits that are part of "total compensation" for tax purposes:

1. Automobile allowance;
2. Awards/prizes over $25 in value (gift cards or certificates in any amount);
3. Back pay awards;
4. Bonuses—cash or noncash;
5. Cafeteria plan;
6. Commissions;
7. Company-owned or -leased airplane;
8. Company-owned or -leased cars;
9. Disability payments;
10. Discount on property or services;

11. Educational reimbursements;
12. Free or subsidized lodging;
13. Golden parachute payments;
14. Life insurance over $50,000 in value;
15. Low-interest loans;
16. Meal allowances and/or reimbursements (when away from home overnight);
17. Memberships in athletic facilities;
18. Mortgage, house insurance, and real property taxes;
19. Moving expenses/relocation allowances;
20. Nonqualified stock bonus plan;
21. Partnership or S corporation distributions;
22. Pension and profit sharing plans;
23. Nonqualified stock option plan;
24. Reimbursements for loss on sale of houses—job-related move;
25. Rent;
26. Severance pay;
27. Scholarships/fellowships;
28. Sick payments; and
29. Vacations (free or discounted).

Of these, Item Nos. 4 (signing and retention bonuses), 5, 11, 14, 16, 19, 22, and 23 are commonly found in hospital employment of physicians. It is rare indeed to find an opinion of fair market value that covers this broad definition of compensation.

The Aid's definition. "Reasonable Compensation is defined by Treas. Reg. § 1.162-7(b)(3) as the amount that would ordinarily be paid for like services by like organizations in like circumstances, and this standard is adopted in Treas. Reg. § 53.4958-4(b)(1)(ii)(A). Thus, the concept has two prongs:

1. "Amount Test—focuses on the reasonableness of the total amount paid; and
2. "Purpose Test—examines the services for which the compensation was paid."

This is one of the more significant statements in the Aid as it is consistent with the regulations under the intermediate sanctions provision that reasonable compensation for tax-exempts is subject to the ordinary and necessary test of Section 162 and its regulations.

The Aid lists the following requirements of Section 162:

3. The employee's qualifications;
4. The nature, extent, and scope of the employee's duties;
5. The employee's background and experience;
6. The employee's knowledge of the business;
7. The size and complexity of the business;
8. The time devoted by the employee to the business;
9. The economic conditions generally and locally;
10. The character and amount of responsibility of the employee;
11. Whether the compensation is predetermined based on activities to be performed or not determined until the end of the tax year;
12. Amounts paid to the employee in prior years;
13. The salary policy of the taxpayer as to all employees; and
14. The amounts paid by similar-size businesses in the same area to equally qualified employees for similar services.

One question that should immediately come to mind is whether and to what extent survey data used in the market approach can address any of these 12 factors. For example, Factor No. 2—"the nature, extent, and scope of the employee's duties"—and Factor No. 6 were key elements in the court's decision in *U.S. v. Campbell*,[1] a case arising out of the University of Medicine and Dentistry of New Jersey (UMDNJ) investigation.

Perhaps the most striking factor where survey data are considered is Factor No. 12, "the amounts paid by similar size businesses in the *same area to equally qualified employees for similar services.*" Looking to the Stark regulations, we find "usually, the fair market price is the price at which bona fide sales have been consummated for assets of like type, quality, and quantity *in a particular market at the time of acquisition, or the compensation that has been included in bona fide service agreements with*

1 *United States v. Campbell*, 2011 U.S. Dist. LEXIS 1207 (D.N.J. Jan. 4, 2011).

comparable terms at the time of the agreement." It is often mistakenly believed that there is a wide disparity between fair market value for Stark and IRS purposes, but the history of the term "fair market value" since 1959's Revenue Ruling 59-60 belies that belief. It is well-established in the facts presented earlier in the chapter that the survey data lack "same area" or "particular market" specificity—even if government regulators have historically failed to ascertain that.

Factor No. 10, "historical compensation," is widely ignored in fair market value compensation opinions, as evidenced by the significant or enormous disparities between survey rates and the amount insurers operating in the local market of a physician actually pay. To pose the question rhetorically yet again: How can a physician who historically has been willing to work for $38 per wRVU suddenly be worth $50 or even $60 per wRVU? Importantly, the Aid states: "A large increase to an employee's compensation may indicate unreasonable compensation unless the duties of the employee changed significantly." In the 2015 *Citizens Medical* qui tam settlement, this wide disparity between historic market rate-driven compensation paid to cardiologists subsequently employed by Citizens Medical at a substantial increase in compensation, which then created losses for the hospital, was key, despite the hospital's defense that an expert report used a survey median. Although the case was settled for a fine and did not go to trial, rulings on motions during the litigation made the likely result inevitable:

> Citizens also argues that Relators' allegations are insufficient because they do not allege that the cardiologists actually made above-market income and, instead, that an expert report they rely on shows that the cardiologists' salaries are below the national median. They thus argue Relators have not sufficiently alleged that the cardiologists are receiving improper remuneration as is required for AKS- and Stark-based liability.
>
> Given the Rule 12 posture in which Relators allegations must be taken as true, the Court disagrees. Relators have made several allegations that, if true, provide a strong inference of the existence of a kickback scheme. Particularly, the Court notes Relators' allegations that the cardiologists' income more than doubled after they joined Citizens, even while their own practices were costing Citizens between $400,000 and $1,000,000 per year in net losses. Even if the cardiologists were making less than the national median salary for their profession, the allegations that they began making substantially more money once they were employed by Citizens is sufficient to allow an inference that they were receiving improper remuneration. This inference is particularly strong given that it would make little apparent economic sense for Citizens to employ the cardiologists at a loss unless it were doing so for some ulterior motive—a motive Relators identify as a desire to induce referrals. Relators' allegations are more than sufficient to satisfy Rule 9(b) as interpreted by Grubbs. The AKS- and Stark-predicated FCA allegations concerning the cardiologist group survive the motion to dismiss.[2]

Financial analysis. In describing the type of financial analysis an examiner should undertake, the Aid states: "The financial performance of the taxpayer's business must be compared with the industry as well as with similar businesses (competitors). From this perspective, it can be determined whether or not the taxpayer's business is below average, average, or above average. The result of this analysis then provides support for selecting the compensation of the employee being analyzed at the lower, middle, or upper end of a range." As *Citizens Medical,*

2 *United States of America, ex. Rel. Dakshesh Parikh, et al., Plaintiffs, v. Citizens Medical Center, et al., Defendants,* United States District Court, S.D. Texas, Victoria Division. Sept. 20, 2013, 977 F.Supp.2d 654 (2013).

Tuomey, and *Halifax,* to name a few, found, losses and compensation were very different in the hospital-employment setting than in the private-practice setting.

Valuation approaches. In its discussion of the approaches to valuing compensation, the Aid notes that the question of reasonable compensation is: "How much compensation would be paid for this same position, held by a nonowner in an arm's-length employment relationship, at a similar company?"

There is an extensive discussion of the independent investor test under the income approach along with the *Mulcahy*[3] case, perhaps the most significant recent case involving compensation of professionals and the use of surveys in establishing reasonable compensation.

Rationale for the independent investor test. "The rationale behind the Independent Investor Test is that investors pay employees to work to increase the value of the assets entrusted to their management. A high rate of return indicates that the assets' value increased and that the employee provided valuable services. Thus, if investors obtain returns above what they should reasonably expect, an employee's salary is presumptively reasonable." Now, the argument is made that tax-exempt organizations are not "profit-making"—something that is not necessarily apparent by looking at financial statements available on Guidestar, for example—but that community benefit or a community needs analysis overrides a need for return. There are certainly examples of where this is true, and one would imagine that the appraiser and/or management should document the disposition of the asset owner's (hospital's) return on investment in a fair market value analysis. If all or a portion of the return is being used to subsidize physician compensation, a community benefit needs to be present.

Reconciliation of approaches. Notably, the Aid concludes that "the reconciliation in the case of Reasonable Compensation will generally rest heavily on the market approach" with the income and cost approaches "used to refine the reasonable compensation amount."

Tax-exempt entities. Section 4948 deals with intermediate sanctions. "A reasonable compensation analysis for the purposes of Section 4958 relies upon the principles of reasonableness in the Section 162 context that have already been discussed." The Aid appendix uses a university example for tax-exempts, with issues specific thereto that provide only limited insight into a healthcare setting, but broadly speaking some useful points include:

1. Plan on preparing a complete compensation analysis using as many data sources and analysis approaches as is feasible, with a minimal reliance on summary figures from databases;

2. Consider the appropriate market population for tax-exempts; generally speaking, we would start with both taxable and tax-exempt comparables (which is expressly permitted in the Treas. Reg. § 53.4958-4(b)(1)(ii)(A)) and make an appropriate decision as to what comparable set is most appropriate for the specific facts and circumstances;

3 *Mulcahy, Pauritsch, Salvador & Co., Ltd. v. Commissioner,* T.C. Memo. 2011-74 (2011).

3. Reference the most reasonable of comparables, striving for at least five comparables if possible; comparables must consider both the position being evaluated (actual activities performed) and the entity in which the position exists;

4. Make appropriate adjustments to the comparable data to reflect the subject and to fully explain the logic of those adjustments;

5. Perform some type of a multifactor analysis such as that of the 5th Circuit in *Owensby & Kritikos, Inc. v. Commissioner*, 819 F.2d 1315 (5th Cir. 1987) (court agreed with Service position that compensation was unreasonable but disagreed on amounts considered reasonable compensation for years at issue);

6. Consider the viewpoint and the financial requirements of an *independent investor* as the 2nd Circuit did in *Rapco Inc. v. Commissioner*, 85 F.3d 950 (2d Cir. 1996) (court agreed with Service position that compensation was unreasonable but disagreed on amounts considered reasonable compensation for years at issue) (emphasis added);

7. Focus on total compensation rather than its individual parts as the 5th Circuit made clear in *Owensby & Kritikos, Inc. v. Commissioner*, 819 F.2d 1315 (5th Cir. 1987) (court agreed with Service position that compensation was unreasonable but disagreed on amounts considered reasonable compensation for years at issue); and

8. Avoid analyzing isolated periods without considering long-term patterns, especially where a bonus plan is in place. See *Dexsil Corp. v. Commissioner*, 147 F.3d 96 (2d. Cir. 1998) (court agreed with Service position that compensation was unreasonable but disagreed on amounts considered reasonable compensation for years at issue).

Summary. The *IRS Reasonable Compensation Aid* requires the following tests or analyses to be performed, which can be met by using the RVU model:

1. *Amount test.* "Total compensation" in the IRS Aid has a broader definition than that appraisers typically employ. Similarly, wRVUs include all physician compensation and benefits, such that using the RVU model enables the appraiser to meet the IRS definition.

2. *Purpose test.* This test can be likened to the prohibition against paying for referrals under the Stark law and anti-kickback statute. The sole purpose of reasonable compensation is to pay for labor. The *Mulcahy* case demonstrates that survey data including profit distributions do not meet the purpose test.

3. *Comparability test.* In a definition close to that in the Stark regulations, the Aid requires use of "the amounts paid by similar size businesses in the same area to equally qualified employees for similar services." The RVU model meets this definition, while surveys rarely do.

4. *Historical compensation test.* Historical compensation in a given market area is the strongest predictor of future compensation since it is based on third-party contracts with local-market payers. The RVU model specifically meets this requirement.

5. *Independent investor test.* As the Aid and many court cases find, differentiating between return on labor and return on investment is critical to the determination of reasonable compensation. By enabling the appraiser to differentiate between: (1) PC and TC revenue and profits; (2) a shortfall or surplus in peRVUs; and (3) wRVUs and peRVUs attributable to midlevel providers, along with physician wRVUs, the RVU model generates the data for use in the independent investor analysis.

Mark O. Dietrich, *CPA/ABV, MBA, MST, is a nationally recognized author, speaker, and expert in the field of healthcare valuation. He serves as Of Counsel to Meyers, Harrison & Pia. Mark's career experience includes serving as partner-in-charge of the annual audit of an 80-physician tax-exempt faculty group practice, representation of tax-exempt and taxable entities in Internal Revenue Service field audits, participation in the development of a 250-physician independent network and negotiation of its managed care and Medicare Advantage contracts, and more than 400 valuation engagements in the healthcare industry.*

Coping With the Challenges of Valuing a Cannabis-Related Firm

Editor's note: Valuing a cannabis-related business is not much different from valuing any other business except for one important fact: This business is based on a product that is illegal to grow or sell under current federal law. How this challenge is dealt with in states that have legalized it is the focus of this article excerpted from a guide[1] to valuing this type of firm. This article is based on material from Jim Marty and Ron Seigneur, both of whom are valuation practitioners in Colorado, one of the first states to legalize adult recreational cannabis.

When valuing a cannabis business, you can often approach the cash flow analysis with the same formula used in many other valuations: Present value of any asset is equal to the cash flow divided by the risk less growth, as shown in Exhibit 1. The critical issue in this industry, though, is the lack of reliable historical cash flow information, which requires the application of a discounted cash flow analysis based on projected performance.

Exhibit 1. Present Value

$$PV = \frac{CF_1}{k - g}$$

Where

CF_1 = cash flow expected in the next period

k = discount rate

g = growth rate (in perpetuity)

As with any business, with a cannabis retail operation or medical dispensary, you have to switch your net income to a cash flow by adding depreciation and taking away capital expenditures. You also have to add (or subtract) your working capital requirements to get to enterprise cash flow and then take away debt service and add loan proceeds. This brings you to cash flow to equity (see Exhibit 2). Nothing changes in the cannabis industry other than to really understand where these numbers come from.

Given that this business has operated in the open—officially legal first in Colorado—for less than a decade and many businesses have been around for only a few months or years, it is no surprise that there are very few reliable benchmarks in the cannabis industry from the point of view of a business valuation. More information is emerging, but it is anecdotal for the most part and very jurisdictional-specific.

1 *What It's Worth: Value and Business Challenges in the Budding Cannabis Industry*, August 2016, Business Valuation Resources, LLC.

Exhibit 2. Cash Flow Analysis	
	Net income after taxes
Plus	Depreciation
Less	Capital expenditures
Plus/minus	Working capital requirements
Equals	Enterprise cash flow
Less	Debt service
Plus	Loan proceeds
Equals	Cash flow to equity

Business appraisers have to come up with workarounds in this situation. Look at what investors expect to receive in the public stock market, add in the additional risk of being invested in this industry, and then apply professional judgment. In a more established industry, an investor might be content with a 20%-to-25% return; in this one—with the regulatory oversight of federal, state, and municipal authorities and leasing, banking, cash, and security issues—the investor might be looking for a 40%-to-50% return.[2]

Other factors to consider include location, competitors, the depth of management, and whether it has good operating procedures and a formalized long-term lease. Is there adequate parking, visibility, and access? As another example of the radical trends in this sector, enterprises involved in the cultivation part of the industry are seeing very dynamic changes as small urban-based grow operations migrate to larger commercial, often rural, facilities, covering many acres and using state-of-the-art technology.

Thus, a cannabis business valuation is similar to any other in some ways, but the particular issues in the cannabis business can affect the cash flow. Pay close attention to vetting forecasts, tax affecting the cash flow, the potential liability to the IRS, and other risk factors unique to the industry. It is important to recognize that finding a dispensary operator with reliable projections will be unusual.

Vetting forecasts. When assessing a forecast, in the cultivation sector, for example, make sure you tour the warehouse and the garden; ask what kind of crop the cannabis growers are expecting to have in the next six months and what their annual capacity is. Get a firm understanding of the expertise involved in the grow and how much tenure these individuals have.

An important factor to consider is the number of plants in the ground. There will be three cannabis harvests or more a year because cannabis growers plant in phases. This "perpetual garden" practice ensures plants can be harvested and dried weekly. Get a thorough understanding of the lighting scheme utilized and the philosophy of the lead cultivator toward target plant sizes and varieties produced.

Ask about crop failures. Even the best operations can have a crop failure, so find out how many failures and why. If the crop failures are minimal, the chance of the business being profitable going forward is very much enhanced. Remember, if you grow it, you can sell it, but price points are beginning to moderate in some markets due to increased capacity, better technology, and competitive pressures.

2 Chris Walsh, "Appraising a Marijuana Business: Q&A With Valuations Expert Ronald Seigneur," *Marijuana Business Daily*, Sept. 10, 2014, mjbizdaily.com.

Various parts of the plant can be sold—not just the desirable flowers that dry into what are called the buds, but the leaves can be harvested and sold to the infused products manufacturers. Ask what the lines of revenue are. Ask about the cannabis growers' expansion plans.

Tax affecting the cash flow. Generally, when tax affecting the cash flow, you want to apply a fairly high marginal rate by taxing the gross profit. If the business has not been handling IRC §280E, regarding the deductibility of business expenses, in compliance with how the IRS would like to see it, you may need to book an unrecorded liability for potential IRS audits. If the dispensary has had IRS audits, ask whether they have been resolved. Remember, many dispensaries have only been in operation for a short period, so check for the possible liability of IRS audits. How is §280E handled? If the dispensaries have been ignoring §280E, consider making a valuation adjustment to record potential IRS tax assessments.

Identifying risk factors. When considering risk in a cannabis business, never forget that the federal government considers selling cannabis illegal. You need to understand the Department of Justice (DOJ) memos (listed in Exhibit 3) and the IRS chief counsel's memo[3] and consider how they affect your risk.

These memos certainly appear to reduce risk; the DOJ is saying, "If the dispensary owner stays compliant, you are actually doing what we want you to do." In fact, the Cole memo basically quotes the Colorado regulatory system, and the guidance it provides is being practiced in Colorado.

3 IRS Chief Counsel Memorandum 201504011.

Exhibit 3. Regulatory Information: Cannabis-Related Businesses
James M. Cole, U.S. Department of Justice, Memorandum, June 29, 2011. www.justice.gov/sites/default/files/oip/legacy/2014/07/23/dag-guidance-2011-for-medical-marijuana-use.pdf.
James M. Cole, U.S. Department of Justice, Memorandum, Aug. 29, 2013. http://1.usa.gov/1da7ofM.
James M. Cole, U.S. Department of Justice, Memorandum, Feb. 14, 2014. http://www.justice.gov/sites/default/files/usao-wdwa/legacy/2014/02/14/DAG Memo - Guidance Regarding Marijuana Related Financial Crimes 2 14 14 (2).pdf.
W. Thomas McElroy Jr., Office of Chief Counsel, Internal Revenue Service, Memorandum 201504011, Jan. 23, 2015. www.irs.gov/pub/irs-wd/201504011.pdf.
Financial Crimes Enforcement Network, Department of the Treasury, "BSA Expectations Regarding Marijuana-Related Businesses," FIN-2014-G001, Feb. 14, 2014. www.fincen.gov/sites/default/files/shared/FIN-2014-G001.pdf.
David W. Ogden, U.S. Department of Justice, Memorandum, Oct. 19, 2009. http://1.usa.gov/11yMHfi.
National Council of State Legislatures, *State Medical Marijuana Laws*, July 20, 2015. http://bit.ly/1udxSs4.
Source: What It's Worth: Value and Business Challenges in the Budding Cannabis Industry, August 2016, Business Valuation Resources, LLC

Nevertheless, even if your clients are playing by the rules, the DOJ is watching. If they break any of the rules—if the cannabis is consumed or grown on public lands, if it gets into the hands of kids, if it crosses state lines—then there is an issue. Residents can buy an ounce of cannabis for recreational purposes legally in Colorado; people from out of state can come in and buy a fourth of an ounce. But there is no tracking of sales. On South Broadway in Denver, you could stop at 10 to 12 different facilities and buy a quarter ounce at each to take back home. It is only a matter of time before somebody gets caught at the airport or at the border. The police on the Kansas and Nebraska borders are watching interstates 70 and 80 for eastbound travelers. These rules will continue to evolve. That is the conundrum of trying to value the risk.

You have to know your client. You want to make sure your client is ethical and not coloring outside the lines because you don't want to be involved in that. The vast majority of the people involved in this industry are honorable and want to do the right thing and want to see this industry succeed. On the other hand, the cannabis industry continues to attract some unsavory types, and it is paramount that professionals working in the space always be on the lookout for client types that are not a good fit. If we have an interview with somebody and we don't have a good feeling, we generally don't take that person on as a client. That is true of any industry but a bit more relevant in this sector.

An internal controls assessment is essential. Controls must be in place to prevent diversion by employees. Even if the owners are unaware of this activity, it could cost them their license.

Cash on hand. How are cash payments handled? Are Form 1099s issued? If it is a retail or wholesale operator, has the business complied with the Form 8300 requirements for large cash deposits? This is a cash-based business, so you want to make sure that the proper Form 1099s are being issued and the businesses have proper internal controls over cash and inventory. How are the businesses handling their cash? How is their banking handled? This industry has had many workarounds in relation to banking.

Competitive landscape. Consider the local area in which the cannabis business operates. A county with a large population may have only one location due to zoning restrictions, and a business there may do very well because of the lack of competition. On the other hand, for example, an area in Denver called South Broadway has a concentration of dispensaries, making for a more competitive environment. A dispensary in northern Colorado gets most of its sales from the east because, between there and Kansas (around 300 miles), there are no other dispensaries. Since 2014, it has been legal to sell to out-of-state customers, and we now are seeing cannabis tourism in Colorado.

Key employees. In terms of personnel, the head gardener is very much a key employee. The best chance for success in the business is a very strong gardener working in combination with a good businessman or businesswoman. If the cannabis growers have a gardener with no business sense, this could be a problem. Owners in it just for the money, with no growing skills, are at higher risk, too.

Do the owners have relevant business experience? Is the main gardener an owner? If that gardener quits or is let go, not only will the job be vacant, but also the disgruntled former employee could go in at night and destroy the harvest. Gardeners can be very protective of their genetics. Do any of the owners have lurking personal issues that can jeopardize a cannabis license? If multiple owners, do they all get along and work cohesively?

Leases. Is the lease ironclad? Is there bank financing on the property that could go awry? During your interview with members of management, discuss their lease and their option to renew. How is the building financed? Here is a possible scenario: The rent is paid every month, and the landlord is happy with the tenant. Then the three-year balloon comes up on the mortgage. The landlord goes to the bank to refinance, and the bank representative asks, "Who is your tenant?"

> *Landlord:* It is Joe Cannabis Co.
>
> *Bank representative:* Sorry, we won't refinance unless you kick them out.

That can happen both at the retail and the wholesale level. If the owners of a cannabis business are going to rent, ask their landlord about the debt structure. You want a building that is free and clear or has private financing. Another option, if it is financially feasible, is for the owners to purchase the real estate for the grow and retail, eliminating the real estate problem. Another issue can arise when an operation initially granted a medical license then becomes authorized to sell to the retail adult-use market. Have the lease arrangements contemplated this expansion? Anticipating and planning for such contingencies is the only way to avoid adverse consequences.

The problem of banks. One reason banks are reluctant to be involved in this industry in the current climate is that, with central bank processing, Colorado checks clear outside the state, in places that do not have legal cannabis. If the federal government stepped in and enforced the law differently, a lot of checks could bounce. Thus, banks need to know a cannabis retail or dispensary client is fully compliant with state laws and that there is complete control of the product from the grow facility to the retail and then to the bank. Armed security guards and armored trucks that move the cannabis and cash are a must if the business wants to have access to banking.

It is very difficult for banks to do business with an industry that is making large cash deposits and operating illegally according to federal law and still comply with their own regulations under the Bank Secrecy Act (BSA) and anti-money-laundering rules.

The Payment Law Advisor provides an excellent analysis[4] of the current risks inherent for financial institutions in providing services to the cannabis industry in the context of the Treasury's February 2014 "FinCEN memo." In that memo, the Financial Crimes Enforcement Network aimed to clarify the requirements of the BSA. In a quest for full transparency, a bill named "The Marijuana

4 Karen Ross, "Marijuana, Banking, and the '10-Foot Pole,'" April 28, 2014. www.paymentlawadvisor.com/2014/04/28/marijuana-banking-and-the-10-foot-pole/.

Businesses Access to Banking Act" has been introduced in both houses of Congress for a number of years, so far without passage.

If the banking problem were easy to solve, someone would have figured it out by now. Colorado has had a robust cannabis industry for seven years, and yet only a few banks are openly accepting cannabis business clients, and they do not accept new applications.

The hardest bills to pay without a checking account are taxes on payroll. You have to do an electronic funds transfer (EFT) to pay federal withholding taxes. Thus a cannabis business needs at least one checking account, perhaps a personal checking account used just for those transactions. The rent and other bills are paid in cash.

One cannabis dispensary owner uses his accounting software to generate checks for his payroll on plain white paper. He tells his employees, "Here is your check, really a voucher, for the last week, $329.66, printed right here out of Peachtree. Oh, and by the way, there is only one place in the world you can cash that check, and that is at the dispensary counter right here." That way, all payroll records are created in his system so that he can generate the W-2s at the end of the year. He uses that system with his vendors as well.

Much of the information presented in this article is relevant for assignments focused on the appraisal of intellectual property rights in the cannabis industry. IP appraisal is substantially needed in this sector due to the value of certain license rights associated with cultivation, retail, and MIPS licenses, in addition to the IP value of branding for operators who have an established brand involving trademarks, trade dress, graphics, and beyond.

This industry is not yet mature, and it is continually evolving. For the authors, it is fascinating to take on appraisal work in more established markets such as Colorado and Washington state, as compared to work assignments in emerging markets, such as Nevada and Maryland, just as examples. A valuation done a year ago in many industries would still be relevant, but, in the shifting sands of this industry, it is likely not to be. There is not yet much activity in terms of mergers and acquisitions. There is pent-up interest. Some people who would love to be involved are waiting on the sidelines for now.[5]

Jim Marty, *CPA/ABV, MS, of Bridge West LLC, can be reached at jmarty@jimmarty.com and 303-651-0304.* ***Ron Seigneur,*** *CPA/ABV, ASA, CVA, CFF, CGMA, of Seigneur Gustafson LLP CPAs, can be reached at* ron.seigneur@cpavalue.com *and 303-980-1111.*

5 Chris Walsh, "Appraising a Marijuana Business: Q&A With Valuations Expert Ronald Seigneur," *Marijuana Business Daily*, Sept. 10, 2014, mjbizdaily.com.

Dietrich Gives Insights Into Latest Issues in Healthcare Valuations

The newest member of the *Business Valuation Update* editorial advisory board is Mark O. Dietrich, CPA/ABV, who is, according to the American Health Lawyers Association, a renowned valuation thought leader in the area of healthcare. Of course, we agree with that assessment. *BVU* talked with Dietrich about his practice and about some of the current hot topics in healthcare valuation.

BVU: *How did you get into valuation? Have you always specialized in healthcare?*

Mark O. Dietrich: Yes, I have always specialized in healthcare. As an undergraduate student, I worked in a law library and at small CPA firms doing tax work. When I finished graduate school, the CPA firm I joined did a fair amount of healthcare and dentistry practices. The firm picked up an 80-physician tax-exempt faculty group practice as an audit client, and that's where I got my audit experience to get certified. I stayed with that client for 20 years, and it gave me a great deal of in-depth knowledge of medical practice operations. By the time I left that firm, I had built up a portfolio of almost exclusively healthcare clients. Along the way, I represented tax-exempt and taxable entities in Internal Revenue Service field audits and participated in the development of a 250-physician independent network and negotiation of its managed care and Medicare Advantage contracts. Overall, I've conducted more than 400 valuation engagements in the healthcare industry.

BVU: *What types of engagements do you typically have?*

MD: Interestingly, it swings between divorce work and transaction work. It's all healthcare-related, but this year I've had a lot of divorce cases involving a physician practice or other healthcare entity caught up in the marital estate. But, last year, I had very little divorce work and a lot of transaction work. It was all healthcare-related.

BVU: *You are the editor and a contributor to a new edition of the* BVR/AHLA Guide to Healthcare Industry Finance and Valuation. *Has the book changed much since its last edition?*

MD: Yes, it's essentially an entirely new book. There are 14 brand new chapters, and almost all of the other chapters have been extensively revised.

BVU: *What are the main issues that can cause problems in a healthcare valuation? How does this book help deal with those issues?*

MD: One of the big issues is the exposure business valuation experts now have to the Health Insurance Portability and Accountability Act of 1996 (HIPAA). This can happen if you receive protected health information when doing a valuation, and the penalties are very severe. The rules have been expanded, and they now apply to a healthcare entity's "business associates," which can include you as an appraiser. There's a new chapter in the book that explains this and gives you some practical ways to avoid exposure.

Retail healthcare is another big issue in the industry as you probably notice with the significant increase in urgent care operations. Hospitals are in this space, and the market is becoming more competitive. There's a new chapter in the book devoted to urgent care centers.

Another issue is reasonable compensation. Most practitioners focus on survey data, especially MGMA, in establishing reasonable or fair market compensation. But this method is based on several false premises, including that the surveys have statistical significance for the 90% or so of physicians not included in the surveys. The book goes into this in much greater detail. The fair market value of physician compensation is an essential issue in the government's qui tam (whistleblower) cases it has been winning in False Claims Act (FCA) lawsuits against a number of hospitals, which have been hit with hundreds of millions of dollars in fines. These lawsuits—and there will be more coming—have been triggered by hospitals acquiring medical practices. This raises the bar for appraisers and employing physicians, and there are several new chapters in the book that address this issue. Also, there is an extensive analysis of the IRS Job Aid on reasonable compensation from a healthcare perspective.

BVU: *You've done extensive research in the issue of physician mobility in the context of determining the fair market value of physician compensation. What have you found?*

MD: Hospitals feel that, if they don't pay their physicians at least the median compensation for their specialty, they will relocate to earn more. The government follows this line of thinking, and it has figured into cases in which the fair market value of doctor compensation is an issue. But research shows that physicians are less likely to relocate than other occupations, which refutes the government's position. For example, 10 years after being trained, two-thirds of physicians are still in the same state, according to the Association of American Medical Colleges, which tracks physician training and practice patterns. When a physician does move, it's most likely after residency is completed. There are exceptions, such as neurosurgeons, who are heavily recruited due to demand for that specialty. But, overall, the notion that a physician will relocate if he or she doesn't get the median compensation does not hold up to scrutiny. However, this is the current mindset among hospitals and appraisers that needs to change.

BVU: *You have a new chapter in the book that talks about a way to compensate physicians that meets business goals but does not cause trouble with government lawsuits. What is this method?*

MD: Instead of paying physicians the median compensation, hospitals could set fair market value compensation based on the resource-based relative value scale (RBRVS). This is a fee schedule that uses a complex formula to determine the payment due a physician for patient services. It also takes into account such factors as the resources used, practice expenses, malpractice expenses, geographic location, and others. It measures direct compensation and benefits for physicians and excludes other costs or revenues unrelated to the physician's personally performed clinical services. RBRVS reveals how much of what is collected should go toward paying doctors instead of overhead. The amount of collections could be allocated to physicians based on compensation vis-a-vis overhead and insurance, which allows the hospital to set malpractice compensation based on conditions in the local market. I explain this in much greater detail in the book.

BVU: *What are some of the other current trends and hot topics in healthcare valuation?*

MD: In addition to HIPAA, reasonable compensation, and retail health, there are two other important matters that we're keeping an eye on. One is accountable care organizations in the Medicare Shared Savings Program. Despite reports of success, these groups are not generating a lot of savings and don't seem to be going anywhere, so this is an area to watch.

The other issue is the merit-based incentive payment system, which is a complete revision that will move a substantial amount of physician payments under the fee-for-service Medicare system to being merit-based. A lot of this will be based on data that can only be extracted from electronic medical records. Those practices that have not yet implemented electronic medical records—and there are many of them—will find themselves with substantially reduced payments from Medicare for their services. It's a very big issue, and it's supposed to be effective in 2017. I did a chapter on it for the next edition of a book that Tim Smith of Ankura Consulting and I are doing on healthcare compensation.[1]

BVU: *There has been a lot of talk about repealing the Stark Law. What are your views on this?*

MD: I think it's highly unlikely that the Stark Law will be repealed. If anything happens, they may modify the rules with respect to the compensation paid by hospitals to physicians because that's the source of most of the qui tam cases. The claims are that doctors are being overpaid because the hospital is buying referrals. That is one area you may see change because the government is pushing hospitals and physicians to closely work together, which will include revenue sharing, which is the source of the trouble. On the other hand, you rarely see Congress or the administration cut big revenue sources, and the Stark Law generates a huge amount of revenue.

BVU: *What advice would you give an individual just starting out in business valuation?*

MD: I would pick an industry and specialize in it. In the healthcare industry, there are too many generalists and not a lot of people who specialize—particularly in the litigation side of healthcare.

1 *BVR/AHLA Guide to Healthcare Industry Compensation and Valuation* (www.bvresources.com).

It's difficult to find someone who doesn't have a conflict. Their firm may do transaction work in healthcare so there may be a conflict if a case comes up.

BVU: *Thanks, Mark, for sharing these insights. We're happy to have you on our editorial board, and we look forward to your helping BVR readers keep up-to-date with what's going on in the exciting area of healthcare valuation.*

Special Considerations in Valuing Wealth Management Firms

By Patrice Radogna, ASA, CBA, CVA, CPA

The valuation of wealth management firms presents a number of special considerations. These firms are brimming with talent, brain power, energy, and, most importantly, revenue-generating capacity. They come in many shapes and sizes and vary widely in terms of the key components that drive value.

As with the typical professional service firm, tangible assets are negligible among wealth management firms. The major driver of value is a "two-legged" asset that goes home every night—the human capital. Business is typically based on close personal contacts, mutual trust, and the collective reputation of the firm and its key professionals. The longevity and predictability of those assets are difficult to ascertain, and, in many cases, firms do not have legal rights to those assets except for those cases in which employment agreements have been signed.

Of the three approaches to valuing a business (asset, income, and market approaches), the asset approach is typically best suited to value tangible asset-rich businesses or non-operating-type entities. Wealth managers are in fact human capital-driven, which is measured through the financial operating results of the business. Thus, the income and market approaches are best relied upon in valuing a wealth management firm. The remainder of this article will focus on elements of the income approach and the market approach and their applicability in valuing wealth management firms.

Income approach. An important consideration when using the income approach to value a wealth management firm is the use of historical financial information or forecasts. The two primary methodologies within the income approach are the capitalization of cash flow (CapCF) and the discounted cash flow (DCF) methodologies. The CapCF measures and determines value, based on capitalizing a normalized cash flow amount that is viewed as representative of normalized financial performance. To the extent that the business is mature and the past is deemed to be a predictor of the future, a valuation professional may find the CapCF the best method to employ. Often times, however, the future direction of the firm is expected to vary from the historical results. This situation is best addressed through use of the DCF methodology. The build out of forecasts often can be a daunting task.

Revenues of wealth management firms are a function of price and quantity. Price is usually stated in terms of basis points earned on assets under management (AUM), and quantity reflects the asset base. Revenues for wealth management firms are not secured by long-term contracts and thus can provide challenges to building (or relying on) defensible forecasts beyond one year (much less two years). While current operating data may be relied upon when there is a high level of client retention and when fee structure is predictable, in some cases, there can be shifts in revenue (due to unpredictable swings in market performance) or cost drivers, or the business is not at a mature state (earlier-stage companies); all of these factors make the use of current operating data tenuous. In the case where there is a reliable track record or there are several likely scenarios on the horizon, my firm (Valuation Research Corp.) has worked with its clients to create sophisticated expected cash flow models, based on various scenarios, which consider all operating characteristics and pertinent drivers of value.

As forecasts are subject to market expectations and are tied to shifting business dynamics, valuation professionals are dependent on management to prepare forecasts based on a soft set of assumptions. When the underlying forecast assumptions the client provides are deemed to depart significantly from historical results, with no supportable rationale (based on the valuation professional's independent examination of the business and/or the company financials) or are subject to attack, a valuation professional will lean more heavily on industry knowledge, market data trends, and drivers, coupled with the client's input, in building defensible, well-reasoned forecasts.

Forecast risk for smaller wealth management firms tends to be higher than for larger firms, due to higher dependencies on both key personnel and client concentration issues. The loss of either of these could significantly change the projected path of the firm. This risk is mitigated in medium to large-size firms as they have deeper benches of seasoned professionals with a larger pool of intellectual capital. Additionally, the intangible assets of a larger wealth management firm tend to be embodied in the collective knowledge of the firm's culture, which is largely recognized as "corporate branding." A wealth management firm that has built a reputation of consistently delivering a superior product, backed by a strong track record and delivered by high-quality professionals, has created distinctive branding, which enhances value.

In general, higher value, developed using the income approach, will be attributed to wealth management firms with the following characteristics: larger size, longevity, depth of personnel, increased brand awareness, diverse client base, and differentiation/sophistication of services. This translates into value to the extent that an investor would attribute lower company-specific risk (in the form of a "required rate of return" for investing in the company) when determining value via an income-based approach or a higher multiple when determining value via a market approach. All other things held equal, holding the average AUM fee constant, the lower the risk attributes, the higher the firm value.

Market approach. In addition to the income approach, the market approach is often applicable to valuing small to medium-size closely held wealth management firms. While a plethora of pricing data is available, valuation professionals must be cautious, however, in not blindly applying the observed market data. There are two primary methods to employ the market approach: by developing valuation multiples implied by outright sales of similar businesses (the transaction multiple method, or TMM) or by obtaining the trading activity and valuation multiples in shares of publicly held companies (the guideline public company method, or GPCM).

Due to the size and the diversity of most publicly traded wealth management firms, and thus the differences between those firms and a small privately held wealth management firm, when dealing with these small/medium-size firms, we tend to focus on the TMM, as opposed to the GPCM. The TMM provides data on more similar-sized private companies, which may have a more similar operating platform to our smaller/medium-sized wealth management firms. While there may be a plethora of data for the GPCM, there are typically significant differences due to: the size of these companies, the fact that they are public companies and subject to differing influences of value, and that these public companies may be significantly more diversified than closely held wealth management firms.

In the end, a valuation professional must simply recognize the strengths and weaknesses of each data set (for either the TMM or the GPCM) when applying one of these methods in performing the market approach. Based on the quality and quantity of market data, the valuation professional may apply the TMM or the GPCM as either a determinant of value or a check to the results set forth in the income approach, depending on the market data available. It is not uncommon for market data to call into question the credibility of client-driven forecasts, which form the basis of the income approach.

Another relevant point regarding market data is that small to medium-size wealth management firms often contemplate the implied value, as a multiple of *revenues*, often in lieu of focusing on value as a multiple of *earnings*.[1] The rationale is that the operating structure, practices, and expense structure could vary widely among firms, especially when it comes to partner compensation and employee bonuses. In addition, many smaller to midsize wealth management firms are not encumbered with external third-party financing and therefore are not required to have audited financial statements. Thus, the financial statements are often not reviewed/audited by an accounting firm, increasing the skepticism by acquiring firms of the expenses represented on the income statement. For these reasons, a buyer will often focus on the revenue-generating capacity of the firm. They will determine value, in relation to the level of expected continuing revenues, and will institute their own practices and expense structure in generating future revenue. The multiple that is considered applicable to a given company is largely determined by an analysis of many of the items previously discussed in this article.

Industry data from MergerStat and Capital IQ databases support the wide range of multiples applied to wealth management firms. Average revenue multiples based on a search for wealth management firms range from 0.25x revenue multiple up to a 6.26x revenue multiple, with a median multiple

1 It is noted that the valuation of larger wealth management firms will typically also incorporate the reliance on a multiple of "adjusted earnings." This may be more applicable when reviewed/audited financials are available and when adjusted earnings can be computed.

of 1.73x revenue. Due to this wide range of multiples, a valuation professional needs to appreciate how the qualitative factors of the wealth management firm business would impact if they are on the low or high range of the stated revenue multiples.

Key drivers of value. The key data that a valuation professional should focus on in valuing wealth management firms are:

- Recurring client base—characterized by the amount of repeat business.
- Revenue growth—segregate organic versus market growth.
- Revenue source—commission-based or fee-based.
- Size of wealth management firm—scale matters.
- Client demographics—client concentrations, client tenure, new client ratio, client age.
- Compensation and expenses of management.
- Life stage of company—startup, expansion phase, mature life cycle.
- Sophistication and quality of services—generally the more differentiated and sophisticated the services provided, the higher the management fees (thus the higher the profitability) for services rendered.
- Understanding of business model—is the wealth management firm offering integrated advice (i.e., financial planning, risk management) with higher margins in addition to traditional asset management services?
- Do alliances exist to generate new business (i.e., does the wealth management firm have an alliance with a broker-dealer that will enable the wealth management firm to offer additional products while continuing to remain independent)?
- Longevity—In general, the longer the wealth management firm has been in business, the more stable the revenue base and the stronger the corporate brand in the marketplace.
- Employee demographics—number of employees, tenure, relationship with clients. These factors will provide insight into the collective knowledge, reputation, and branding of a company.

Case example. We have valued many wealth management firms over the past several years. Below is a case study of two wealth management firms that operate similar business platforms but differ significantly in key characteristics. The exhibit illustrates the variety one can encounter when valuing two companies operating in the same industry.

Firm 1. The purpose of the valuation of Wealth Management Firm 1 was for shareholder buy-ins and buy-outs. We completed these valuations annually in order to set equity value for the purpose of the buy-in/buyout related to shareholder transactions.

The primary valuation approach that we relied on was the income approach. Specifically, we performed a five-year discounted cash flow analysis, with a relatively low discount rate (due to the perceived low forecast risk for this company). We also considered a significant sample size of transactions in the marketplace and used the market approach to compare how the implied market multiples, developed from the income approach, compared to market multiples from private transactions in the marketplace.

Tale of the Tape: Key Issues in Valuing Two Wealth Management Firms

Key Characteristics	Wealth Management Firm No. 1	Wealth Management Firm No. 2
Longevity	In business for 25 years	Business division (of a larger firm) commenced three years prior to valuation
Branding	Ranked as one of the top 25 wealth management firms in the U.S.	Reputation of the firm is closely aligned to the founder of the company
Size	Almost $250 billion AUM	Approximately $1 billion AUM
Historical Growth	Compound annual growth rate (CAGR) of 15% over the past 12 years	Growth—from no meaningful revenue in 2011 to approximately $4 million revenue in 2013
Revenue Model	Flat fee revenue model—to respond to client desire for a flat fee model versus a commission-based model (over 70% of revenues derived from flat fee model)	Commission-based model
Profitability	Profit margins exceed industry norm	Profit margins below industry norm
Top Management	Twenty directors who manage the firm and bring in revenue	One director who is also the chief investment officer
Depth of Employee Base	Deep bench of employees	One credentialed employee in the investment division
Client Concentration Risk	Diverse client base with less than 10% of revenues coming from the aggregate of its top 10 clients	Approximately 83% of revenues are derived from the top two clients. One of the two clients has only been a client for approximately one year
Client Retention	Client loss ratio of less than 5% over the past 15 years	Client No. 1 (first institutional client with track record for this wealth management firm) has been a client for two years, but the client relationship is in jeopardy as the investment return is below the client's established benchmark return
Industry Risk Concentration (Market Sector)	Diverse market sectors (attracts funds from different market sectors), with not more than 28% of revenues coming from any one sector	Two top clients are both pension clients, which to date represent the only institutional money

Firm 2. The purpose of the valuation of Wealth Management Firm 2 was for stock equity compensation. We were hired to determine the base price of the company in order to determine growth in value in subsequent years for the existing shareholder base.

The primary valuation approach that we relied on was the income approach. Unlike Management Firm 1, we could not rely on a single-point DCF due to the risk patterns shown in the above facts (see the exhibit) as well as the myriad of possible paths in the near future for this firm. In this case, with significant input from management, we prepared a probability-weighted cash flow scenario, considering four different scenarios (including using a 25% weight in a scenario that the company would be out of business and dissolved in three years and consistent with the fallout of the potential loss of its founding and largest client). The preparation of each set of these cash flows considered the following: (i) compensation schemes; (ii) changes in significant value drivers; (iii) differing market expectations; and (iv) risk characteristics.

Although both of these wealth management firms have highly talented personnel providing sophisticated services to their respective client base, there are significant differences in the fact pattern between the two companies. It should be of no surprise that the value results of Wealth Management Firm 2 were much lower in terms of a concluded value and implied valuation multiple than Wealth Management Firm 1.

Concluding thoughts. Wealth management firms are sensitive to many assumptions, which need to be carefully contemplated in the valuation process. If significant value-driving factors and potential risks for a company are not identified, or are mischaracterized, the results may be illogical in relation to the underlying fact pattern. A deep understanding of any wealth management firm, and analysis of meaningful documentation and facts in each case, could be the difference between a supportable value conclusion and one that a third party can easily challenge.

***Patrice Radogna,** ASA, CBA, CVA, CPA, is senior vice president at Valuation Research Corp. She has more than 17 years of experience in the valuation of privately held businesses, professional practices, pass-through entities, and intangible assets. Her areas of specialty lie in the disciplines of ESOP valuations, trust and estate planning, and shareholder transactional work. Patrice has experience as a valuation advisor to clients in various industries with a particular expertise in the professional services practices. She can be reached at PRadogna@ValuationResearch.com.*

Section III.
From the Courtroom

10 Best Valuation Cases for 2015

Valuation plays a key role in most civil litigation. Appraisers testify in divorce cases, contract disputes, bankruptcy proceedings, statutory appraisal actions, patent litigation and a host of other suits. All of this activity produces a continuous stream of case law. But some cases are more impactful than others. Here are 10 cases that stood out in 2015.

1. *Bank of Am., N.A. v. Veluchamy (In re Veluchamy)*, 2014 Bankr. LEXIS 5106 (Dec. 18, 2014); affirmed in *Bank of America, N.A. v. Veluchamy*, 2015 U.S. Dist. LEXIS 110083 (Aug. 19, 2015). This gnarled bankruptcy case contains a short but significant discussion about tax affecting in valuing the stock in one of the defendants' S corporations. Unswayed by U.S. Tax Court rulings on this issue, the Bankruptcy Court says it is appropriate to account for the effect of taxation on the shareholder level.

2. *Bohme v. Bohme*, 2015 Ohio App. LEXIS 325 (Jan. 30, 2015). In a first blow to its own 2008 Heller decision, which prohibited double dipping in divorce cases, the Ohio Court of Appeals says using income "as a tool" for valuing a professional business and then considering that income "as actual income for a spousal support calculation" does not per se amount to impermissible double dipping.

3. *Gallo v. Gallo*, 2015 Ohio App. LEXIS 938 (March 17, 2015). This may well be the coup de grâce to the Heller double dip framework. Not even two months after the *Bohme* decision, the Court of Appeals in Gallo says there is no prohibition against double dipping. Ultimately, what matters is for the trial court to craft a fair and equitable resolution to divorce proceedings.

4. *AstraZeneca AB v. Apotex Corp.*, 2015 U.S. App. LEXIS 5543 (April 7, 2015). Do concepts such as apportionment and the entire market value rule (EMVR) have a role to play in big pharma patent infringement cases? This opinion from the Federal Circuit involving AstraZeneca's "Prilosec" explains why EMVR is inapplicable in this case and how to calculate damages in drug cases.

5. *Washington v. Kellwood Co.*, 2015 U.S. Dist. LEXIS 63457 (April 21, 2015). Is there a there there? Facing a dearth of financial evidence on which to base damages in support of the client's breach of contract claim, the plaintiff's expert develops a questionable yardstick analysis using sales figures from the leading seller of similar products. The expert's conclusions may be "improbable," the court says, but his analysis is good enough to warrant admission under *Daubert*.

6. *Owen v. Cannon*, 2015 Del. Ch. LEXIS 165 (June 17, 2015). A first pronouncement on tax affecting from the Delaware Court of Chancery's new chief. In ruling on the propriety of this "blitzkrieg"-style merger, the court opts for the discounted cash flow analysis to determine the fair value of the plaintiff's shares and uses the controlling Kessler model to calculate a 22.71% hypothetical corporate tax rate.

7. *Tri Cnty. Wholesale Distribs. v. Labatt USA Operating Co. LLC*, 2015 U.S. Dist. LEXIS 81914 (June 24, 2015). A contract dispute with a twist. After the manufacturer of Labatt beers lawfully terminates its agreement with two distributors, they ask the court to quantify the "diminished value" of the businesses stemming from the loss of the franchise contracts. The court prescribes a "hybrid" approach and provides a useful analysis of the factors affecting the value of beer distributorships and brands.

8. *LongPath Capital, LLC v. Ramtron Int'l Corp*, 2015 Del. Ch. LEXIS 177 (June 30, 2015). Ever heard of "negative synergies"? This statutory appraisal decision from the Chancery aligns with other decisions in which the court favored the merger price over other techniques, including the DCF model, to determine fair value. What adds spice to it is the embedded discussion on synergies. The seller's "negative" synergies need to offset the "positive" synergies that bring down the price, the plaintiff's expert argues—successfully.

9. *Guardian Energy, LLC v. County of Waseca*, 2015 Minn. LEXIS 437 (Aug. 12, 2015). Experienced appraisers are the first to admit that determining external (or economic) obsolescence is a formidable task. Yet in this tax assessment case involving a special purpose property, the Minnesota Tax Court rejected the proffered expert opinions and developed its own methodology. The state Supreme Court's opinion explains where the Tax Court went wrong.

10. *Moore v. Moore*, 2015 S.C. LEXIS 343 (Oct. 7, 2015). A South Carolina divorce case featuring a successful light fixtures retail store and illustrious valuators presents the state high court with an issue of first impression: Can enterprise goodwill be a marital asset subject to division? In answering "yes," the court provides a thorough review of goodwill jurisprudence and an informative discussion of other valuation issues such as the discount for lack of marketability.

Defending the Use of a Monte Carlo Analysis in Court

In a survey conducted by BVR, a third of valuation experts say they don't use Monte Carlo analysis because they are "concerned about defending this method if challenged by third parties." Of course, such a challenge will typically occur in a litigation context. This is a valid concern, as Monte Carlo is "rarely used in court," says Michael Pellegrino (Pellegrino & Associates LLC). But Pellegrino has used it hundreds of times in practice and dozens of times in litigation-related analysis, and he shares his experience and advice for those who may come up against a challenge.[1]

"We have used Monte Carlo analysis for firms in every major sector of the economy and in every variety of damages models," he says. He makes the point that the problems and questions that you are trying to resolve have no dependence or reliance on a particular sector of the economy.

Overall objections. One of the broad objections the opposition has about Monte Carlo is that not many people use it in court. Pellegrino points out that, if you search for Monte Carlo on Google Scholar, you'll get about 2.7 million hits, but, if you limit the search to a legal context, you only get 27 hits. However, this is not a reflection on the lack of acceptance of Monte Carlo simulation, which has been around for over 70 years. Contemporary literature and current trends point to broad use and acceptance of the method. For example, every time you look at a weather report, you see the results of a Monte Carlo simulation.

Another point about the validity of the model itself is that it can also be said that no court has ever validated the use of Microsoft Excel, but it's used extensively. Excel's use is accepted even though there has been some interesting analyses of possible errors in its statistical functions, he observes.

***Daubert* hurdle.** In terms of a Monte Carlo analysis, four *Daubert* factors will basically have to be addressed: (1) whether the method is testable; (2) whether it has undergone publication and peer review; (3) whether it has an acceptable rate of error and maintenance of the standards concerning its operation; and (4) whether the scientific community has accepted it.

1 Michael Pellegrino (Pellegrino & Associates LLC) and Dave MacAdam (Novelis), Advanced Workshop on Monte Carlo: From Classroom to Boardroom to Courtroom, BVR webinar, Sept. 29, 2015.

As for whether the Monte Carlo simulation is testable, the answer is "yes." The basic theory can be tested on paper, Pellegrino notes. You can do the random sampling yourself using a table of random numbers, plug in values based on a look-up table, and look at the outputs—and do this over and over again. It might take a long time, but it's certainly testable. The almost 3 million hits on Google Scholar demonstrate that it has been well published.

The question as to whether there is an acceptable rate of error and maintenance of standards concerning its operation can also be answered affirmatively. Pellegrino points out that the errors associated with Monte Carlo simulation typically relate to the construction of the model and the parameters used, not the model itself. "There has not been a single decision I am aware of that said that Monte Carlo simulation is improper," he says. Has the scientific community accepted it? In terms of a broad adoption across the world, the answer is a definite "yes," although, if you stay within the valuation profession, the "jury might be mixed about that."

Key cases. Two important court cases back up the use of Monte Carlo simulation: *Lyondell Chemical*[2] and *Nanovation Technologies*.[3] In the *Lyondell* case (an environmental cleanup case), the side opposing the use of Monte Carlo actually conceded that the method is reliable. The case provides several good quotes from the court, including "just because Monte Carlo simulation produces a range of outcomes ... does not mean it is speculative" and "the EPA itself has endorsed the use of Monte Carlo analysis." The court did note that a Monte Carlo analysis "is unreliable when injected with faulty inputs, but nothing more." In a 2014 valuation case, *Myservice Force*,[4] the judge invalidated the Monte Carlo analysis not because of the model but because the expert based it on the wrong assumptions.

Nanovation was a bankruptcy case in which Monte Carlo was used to calculate common stock value. The expert opposing Monte Carlo was not challenging the model but said that he had never seen it used in similar circumstances. But the court said that it is a "generally accepted statistical tool" and there was "no evidence that might provide a reason to believe that [the analysis] is unreliable."

Therefore, when the opposition challenges the reliability of the method itself, you can point to court rulings that say it is reliable.

Attack points. Once the *Daubert* hurdle is cleared, the the opposition will likely attack the Monte Carlo analysis on the following points:

- *Is the structure of the model correct?* Of course, if the valuation model structure is wrong, then every derivative conclusion will also be wrong.

- *Are the inputs correct?* If the structure is right, but the inputs are wrong, then it's a case of garbage-in, garbage-out.

2 *Lyondell Chemical Co. v. Occidental Chemical Corp.*, 608 F.3d 284 (5th Cir. 2010).

3 *In re Nanovation Technologies, Inc.*, 2007 Bankr. LEXIS 1862 (May 17, 2007).

4 *Myservice Force v. American Home Shield*, 2014 U.S. Dist. LEXIS 61207 (May 2, 2014).

- *Are the variances and distributions associated with each input appropriate?* If not, that may elevate or demote the importance of the variables.
- *Are the outputs appropriate?*

A case Pellegrino discusses in which he had to deal with these issues is *Vernon v. Cuomo,*[5] which was a dissenting shareholder and statutory buyout case. Pellegrino was the court-appointed expert whom both parties agreed to. The task was to value an early-stage company with no assets other than untested technology. He used algorithms ("Latin hypercube") and Monte Carlo simulations, and his approach was "appropriate for this type of business and [was] clearly in the mainstream of IP valuation methodologies," the court said. His report indicated a range of value and selected the statistical median as the expected value. The report expressed a 90% confidence level in its range of value and its conclusions because it had reasonable access to the company's financial data and the new technology was ready for sale, Pellegrino said.

Because he was a court-appointed expert, he had to deal with opposition from both sides, one wanting a high value and the other wanting a low value. The majority shareholders criticized the report for using "hypothetical information and extraordinary assumptions" and for overstating the value of the technology. "They put forward a dim outlook," the court said, "emphasizing a number of worst-case scenarios." The minority shareholders, on the other hand, accused the report of underestimating value, particularly in Pellegrino's rejection of the market approach and his selection of a discount rate.

Pellegrino addressed each criticism at trial, satisfying any concerns of the court. "Any shortcomings … can be attributed to the intrinsic uncertainty of early-stage IP valuations," it said, and accepted Pellegrino's range.

For more information. Pellegrino and Dave MacAdam (Novelis) go into a great deal more detail during their recent four-hour Advanced Workshop on Monte Carlo: From Classroom to Boardroom to Courtroom. It is available at www.bvresources.com/dlc.

5 A redacted copy can be found at ocoee.files.wordpress.com/2010/04/vernon-v-cuomo-phase-2-opinion-2010.pdf.

Judge Laro Toplines Panel on Hot Issues in Tax Valuation

A panel session by several of the leading minds on taxation to discuss hot topics in valuation was a highlight of the 2015 AICPA FVS conference in Las Vegas. David Laro, a senior judge of the U.S. Tax Court, was there with Judge Kathleen M. Kerrigan. Also on hand was Michael R. Devitt (professor of law, University of San Diego School of Law) and attorney Lawrence A. Sannicandro (Agostino & Associates PC). The moderator was John I. Forry (University of San Diego School of Law).

Audit risk. Because valuation is involved in so many different situations, there's an overall 50% chance that the IRS will question a valuation, noted Sannicandro. However, this takes into account all valuations, including those for charitable contributions. In many of those cases, the required qualified appraisal is omitted from the return.

He presented some interesting statistics on the prevalence of valuation in Tax Court cases. In 2014, the Tax Court published 422 opinions, of which 148 involved taxpayers represented by counsel (the others appeared pro se). Questions of valuation were resolved, in one form or another, in roughly 52 of those 148 cases, which means that valuation was at issue in about 35% of represented taxpayer cases in 2014. This is up from 20% in 2013.

Smart court. None of the judges on the U.S. Tax Court are specialists, Judge Kerrigan explained. "We all have different backgrounds," she said. Judge Laro mentioned that today's Tax Court judges are "very smart and sophisticated" when it comes to business valuation and they do their own analysis.

Judge Kerrigan gave a brief review of the different types of opinions the Tax Court issues and the weight they carry:

1. *Summary opinion:* This type of opinion is used in small cases ("S cases," no more than $50,000), and there is no right of appeal.

2. *Bench opinion:* This is an oral opinion the judge may issue from the bench during trial. It cannot be relied on as precedent.

3. *TC memo opinion:* This opinion generally is issued in a regular case that does not present a novel legal issue. It addresses situations in which the law is settled or fact driven. It may be cited as legal authority and may be appealed, but it is not binding precedent.

4. *TC opinion:* This type of opinion carries the most weight. It is issued in regular cases that present an important legal issue or principle. It is appealable and may be cited as legal authority.

Judge Kerrigan cautioned the audience that the applicable standard of value in federal tax cases is the fair market value. Be careful not to use the market value (e.g., an actual sale or transfer) because using the wrong standard of value invalidates your analysis.

Judge Laro gave a rundown on key valuation issues, noting that he was speaking for himself, not the Tax Court. After serving 20 years on the court and immersing himself in valuation issues, he has become an authority on valuation.

Tax affecting. Practitioners should check out the IRS's Job Aid that explains the agency's thinking on valuing S corporations, Judge Laro advises. The IRS's position of no tax affecting leans on *Gross v. Commissioner* and progeny (there are at least five such cases), but it contradicts sound valuation practices, he says. All of the cases were Tax Court memos, so he says to keep in mind that these opinions are not binding on other judges. Therefore, "the final chapter on tax affecting has not yet been written."

DLOM. Simply pulling the discount for marketability rate from restricted stock and pre-IPO studies spells trouble, the judge cautions. "I'm bothered by those studies," he says. "Look how old they are. Be careful when you offer them as part of your technique." Today's Tax Court judges know valuation in a way the prior generation did not. And they expect experts to tailor their DLOM to the facts of a particular case. Judge Laro recommends using his *Mandelbaum* decision (in which he sets forth a multifactor analysis) as guidance for your DLOM determination. (A digest of *Mandelbaum v. Commissioner*, T.C. Memo 1995-255, along with Judge Laro's opinion, is available at *BVLaw*).

Subsequent events. The general rule is that events subsequent to the valuation date should be excluded from a valuation analysis. However, Judge Laro says that there are exceptions to this rule. Some courts have examined subsequent events that are relevant to the taxpayer's perceptions at that time. In some cases, subsequent events were reasonably foreseeable as of the valuation date, so they are relevant to the valuation. "Consult the attorney to see if subsequent events could be considered in your circuit," he says.

USPAP. Mere compliance with the profession's standards does not make you a reliable expert for Tax Court purposes, Judge Laro says. Conversely, failure to comply with the standards does not exclude your testimony from consideration.

A key step to ensuring the testimony is admissible is using the correct standard of value, Judge Laro cautions. Like Judge Kerrigan, he warned experts to use fair market value, not market value. While the Tax Code does not provide a definition of fair market value, estate tax regulation §20.2031-1 does. It describes FMV as "the price at which the property would change hands between a willing buyer and a willing seller, neither being under any compulsion to buy or sell and both having reasonable knowledge of relevant facts." In other words, the focus is on a hypothetical willing buyer and seller that engage in an arm's-length transaction, not on actual sales data. Apply the wrong standard of value and the Tax Court will disregard your valuation opinion.

Attorney involvement. Protect your independence, Judge Laro warns. Most experts have dealt with retaining attorneys who want to steer the valuation by reviewing draft opinions and suggesting (or even ordering) recalculations that favor their side. Know the discovery rules; much of the communication between attorney and expert may be discoverable. If the attorney's involvement crosses the line, the valuation evidence may be spoiled.

Judge Laro mentioned a recent billion-dollar case in which a major law firm told the valuator in writing what number it wanted the expert to reach. The communication was discoverable and ended up in court. "Think of what that does to the valuator's credibility in court," the judge says.

Professor Devitt also cautioned appraisers about their dealings with the attorneys. "Don't let overzealous lawyers push you into untenable positions," he warns. He advised experts to know the *Daubert* case and the factors it sets forth inside and out because it is almost certain that the other side will file a *Daubert* challenge. "Sort of" knowing the case is no longer enough to overcome the hurdle *Daubert* has become.

Hot-tub technique. Devitt also talked about a method of testifying that he dubbed "hot tubbing." It is also known as "concurrent witness testimony." Devitt says he has been a strong proponent of the technique for the past 10 years (see his detailed article in the October 2012 issue of the *Journal of Taxation*). Hot tubbing has become Judge Laro's preferred technique of receiving expert testimony. It replaces the blood sport of cross-examination with a collegial discussion involving the judge and both sides' experts but excluding the attorneys.

In the case of *Rovakat*,[1] following the traditional cross-examination and rebuttal of the expert witnesses, Judge Laro asked the parties whether they would allow the experts to talk directly to one another (under oath) and the judge in the presence of the attorneys. After the parties agreed, Judge Laro held two successive hot-tub sessions in which the petitioner's sole expert had separate discussions with the government's two experts. Only the experts and the judge sat around a table. Since this was the first time the hot-tub technique had been used in the Tax Court, Judge Laro allowed the attorneys to make objections during the session. The judge engaged the experts in conversation and occasionally interjected to ask whether the opposing expert agreed or disagreed

1 *Rovakat, LLC. v. Comm'r*, T.C. Memo 2011-225.

with what the other expert had just said. He also asked whether they would talk directly to one another.

After the sessions, Judge Laro was able to narrow in on specific points on which the experts disagreed: They varied in their appraisal methodologies and differed on book values and fair market value. The resulting dialogue helped the judge assess the strengths and weaknesses of all expert opinions in the case.

According to Judge Laro, when experts need not fear attacks on their credibility, they are able to express their thoughts more freely and provide the judge with a more meaningful valuation than the adversarial system allows. Not everyone is on board, but it's a technique that is catching on—the AICPA is now providing training in this method.

Ongoing series. Moderator Forry explained that this was the first in a series of annual sessions on valuation and tax and is part of the USD Law School's Thought Leadership Program. The next installment, building on another year's experience with the technique, should be interesting.

Recent Case Points Up Danger of the Discovery Trap

By Sylvia Golden, Esq.

In a typical valuation engagement for litigation, there can be a slew of written communication between the expert and the client or attorney. Draft reports, emails, letters, and memos can fly fast and free. The trouble is, this material may be discoverable and you may find yourself on the witness stand trying to explain a seemingly innocent document that has fallen into the hands of the opposition.

What's at stake. An appraiser's reputation is at stake if documents come to light that even hint at being an advocate or "hired gun" for the client. In a recent case, letters between the appraiser and the client and the client's attorney suggested that the appraiser used the client's valuation as the basis for the valuation. These letters, produced as part of the discovery process, cast doubt onto the appraiser's independence. The opposing side ended up winning the case. See *TWC I, L.L.C. v. Damos*, 2015 Iowa App. LEXIS 438 (May 20, 2015) (available at *BVLaw*).

The best protection against this kind of nightmare is familiarity with the discovery rules. Here is a quick review of Rule 26 of the Federal Rules of Civil Procedure, which applies in federal courts. States have their own rules, so make sure you check those out.

2010 Amendment. Rule 26 was amended in 2010 to simplify discovery obligations, limit disclosures, and protect the attorney's thoughts, opinions, and mental impressions (work product). The amendments require only disclosure of "facts or data" considered by the expert. But since courts have been slow to clarify the scope of protection, a sense of uncertainty remains among experts and attorneys.

Expert reports. Rule 26 (b)(4)(B) protects drafts of expert reports "regardless of the form in which the draft is recorded." But courts don't agree on what constitutes a nondiscoverable draft expert report. Some have said that an expert's notes, memos, lists, and outlines are discoverable because they are not strictly speaking "draft" expert reports. Others have considered them parts of the draft, which can be in any form, and protected them, or they have said that discoverable "facts or data" does not mean everything the expert needs to do his or her analysis.

Expert-attorney communication. The rules now protect all communication between counsel and testifying experts, "regardless of the form of the communication." But they still permit discovery of: (1) communications related to the expert's compensation; (2) communications that "identify facts or data that the party's attorney provided and that the expert considered"; and (3) communications that "identify assumptions that the attorney provided and that the expert relied on."

This means communications in which the attorney and expert discuss general hypotheticals using the assumptions are protected, but communications in which the attorney identifies facts or data on which the expert later relies in developing his or her opinion are not. And there is no protection for communication between the testifying expert and someone other than counsel.

Open questions. A host of questions remain unanswered. How much work product can the expert put in the draft? What happens when the attorney conveys facts, data, or assumptions that the expert already knows? What about an expert's notes of communication with the attorney? Under the rules, the communication itself is protected if it doesn't fall within one of the three exceptions, but a court may find the notes are discoverable.

What to do. Here are a few things experts can do to limit their exposure:

- Be careful in your collaboration with attorneys;
- Limit the number of draft reports. Fewer means less exposure;
- Limit communication with the attorney;
- Assume all notes and work papers will be discoverable, even if they summarize discussion with counsel;
- Limit the need for counsel to provide facts, data, and assumptions; and
- Consider using technology such as GoToMeeting for conferences with counsel.

***Sylvia Golden, Esq.**, is executive legal editor at Business Valuation Resources. She received her J.D. from the University of California at Berkeley (Boalt Hall) and is an active member of the State Bar of California.*

Attorneys Reveal Seven Surprising Views on Expert Depositions

By Sylvia Golden, Esq.

Workshops on expert testimony abound, but too many paint the same picture of what it's like for an expert to become an actor in a litigated dispute. However, a recent presentation, "Deposition of the Expert Witness," by the Multnomah Bar Association in Portland, Ore., offered some unusual views from two experienced litigators on how to work with and against experts. The presenters, Paul Conable (Tonkon Torp LLP) and Chris Kayser (Larkins Vacura), spoke primarily to an audience of attorneys, but their tips can help experts in landing engagements and getting battle-ready.

1. *Clueless on experts.* Most attorneys don't know what an expert is. That's how Conable and Kayser started their discussion. Knowing this simple truth may help the expert in his or her interaction with the retaining attorney.

Also, even though expert deposition testimony is almost always available in federal court (under FRCP 26(b)(4)(A)), it's almost never available in Oregon state court—unless the parties agree to take depositions. If you are an expert on a state law case, check with the retaining attorney whether there are going to be expert depositions.

2. *It's not cross-examination.* The common take on expert depositions is that they serve as a form of cross-examination or a dress rehearsal for trial. Conable and Kayser disagree. The last thing an attorney wants is to give away his or her case before trial, which can happen when you ask the expert too many questions or ask too aggressively during a deposition. If an attorney discovers weaknesses in an expert's report, the attorney should use the deposition simply to commit the expert to the statements in the report.

From the expert's perspective, this means, "be on your guard." Gentler interaction with the opposing attorney during your deposition may mean the attorney is saving the full-frontal attack for trial.

3. *Boxing in the expert.* A main objective of a deposition is to "box the expert in," Conable and Kayser agree. Smart attorneys use depositions to find out what's the worst the expert is going to say, to limit the scope of what the expert is going to testify to, and to uncover what the expert did or did

not rely on. In other words, the deposition serves as a record with which the attorney will try to exclude parts or all of the expert testimony at trial.

Finally, as an expert, be prepared to hear a catchall question along the lines of: "Other than the opinions you have already expressed today, are there opinions you intend to give at trial?" Your reply limits what you as an expert can say at trial and helps the attorney protect against surprises in the courtroom.

4. *Battle shifts to facts.* Experts know a lot more about issues in their area of expertise than the attorneys working on the case. But, Conable and Kayser point out, experts likely know far less about the specific facts of the case. Therein lies their weakness. Veteran attorneys use depositions to home in on the facts underlying the expert's analysis. Is a calculation based on sufficient facts, on relevant facts? Does the expert tie the analysis to the facts? Is there material the expert did not see prior to developing his or her analysis? The goal is to make the expert doubt the relationship with the retaining attorney rather than feel under attack from the opposing attorney.

From the expert's point of view, this signals a need to be continually informed about the case and to scrutinize the facts and assumptions you are being handed.

5. *Forget the glittering CV.* "Don't fall in love with an expert's CV," Conable and Kayser warned the audience. Both say the most important thing when choosing an expert is that he or she is a good communicator—someone who's likable and can connect with the jury. An expert who is enthusiastic about his or her work often can convey that sense of excitement to a jury even if he or she never testified before, the attorneys believe. On the other hand, an experienced but smug witness may turn into a liability.

6. *Early engagement preferable.* Both attorneys say they like to engage experts in the early stages of a case for a number of reasons, including giving the client a heads-up as to the cost of the case, allowing the expert sufficient time to develop his or her testimony, and enabling the attorney to rely on the expert to evaluate the opposing expert's credentials and testimony.

7. Daubert *reminder to attorney.* Both attorneys also reminded the attorney audience how crushing a *Daubert* exclusion is to an expert. It's easy for the attorney to forget about the expert once the motion has been decided and to take the defeat personally—since, in the final analysis, it's the attorney's, not the expert's, case—Kayser said. But that's nearsighted. When it comes to *Daubert,* the expert's reputation is just as much on the line as that of the attorney, he emphasizes. Therefore, it's critical to empower your expert by giving him or her the complete pertinent information in a timely manner.

Sylvia Golden, Esq., *is executive legal editor at Business Valuation Resources. She received her J.D. from the University of California at Berkeley (Boalt Hall) and is an active member of the State Bar of California.*

Pitfalls for Expert Witnesses Doing a Valuation Report Review

One of the highlights of the recent ASA Advanced Business Valuation Conference in Florida was a mock trial session. It demonstrated how skilled opposing counsel can skewer even the most experienced valuation expert in court.

All six valuation disciplines gathered to attend the session (no easy feat), and an expert from each discipline was put on the "witness stand." For the business valuation part, an expert who prepared a review of another expert's valuation report was called to testify. Because this was based on a real case, the names of those involved and relevant details of the case are not disclosed here. Also, some of the situations have been changed for educational purposes. Attorney Peter L. Gladstone (Gladstone & Weissman PA) played the role of counsel for both sides. First, he elicited direct testimony, and some excerpts are below.

Q: *You were asked by me to critique a business valuation report of another appraiser?*

A: Yes.

Q: *And you wrote me a letter explaining what the flaws in the report were?*

A: That's correct.

Q: *Among other things, you concluded that the appraiser, Mr. Smith, failed to comply with numerous standards, including USPAP Standards 9 and 10?*

A: Not just USPAP, but Smith didn't comply with any set of standards I've ever seen.

Q: *In your letter, you write that it's your opinion that the Smith report contains conclusions of value that are overstated?*

A: Yes. I also wrote that not only are the values calculated incorrectly, but they don't make any sense.

Q: *One of the issues is discounts. Did Smith take any discounts into account in his report?*

A: There were no discounts reflected in his report. I don't know all of the facts, but this is a closely held company and clearly there are some illiquidity issues.

The attorney asks a few more questions along these lines and then ends his direct testimony. The attorney asks the court to strike the Smith valuation report. It appears that the valuation expert did a good job, and it was all pretty straightforward.

Cross-examination. Attorney Gladstone puts on his other hat to do the cross-examination.

Q: *In one of your answers just a moment ago, did you say, "I don't know all the facts?"*

A: Absolutely.

Q: *Then how, sir, can you have the gall to sit there and critique Smith's appraisal if you don't have all of the facts?*

A: The concept of writing a proper appraisal report is to allow the reader to understand the thought process that went into formulating an opinion. Smith's report failed to do that because there were many items missing from the report. So all I can do is provide a critique of what's in the report. I have not provided an independent opinion of value—I was not asked to do that.

Pitfall No. 1. Note the tone of the cross-examining attorney in his question. You can expect this, so don't let it rattle you. In this case, the expert handled it very well. However, his statement that he didn't provide an opinion of value triggers some questions along these lines.

Q: *You say you didn't provide an opinion of value. But you did recalculate some of the figures in the Smith report?*

A: Actually, what I said was that, if a rule of thumb were used, then Mr. Smith's value would be different. I said many times in the report that I'm not giving an opinion.

Q: *You write in your critique that the Smith report contains conclusions of value that are overstated and the calculations defy logic. Is that correct?*

A: Yes.

Pitfall No. 2: In an appraisal review, never go after the appraiser—go after the report! You should not call the other appraiser "incompetent" because then you could get into defamation issues, which could be very serious, the speakers say. Also, don't use the word "violation" because only a court can determine whether a violation was made. Instead, use language such as "he did not comply" with standards. Speakers also advised the proper way to lay out another appraiser's transgression. You find what you think he or she did wrong, and then you find the rule that governs it to show noncompliance. Let's go back to the cross-examination.

Q: *So aren't you rendering an appraisal opinion if you're stating that you disagree with the value?*

A: I did not do an appraisal.

Q: *That's all well and good, but you've assigned a value to this entity, and the judge is entitled to review these amounts.*

Pitfall No. 3. You must be very sensitive to the language you use in an appraisal review, the speakers advised. Don't get boxed into providing an opinion of value. If you fall into that trap, you will be subject to Standards 9 and 10 of USPAP. In this case, the language the reviewer used such as calling the values "flawed" and "defying logic" constitute evidence of a value opinion. The proper language to use would be "if Smith had used such-and-such figure, his value would have been thus-and-so."

Q: *You state in your review that Smith only used the income approach even though there was a great deal of market data to support a market approach.*

A: That's correct. All of the leading business valuation treatises indicate that the correct way to …

Q: *Excuse me, but you say "all of the leading business valuation treatises." Did you cite in your review what these treatises are?*

A: No.

Q: *So you're saying it is so just because you say it?*

Pitfall No. 4. Without the citations, the authority is implied in the reviewer himself. This is the legal concept of ipse dixit (literally, "he himself said it"). You can't simply make statements without support, or the other side will jump on it. The attorney now picks up on another weakness in the reviewer's report.

Q: *Are you familiar with USPAP Standard 3?*

A: I've heard of it.

Q: *What is it?*

A: It has to do with appraisal review.

Q: *Are you not aware that Standard 3 requires you to identify the client for whom you're doing the review?*

A: That's in Standard 3, yes.

Q: *But you did not do that, correct?*

A: That's correct. I didn't follow Standard 3 because this was for litigation. I felt I was disclosing enough information to you.

Q: *So it's your understanding that litigation is an exception to Standard 3?*

A: At the time I did the report, I thought that, yes.

Q: *So sitting here today in this court, before all of these fine people, you know that Standard 3 applies to every appraisal review whether it's for litigation or not?*

A: My opinions wouldn't be different whether I complied with Standard 3 or not.

Q: *Sir, you are required as an ASA certified business appraiser to comply with USPAP Standard 3, and you failed to do so.*

Pitfall No. 5. Know your standards. Note how the attorney raked the appraiser over the coals because of this. The over-the-top wording he uses is designed to make the reviewer look really bad. In this case, the reviewer criticized the other appraiser for not following USPAP, but he was not in compliance himself! However, he turned it around fairly well by saying he knew it was wrong and that it shouldn't be done that way. But when he did it he thought it was OK. Standard 3 also requires the reviewer to state the scope of the work and provide a signed certification, which the reviewer also failed to do in his report.

What happened in this case? The court tossed out the expert's report, and the strategy the attorney used with the reviewer worked out. That is, the reviewer's recalculation of value assisted the court in coming up with a value. So the lesson is to follow the strategy of the attorney in terms of whether to just do a rebuttal or offer an alternative number in terms of value. But, as this case illustrated, this is a risky move that can open up the reviewer to attack and all types of ethics violations.

One final piece of overall advice for any expert: Tell your attorney about weaknesses that could undermine your report so that you can be prepared for the witness stand. Gladstone warns: "Don't keep it to yourself."

Section IV. Business Valuation Profession and Practice Management

Business Valuation Year in Review 2015

Here's a rundown of some of the major developments in the business valuation profession during 2015, which marked the 20th anniversary of *Business Valuation Update*. The October 2015 issue presented a retrospective as well as insights into the profession from leading practitioners and thought leaders. The issue also featured an interview that included Shannon Pratt, who was the founding editor of *BVU*.

Legal. The courts continued to provide a steady stream of cases involving various business valuation issues. You can see a listing of the top-10 BV-related cases elsewhere in this issue. In addition to those cases, the fair market value of physician compensation played an important part in a number of cases in the healthcare industry. The cases include *DaVita,*[1] *Tuomey,*[2] and *Citizens Medical,*[3] which follow on the heels of several others—and others are now in the works. The government has been suing hospitals, challenging the fair market value of certain transactions, including the acquisition of medical practices. However, valuation experts point to many flaws in the government's arguments and methodology, including the use of faulty survey data (see the November 2015 *BVU* and the article elsewhere in this issue).

Data and publications. Duff & Phelps released a vibrant new product, the *Valuation Handbook – Industry Cost of Capital,* as a companion to its *Valuation Handbook – Guide to Cost of Capital.* It's the second book in a series that replaces the now discontinued material from Morningstar/Ibbotson (see the January 2015 *BVU).* A third book was also released, the *International Valuation Handbook – Guide to Cost of Capital,* which provides the same type of country-level cost of capital analyses previously published by Morningstar/Ibbotson.

D&P also updated its Risk Premium Calculator, an online tool used to calculate the cost of equity capital (see the February 2015 *BVU*).

Private-company business transaction data enjoyed significant expansion: *Pratt's Stats* now has over 24,000 transactions with up to 89 data fields per transaction. BIZCOMPS, Done Deals, and the IBA

1 *United States of America et al ex rel. David Barbetta vs DaVita, Inc.*

2 *U.S. ex rel. Drakeford v. Tuomey,* No. 13-2219 (4th Cir. 2015).

3 *United States ex rel. Parikh, et al. v. Citizens Medical Center, et al., Case No. 6:10-cv-64 (S.D. Tex.).*

Market Database also expanded their number of transactions. An excerpt from *The Comprehensive Guide to the Use and Application of the Transaction Databases,* written by Heidi P. Walker (Meyers, Harrison & Pia LLC), is in the April 2015 *BVU.*

A new book, *Taxes and Value: The Ongoing Research and Analysis Relating to the S Corporation Valuation Puzzle,* challenged some conventional wisdom. The book by Nancy J. Fannon (Meyers, Harrison and Pia LLC) and Keith Sellers (University of Denver) contains an abundance of research showing that shareholder-level taxes do indeed affect a firm's value. Up until now, the IRS and the Tax Court have refuted this position, largely because data have never been presented to support it. This work should provide valuation professionals with the evidence they need to support their valuation conclusions. It also provides a suggestion for a new, more direct approach to pass-through entity valuation (see an article in the April 2015 *BVU* and a review of the book in the June 2015 *BVU*).

Business Valuation Resources added a new line of industry-specific special reports under the series title *What It's Worth.* The first two have been released, accounting firms and veterinary practices, with several more in the pipeline.

Standards. There has been the perception that the various valuation standards conflict with each other. Mark Hanson (Schenck SC) and Mark Kucik (Kucik Valuation Group) prepared a side-by-side comparison of the standards set by NACVA, IBA, AICPA, ASA, and USPAP, which reveals that they do not conflict with each other (see the February 2015 *BVU*).

The Appraisal Foundation issued the 2016-17 version of USPAP and held its third annual Business Valuation Roundtable. This event brought together business valuation leaders to discuss a number of topics and trends in the profession (see the December 2015 *BVU*).

At the annual meeting of the International Valuation Standards Council (IVSC) in Paris, the new version of IVS was discussed. The exposure draft of the newest update is planned for January 2016, followed by a three-month review period (see the December 2015 *BVU*).

Regulatory. Two new job aids from the IRS were released. *Reasonable Compensation: Job Aid for IRS Valuation Professionals* has a wealth of information to help valuators anticipate the challenges the IRS will make to reasonable compensation estimates (see the January 2015 *BVU*). *Valuation of Non-Controlling Interests in Business Entities Electing to be Treated as S Corporations for Federal Tax Purposes* explains the agency's thinking on valuing S corporations, but it does not reflect sound valuation principles (see the June 2015 *BVU*).

The Department of Labor (DOL) eliminated the "appraiser-as-fiduciary" rule from its newly reissued proposal of a broader fiduciary rule. However, there is still a need for peer review of ESOP valuation reports (see the March 2015 *BVU*).

Methodologies. Valuation concepts have undergone significant changes in thinking over the years (see the October 2015 *BVU*), and change will continue. Conventional thinking is being challenged in a number of areas, including the size premium (see the February 2015 *BVU*), the double dip (see the July 2015 *BVU*), and personal goodwill (see the August 2015 *BVU*).

An interesting interview was conducted with Pablo Fernandez (University of Navarra—IESE Business School, Spain). He is a widely published author, and he conducts a survey of market risk premiums and risk-free rates used in countries around the world. His paper, "CAPM: An Absurd Model," created a stir in the business valuation community. Fernandez was interviewed by Michael Crain (Financial Valuation Group), a valuation practitioner who has done academic research, most recently on the size premium (see the July 2015 *BVU*).

Conferences. Attendance at valuation conferences was up this year from last. *BVU* attended many of these events and provided recaps and some detailed coverage. At the ASA-CICBV Business Valuation Conference in Toronto, a session on new scrutiny on valuation and fairness opinions in M&A was presented by Steven M. Davidoff, a professor of law at the University of California, Berkeley (see the January 2015 *BVU*).

Business valuation professionals from all corners of the globe gathered in Atlanta for an event sponsored by the International Association of Consultants, Valuators and Analysts (IACVA). One of the fascinating sessions showcased practitioners from different countries who gave an overview of BV practice and the profession in their land (see the June 2015 *BVU*). The New York State Society of CPAs (NYSSCPA) annual business valuation conference covered some of the profession's hottest topics. Of particular interest were the session on S corp valuations and a panel discussion on DLOM (see the July 2015 *BVU*).

NACVA held its annual conference in New Orleans (see the recap in the August 2015 *BVU*), and the ASA's annual event was in Las Vegas (see highlights in the December 2015 *BVU*). Over 1,100 attendees were at the AICPA FVS Conference and about 350 attended its Healthcare Industry Conference, which included a valuation track (see articles on both of these events elsewhere in this issue).

It looks as if 2016 will be another year of changes, challenges, and opportunities in the field of business valuation, and we at *BVU* will keep our readers ahead of the curve on developments.

BVU Profile:
Newest *BVU* Editorial Board Member Is a Strong Advocate of Education

One of the busiest people at the recent AICPA FVS conference was Harold G. Martin Jr., who is the partner-in-charge of Valuation and Forensic Services for Keiter, a CPA and consulting firm located in Richmond, Va. Not only did he teach the ABV Exam Review class, but he also conducted a four-hour workshop on cross-examination of expert witnesses—and then did three regular sessions to boot. This reflects his passion for BV education. He is also the co-author of *Financial Valuation: Applications and Models* (1st, 2nd, 3rd, and 4th editions) and a contributing author to *Cost of Capital: Estimation and Applications* (2nd, 3rd, and 4th editions). In 2012, he was inducted into the AICPA BV Hall of Fame. *BVU* is happy to welcome him to its Editorial Advisory Board.

BVU: *How did you get into business valuation?*

HM: After graduating with a degree in English from The College of William and Mary in 1979, my first job was in retail banking where I became interested in accounting and finance. I then completed the required courses to sit for the CPA exam. I joined Price Waterhouse's Richmond office in 1983 as an auditor and completed my MBA in night school. I did not begin my career in public accounting with the objective of specializing; instead, my career evolved as opportunities presented themselves. After about two years in audit, I transferred to the consulting practice where I worked on systems development projects, including a large litigation project. Following that experience, I transferred to the Philadelphia office where I specialized in litigation. In 1992, I joined Coopers & Lybrand's Financial Advisory Services group, where I served as a director responsible for managing the Richmond litigation practice. It was during this time that my father sold his insurance agency and requested my assistance in valuing it. I collaborated with a specialist in C&L's valuation group, and this project piqued my interest in valuation.

BVU: *Can you describe the valuation practice at Keiter?*

HM: In 1996, I had the opportunity to join Keiter and develop a valuation and forensic services practice. Since that time, our practice has grown into one of the largest full-time practices in Virginia outside of the metro-D.C. market. Our practice focuses on valuations of closely held businesses for tax, transactions, financial reporting, shareholder agreements, stock-based compensation, intellectual property, and transfer pricing.

BVU: *Are you still doing economic damages work?*

HM: Yes, our forensic services include litigation consulting and expert witness services for business litigation and family law. The types of business litigation matters for which we have served as a consultant or expert include breach of contract, business interruption, divorce, fraud, intellectual property infringement (trade secrets, patents, copyrights, and trademarks), post-acquisition disputes, professional malpractice, securities, shareholder disputes, tortious interference, wrongful death, and wrongful termination. Our forensic services also include financial investigations. While litigation consulting and expert witness work can be very stressful and challenging, it is also is a very rewarding experience when you are successful in assisting a client. In this venue, I have had the privilege of being appointed as an expert by both federal and state courts.

BVU: *When you need staff members, how do you recruit them?*

HM: We recruit, develop, and train our staff from the pool of accounting and finance majors directly from undergraduate and graduate schools. We also send them to training sponsored by the AICPA and ASA.

BVU: *When you're looking for new recruits on campus, what do you tell them about the profession?*

HM: I tell recruits that I have been in practice for over 30 years and still enjoy the work because I learn something new every day. Valuation is an interesting and challenging discipline and requires knowledge of many diverse areas such as finance, accounting, tax, economics, statistics, marketing, information technology, as well as written and oral communications skills. It's also a great profession in which to begin a career because you will be exposed to a lot and learn a great deal, which will help you no matter what career path you ultimately pursue. I always conclude by advising prospective recruits to select a career about which they are passionate and they will be successful.

BVU: *I see from your CV that you do a lot of teaching.*

HM: Yes, I'm a very strong advocate for serving as an instructor as it is a way of giving back to the profession. I have served as an instructor for the AICPA since 1997, and I teach the AICPA National BV School, AICPA ABV Exam Review Course, and the AICPA Expert Witness Skills Workshop. I created and serve as chair of the Virginia Society of Certified Public Accountants Annual Business Valuation, Fraud, and Litigation Services Conference, which is now in its 16th year. Also, for the past 11 years, I have served as an adjunct faculty member of The College of William and Mary Raymond A. Mason Graduate School of Business and have taught forensic accounting in the Master of Accounting program, and have also served as a guest lecturer on valuation for the MBA program and the Marshall-Wythe School of Law. I also speak frequently at seminars, most recently presenting at the Federal Bureau of Investigation Supervisor Forensic Accountant Summit.

BVU: *You co-presented a session on cost of capital at the recent AICPA FVS conference in Las Vegas. From your perspective, what are the major areas of controversy regarding cost of capital?*

HM: One area of controversy is the appropriate data to use in computing the different variables in the cost of capital (e.g., computing the equity risk premium using long-term historical returns or expected future returns). Another is whether certain adjustments should be made to certain variables in computing cost of capital (e.g., adjusting the risk-free rate to reflect a sustainable average return, adjusting the equity risk premium to reflect current market conditions). Yet another example is the source of data to be used in computing a size premium (e.g., CRSP data or Duff & Phelps data) or even whether or not a size premium exists. Finally, the quantification of company-specific risk is an issue given the lack of empirical data.

BVU: *You do a lot of litigation work, so how do you handle these differences in practice?*

HM: We recognize that in litigation our work will be subject to scrutiny by opposing counsel and the adverse expert. To address this, we calculate the discount rate using alternative models and develop a range of rates to value a company. We then select a rate from this range based on our professional judgment and in consideration of the particular facts and circumstances. Using this approach, we are able to demonstrate that we have considered the alternatives, and then we explain the reasons for selecting the rate we ultimately used. We also compare our discount rate with the range of total rates of return observed in the market. Finally, we corroborate the value derived using the income approach with estimated values using alternative valuation approaches.

BVU: *What do you do in your spare time?*

HM: My hobbies are reading, playing the guitar, and keeping up with my children, who are all grown and the last one is in college. I also help my wife in the garden. Well, let me get that straight—she is a master gardener, and I'm just the hired help!

BVU Profile:
NACVA Thomas R. Porter Award Winner Offers Advice and Insights to Valuation Experts

Editor's note: P. Dermot O'Neill has over 40 years of experience as a CPA with a diverse background and practice. He is the president of P. Dermot O'Neill, CPA PC, which concentrates on business valuation, forensic accounting and litigation support, transaction consulting, financial analysis, and income taxation. In addition to being a CPA, he holds the ABV, CFF, CVA, MAFF, and ABAR credentials. He has served as an expert witness, teaches business valuation in a graduate program, and is managing editor of the National Litigation Consultants Review. *In 2015, he was the recipient of NACVA's Thomas R. Porter Lifetime Achievement Award, which recognizes a member's exemplary character, leadership, and professional achievements.* BVU *was fortunate to be able to talk with him about his career and his insights into the practice of business valuation.*

BVU: *How did you get into valuation?*

O'Neill: In college, I started studying engineering but after my first year switched to business. I went to work for an accounting firm and got into accounting systems design. This was in the late 1960s and early 1970s, when clients were moving from manual books to an automated system, so I designed custom systems. I liked the analytic aspect of that work, and it was very beneficial to me later on. I then moved into tax and took graduate courses in taxation. I was working in a tax practice, and the owner was the local divorce guru who also did some business valuation for divorce. I liked valuation and the analytics involved, so in 1994 I started to do the training for business valuation. I got my CVA from NACVA, and then when I had enough experience I was able to take the test for the ABV from the AICPA. I went to work in the valuation and litigation services group at a national consulting firm that was affiliated with a national CPA firm. They had about 20 partners and about 100 staff, so there was always someone who needed a valuation of some type. If you're with a CPA firm, the best marketers are the partners in the firm who know what valuation is all about—they're your best source of business.

BVU: *You are accredited in business appraisal review (ABAR). Can you comment on that credential?*

O'Neill: It's a very powerful credential because you are able to opine on the credibility of a valuation report, which is very critical to a judge. I'm often called in to review the appraisal reports of the opposing side in litigation matters. The most recent ones I've done involved very contentious matters that were ready to go to court. In all of the cases, the parties settled after reading my reports.

***BVU:** What is the most common error you see in reviewing valuation reports?*

O'Neill: One of the most common issues I see is advocacy, where the valuation expert, through the use of chosen methodologies, is being an advocate as opposed to being objective. Another issue is a lack of foundation for the numbers utilized. For example, the report will state that a certain percentage is used for a discount for lack of marketability, but there will be no explanation as to why that number was used. The report may include data from restricted stock studies or pre-IPO studies, but there is no specific explanation as to why the particular percentage was chosen. It may point out that the percentage used is an average of the relevant data, but that's the "flaw of averages."[1] Unless the company is "average," the average number may be misleading.

***BVU:** What do you feel are the most controversial issues today in terms of business valuation theory or methodology?*

O'Neill: I see two issues as particularly controversial: the tax-affecting issue and the control premium. In terms of tax affecting, for years I've been an advocate of using a pretax discount rate as opposed to taking a tax deduction from earnings or cash flow. From a litigation standpoint, it's practically impossible to explain tax affecting to a judge or jury. Adjusting the discount rate ties into what Nancy Fannon, Keith Sellers, Aswath Damodaran, and others have been advocating. It also ties in to what the Tax Court has been saying—that they don't throw out tax affecting but no expert has adequately explained why the court should consider it. There needs to be more work done in this area, but there have been steps made so far.

As for the control premium, it was thought that the prices in the public market represented minority interests. Therefore, in an M&A situation, a company was really buying control. I think that's a fallacy because we really don't know what they're buying. We know they're buying future synergies and strategic positioning, so looking to the public market for a control premium is probably not the best thing to do, although we do it. Maybe in the future someone will take a look at private-company information, such as *Pratt's Stats* data, to see if there's some way to glean control premium information from that data.

***BVU:** You've done a great deal of testifying in court. How can a valuator break into expert witness work?*

O'Neill: Typically, the most successful way is to do pro bono work for nonprofits or charities to build up your CV. You may not get paid, but it's an investment to make in order to gain experience.

1 Sam L. Savage, The Flaw of Averages; Why We Underestimate Risk in the Face of Uncertainty, John Wiley & Sons Inc., Hoboken, N.J., 2009-2012.

Another good idea is to represent the nonpropertied spouse in a divorce matter who typically doesn't have the funds to pay a retainer or your regular fee. You don't take the engagement for free, but you charge what the client can afford. You may or may not have to write it off, but it's critical to build up your CV if you want to do expert witness work. I did one recently for a public agency that involved a wrongful death case. The agency is on a limited budget, so I charged about a third of what I would normally charge because it increases my experience testifying in a wrongful death case.

If you're in a CPA firm, you may get some resistance to these ideas, so you'll need to garner the support of the partners and the other people in the firm. Educate them as to what you do and how you'd like to get into the expert witness area.

BVU: *Over the years, you've developed a diverse practice. If you were starting out today, would you specialize in a particular area of business valuation?*

O'Neill: The first thing I would do is look for a mentor, which is extremely important for someone to have. Hopefully, that mentor would tell me that before I make a decision about specializing that I should get some basic experience and training in accounting, finance, and economics. I teach business valuation in the graduate business program at Rider University, under the MAcc program [Master of Accountancy], so many students have an undergraduate degree in accounting. I tell them that they have all the accounting that they need to know for business valuations, so their graduate studies should include finance, for example, because valuation is not just about accounting. The students who get their master's in accounting and want to jump right into business valuation should consider first going into public accounting or consulting to gain a range of experience.

BVU: *Do you see any valuation growth areas on the horizon, such as litigation, divorce, or fair value?*

O'Neill: Litigation and divorce are growth areas, and one of the reasons I sense is that many of the "dabblers" are getting weeded out. The CPAs who primarily did accounting and tax work but also valuations on the side have found that it is not something you dabble in. But this has created some pricing pressures because clients are looking for the lower fees that the dabblers charged. There are also opportunities related to the fact that the baby boomers are retiring, so there will be some growth in valuations for that market as they sell or gift their businesses to family members.

I don't think that fair value is going to be a growth area per se. Back in 2013, the FASB decided not to require the fair value standards for closely held companies, so that cut into the market. Some colleagues of mine who felt that closely held companies were looking to be acquired by private equity funds or funds looking to go public found they had to expand their practices into litigation, for example.

BVU: *Congratulations on receiving the Thomas R. Porter award from NACVA. The award recognizes an individual's achievements in both the business valuation and financial forensics communities. Can you comment on the use of financial forensics from a valuation standpoint?*

O'Neill: Business valuation and forensics both come down to analytics—looking at a situation, analyzing it, and coming up with a conclusion. I look at it from the standpoint of skills. Business valuation and forensics both require the same skill sets; they're just applied differently.

Years ago someone asked me what I did for a living, and I said that I was a forensic financial analyst. The person said: "Oh, just like 'CSI.'" Yes, it's exactly like "CSI"—but instead of dead bodies, we're dealing with dead transactions, dead financial relationships, etc. We look at evidence and draw conclusions and express opinions, which is really what forensics is all about. And it can be in various contexts, such as business valuation or lost profits. Right now I have a case where someone at a third-party payroll service took a client's money by taking the withheld payroll taxes and not turning them over to the IRS. This is not business valuation or lost profits—it's an analytics situation. You need to look beyond the labels.

BVU: *You have both the CFF and MAFF credentials in financial forensics. How did getting these make you a better valuator?*

O'Neill: It was an opportunity to improve my analytical skills and also my report writing skills. It also helps you look at things in different ways through the eyes of other practitioners. It also expands your networking, which is invaluable. You come in contact with some great people as you go through this kind of continuing education.

Another reason for getting the credential was that, when I was doing forensic work for litigation, I would get the question of why I didn't have the forensics credential that's issued by my own organization [the AICPA].

BVU: *How does forensics come into play in a typical valuation?*

O'Neill: Forensics, or analytics if you will, is intertwined with valuation. For example, if I'm looking at a company's revenue, I know it's made up of two components: units and price. So I will ask for that information. Then I will look at the units and prices and see how they may be correlated with the industry, local demographics, and so on. The forensics piece of it is the ratio analysis that is done to correlate what's going on in the industry with what I'm seeing in the subject company. You do this in order to determine whether the historical financials relate closely enough to the industry and market so that you can use them as a basis for the forward-looking valuation such as a single period capitalization model. That's how I apply the forensics—or analytics—to the business valuation.

BVU: *How can the business valuation profession improve itself?*

O'Neill: I think that to improve the profession you need to educate the users about how to use our services. Some of the attorneys and clients who think they know what business valuation is don't know how to use it. We need to educate them on how to use the process.

P. Dermot O'Neill's practice is located in Glen Mills, Pa. He can be reached at damages@comcast.net.

BVU Profile:
What Is the Practice of BV Like in the Middle East?

Editor's note: Faisal Alsayrafi, ASA, CVA, CMEA, CPA, is founder, president, and CEO of Financial Transaction House (FTH) in Saudi Arabia, which offers a wide range of corporate finance advisory services to a diversified client base in the Middle East. He can be reached at faisal.alsayrafi@fthgulf .com or at +966 12 657 3030.

BVU: *How did you get into business valuation?*

Faisal Alsayrafi: I joined Arthur Andersen after graduating with a masters in accounting and MBA in finance from a U.S. graduate school. I worked closely with senior management providing consulting and became managing partner of corporate finance, M&A, and advisory services for the Middle East region where valuations services were a critical concern.

BVU: *Is business valuation regulated in your country?*

FA: Yes, valuation services are now regulated by TAQEEM for most of areas and disciplines of valuation. TAQEEM is the Saudi Authority for Accredited Valuers, a government regulator for business valuations in Saudi Arabia.

BVU: *What is the nature of the typical valuation engagements in your market area?*

FA: The environment is competitive and evolving. The engagements range from valuations for financial reporting, goodwill impairment to buy-/sell-side engagements (for business and machinery and equipment).

BVU: *What countries are in your market area?*

FA: Saudi Arabia, UAE, Qatar, Bahrain, Kuwait, Oman (GCC countries), and Egypt.

BVU: *Are there any areas of valuation practice that are particularly growing?*

FA: There is a growing interest in intellectual property and the valuation of IP assets, as well as valuation of machinery and equipment in connection with purchase price allocations.

BVU: *What sources of financial data do you use for business valuations?*

FA: One important source is the Tadawul, the Saudi stock exchange. As regulations have relaxed to allow more foreign investment, it has become more important as a barometer of value. Accredited valuers also use U.S.-based databases as a benchmark for valuation purposes (i.e., Business Valuation Resources for private company data).

BVU: *Are private equity or venture capital groups active in your market?*

FA: Private equity (PE) and venture capital (VC) are active, but they tend to acquire minority interests in vertically integrated companies and serve as family advisors. They are also very important in those instances where firms are in distress and in need of capital because the laws involving bankruptcy and turnarounds are new and evolving and PE and VCs offer more certainty.

BVU: *Are valuers involved in litigation? Is there a court system similar to ours in the U.S.?*

FA: Yes, there is a role for litigation support in facilitating dispute resolution. The court system in Saudi Arabia (independent) does not have judges that specialize, such as the Delaware Court of Chancery or courts in the U.S. where IP disputes are presented to judges with the training and education to handle those matters. As the number of businesses grow in response to diversification efforts, the need for specialized courts will increase and we may see those become a reality.

BVU: *Is there anything unique to business valuation in your market area (e.g., scope of services, methodology, or reports)?*

FA: Most professional firms and qualified practitioners use U.S.-based approaches and standards such as USPAP/AICPA standards. In Saudi Arabia and most of the GCC, the International Valuation Standard (IVS) provides the governing standards as per Saudi TAQEEM regulations in connection with iiBV (International Institute of Business Valuers) advisory contractors.

BVU: *How do you develop a cost of capital?*

FA: Normally, professionals will develop a cost of capital in accordance with international cost of capital and CAPM methodologies.

BVU: *What set of standards do valuers use?*

FA: Currently, in Saudi Arabia, we all use the IVS.

BVU: *Are business valuers certified? What credentials do they have?*

FA: Currently, TAQEEM has developed licensing and accreditation requirements for appraisal practices using the help of the iiBV for business valuation discipline, which eventually will be the ASA basic course material (regulations are in draft form at this stage).

BVU: *In addition to the iiBV, are business valuers active in other valuation or finance organizations, such as the CFA, ASA, or RICS?*

FA: I believe the answer is "yes," and TAQEEM is reaching out to various professional institutes in the world. The most committed and networked entities are the iiBV, AI, RICS, and Malaysian Institute of Appraisals. There are other professional organizations that have expressed an interest in participating in training but have not executed as of yet. As for professionals providing valuation services across the various disciplines, there are those holding designations earned through the ASA, CFA, RICS, and NACVA. I'm the only person qualified in ASA, as Accredited Senior Appraiser, in the whole region! Then, there are a few others that have earned the CFA designation, others that have earned the CVA from NACVA and the RICS accreditation, which focuses on real estate.

Exclusive Survey:

Most BV Firms Expect 2016 Revenues to Top Last Year

The majority of business valuation firms we polled say they expect to do more business in 2016 than last year. Most of the revenue is coming from certain areas, the top area being tax, gifts, and estates. This is according to preliminary results from BVR's Firm Economics Survey conducted during June and July of this year.

About 170 BV firms, sole practitioners, CPA firms, and other entities with business valuation practices responded to the survey. The responses reveal how firms stack up in terms of performance, compensation, billing rates, marketing and practice development, and more. Responses are being analyzed, and a full report will be available soon.

2015 vs. 2016. Practitioners are more optimistic about 2016 compared with actual results for 2015. About two-thirds (64%) expect revenues for 2016 to be higher than 2015 (Exhibit 1). A slightly higher percentage of practitioners feel they will see an increase in 2016 as opposed to their performance in 2015, when 58% of respondents saw a year-to-year increase (Exhibit 2). For 2016, a third of practitioners feel revenue will stay the same, and only 4% expects revenue to decline.

Exhibit 1. Do You Expect That Your Firm's Business Valuation Revenues in 2016 Will:

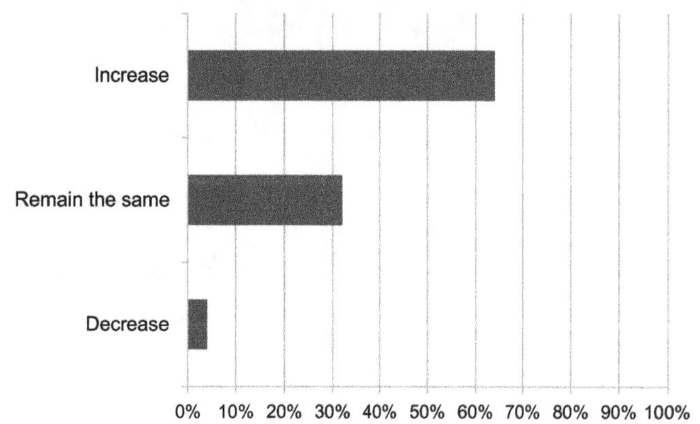

Some respondents who posted comments report increased staff and merger activity. "We expect a 10% increase in 2016. Our backlog is strong and we're seeing robust proposal activity." (Public accounting—tax or audit/accounting with three FTE valuation staff). "Business is expected to increase 25% in 2016—we added a new partner during past year." (BV firm with three FTE valuation staff). "We don't know yet about a percentage change because we merged with a smaller firm at the beginning of

Exhibit 2. In 2015, How Did Your Firm's Business Valuation Revenues Compare With 2014?

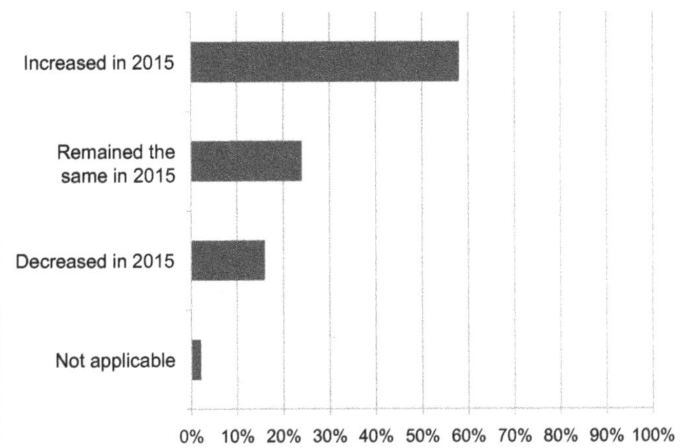

the year." (Public accounting—tax or audit/accounting, sole practitioner)

Also, a number of respondents who report decreasing revenues say they are winding down their practices and retiring. "I project about 20% less revenue than last year as I am going into partial retirement." (Public accounting—forensic or litigation services firm with two FTE valuation staff)

Several respondents who reported a decrease in 2015 say the reason was due to the nonrecurring nature of some engagements. "We had a few large engagements in 2014 that did not recur." (Public accounting firm—forensic or litigation services with eight FTE valuation staff.). "We had a large unusual project in the prior year." (BV firm with 13 FTE valuation staff).

Revenue sources. The largest percentage of total revenue comes from the tax, gift, and estate specialty area, respondents say, which represents about one-third of total revenue on average. The other top specialty areas are: family/matrimonial, fair value for financial reporting, transactional (including brokerage, mergers, and acquisitions), and shareholder/corporate, which includes buy/sell agreements and shareholder disputes (Exhibit 3). A material percentage of respondents report "other" revenue sources not listed. Some of the more prevalent sources include:

Exhibit 3. What Percentage of Your Total Business Comes From the Following Specialty Areas (Total Should Equal 100%)

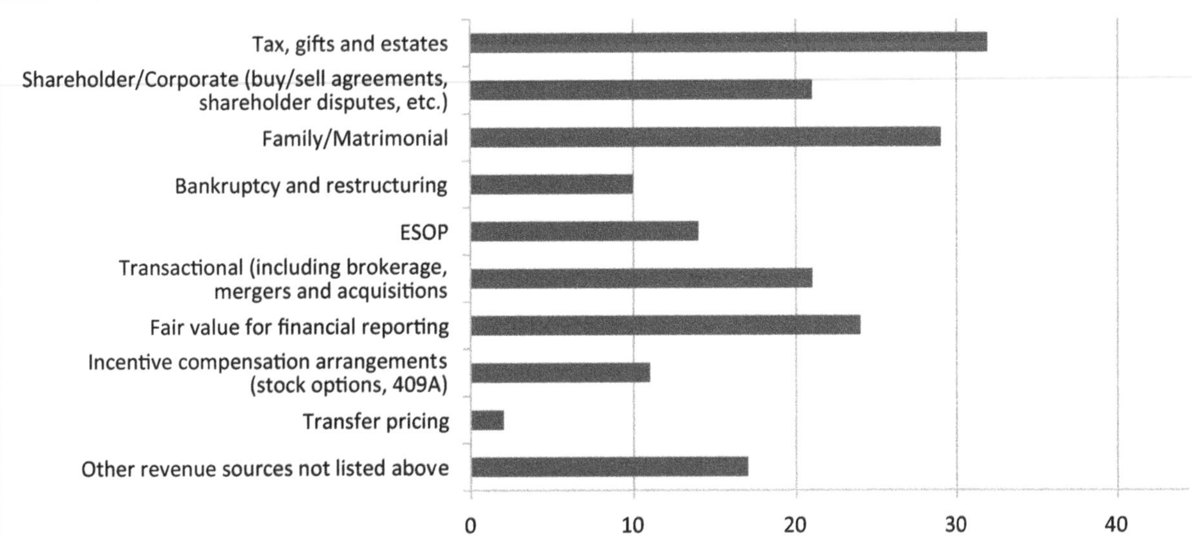

- Economic damages/lost profits;
- Fairness and solvency opinions;
- Litigation support, including expert witness services;
- Exit planning/owner transition services; and
- BV review services.

Respondents were also asked about their fastest growing area of practice over the past year. The top five they cited are:

1. Matrimonial/divorce;
2. Tax, gift, and estate;
3. Transactional (M&A);
4. Shareholder issues, disputes; and
5. Exit/succession planning.

Survey demographics. The vast majority (88%) of respondents are business valuation firms (46%) and public accounting firms either in tax or audit/accounting (32%) or forensic/litigation services (10%). A third of all respondents are sole owners.

More details on the results will appear in future issues of *Business Valuation Update*. Complete results and analysis will be included in a special report that will be available from BVR later this year.

Exclusive Survey Reveals BV Research Sources of Choice

Information is the lifeblood of a business valuation practice. Your credibility and competitive advantage hinges on the sources of data you use. BVR recently collected data concerning research sources valuation experts rely on most. *BVU* has examined the preliminary results, and we have broken down the responses into product categories.

Key trends. The top research sources shown in the following exhibits are familiar to every business appraiser: Duff & Phelps, *Pratt's Stats,* Mergerstat/BVR, BIZCOMPS, RMA, FMV, IBISWorld, and others. In looking at the survey data, some general observations can be made:

- Sources for industry-specific data and risk have increased over the years as appraisers recognize how important—and conclusive—a thorough analysis can be.

- Most appraisers are still getting guideline public company data from inexpensive sources, but some of the large, expensive databases are beginning to find favor.

- Research sources can become firmly entrenched, making it difficult for a new entrant to make significant inroads (even if the data are good). One good example is cost of capital data sources. A reason for this is the precedential nature of defending valuations and the need to use recognized unimpeachable sources.

- In some cases, favored sources of data have fluctuated, with one source gaining favor over another. One reason can be concerns about data quality.

- We should note that responses from NACVA members who purchase subscription plans from ValuSource or KeyValueData can slightly influence the absolute numbers in the following exhibits. Subsets (or all) of a few of these independent products are mixed in with the offerings available from those websites.

Transaction databases. The most widely used transaction databases appear in Exhibit 1. *Pratt's Stats* and BIZCOMPS continue to be the most widely used. CapIQ has had a significant increase in use among respondents. Other databases mentioned include IBISWorld, Partnership Profiles,

Exhibit 1. Which Private- and/or Public-Company Transaction Databases Do You Use?

	2016	2010	2008
BVR's *Pratt's Stats*	76.7%	74.8%	77.2%
BIZCOMPS	46.6%	64.4%	72.4%
NACVA/IBA Transaction Database	24.1%	39.1%	34.4%
CapIQ	23.3%	8.4%	1.9%
Factset/Mergerstat	16.4%	29.1%	31.2%
PitchBook	15.5%	NA	NA
Done Deals/Mid Market Comps	13.8%	11.3%	2.4%
BVR's Public Stats	12.9%	18.3%	NA
GFData	6.0%	NA	NA
Thomson Financial M&A Database	5.2%	4.0%	NA
None of the above	6.9%	5.5%	5.4%

Note: "NA" means that this source wasn't included in the survey questionnaire for the year.

Exhibit 2. Which of the Following Equity Risk Premia Data Do Your Firm Use?

	2016	2010	2008
*The Valuation Handbook - Guide to Cost of Capital**	80.2%	83.7%	81.0%
*Risk Premium Toolkit***	37.1%	56.5%	51.2%
Damodaran's cost of capital data	32.8%	NA	NA
Pepperdine Private Capital Markets Study	12.1%	0.6%	NA
Implied private company pricing line (IPCPL)	0.9%	NA	NA
None of the above	8.6%	8.9%	NA

* formerly Morningstar/Ibbotson

** formerly the *Duff & Phelps Risk Premium Calculator*

Note: "NA" means that this source wasn't included in the survey questionnaire for the year.

SNL Financial, Hoovers, BizExchange, and a few others.

Risk premium resources. Since the last time this survey was done, there have been some changes to the providers of discount rate and cost of capital data. Morningstar/Ibbotson discontinued its cost of capital products, which have been incorporated into the *Valuation Handbook* series from Duff & Phelps. Also, the *Duff & Phelps Risk Premium Calculator* and *Reports* were expanded to include industry risk premia, additional small-company cost of capital exhibits, and other features. The offering is now called the *Risk Premium Toolkit*. In addition, Duff & Phelps acquired the rights to the *SBBI Classic Yearbook* from Morningstar.

The most widely used resources for calculation of the risk premium and discount rates appear in Exhibit 2. Duff & Phelps dominates, but Damodaran's data-rich (and free) data have popped onto the radar and are used by a third of respondents. Going "beyond CAPM," other sources have begun to emerge, such as the implied private company pricing line (IPCPL), which is designed to measure cost of capital for small private companies.

Industry research. The historical survey results underscore the fact that there is a great deal more accessible industry-specific information than years ago. Gone are the days when a valuation report could get by with scant industry information. We point out, however, that a good number of appraisers do not use commercially available industry research databases largely because they rely on materials from trade associations, their own experience, or other vertical market sources.

Exhibit 3. Which of the Following Do You Use for Industry Benchmarks or Industry-Specific Risk Analyses?

	2016	2010	2008
IBISWorld	56.9%	29.7%	NA
RMA industry studies	48.3%	60.9%	61.1%
First Research industry reports	39.7%	29.1%	NA
Business Reference Guide	29.3%	20.3%	NA
Integra industry studies	20.7%	20.3%	32.8%
BizMiner	19.0%	21.1%	NA
None of the above	9.5%	14.4%	NA

Note: "NA" means that this source wasn't included in the survey questionnaire for the year.

Exhibit 4. Which of the Following Do You Use to Support Discounts for Lack of Marketability (DLOM), Lack of Control (DLOC), Lack of Liquidity (DLOL), or Implied Discounts?

	2016	2010	2008
Mergerstat/BVR Control Premium Study	52.6%	65.3%	45.8%
FMV Restricted Stock Study	51.7%	61.9%	36.8%
Partnership Profiles calculations	51.7%	NA	NA
Valuation Advisors Lack of Marketability Discount Study	23.3%	33.2%	23.8%
Option pricing model(s)	23.3%	6.8%	NA
Mercer Capital QMDM	12.9%	16.9%	11.2%
Pluris	11.2%	NA	NA
"Bajaj" methods	0.9%	2.5%	NA
None of the above	16.4%	14.4%	NA

Note: "NA" means that this source wasn't included in the survey questionnaire for the year.

While RMA continues to be a widely used industry research source, IBISWorld has emerged as the most cited source in this year's survey. It's pricey, but it gives you an assessment of three dimensions of risk: industry (structural), performance (growth), and economic forces (sensitivity) risk. IBIS uses a measuring system that assigns weights and comes up with a mathematical computation to determine whether the company has low, medium, or high risk.

Some of the other sources mentioned but not listed here include 10-K filings, analysts' reports, and academic studies.

Minority share discount research. Arguably, the most contested area in business valuation is the need to substantiate discounts for lack of marketability, control, or liquidity. Discounts are being challenged more frequently these days, particularly in the courts. Therefore, most appraisers rely on more than one research source and are able to choose from a number of respected and widely used resources, as shown in Exhibit 4.

Since the last survey, Pluris entered the DLOM market, and Partnership Profiles (FLP data) has made a strong showing. Also, note that more appraisers are using option pricing models (OPM) as a way to test their discount conclusions. Models from Finnerty, Chaffe, Longstaff, and comparisons to the *Mandelbaum* factors are often cited.

One respondent answered "professional judgment" as the support for discounts. In today's world of increasing *Daubert* challenges, this is a courageous strategy.

Guideline public-company method analyses. Most appraisers continue to pull GPCM comps on their own from EDGAR and Yahoo!

Exhibit 5. Which of the Following Do You Use for Guideline Public Company Method Analyses?

	2016	2010
SEC/EDGAR or EDGAR Online	54.3%	49.1%
Yahoo! Finance	43.1%	55.0%
BVR/PitchBook Public Company Comps Tool	12.9%	6.1%
Morningstar 10K Wizard	8.6%	12.4%
Hoovers	7.8%	17.8%
TagniFi (formerly FetchXL)	4.3%	5.7%
None of the above	32.8%	26.2%

Note: As with all exhibits in this section, the total is not 100% since most firms use more than one resource.

Exhibit 6. Which of the Following Tools Do You Use for Compensation Research?

Economic Research Institute	77.1%
CEO and Senior Executive Compensation Report for Private Companies	20.8%
Milliman NW Executive Compensation Survey	10.4%

Exhibit 7. Which of the Following Tools Do You Use for Valuation Case Law Research?

	2016	2010
BVLaw	26.2%	39.4%
Lexis-Nexis	19.4%	11.0%
KeyValueData's federal and state law cases (EconAssist)	13.6%	8.1%
Westlaw	4.9%	7.1%
Bloomberg Law	3.9%	NA
None of the above	40.8%	48.8%

Finance and download the financial data into their own Excel spreadsheets for ratio and other analyses. Some expensive tools automate this process, and they appear in Exhibit 5. The last survey was the first year that included data on tools used to help with this essential but time-consuming method.

Other sources survey participants reported included CapIQ, Bloomberg, SNL Financial, and Economatica (for Brazil).

Compensation research. Data on sources for compensation research have been added to the survey for the first time. ERI dominates the space with respondents as per the results shown in Exhibit 6. Other sources mentioned include PayScale, Salary.com, RMA's annual statement studies, and industry associations. Interestingly, one source the IRS uses the most to examine reasonable compensation was not mentioned: Watson Wyatt.

Valuation case law analysis. Regardless of whether you are preparing a valuation report for litigation purposes, it's essential that appraisers have a general understanding of the relevant case law. As shown in Exhibit 7, *BVLaw* is the source most respondents cite. Of those who responded "none of the above," sources include Docket Navigator, CanLi (Canada), and PACER. One respondent said they "rely on legal counsel" (conventional but effective).

Valuation-related periodicals. The most widely read business valuation periodicals appear in Exhibit 8. BVR's *Business Valuation Update* and its weekly *BVWire* came out at the top, though it should be noted that BVR's distribution list was used to collect responses for this survey. The ASA's *Business Valuation Review* is also a leading

Exhibit 8. Which Business Valuation Journals, Publications, or Blogs Do You Read?

	2016	2010
BVR's *Business Valuation Update*	66.7%	63.1%
BVR's *BVWire*	55.0%	76.7%
Business Valuation Review	45.0%	71.7%
Value Examiner	44.1%	43.0%
Forensic & Valuation Section (FVS) newsletter (AICPA)	32.4%	NA
Aswath Damodaran blog	32.4%	17.1%
ASA BV E-Letter	28.8%	40.9%
Financial Valuation and Litigation Expert (VPS)	22.5%	NA
Valuation Strategies	15.3%	21.3%
CFA Institute publications	12.6%	NA

Exhibit 9. Which of the Following Royalty Rate/Licensing Products Do You Use to Support Intellectual Property Valuations?

	2016	2010
RoyaltySource	39.0%	28.7%
ktMINE	30.5%	17.0%
MARKABLES	6.7%	NA
RoyaltyStat	5.7%	6.3%
Royalty Range	1.0%	NA
None of the above	41.9%	59.6%

Exhibit 10. What Additional Research Tools Do You Use in Your Appraisal Work?

	2016	2010	2008
IBISWorld (mostly industry research)	58.7%	34.9%	NA
BVR's *Economic Outlook Update* (economic conditions)	55.0%	53.7%	32.9%
Partnership Profiles (FLP database)	49.5%	54.9%	48.2%
BVR books, guides, and special reports	49.5%	NA	NA
ValuSource/KeyValue data (multiple topics)	31.2%	35.9%	26.8%
BVR's BVResearch (white papers, general research)	37.6%	34.5%	30.2%
Morningstar (stock research)	22.9%	32.0%	NA
ERI executive compensation studies (reasonable comp)	24.8%	15.4%	NA
BVR Digital Library	19.3%	NA	NA
Bloomberg	15.6%	NA	NA
Hoovers	11.0%	NA	NA
OneSource	4.6%	NA	NA
Alacra (transaction database)	0.9%	4.5%	NA

Note: "NA" means that the resource was not listed as an option on the 2008 questionnaire.

paid periodical, but it was cited much less than in the previous survey. This is by no means an all-inclusive list, and respondents mentioned many other great publications, including Willamette Management Associates *Insights,* Chris Mercer's blog, *Business Appraisal Practice* (from the IBA), and more.

Royalty rate, licensing, and other intellectual property valuations. IP valuations are a growth area, as the responses in Exhibit 9 indicate. RoyaltySource continues to be a leader in this specialized field, as it has been for some time, but ktMINE is becoming more widely used. Two sources, MARKABLES (trademark data) and RoyaltyStat, are new to the survey results. Of course, all of these databases are also popular with IP owners and licensees.

Other popular research sources appraisers mentioned. One theme is clear from Exhibit 10: Business appraisers are using more research sources than before—and they're using most of them more frequently. One veteran appraiser says he spends two hours a day reading these sources. Of course, each appraiser develops his or her own set of sources to help keep up with what's going on in the profession—and best help him or her support his or her assumptions and conclusions.

The results reported here are from a larger survey designed to examine valuation firms in terms of performance, compensation, billing rates, marketing and practice development, and so on. Over 170 valuation firms, sole practitioners, CPA firms, and other entities with business valuation practices responded to BVR's Firm Economics Survey conducted this summer. All of the responses are being analyzed, and a full report will be available soon. *BVU* will present more results in future issues.

Exclusive BVR Survey Examines BV Firms' Mix of Practice Revenue

Business valuation firms continue to see the largest percentage of their revenues from tax-related matters and family law engagements, according to a BVR survey. Over 170 valuation firms, sole practitioners, CPA firms and other entities with business valuation practices responded to the survey conducted earlier this year. This information may spark one—or more—ideas in terms of strategic direction or marketing efforts

Exhibit 1. Percentage of Total Business Valuation Revenue Comes From the Following Specialty Areas (Average for Firms Reporting Any Revenue in Each Specialty):

Practice Specialty	2016	2010	2008
Tax, gifts, and estates	32%	36%	32%
Family/matrimonial	29%	29%	35%
Fair value for financial reporting (ASC 820, ASC 805 purchase price allocations, etc.)	24%	18%	19%
Transactional (including brokerage, mergers and acquisitions)	21%	24%	23%
Shareholder/corporate (buy-sell agreements, shareholder disputes, etc.)	21%	17%	18%
ESOP	14%	11%	14%
Incentive compensation arrangements	11%	12%	7%
Bankruptcy and restructuring	10%	5%	7%
Transfer pricing	2%	5%	3%
Other revenue sources not listed above	17%	14%	19%

Note: Total does not equal 100% because each calculation includes average percentage of revenue only for firms that reported revenue in each specialty area.

Revenue breakdown. As shown in Exhibit 1, valuations for estate and gift tax purposes continue be the prime source of business since it leap-frogged over divorce valuations by 2010. It's natural to assume that this is evidence of the ongoing increase in business transfers as baby-boomer owners look for the exit. Valuations for fair value for financial reporting purposes increased and catapulted this area into third place. Valuation revenue percentages also increased for shareholder matters, ESOPs, and bankruptcy/restructuring.

As for "other revenue sources," there is an increasing presence of niche practices with significant revenues in one or more specialty areas. The most cited areas are damages/lost profits and other litigation work (such as support services). Exhibit 2 lists some of the business valuation specialties that respondents chose to categorize individually. A few areas

Exhibit 2. Other Areas of Practice Specialization
Quantification of damages/loss analysis (9 responses)
Other litigation (8 responses)
Exit planning (3 responses)
Fairness and/or solvency opinions (3 responses)
General management consulting (2 responses)
SBA/banking advisory/lending
Business planning services
Valuation review
Expropriation
Minimum compensation
Intellectual property
Pension valuations

Exhibit 3. Fastest Growing Business Valuation Practice Specialty

Rank		2010	2008
1.	Divorce/ matrimonial	Fair value for financial reporting	Tax/estates
2.	Tax/estate planning/gifts	Tax/estate planning/gifts	Family/ matrimonial
3.	M&A/buy-sell	Divorce/ matrimonial	Fair value for financial reporting
4.	Shareholder disputes	M&A/buy-sell	Business trans-fer/succession/ M&A
5.	Fair value for financial reporting	Healthcare	Healthcare
6.	ESOP	Incentive stock	Incentive comp/stock options/409a/ FAS 123R
7.	Exit/ succession planning	ESOP	Shareholder disputes (particularly litigation)
8.	Litigation—other	Damages/lost profits	Forensic services

saw declines in mention or disappeared completely. General management consulting was mentioned much less than in 2010 and buy-sell/brokerage or investment banking services vanished from the "other" category.

Growth areas. A question was asked: What is the fastest growing specialty in your practice? The most often cited areas for growth, in descending order, appear in Exhibit 3. Of note is that divorce-related work has jumped to the No. 1 position, while fair value for financial reporting dropped sharply, to the No. 5 slot. One respondent's remarks indicate that this type of movement is no surprise: "It swings back and forth between years, between matrimonial and tax." However, one surprise may be the disappearance of healthcare valuations from the list of growth areas. The question of growth will be dependent in part on the geographic area in which a practice is located, as one respondent pointed out: "There is a decrease in the bankruptcy area consistent with the overall decline in Chapter 11 bankruptcies in venues where we practice."

Most profitable work. Interesting here is a flip-flop in the list of most profitable practice areas since the last survey in 2010. Estate/gift tax and divorce work are now the top two most cited profitable areas, while litigation and transactional services dropped to the No. 4 and 5 slots, respectively. In 2010, it was the other way around, as shown in Exhibit 4.

Shareholder disputes and related matters now appear on the list of most profitable areas, while fair value for financial reporting has disappeared from the top five. It's still cited as a most profitable area, and so are these areas respondents specifically named: fairness/solvency opinions, damages, ESOPs, 409a work, bankruptcy, buy-sell agreements, and exit planning.

Exhibit 4. Most Profitable Business Valuation Practice Specialty

Rank	2016 Area of Practice	2016 Percentage of Firms Ranking No. 1	2010 Area of Practice	2010 Percentage of Firms Ranking No. 1
1.	Estate/gift tax	25%	Litigation—all types	26%
2.	Divorce/ matrimonial	13%	Transactional/M&A	14%
3.	Shareholder matters	13%	Fair value for financial reporting	12%
4.	Litigation—all types	11%	Estate/gift tax	9%
5.	Transactional/M&A	6%	Divorce/matrimonial	8%

Exhibit 5. Litigation-Related Revenue as a Percentage of Total Business Valuation Revenue

Percentage of revenues	Firms reporting
0%	14%
1%-25%	40%
26%-50%	22%
51%-75%	12%
76%-99%	11%
100%	1%

Litigation-related revenue. Almost half (46%) of firms say they receive a substantial portion (over 25%) of revenue from litigation-related services (Exhibit 5). Generally, these firms tend to be larger and more diversified than a smaller, more specialized firm. However, small firms and solo practitioners are also successfully working in litigation. The percentage distribution overall has not changed materially over the years we have done this survey. The percentage of respondents who claim they do no litigation work at all has dropped from 17% in 2008 to 14% now.

The results reported in this article are from a larger survey designed to examine valuation firms in terms of performance, compensation, billing rates, marketing, and practice development, and so on. All of the responses are being analyzed, and a full report will be available soon. *BVU* will present more results in future issues.

Section V.
Reviews of Data Sources and New Books

Appraiser Review: How *Pratt's Stats* Upgrades Improve Your Search for Comps

By Jessica Landay, CVA, and Ron Seigneur, CPA/ABV/CFF, ASA, CVA, CGMA

The guideline company transaction method[1] is commonly used by valuation professionals and is one of the most contentious methods of valuation, often due to the appraiser's general lack of knowledge of the underlying transactions. The *Pratt's Stats*[2] transaction database has recently added enhancements to help appraisers identify transactions of companies comparable to the subject company being valued, as well as to better determine comparability of the transacted companies and the subject entity. The new enhancements were released to *Pratt's Stats* subscribers through BVR on January 6.

New search criteria. The first change users will notice is that you can now search by secondary (or tertiary) SIC or NAICS code by checking a box below the SIC or NAICS code drop down list. This option allows the user to capture companies in the database that have more than one line of business. For example, if a reported transaction is of an enterprise with more than one identifiable line of business, the database will now search for all lines of business for the transacted company, since it has been expanded to include the secondary and tertiary SIC/NAICS codes of all transacted companies in the database. Including secondary industry codes in the search criteria will prompt the database to search for acquired businesses in which the selected SIC/NAICS code is an additional product or service line of the acquired business that generates less revenue than the primary SIC/NAICS code. If applicable, each transaction will have up to three SIC and NAICS codes assigned. Selecting this option allows the user to find more companies when searching by industry. The search results only show the primary SIC/NAICS code when viewing in the results summary page, but when exported to Excel or the *Pratt's Stats* Analyzer, the secondary and tertiary SIC/NAICS codes are provided for each transaction, if there are any. Also, when looking at the individual transaction detail, the secondary and tertiary industry codes are provided.

1 This method is also referred to as the merged and acquired company method or direct market data method.

2 Go to www.bvmarketdata.com.

Another added function is that users can now select to include or omit transactions of companies classified as franchises, development-stage companies, and transactions in which real estate was acquired by using the drop down menu and selecting "all," "yes," or "no" for each of the three categories (the default setting is "all"). A search of the entire database for sales of development-stage companies resulted in only 19 transactions, of which only seven reported net sales, and therefore only seven transactions have transaction multiples. The database includes 791 transactions of franchises and 1,046 transactions in which real estate was acquired.

Users now have the ability to search for transactions by "sale region," whereas previously users could only search by country, state, and city. These nine regions are: East North Central, East South Central, Mid-Atlantic, Mountain, New England, Pacific, South Atlantic, West North Central, and West South Central. These regions are further defined in the updated FAQ. The advantage of this is that previously the user could only narrow the sale area to one state and would have to run multiple searches to find transactions by more than one state (or search by the entire country and eliminate the unwanted states from the results). Now, users can perform one search for a selected geographical region including multiple states.

The final enhancement to the search criteria is the user can now search by EBITDA (earnings before interest and taxes, depreciation, and amortization) and discretionary earnings (defined by *Pratt's Stats* as operating profit plus owner's compensation plus depreciation and amortization), in addition to net sales, operating profit, net income, and total assets, which were previously available in the database. The EBITDA range for all transactions in the database is -$1,449,989,000 to $4,092,000,000. The discretionary earnings range for all transactions is -$828,740,000 to $224,940,000.

Improved layout. In addition to the new search criteria, *Pratt's Stats* has created a new layout in the transaction detail view. In addition to the information that was previously available for each transaction, now there is a dedicated section for "Purchase Price Allocation Data" with 23 fields, as well as additional fields in the "Transaction Data" and "Income Data" sections. The purchase price allocation data allow users to determine the value of the various assets that were purchased in the transaction, providing greater opportunity for comparability to the subject company. Previously, the "Asset Data" section of the transaction detail contained a line item that said "Data is Purchase Price Allocation agreed upon by Buyer and Seller," and it was marked with a "Yes" or "No" to indicate whether it was balance sheet or purchase price allocation data. This new addition of a separate section specifically for Purchase Price Allocation data reduces confusion for the user.

Transaction costs are another new addition, which are captured and reported in the "Transaction Data" section of the transaction detail, when available. The user must determine the effect of the transaction costs on the value of the business being acquired and make the appropriate adjustments for use in valuing the subject entity.

The transaction detail now includes additional line items for interest income, other expense, other income, and tax benefit in the "Income Data" section of the printout. The inclusion of these items allows the user to determine why operating profit differs from earnings before taxes (EBT). Previously, only interest expense was provided, and the operating profit less interest expense did not always equal earnings before taxes. This information was previously noted in the "Additional Transaction Information" section of the transaction detail, when available, and required the user to carefully read the notes of each transaction.

Revised print formats. Because of the additional information included for each transaction on the transaction detail view, the printable report is best viewed on 8.5-inch-by-14-inch paper; if it is viewed or printed on 8.5-inch-by-11-inch paper, each transaction will now take up two pages, as opposed to the one 8.5-inch-by-11-inch page each transaction formerly occupied.

The report package print function (the red box appearing on some transactions to the left of the industry code in the transaction results summary view) now prints 25 transactions compared to 10 transactions previously. This saves time for the user, allowing he or she to print more transaction details with less mouse clicking (100 transactions can now be printed in four print operations compared to 10 before the change).

The downloadable versions of the transaction data—*Pratt's Stats* Analyzer and Excel format—include 45 new fields, as well as changes to some of the previously included fields. For example, "Company Name" is now "Target Name," "COGS" is now "Cost of Goods Sold," and "Liabilities Assumed" is now "Debt Assumed." Columns have been added to provide the contact information of the acquiring company, if available. Another addition is the amount of the selling price that the seller financed. All historical transactions in the database have been updated to include the newly added transaction information, if that information was available for the transaction. A total of 149 columns of data is now included in the Excel download. Additionally, some columns in the *Pratt's Stats* Analyzer and Excel format downloads were reordered to group related items together. Because of this, analysts using a template previously built from the Excel exports or the *Pratt's Stats* Analyzer will be required to modify their templates in order to accommodate the recent changes.

The FAQ page[3] has also been updated to reflect the recent changes to the database. To update templates due to the field name changes and placement, the FAQ page provides a crosswalk between the old field names and the new field names (located in the first question under the Data Principles and Collection section of the FAQ page).

The more data that are available about transactions for use in the guideline company transaction method, the easier it is for valuation professionals to determine the comparability of the transacted company to the subject company. While these enhancements to the *Pratt's Stats* database improve the usefulness of the transaction data, they do not make the expanded transaction information appropriate for use in the business appraisal process without proper scrutiny and application by the valuation analyst. We have yet to see any transaction database that includes enough transaction

3 Go to www.bvmarketdata.com/pdf/PrattsStats-FAQ.pdf.

data to be perfectly used in the market approach. However, *Pratt's Stats* provides the most data of any database we have considered and utilized, and these enhancements add to the utility of the data. A future enhancement that would be incredibly helpful to the business valuation community would be the inclusion of historical financial data of the transacted ("target") company, allowing analysts to dig deeper into selling price of the company, as well as make better comparisons to the valuation subject.

Jessica Landay, *CVA, is a senior financial analyst at Seigneur Gustafson LLP in Lakewood, Colo. She has passed all exams en route to completing the Accredited Senior Appraiser (ASA) designation from the American Society of Appraisers. She can be contacted at jessica.landay@cpavalue.com.*

Ronald L. Seigneur, *CPA/ABV/CFF, ASA, CVA, CGMA, is managing partner at Seigneur Gustafson LLP in Lakewood, Colo. He can be reached at ron.seigneur@cpavalue.com.*

Fannon and Dunitz Bridge the Gap in the Practice of Economic Damages

There are a lot of books on economic damages, but *The Comprehensive Guide to Economic Damages* is the only book that bridges the gap between the economics and what the courts have to say about the calculations and evidentiary requirements. The book's editors, Nancy J. Fannon, CPA, ABV, ASA, MCBA (Meyers, Harrison & Pia), and Jonathan M. Dunitz, Esq. (Verrill Dana), have completed the fourth edition of the book, and *BVU* recently talked with them about it.

BVU: *With this new edition, the title has changed from* The Comprehensive Guide to Lost Profits and Other Commercial Damages *to* The Comprehensive Guide to Economic Damages. *Why?*

Nancy Fannon: We did the first edition of the book because there was a dearth of guidance concerning lost profits damages. Over time, I also realized that there was a lack of meaningful guidance on other types of damages, so Jonathan and I expanded the book. This new edition covers not only lost profits damages, but also many kinds of damages, so the title of the new edition has changed to reflect that.

BVU: *What are the major changes to this edition?*

NF: There are nine new chapters from 14 terrific new contributors. We added over 300 pages to Volume 1, so it has gone from just under 1,000 pages to over 1,300 pages. We also added 100 cases to Volume 2 (case law), bringing the total cases to about 240. Of course, not all of the added cases are recent cases—many of them are related to the new chapters.

Some of the new chapters deal with compensation forfeiture, fraudulent transfer, the use of surveys in trademark litigation, personal injury and wrongful termination, the use of statistics in damages claims, and the use of event studies in securities litigation. [See Exhibit 1 for a listing of the new chapters and their respective authors.]

BVU: *What are the main issues that can cause problems in a damages analysis or report? How does this book help deal with those issues?*

Exhibit 1. New Chapters and Authors in 4th Edition of *Guide to Economic Damages*

The 4th edition of *The Comprehensive Guide to Economic Damages* is in two volumes: Volume 1 is the main text, and Volume 2 is the case law text. Volume 1 contains six parts: Part I, "Expert Testimony in the U.S. Courts"; Part II, "Lost Profits Damages"; Part III, "Intellectual Property Damages"; Part IV, "The Unjust Enrichment Remedy"; Part V, "Other Commercial Damages"; and Part VI, "Personal Injury and Wrongful Termination."

The new chapters and authors in Volume 1 of the 4th edition are:

- "Projecting But-For Profits" (in Part II, "Lost Profits Damages"), Stacey Udell, CPA/ABV/CFF, CVA (Gold Gerstein Group LLC). This chapter discusses methods for determining lost revenues and avoided expenses, use of management projections, growth considerations, industry/economic data, and other topics.
- "Uses of Survey Research in Damages Estimation" (in Part III, "Intellectual Property Damages"), Larry Chiagouris, Ph.D. (Lubin School of Business, Pace University) and Leon Kaplan, Ph.D. (Princeton Research & Consulting Center Inc.). This chapter provides a summary of the key guidelines used to design and execute surveys, a case study, and special topics that can help ensure success.
- "Using Internet Analytic Tools for Valuation and Damages Calculations in Internet IP Infringement and Defamation Cases" (in Part III, "Intellectual Property Damages"), Doug Bania and Brian Buss, CFA (both with Nevium Intellectual Property Solutions). This chapter describes the ways in which Internet and social media analytics can be used to accurately measure and quantify IP misuse.
- "An Overview of Accounting and Financial Analysis in Fraudulent Transfer Matters" (in Part V, "Other Commercial Damages"), Jeffrey L. Baliban, CPA, ABV, CDBV (Citrin Cooperman & Co. LLP). An introduction to the accounting and solvency issues within the context of fraudulent transfer claims and the kinds of problems that can arise in such engagements.
- "Compensation Forfeiture: Stacking Remedies Against Disloyal Agents and Employees" (in Part V, "Other Commercial Damages"), George P. Roach, J.D. Compensation forfeiture is a simple but substantial enhancement for the remedies awarded for a breach of fiduciary duty. It requires no special proof or expert testimony—and it can be stacked onto any other damage claim or remedy.
- "Event Studies in Securities Litigation" (in Part V, "Other Commercial Damages"), Adrian M. Cowan, Ph.D., and Paul J. Seguin, Ph.D. (both with Analytic Focus LLC). An event study is based on a set of statistical methods to assess the impact of an event on the value of a firm. This chapter discusses how event studies are used in securities litigation.
- "Use of Statistical Analysis to Measure Damages" (in Part V, "Other Commercial Damages"), Charles D. Cowan, Ph.D. (Analytic Focus LLC). This chapter explains numerous methods and situations where statistical analysis can be used for damages analysis. It also discusses the potential pitfalls in the use of such methods.
- "Economic Damages From Personal Injuries" (in Part VI, "Personal Injury and Wrongful Termination"), Jonathan Brogan, Esq. (Norman, Hanson & DeTroy LLC) and Joseph A. DeCusati, CPA, ABV, ASA, CFE (Meyers, Harrison & Pia Valuation and Litigation Support LLC). This chapter discusses some of the basic elements of the calculation of economic damages from personal injuries and wrongful death. It also considers some of the common issues confronted by the expert calculating the dollar value of personal injury damages.
- "Damages in Common-Law Employment Cases" (in Part VI, "Personal Injury and Wrongful Termination"), Joseph D. Garrison, Esq., and Joshua R. Goodbaum, Esq. (both with Garrison, Levin-Epstein, Richardson, Fitzgerald & Pirrotti PC). This chapter addresses the damages available (contract and tort) for violations of the common law in the employment context.

Jonathan Dunitz: The book helps with a broad range of issues, such as the difference in preparing an economic analysis that will be used in court versus one that will not. A valuation report written by an expert who does not have experience with litigation may find that his or her report is not admissible. There are certain things the expert needs to understand to help make the analysis admissible, such as the amount and types of evidence that are needed. Preparing a report for a damages analysis for litigation is not necessarily the same as doing one for a company's internal use or some other purpose.

The book is also helpful to both attorneys and experts in that it describes the different methodologies, the different types of damages, and how to calculate them. It also describes the procedural rules that are very important and presents the problems that may arise and how to address them.

NF: I see two main issues that cause problems with a damages analysis. One is that experts often do not understand the appropriate remedy for a particular action. The book contains a great deal of guidance as to when to use one remedy versus another. The second main issue is how to calculate the damages. There are a lot of nuances that some experts are not aware of, including nuances with respect to the jurisdiction you're in or the particular remedy that is appropriate. The book contains a great deal of guidance in this regard.

BVU: *Does the state of the economy affect the amount of economic damages litigation?*

NF: During the worst of the economic downturn, my observation was that litigation was down somewhat, but it's definitely back up now. People are pursuing things more than they have in prior years.

JD: To me, it doesn't seem to be cyclical—it depends on the type of litigation. Litigation related to intellectual property is definitely a growth area. Also, I think that cybersecurity issues will trigger a huge amount of litigation.

BVU: *Is there any particular concept that practitioners have the most trouble with? How will this book help with that?*

NF: The concept of unjust enrichment is by far the most troublesome. It's been called the "most misunderstood remedy," a characterization that I agree with from my observation reviewing expert reports purporting to calculate unjust enrichment. On its face, the concept seems simple, but in execution it is not. As a result, analysts can really botch this.

JD: The concept of unjust enrichment is difficult, in part, because it is both a cause of action and a remedy, so that creates confusion and it affects how analysts calculate it. Most of the other concepts are exclusively remedies. For example, there is no "lost profits" cause of action. Lost profits is a remedy that is available for a number of causes of action.

NF: Also, there are significant differences in how it's calculated from one jurisdiction to another. Experts tend to get it mixed up with lost profits and often it's double counted. George Roach, an attorney who provides consulting or testimony on corporate damages and valuation, is the author of the book's chapters on unjust enrichment. He has written very extensively on this topic, and the material in the book provides excellent guidance on this important remedy.

[*Editor's note: According to the latest analysis by the author of the unjust enrichment chapters, cases involving disgorgement for unjust enrichment are growing faster than lost profits cases and it now greatly outnumbers lost profits (see Exhibit 2).*]

BVU: *From the litigation perspective, have there been any significant new developments since the last edition?*

JD: There has been an important change to the Federal Rules of Evidence that went into effect Dec. 1, 2015. The new rules add a "proportionality" standard to the amount of material that can be requested during discovery. That is, the material requested should be reasonable in relation to the needs of the case and the resources of the parties. There is a huge cost involved with broad discovery, so the new rules are designed to alleviate this. Nancy often talks about how the material she receives on a matter used to be one banker's box and now there is the equivalent of many boxes contained on disks or in some other digital format because of the huge amount of data. The new rule will hopefully reverse the trend, but it remains to be seen how the courts will interpret these new rules.

BVU: *Can you give some advice on how to optimize the attorney-financial expert relationship with respect to damages cases?*

NF: The new edition contains the knowledge base that will allow a better working relationship between the expert and the attorney. Experts can be most beneficial to attorneys when they're highly knowledgeable about damage remedies and the context in which they are calculated. When an expert is more knowledgeable, he or she can be much more helpful to the attorney in terms of the various options for remedies, given a particular context. For example, I had a case recently where it was clear to me that the damages could best and most easily be calculated in a particular way, but the attorney had never even considered that method.

Exhibit 2. Growth in Cases That Mention Unjust Enrichment

	"Disgorgement"		"Lost Profits"	
	Federal	All States	Federal	All States
2011	4,214	1,888	725	377
2007 to 2011 avg.	3,364	1,697	714	366
2002 to 2006 avg.	1,459	1,131	472	334
1997 to 2001 avg.	807	722	317	266
1992 to 1996 avg.	591	523	313	254
1992	527	518	318	261

Based on a simple word search on Lexus Nexus for cases that mentioned unjust enrichment or lost profits. As of the time of this analysis, unjust enrichment is mentioned much more frequently than lost profits (by about five to one) and opinions from federal courts outnumber the state courts (by about two to one).

Source: Measuring Unjust Enrichment, George Roach, BVR Webinar Sept. 10, 2013

JD: I agree. In the book, the procedural chapters and the material on jurisdictional differences are a great help to make the relationship go well between the expert and attorney. It's important for the expert to talk upfront with the attorney concerning these jurisdictional issues. For example, some jurisdictions don't allow depositions, so that's important to know. There are also differences between jurisdictions governing what damages are available and how certain damages are calculated.

BVU: *I see that both experts and attorneys prepare the chapters. Why did you do it this way?*

NF: Having both an expert and attorney prepare a chapter is so that you get both perspectives—case law and the economic aspect in terms of calculating damages. Of course, the calculations flow from the case law, so it is critical to have both perspectives.

BVU: *You both will be co-presenting a session on economic damages at the NACVA conference this June in San Diego. Can you give us a sneak preview of what you will talk about?*

NF: We will discuss advanced damages concepts including areas that experts often get tripped up by or excluded. We will focus on the right remedy for different circumstances. This is the area where I see experts tripping up the most—understanding the proper remedy.

For more information: *The Comprehensive Guide to Economic Damages,* 4th edition, is available at www.bvresources.com/publications.

Book Review: *A Consensus View—Q&A Guide to Financial Valuation*

By Harold G. Martin Jr., CPA/ABV/CFF, ASA, CFE

All valuation practitioners have been confronted with a difficult issue that was not addressed in a traditional textbook. Moreover, there appear to be alternative schools of thought without a clear consensus for numerous controversial issues. When faced with such predicaments, if one could consult a thought leader in the profession, surely the names of Jim Hitchner, Shannon Pratt, and Jay Fishman would be on everyone's short list! *A Consensus View – Q&A Guide to Financial Valuation* presents these three nationally recognized experts' consensus opinions on selected issues in business valuation—ranging from basic to advanced and including controversial topics.

In this first edition, the authors discuss four topics they consider to be of critical importance in business valuation: the income approach, cost of capital, discounts and premiums, and professional standards and ethics. The discussion is detailed, well-documented, and illustrated with numerous examples. As the title implies, the text is well organized in an easy-to-use, question-and-answer format. The following is indicative of a typical question and the authors' response:

> **Improper Use of the Discounted Cash Flow and Capitalized Cash Flow Methods**
>
> **Question:** *Have you ever seen analysts use both the capitalized cash flow and discounted cash flow methods to manipulate the value?*
>
> **Answer:** Unfortunately, some analysts will use both in order to manipulate their conclusion of value. This happens when the two values are very different. They will use a CCF method to obtain a higher or lower value when historical performance is expected to decline or improve. Let's take two examples, one where the best method is the DCF method and the other where the best method is the CCF method:
>
> **Example 1** (Assume the DCF is the most reasonable method with higher interim growth) Calculate value under a DCF method and a CCF method and apply weights:

DCF value = $10 million@ 50% weight = $5.0 million
CCF value = $ 7 million@ 50% weight = $3.5 million
$8.5 million

So, what's the appropriate value, $8.5 million or $10 million? Obviously, it is $10 million.

Example 2 (Assume the CCF method is the most reasonable method due to flat growth) Calculate value under a DCF method and a CCF method and apply weights:

DCF value = $10 million@ 50% weight = $5.0 million
CCF value = $ 7 million@ 50% weight = $3.5 million
$8.5 million

So, what's the appropriate value, $8.5 million or $7 million? Obviously it is $7 million.

The following is a representative sample of other questions presented in the text. (You'll have to read the book for the answers to these questions!)

Chapter 1. "Income Approach"

- What do you do when you believe a discounted cash flow method is the correct method to use but may not be accepted in the venue for which you are preparing the valuation?
- Many analysts make depreciation and capital expenditures equal in the capitalized cash flow model and the terminal year of a discounted cash flow model. Is that the correct assumption to make?
- Should I rely on tax depreciation or book depreciation when determining the cash flow to be discounted or capitalized?
- How do you determine whether your long-term growth rate is too high, whether in a capitalized cash flow or discounted cash flow method?
- What methodology is better in the terminal year of a discounted cash flow model: the Gordon growth model or exit multiples?

Chapter 2. "Cost of Capital/Rates of Return"

- Do you think the modified capital asset pricing model or the build-up model is better?
- How does one use the Duff & Phelps recommended equity risk premium?
- When valuing a small business, can I rely on both the Duff & Phelps CRSP 10th decile and the *Duff & Phelps Risk Premium Report* 25th portfolio?

- I have heard that when using Duff & Phelps size premium data the extrapolation beyond the regression line (the lower end) should not be used for smaller companies. What is your stance on using the extrapolation?
- Can the data in the Duff & Phelps CRSP subdeciles 10b, 10y, and 10z premiums be relied upon or do they produce incorrect discount rates?
- How do you reconcile the size risk premia from the Duff & Phelps CRSP deciles premia and the *Risk Premium Report* data implied for a subject company when they are very different?
- Is it correct to apply an industry risk premium to a build-up model when using the *Duff & Phelps Risk Premium Report* data from the A exhibits where the industry risk premium and the size premium are combined?
- Is there an accurate way to estimate company-specific risk?
- How do you apply and reconcile all the many data choices in the new Duff & Phelps *Valuation Handbook*?

Chapter 3. "Discounts and Premiums"

- Is there a difference between marketability and liquidity or a discount for lack of marketability and discount for lack of liquidity?
- Does illiquidity apply to controlling interests as well as minority interests?
- Are benchmark-type analyses using restricted stocks still valid for a discount for lack of marketability?
- Are the so-called *Mandelbaum* factors still relevant?
- Does the application of the guideline public company method under the market approach result in a control value or minority value?
- What if the cash flows need no adjustment (i.e., minority and control are the same)? Is the value the same for minority and control?

Chapter 4. "Business Valuation Standards and Ethics"

- If I am a CPA, can I ignore the standards of the ASA, USPAP, NACVA, and the IBA?
- What is the level of certainty or reliability that is required when offering a court your opinion of value?

- Do attorneys and judges really care about business valuation standards?
- How can analysts protect themselves (manage risk) in a valuation engagement, including compliance with the ethics and standards of the organization they belong to?
- Can a valuation analyst have an opinion of a calculated value in a litigation setting where the valuation analyst is an expert witness?
- Can a member of the ASA perform a calculation engagement in compliance with USPAP?

The authors note that they plan to update the *Q&A Guide* annually, expanding on the existing chapters and adding new chapters to address additional topics.

Both novice as well as experienced appraisers will find *A Consensus View – Q&A Guide to Financial Valuation* to be an excellent technical resource. I highly recommend this text for every valuation practitioner's library!

(*A Consensus View – Q&A Guide to Financial Valuation*, James R. Hitchner, Shannon P. Pratt, and Jay E. Fishman, Valuation Products and Services LLC, 2016, 337 pages. Available from BVR at www.bvresources.com/publications.)

Harold G. Martin Jr.*, CPA/ABV/CFF, ASA, CFE, is the partner-in-charge of valuation and forensic services for Keiter, a certified public accounting and consulting firm located in Richmond, Va.*

What's New and Noteworthy in the DP *2016 Valuation Handbook*

By Ronald L. Seigneur, CPA/ABV/CFF, ASA, CVA, CGMA

It has now been three years since Duff & Phelps (DP) took the baton from Morningstar/Ibbotson (MI) to continue the production of arguably the key resource for cost of capital determinations in business and intellectual property appraisal. The Duff & Phelps *2016 Valuation Handbook – Guide to Cost of Capital (DP Handbook)* was released in March 2016 as the third annual edition of the combined DP *Risk Premia Report* and the continued market return data that MI had become legendary in producing in its valuation edition of the *Stocks, Bonds, Bills and Inflation (SBBI) Valuation Yearbook,* which was an ancillary version of the MI SBBI Classic Yearbook, which had been published for over 30 years prior to the launch of the *SBBI Valuation Yearbook.* The *SBBI Valuation Yearbook* was published from 1999 through 2013 with a specific business valuation focus on the CRSP deciles size premia.

Together with my colleague, Stacey Udell (Gold Gerstein Group LLC), I co-wrote a review article on the first DP *Valuation Handbook,* which appeared in the September 2014 issue of *Business Valuation Update*. In that review, we were both impressed with not only the integrity of the 2014 DP *Valuation Handbook* in maintaining the flow of information previously available to valuation analysts in the prior DP *Risk Premia Report* and *SBBI Valuation Yearbooks,* but also with its ability to produce the combined work in the 2014 *Valuation Handbook* on the same timeline as we had been accustomed to in prior years.

Readers are encouraged to access and read this prior article on the DP *Valuation Handbook,* which provides detailed descriptions of Chapters 1 through 10, which remain unchanged in the 2016 edition in terms of cost of capital issues covered. However, the 2016 *Valuation Handbook* has many refinements and additions, including a new Chapter 11 (in 2015) on real estate-related assets and related valuation metrics and an expanded Chapter 12, which provides detailed answers to questions submitted to DP by handbook users.

The DP *2016 Valuation Handbook* is the cornerstone volume of a series of four separate "handbooks," all published annually with updated data and optional intrayear updates.

There are two "U.S.-centric" DP handbooks: (i) the *Valuation Handbook – Guide to Cost of Capital,* which provides size premia, equity risk premia, industry risk premia, and other critical valuation inputs (and is the subject of this review); and (ii) the *Valuation Handbook – Industry Cost of Capital*, which provides industry-level cost of capital statistics for around 180 U.S. industries.

There are two "international" DP handbooks: (i) the *International Valuation Handbook – Guide to Cost of Capital*, which provides country-level base cost of equity and other information for around 180 countries, from the perspective of investors in up to 56 different countries; and (ii) the *Valuation Handbook – Industry Cost of Capital*, which provides the same type of rigorous industry-level analysis published in the U.S.-centric *Valuation Handbook – Industry Cost of Capital*, on a global scale.

New highlights of the 2016 handbook include:

- The previously named Risk Premium Calculator is now called the Risk Premium Toolkit and is available as an ancillary add-on to the *Valuation Handbook*. This online calculator provides a customizable package of reports in Microsoft Word format of cost of capital estimates using both a traditional build-up and CAPM method. The inputs, outputs, and calculations are exported to a "Support and Detail" report in Microsoft Excel format.

- Appendix 2, "Changes to the Risk Premia Report Study Over Time," outlines the evolution of the DP Risk Premia studies since their introduction in 1996. This appendix lists the changes to the DP risk premia data from what first appeared in a 1995 article in *Business Valuation Review*, titled "The Size Effect and Equity Returns," as well as changes from information previously published by Ibbotson Associates, prior to its merger into Morningstar.

The detail for the industry risk premia has been moved from Chapter 5 to Appendix 3a, near the back of the handbook. I note that this industry risk premia now covers approximately 250 industry classifications with a much larger proportion reporting for four-digit SIC codes versus two- and three-digit codes, which makes the data more useful in terms of correlating a specific data point to a target business. In the first year of the industry data appearing in the prior SBBI publication, far less categories were provided and most were only by the more general two- and three-digit SIC codes. Updates to the industry risk premia and debt betas are available in the optional quarterly updates.

Appendix 3b is a nice addition that provides a table of debt betas on a quarterly basis for 2014 and 2015 for measured corporate debt instruments ranging from Aaa to Ca-D grade ratings as provided by Moody's based on Barclays US Corp Risk Analytics. An example of unlevering an equity beta that requires a debt beta as an input is provided in Appendix 3b.

As I read through the 2016 handbook, certain sections pop out at me as worthy of specific note, including:

- "Basic Cost of Capital Concepts" (Chapter-Pages 1-6/9)—This section provides a great overview of the fundamental cost of capital concepts in a very succinct fashion;

- "Estimates of Cost of Capital Are Imprecise" (1-19)—I mention this section merely to remind folks that there is no holy grail when it comes to estimating a discount rate and a solid dose of informed judgment and common sense are always in order;
- "Defining Risk" (2-2/8)—This section has a very nice discussion on the various risk elements that are the cornerstones to deriving cost of capital estimates;
- "Spot Risk-Free Rates Versus Normalized Risk-Free Rates" (3-2/20)—This section provides a thorough discussion of the rationale for using normalized risk-free rates when the risk-free rate shows signs of being abnormally low, as it has in recent periods;
- "Ex-Post and Ex-Ante" (3-22/23)—I mention this short section just as a good reminder of what ex and post ante are in the realm of cost of capital;
- "World War II Interest Rate Bias" (3-27/29)—This section shows the impact of the downward bias in interest rates for the years following World War II and suggests excluding these years from the measurements otherwise provided in the handbook;
- "Comparing Investor Expectations to Realized Risk Premium and the DP Recommended ERP" (3-29/41)—This section provides the rationale and measurement of the alternatives of the equity risk premium;
- "Has the Size Effect Disappeared in More Recent Periods?" (4-17/20)—This section provides a decent summary of the ongoing debate on the existence and magnitude of a size premium and how best to quantify it from the view point of DP;
- "Relationship of Size and Liquidity" (4-21/22)—This section provides some good discussion on the liquidity element in relation to the size of the enterprise;
- "Industry Risk Premia" (5-12/16)—This section and the accompanying Appendix 3a provide the details on the expanded list of industry risk premia provided in the handbook and how to utilize the data in practice in a build-up estimate of cost of equity capital;
- "Debt Betas" (5-17/18)—This section and the accompanying Appendix 3b provide info on the calculation of debt betas for use when applicable in cost of capital calculations; and
- "Specific Company Risk/Beta Suffers From Measurement Errors" (6-2/5)—This section highlights the shortcomings of using beta and CAPM to derive cost of capital estimates as compared to the use of unsystematic risk within other cost of capital models.

This list is obviously not all inclusive but is intended to provide some highlights of some of the interesting insights within the body of the DP *Valuation Handbook*.

I would suggest the owner of a 2016 DP *Valuation Handbook* put the stickie tab of the reader's choice on several pages:

- Page 3-41: "Duff & Phelps Recommended U.S. ERP and Corresponding Risk-Free Rates, January 2008-Present";
- Page 7-11: Exhibit 7.3 "CRSP Deciles, Returns in Excess of CAPM";
- Page 7-15: "Comparison Table for the Risk Premium Report and CRSP Deciles Size Premia Study";
- Page 10-7: "Size Characteristics of the Companies Portfolio 25";
- Appendix 3a: Industry Risk Premium data; and
- Appendix 4-2: Risk Premium Report Study exhibits.

Obviously, there are many more noteworthy pages, but these stand out as just a starting point when using the DP handbook as a cost of capital resource. Readers are encouraged to take the *Valuation Handbook* on their next plane trip or home for an evening to spend a bit of time going from front to back in a bit more detail than is often allowed in the heat of the average work day when the *Valuation Handbook* is there and available to grab key cost of capital inputs from for a particular project.

Ronald L. Seigneur, *CPA/ABV/CFF, ASA, CVA, CGMA, is managing partner at Seigneur Gustafson LLP in Lakewood, Colo. He can be reached at ron.seigneur@cpavalue.com.*

Sneak Preview of New Material in the *BVR/AHLA Healthcare Valuation Guide*

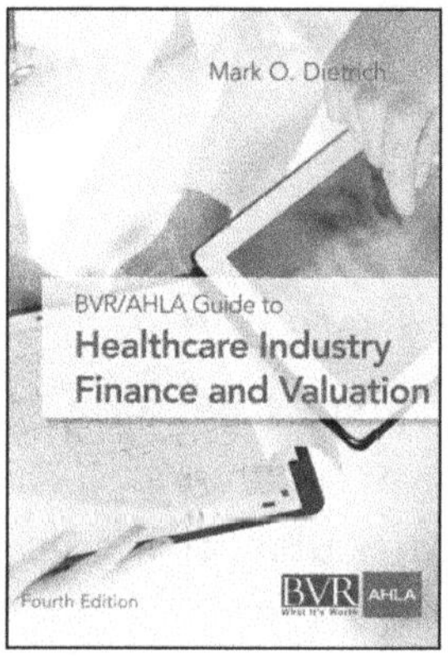

A "complete revision" has been made to the *BVR/AHLA Guide to Healthcare Industry Finance and Valuation* (available at www.bvresources.com/publications) in creating the newly released fourth edition, according to Mark O. Dietrich (Mark O. Dietrich, CPA, PC), the guide's editor. There are 14 new chapters covering new topics not in the prior edition. Plus, most of the other chapters from the last edition have been rewritten.

Tim Smith (Ankura Consulting) has contributed four new chapters on the use of the cost approach, including its use in valuing a trained workforce (more on that later). Robert Reilly (Willamette Associates) has completely revamped his chapter on tax-exempt organizations in the healthcare industry. "He's added an extensive discussion on the Stark Law and Anti-Kickback statutes in addition to the prior material on prohibited private inurement," Dietrich says. "He also has a very important section on 10 things that most people don't understand about healthcare valuation that I think is a great read."

Groundbreaking research. Dietrich himself added three new chapters, the most significant of which discusses the common uses of surveys in determining the fair market value of physician compensation. "I believe that this chapter will be revolutionary in that it exposes things about the surveys and the ways the surveys are used that seemingly in the past have not been recognized," he says. "One of the many things I discovered in my research is that the statistics that come out of those surveys are really best described as descriptive statistics, meaning they only tell you something about the people who participated in the surveys. They don't tell you anything about the vast number of doctors in the country who aren't sampled in the survey. Therefore, you can't draw any statistical conclusions about their compensation. That type of inference, if you will, is from inferential statistics, which is a completely different discipline than descriptive statistics."

The following is an excerpt from that chapter.

FMV of physician compensation.[1] The chapter's analysis starts with Section 3.0, "Failings of the Surveys," which contains a comprehensive analysis of the manner in which physician compensation surveys are presently employed in fair market value opinions. The most significant finding is that the commonly used surveys, using the MGMA survey as an example, are not used in a manner that is statistically valid. Simply stated, statistics generally require that all the members of a population about whom information is being sought—here physicians and their compensation—have a chance to be randomly selected as part of the survey. The MGMA *Physician Compensation and Production Survey* contains a self-selected sample of MGMA members and certain others who choose to provide data—the self-selected sample represents less than 6% of practicing physicians in the country. Any statistics drawn directly from the survey are deemed descriptive statistics, i.e., they tell you something about the physicians who submitted data to it; they do not tell you anything about physicians who did not submit data to it. Thus, the commonly cited median compensation rates are not the median for the United States; they are simply the median for physicians who chose to participate in the MGMA survey.

Using a survey such as this to draw inferences about the 94% of physicians or so who were not asked to submit data (i.e., not sampled) is called inferential statistics, a different discipline than descriptive statistics. That discipline requires considerable knowledge of the science of statistics that is not presently utilized in expressing fair market value opinions. The surveys are not able to explain the vast regional, state, and local differences in physician compensation (that explanation is contained later in the chapter).

The conclusion in this section is that willingness to relocate is the exception not the rule for established physicians, and this has substantial implications in compensation valuation, especially in light of the prevailing assumption that all physicians will relocate to earn at least the median (that median assumption is debunked later in the chapter). Those most likely to move are physicians who recently completed their residency in a state with a surplus of the specialty that they trained in. Supply and demand at the local-market level are the primary factors in physician recruitment and retention. Health systems in urban areas with a high ratio of physicians to population confront a justification issue when "recruiting" physicians already practicing in their service area, especially when paying compensation in excess of that supported by local-market payers. Section 4.0 of this chapter provides a comprehensive solution to the limitations of the surveys, based in part on published studies of the dramatic differences in local-market payment rates for physician service and the commonly accepted use of work relative value units (wRVUs) as a means of measuring fair market value physician compensation. The appendix to the chapter contains a detailed mathematical example of the application of the solution, intended for valuation professionals.

The use of surveys (in a failed attempt) to establish fair market compensation is then presented in an example utilizing internal medicine data. The example demonstrates that the commonly

1 The *BVR/AHLA Guide to Healthcare Industry Finance and Valuation*, 4th edition, Chapter 17, "Using Work RVUs and 'Particular Market' Rates to Establish Fair Market Value Physician Compensation."

accepted practice of utilizing the median compensation rate per wRVU fails a sanity check as it results in nearly 72% of each dollar of collected revenue being used to pay physician compensation and benefits, leaving only 28% to cover practice overhead. In point of fact, real overhead rates for internal medicine practices are closer to 60%—and certainly nowhere near 30%! Every reader should study this section.

For example, the MGMA compensation-to-wRVU ratio data on "orthopedic surgeons: general," used in the comprehensive example in the appendix, show a standard deviation of $30.42 in the 592 sample items, with a median of $68, a mean of $73.12, a 25th percentile of $54.17, a 75th percentile of $84.34, and a 90th percentile of $108.95. If the data set were normally distributed (which appears unlikely), this standard deviation would mean that 68% of the 592 respondents in the sample are between $57.91 per wRVU ([$73.12 - $30.42]/2) and $88.33 ([$73.12 + $30.42]/2). A range of $57.91 to $88.33 is a significant spread for 68% of the sample. This can be easily seen by multiplying those rates by an assumed number of wRVUs generated by a physician to see the range of compensation that results.

The use of standard deviation measures when a data set is not normally distributed, especially when it is right-skewed (here meaning data points of high rates per wRVU as suggested by the 90th percentile of $108.95, double the 25th percentile) is more likely to mislead than inform. As such, the extent to which the median, mean, or 75th percentile is predictive of fair market compensation per wRVU would be suspect. There is often a very large spread between the 25th and 75th percentiles, as is the case here. Thus, selection of these numbers as the so-called market range is arbitrary and imprecise. After all, would one be willing to accept an appraisal for their home as between the 25th and 75th percentiles of all homes sold last year in the United States?

Here are some other excerpts that discuss major issues in the new edition.

Cash flow forecasting.[2] Perhaps the single largest error made in forecasting cash flows for a medical practice or other entity that relies on the Medicare Physician Fee Schedule (MPFS) is failure to evaluate the likely direction that reimbursement for that particular sector is headed.

Additionally, as a general rule, no single location, market, or service line healthcare entity will have reimbursement growth rate assumptions greater than 2% to 3% over the long term. Growth of this magnitude is possible in the discrete periods of the forecast, but, given the complexity of the regulations, it is highly unlikely, and quite likely impossible, for any sector to grow at a rate greater than 2% to 3% over the long term. The key to identifying and addressing risk and future cash flows is understanding that frequently utilized, high-cost procedures and tests will be targeted for dramatic cutbacks. It is not a matter of if, but when, the cuts will be implemented.

2 The *BVR/AHLA Guide to Healthcare Industry Finance and Valuation*, 4th edition, Chapter 3, "Factors in Estimating Cost of Capital and Forecasting Cash Flow in Healthcare."

Medical records.[3] The asset value of patient charts or medical records involves two basic issues: allocating a portion of any intangible value derived from a method under the income approach and valuing the charts directly as a stand-alone asset using the cost approach. The directly related issue of measuring the liability assumed when taking possession of charts is described separately.

One typical application of the cost approach to paper record value under either scenario is the cost of labor and supplies associated with photocopying, something that is consistent with HIPAA. However, given the HITECH Act's requirement that a patient be able to obtain a copy of his or her record electronically if an EHR is in place, this approach may be different for electronic health records where the cost is likely different. The difference between the cost of electronic copies and paper copies should be built into any valuation model. Of course, given the requirement to adopt electronic health records to avoid Medicare and other payer penalties, paper medical records will soon be functionally obsolete and that obsolescence would have to be computed under accepted use of the cost approach.

HIPAA and the HITECH Act have, or should have, a dramatic impact on the stand-alone value of medical charts or records. No charge can be made for search and retrieval of the record or any other arguably incurred cost. For a prospective purchaser of a medical practice still using paper charts, storing those paper charts securely in accordance with HIPAA's Privacy Rule and providing access to patients within the period mandated by state law and HIPAA can be expensive indeed.

Valuation fraud.[4] In presenting some concluding thoughts on the *Citizens Medical*[5] fraud case, the guide points out that losses are the crux of the issue in many compensation valuation engagements and many business valuation engagements, which are part and parcel of compensation arrangements. One can imagine that, if the hospital in this case had purchased the cardiology practice as well as paying salaries that generated dramatic losses, the result would have been the same. Hundreds of such transactions took place with large payments for cardiology practices based on the cost approach and then salaries higher than that earned by the physicians historically. Whether for tax purposes or financial reporting, buyers have to amortize or impairment test most intangible assets, which in turn would increase the operating losses. The court might have said in this scenario: "This inference is particularly strong given that it would make little apparent economic sense for Hospital to purchase the cardiologists' practice and then employ the cardiologists at a loss unless it were doing so for some ulterior motive." Or, perhaps more straightforward: "This inference is particularly strong given that it would make little apparent economic sense for Hospital to purchase the cardiologists' practice then lose money operating it."

3 The *BVR/AHLA Guide to Healthcare Industry Finance and Valuation,* 4th edition, Chapter 9, "Patient Medical Records, HIPAA, and State Medical Records Law."

4 The *BVR/AHLA Guide to Healthcare Industry Finance and Valuation,* 4th edition, Chapter 10, "By the Numbers: A Case-Based Understanding of Healthcare Valuation Fraud."

5 *United States ex rel. Parikh, et al. v. Citizens Medical Center, et al.,* Case No. 6:10-cv-64 (S.D. Tex.).

Physician practices.[6] Public and private equity players carefully tie physician compensation and productivity to the forecast used to value the practice. Many, but not all, hospital and health system players have taken a lesson from this basic element of economics and finance. However, some appraisers have sidestepped the requirement for consistent post-transaction compensation by using the cost approach as the sole means to value the practice. The importance of focusing on post-transaction compensation was re-emphasized in *Derby*,[7] a 2008 Tax Court case. Physician compensation is typically linked to productivity—and increasingly as measured by work RVUs, or wRVUs—and not fixed, the latter practice having led to low patient volumes and large operating losses. Oftentimes, however, the rate paid per wRVU is taken from national physician compensation survey data that are inappropriate for the local market area in which the physician works. Recent government enforcement activity has focused on the commercial reasonableness of losses incurred by hospital operators of formerly privately owned physician practices, many times due to improper use of survey data to set compensation.

Future physician compensation is typically a more significant element of a transaction than is the value of the practice. In many circumstances, hospitals and integrated delivery systems have superior contracts with insurers that in turn permit physicians to receive better compensation for the same amount of work, something published research in a variety of publications supports. Over the course of five years or more, compensation is typically more valuable than sales proceeds to a physician, given the range of valuation multiples. Readers should note that it is not appropriate to value the practice using the buyer's better insurer contracts because that is inconsistent with fair market value although, as described in the chapter on fair market compensation, those rate differences have become significant for evaluating post-transaction compensation. Revenue normalization adjustments the practice might achieve on a stand-alone basis can be considered.

There is no generic "deal" in physician practice transactions. Appraisers with no experience in actual transaction valuation will construct some form of hypothetical transaction to value—as might be the case for estate or divorce valuation, for example. Such a hypothetical transaction construct is unlikely to reflect the actual assets and liabilities involved in the transfer and therefore will be incorrect. Fair market value in transactional valuation involves an actual business, or actual assets and related liabilities, with an actual set of transaction documents at the price a hypothetical buyer and seller would reach.

Reasonable compensation under IRC.[8] In both a hospital employment setting and private practice, physician supervision of midlevel providers such as nurse practitioners and physician assistants can be a critical element of determining reasonable compensation. Particularly in the primary care specialties, this will become an increasingly important issue as midlevel providers likely

6 The *BVR/AHLA Guide to Healthcare Industry Finance and Valuation*, 4th edition, Chapter 16, "Choosing and Using the Right Valuation Methods for Physician Practices."

7 *Derby v. Commissioner*, T.C. Memo 2008-45 (2008).

8 The *BVR/AHLA Guide to Healthcare Industry Finance and Valuation*, 4th edition, Chapter 19, "Reasonable Compensation for Physicians Under the Internal Revenue Code."

meet the dramatic provider shortfall in primary care. Specialty practices such as orthopedics and dermatology are also significant users of midlevel providers. Like law firms and accounting firms, profits earned on income-producing staff pose dividend risk. However, the scope of practice for nonphysicians is not the same in all states, and direct supervision may not be required of nurse practitioners or physician assistants, for example. Intensive activity to expand the scope of practice is underway as well. It is incumbent on the appraiser to be familiar with state scope of practice law when opining on reasonable compensation.

To determine "reasonable compensation" in the context of the independent investor test, it is incumbent upon the valuation analyst to determine what underlying assets the independent investor is entitled to a return on. Because the *Norwalk*[9] case involved a professional practice, it is an important element for determining ownership and investment return as well as reasonable compensation since earnings from personal goodwill not subject to a noncompete should not be considered distributions of corporate profit. Key takeaways from the case include the need to carefully review employment contracts and noncompete provisions. Although not specifically addressed in the case, the enforceability of noncompete agreements varies widely from state to state, and thus the valuation analyst should be familiar with state law as well.

Noncompete agreements are significant because they play a large part in determining who owns any goodwill that is attached to the individual physician: the practice entity or the physician himself or herself. Assume that the seller has the ability and intent to compete post-transaction absent a contractual provision precluding that competition. A hypothetical buyer would pay less for the business—if pay anything at all—absent the noncompete, while a hypothetical seller expects to be paid for not competing in addition to being paid for the value of the other assets being sold. Thus, the noncompete has an identifiable value, and two different fair market value prices would be determined for the practice based upon the terms of the deal.

The chapter also discusses differentiating the return on labor from the return on assets/capital/equity. The key to isolating reasonable compensation from return on the practice's capital or equity is determining what the return on the labor of the physicians is versus the return on assets. In some circumstances, especially where physician services are poorly paid, what would otherwise be a return on capital may be necessary to subsidize reasonable compensation. Assets can be financed with equity or debt, the combination of which is capital. The return on debt capital is paid as interest to the lender. As to who is entitled to the return on assets, the equity owners or the physician as part of the payment for labor, ownership of "goodwill" and other intangible assets are critical. Thus, an understanding of noncompete law in each state, the employment agreements, and cases including *Norwalk*, *Martin Ice Cream*, and *Howard* is required.[10]

9 *William Norwalk, et al. v. Commissioner*, T.C. Memo. 1998-279.

10 *William Norwalk, et al. v. Commissioner*, T.C. Memo. 1998-279; *Martin Ice Cream Co. v. Commissioner*, 110 T.C. Memo. 1998-279; *Howard v. United States*, 2010 WL 3061626 (E.D.Wash.) (July 30, 2010).

Cost approach debate. "Perhaps the most significant contribution to the guide comes from contributor Tim Smith, who did four extensive chapters on the cost approach in valuation of a trained workforce," says Dietrich. "Two of the chapters were written with his co-author, Angie Smith. I believe that this should constitute a definitive resolution of the use of the cost approach in healthcare valuation, an issue that has challenged the industry for the past seven or eight years."

BVU will provide excerpts from those chapters in the next issue.

Book Review: *The Comprehensive Guide to Economic Damages*, Volume 1 and 2, 4th ed.

By Michael D. Pakter

For many years now, my expert reports on lost profits and other economic damages have referenced the Nancy J. Fannon (Fannon) and Jonathan M. Dunitz (Dunitz) publication as one of the few treatises that provided me with peer-reviewed economic damages guidelines. (The other treatise I routinely reference in my expert reports is *The Litigation Services Handbook: The Role of the Financial Expert*, 5th ed., by Roman L. Weil, Daniel G. Lentz, and David P. Hoffman.)

The Fannon and Dunitz text, titled *The Comprehensive Guide to Economic Damages*, was previously titled *The Comprehensive Guide to Lost Profits and Other Commercial Damages*—both published by Business Valuation Resources, LLC (BVR) at www.bvresources.com/publications. The broadened title is appropriate as the Fannon and Dunitz text is a broader, richer, and more detailed analysis of the issues that pertain to economic damages taken as a whole—including, but not limited to, damages in instances of personal injury and wrongful termination, intellectual property issues, post-acquisition disputes, and internal investigations. Accordingly, for forensic and valuation services practitioners, it serves as a serious and useful companion to *The Litigation Services Handbook: The Role of the Financial Expert*.

Fannon is the partner in charge of litigation services with Meyers, Harrison & Pia Valuation and Litigation Services LLC. She is a nationally known author and expert in the area of economic damages and corporate valuation. With over 25 years of experience as a financial analyst, Fannon frequently serves as an expert witness or a financial consultant in matters involving complex corporate litigation for public and private companies and testifies or consults on matters involving economic damages, unjust enrichment/disgorgement, shareholder disputes, and other damages analyses.

Dunitz is counsel with the Portland, Maine, law firm of Verrill Dana LLP, where he is chair of the Insurance Coverage and Litigation Group. He has over 20 years of experience, including complex commercial and business litigation, complex family law matters, appellate advocacy, and insurance coverage. Dunitz is admitted to practice before all state and federal courts of Maine and the United States 1st Circuit Court of Appeals. He has written and spoken extensively on the issue of expert exclusion, particularly in the area of financial damages.

The publication that these two co-editors have produced is every bit as comprehensive as its title promises. The material is laid out in an extremely useful and logical way, making it a valuable tool for reference and research. The available PDF version adds the additional functionality of keyword searches and hyperlinks from the table of contents and to sections within the text.

In summary, the two-volume set is logically set forth as follows (see the accompanying sidebar for details):

- Part I, "Expert Testimony in the U.S. Courts";
- Part II, "Lost Profits Damages";
- Part III, "Intellectual Property Damages";
- Part IV, "The Unjust Enrichment Remedy";
- Part V, "Other Commercial Damages";
- Part VI, "Personal Injury and Wrongful Termination"; and
- Part VII, "Case Digest."

The Fannon and Dunitz text is truly an impressive body of work. As the editors themselves have acknowledged, "[t]he ability to create a text with deep insights into the breadth of issues that affect financial damages requires the talents of many individuals, and there is no group more qualified than this group of contributing authors. They are specialists in the particular area on which they have written." The contributing authors hail from public accounting and consulting firms and colleges and universities and possess, among others, CPA, ABV, CDBV, CFF, CFA, CLP, ASA, CVA, CFE, CAMS, Ph. D., and Esq. certifications, qualifications, and/or degrees. Contact information for each of the contributing authors can be found at the beginning of Volume 1.

I selected Volume 1, Chapter 11, "Projecting But-For Profits,"[1] to illustrate the construction, power, and value of the Fannon and Dunitz text. That chapter, written by Stacey Udell, CPA/ABV/CFF, CVA, is divided into the following topics:

- "Methods for Determining Lost Revenue";[2]

1 *The Comprehensive Guide to Economic Damages,* Volume 1, 4th ed., page 265.

2 Id., page 270.

Organization of the The Comprehensive Guide to Economic Damages, Volume 1 and 2, 4th Ed.

The two-volume set is logically organized as follows:

- Part I, "Expert Testimony in the U.S. Courts":
  - "Professional Standards for Experts";
  - "A Brief Introduction of the U.S. Court Systems";
  - "Spoliation of Evidence";
  - "A Guide to Electronic Discovery and Evidence";
  - "Expert Depositions";
  - "The Reasonable Certainty Requirement in Lost Profits Litigation"; and
  - "Motions to Exclude Financial Experts."
- Part II, "Lost Profits Damages":
  - "Motions to Exclude Expert Testimony";
  - "Context of the Lost Profits Damages Claim";
  - "Performing Credible Lost Profits Analyses";
  - "Projections of But-For Profits";
  - "Establishing Evidence in Lost Profits Cases";
  - "Calculating Damages for Early-Stage Companies":
  - "Lost Profits Versus Lost Business Value";
  - "Discounting Lost Profits in Damage Measurements";
  - "Case Law on Discounting Damages";
  - "Use of Forensic Evidence in a Lost Profits Case";
  - "Financial Forensic Services for Internal Investigations"; and
  - "Business Interruption and Damage Claims."
- Part III, "Intellectual Property Damages":
  - "Intellectual Property Overview";
  - "Patent Infringement Damages: Lost Profits and Royalties";
  - "Lost Profits (and Other Damages) in Trademark and Copyright Cases";
  - "Uses of Survey Research in Damages Estimation"; and
  - "Using Internet Analytic Tools for Valuation and Damages Calculations in Internet IP Infringement and Defamation Cases."
- Part IV, "The Unjust Enrichment Remedy":
  - "Introduction to Remedies in Equity";
  - "Unjust Enrichment and the Defendant's Overhead"; and
  - "Restitution Rollout."
- Part V, "Other Commercial Damages":
  - "An Overview of Accounting and Financial Analysis in Fraudulent Transfer Matters";
  - "Compensation Forfeiture: Stacking Remedies Against Disloyal Agents and Employees":
  - "Post-Acquisition Disputes and Related Damages";
  - "Event Studies in Securities Litigation";
  - "Use of Statistical Analysis to Measure Damages";
- Part VI, "Personal Injury and Wrongful Termination":
  - "Economic Damages From Personal Injuries"; and
  - "Damages in Common Law Employment Cases."
- Part VII, "Case Digest":
  - "A Court Case Summary Table"; and
  - "Court Case Digests."

- "Whether and the Extent to Which Historical Information May Be an Indicator of the Future";[3]
- "Alternatives to the Average, Weighted Average, or Most Recent Year";[4]
- "Startup Companies, Businesses in a New Industry, and Businesses With Limited Operating Histories";[5]

3 Id., page 276.
4 Id., page 281.
5 Id.

- "Use of Projections Prepared in the Ordinary Course of Business";[6]
- "Consideration of Growth";[7]
- "Consideration of Industry and Economic Information";[8] and
- "Methods to Forecast Expenses."[9]

Each of the above eight topics is discussed in a comprehensive and articulate way. Terminology (for example, the differences between a "forecast" and a "projection") is carefully defined, and the listed factors to be considered by the practitioner are thoroughly explored (for example, the subject company's historic operations and its financial position, etc.).

Within each of the eight topics, the text articulates carefully, completely, and articulately the underlying issues, often exploring them with on-point examples, illustrations, and exhibits. The text is replete with important and useful cross-references to professional standards (including but not limited to AICPA standards), published articles (such as those from the *Harvard Business Review*), and—most importantly—decided court cases (such as the *Celebrity Cruise* case that provided additional information on the "yardstick method"). Taken as whole, the presentation provides essential and useful sources and other information for economic damages practitioners.

The Udell chapter goes on to discuss the most common techniques of comparing (say) current and prior financial information, methods for appraising actual past results with comparable budgets and forecasts, how to use ratios and/or amounts based on expectations developed by management, and techniques for using projected ratios and industry averages. Helpful ratios are listed, best practices are described, and different analytical methodologies are presented. Specific computations are set forth in detail—for example, a systematic guide on how to calculate a compound annual growth rate (CAGR)[10] is presented.

The Udell chapter includes perfectly placed quotes from renowned professors (for example, Dr. Aswath Damodaran, the professor of finance at New York University's Stern School of Business)[11] and case law (for example, a 2004 Delaware Chancery case on the use of projections prepared in the ordinary course of business).[12,13]

The Udell chapter ends with the following useful and quotable summary of its contents:[14]

6 Id.
7 Id., page 283.
8 Id., page 286.
9 Id., page 287.
10 Id., page 278.
11 Id., page 280.
12 Id., page 281.
13 *Doft & Co. v. Travelocity.com*, 2004 Del. Ch. LEXIS 75, *22 (Del. Ch. May 20, 2004).
14 *The Comprehensive Guide to Economic Damages*, Volume 1, 4th ed., page 287.

> Quantifying lost profits is complex and heavily dependent on the unique facts and circumstances of each case. Analysts should take logical and defensible positions supporting (and documenting) all assumptions utilized. While it is helpful to utilize company-prepared forecasts/projections, experts should not rely on such documents without further analysis, testing, and questioning. The analyst should consider the facts and circumstances specific to the company and the case in conjunction with industry and economic conditions and any other outside factors affecting the company. Lastly, experts must look behind the numbers, use sound methodology, and, most of all, be credible and reasonable.

As this single chapter clearly illustrates, the Fannon and Dunitz text is an extremely useful professional research tool for practitioners who routinely prepare expert reports (or similar analyses not concluding in an expert report) on lost profits, lost earnings, and other elements of economics damages or business interruption claims.

The Fannon and Dunitz text is not simply a primer on economic damages—it is a detailed drill down analysis of the current common body of knowledge on economic damages. The text covers basic and complex issues relating to economic damages generally—and goes further by presenting in-depth research and analyses in specialized areas including, but not limited to, intellectual property damages and damages involving physician practices, construction claims, automobile dealerships, eating establishments, and specific issues unique to government contracts.

If you testify as to economic damages, the two-volume Fannon and Dunitz text belongs in your server or in your library or even center stage on your desk.

***Michael D. Pakter,** CA, CPA, CFE, CIRA, CDBV, CFF, CFFA, CVA, CGMA, has more than 35 years' experience in accounting, financial analysis, financial forensics, and investigations, including more than 15 years' experience in economic damages and business valuation issues. Mr. Pakter can be reached at 312-229-1720, mpakter@litcpa.com, or www.litcpa.com.*

Reprinted with permission from the *National Litigation Consultants' Review, a publication of* The National Association of Certified Valuators and Analysts (NACVA).

Latest Data on Private-Company Transactions in the United Kingdom

What industry saw the highest—and lowest—transaction multiples paid for U.K. private companies in 2015? The answer and a great deal more insight is included in a new guide, *BVB Insights: Data and Analysis on UK Private Company Multiples*, 2016 edition. The guide, published by Business Valuation Benchmarks Ltd., includes details on about 230 private-company transactions in over 40 industry categories.

The majority of transactions (57%) involve U.K. buyers, followed by U.S. buyers (19%), Western Europe (10%), and Asia (4%). Corporate buyers made the lion's share (84%) of the transactions. Private equity firms did the remainder of the transactions as direct investment (10%) and in the form of management buyouts (MBOs) backed by PE firms (6%).

Key insights. The highest multiples (EV/EBITDA) paid in 2015 were in the consumer staples, healthcare, and energy sectors (see exhibit). Consumer discretionary, financials (excluding banks), and IT sectors also saw high multiples. High multiples in the consumer staples industry were largely due to branded food manufacturers. The IT sector saw high multiples in application software, an industry poised for solid growth over the next few years. Consumer discretionary further continued its strong EBITDA multiples on average, largely driven by local and foreign PE acquiring strong branded companies, continued consolidation in the advertising and marketing sector, and leisure businesses that are forecast to grow due to increased consumer confidence and disposable income.

The lowest multiples were paid in the industrials (7.9x), industrials—services (6.9x), and utilities (7.8x) sectors. The lower multiples were largely due to the targets in these industry categories being the smallest and having relatively lower margins amongst the industry categories.

It's important to note that the earnings multiples of the target companies are derived from normalized earnings. Adjustments have been made for items such as discontinued operations, nonrecurring revenue items (e.g., asset disposals, government incentives, rebates), and other factors (that are identified). In some cases, acquirers provided their own calculated normalized revenue for the target company.

Industry	No. of Txns.	Average Transaction Size (m)	Average Revenue (m)	Average EBITDA (m)	Average EBITDA Margin (%)	EV/ Revenue	EV/ EBITDA
Consumer discretionary	58	£46.2	£51.4	£4.7	11.9%	0.9	9.1
Consumer staples	12	£65.1	£52.0	£5.0	14.3%	1.6	11.3
Energy	2	£11.5	£4.7	£0.9	19.6%	2.6	15.1
Financials (excl. banks)	15	£25.9	£11.6	£2.7	20.7%	1.7	9.4
Healthcare	21	£20.3	£10.1	£2.4	18.7%	2.2	11.0
Industrials	49	£23.0	£23.2	£3.7	16.7%	1.0	7.9
Industrials—services	37	£18.0	£15.7	£2.5	16.5%	1.2	6.9
Information technology	28	£15.7	£9.8	£2.3	25.3%	2.4	9.2
Materials	2	£372.6	£245.7	£49.9	15.5%	1.1	6.4
Telecommunications	4	£37.5	£22.6	£5.1	20.3%	1.6	10.1
Utilities	3	£12.5	£7.2	£1.6	23.2%	1.8	7.8

Details included. There is detailed information on transaction information that includes descriptions of the buyer and target as well as the motivation of the buyer. For example, Shutterstock Inc., a U.S. company that's a leading global provider of high-quality licensed photographs, purchased a U.K. firm, Rex Features Limited, one of the world's leading independent photographic press agencies and picture libraries. The report gives the target's enterprise value (£20.6m), revenue (£10.8m), EBITDA (£2.3m), EBITDA margin (20.8%), EV/revenue (1.9), and EV/EBITDA (9.1). In addition, management comments are included: "Jon Oringer, Shutterstock founder and CEO, said: 'The acquisition of Rex Features marks our substantive entry into editorial imagery—a new market for Shutterstock with significant potential and many opportunities to better serve global media companies.'"

The guide also examines M&A trends in all of the industry sectors covered. It also has some interesting observations on private equity investments:

> Over 2015, PE acquired a number of businesses in the consumer discretionary market, particularly leisure businesses such as restaurants and retail with strong brands. Continuing the trend we observed last year, PE dominated the acquisition of strong-branded businesses with acquisitions in 2015 of Yo Sushi!, Prezzo, New Look, T.M. Lewin, Ben Sherman, Evans Cycles, Dr Organic, and Waterlogic. These purchases are on the back of increasing consumer confidence and an upturn in the economy, which will boost discretionary spend and thus growth for businesses in this sector. Industrials was also an active industry where PE firms targeted businesses in aerospace and defense, automotive/services, and industrial products and services.

Data sources. The guide uses information from sources that include Experian Corpfin (a U.K. database of M&A transactions over £500,000), IbisWorld, Companies House, and publicly available information (e.g., annual reports, press releases, and articles in the financial press).

The guide is available from BVR at www.bvresources.com/publications.

Experts Reveal Details of the Business Valuation Market in India

Valuation practitioners from India believe that the BV industry will grow significantly in their country as well as in global markets. Bharat Ramnani, director of valuation services for Aranca; Aroop Cherian, founder of Cherian Advisors; and Bharat Kanodia, founder of Veristrat, all provide cross-border business valuation services from Indian offices. They were part of a panel moderated by Ray Moran, CEO of MG Valuation LLC, a firm serving clients in the Americas, Europe, and Asia/ Pacific. Moran has 35 years of experience with international valuation and accounting firms and is on the board of the International Institute of Business Valuers (IIBV) and is chair of its marketing committee. During the panel discussion, they shared their thoughts on the industry, markets and services, growth opportunities, and professional education.

Ray Moran: *What is the state of the valuation industry in India?*

A: All three practitioners agreed that there are not any regulatory agencies in India with direct oversight of the valuation profession, nor any professional business valuation organizations. However, the Ministry of Company Affairs, the Institute of Chartered Accountants of India (ICAI), and laws such as the Foreign Exchange Management Act, 1999 (FEMA) set procedures and standards in performing valuation engagements.

Aroop Cherian indicated that services provided include financial and tax reporting valuations, M&A, and valuation of financial instruments. Indian accounting standards are making a transition toward fair value for financial reporting and have issued Indian AS 113 in 2011.[1] After delays in implementation, India is expected to embrace IFRS shortly, which will increase the scope of financial reporting valuation work in India. Tax reporting issues include transfer pricing, where the Foreign Exchange Management Act, 1999 lays down guidelines on valuation methodology to be considered as foreign entities invest in Indian companies. Merger and acquisition services may include help with acquisitions and raising funds for corporate finance, while additional valuation services are provided for private equity and hedge funds.

1 www.mca.gov.in/Ministry/pdf/INDAS113.pdf.

Bharat Kanodia added that "the introduction of the concept of Registered Valuer in the Companies Bill, 2011 has provided a framework to enable fair valuation in companies. Thus, there will be a need for professional valuers to standardize the use of valuation practices in India, leading to transparency and better governance."

Aroop Cherian further described the BV market segments as:

1. Big Four consulting and audit firms with CPA equivalent professionals; operations are separate for professionals serving Indian clients (front-facing professionals) and non-Indian clients (back-office operations);

2. Back-office operations for established firms in the United States and other regions;

3. Third-party operations that work independently with firms in the United States and other regions; and

4. Domestic independent appraisers who appraise real estate, property, plant, and machinery for collateral and transaction purposes.

RM: *What business valuation education is currently available in India?*

A: There are no organized professional business valuation programs in India, the panelists say. Students take graduate-level programs or in-house valuation programs through their companies. It's interesting to note that the panelists all prefer in-class programs in India versus online offerings.

"Except for a few basic short-term courses provided by ICAI and Securities and Exchange Bureau of India (SEBI), there are not many professional development programs or university programs which provide thorough business valuation education," says Ramnani. "Given the lack of competent education programs relating to business valuations, there is a need and scope for organized education programs in India."

RM: *Is there interest in national or international valuation designations, following initiatives in the U.S. and elsewhere, particularly in financial reporting?*

A: All three panelists believe that the Chartered Financial Analyst® (CFA) designation is the most recognized business valuation brand in India. As fair value becomes mandatory from a reporting standpoint, a professional valuation designation could become a major differentiator for firms providing valuation services.

Through revised guidelines in 2014, the Reserve Bank of India (RBI) has specifically mandated that internationally acceptable pricing methodology should be utilized that a Chartered Accountant or a Registered Merchant Banker should duly certify. While that implies only CA's or bankers should certify the majority of work in India, Kanodia further commented "different regulators in

India such as RBI, taxing authorities, SEBI have prescribed different, and in some cases conflicting, valuation methodologies."

RM: *What is the size of the Indian valuation market, in terms of business valuers? How many firms are there in business valuation?*

A: Firms providing business valuation services range from the Big Four to medium-sized organizations and smaller firms, the panelists point out. It appears that the Big Four and medium-sized organizations perform the majority of the business valuation business. It's difficult to measure the size of the market without a business valuation organization, although it's believed there are several hundred business valuers in India.

RM: *The valuation industry in India includes a domestic and international market. Can you comment on each?*

A: The valuation industry in India does have an international market, the panelists agree. Private equity and hedge fund engagements include quarterly valuations for portfolios, which are business and equity valuations. Many companies focus on 409A work where, because of their significant value, Indian firms have had a major impact on this U.S. market. IRC Section 409A is the tax code regarding stock option plans, where valuations assist in the issuance of options, particularly serving startup firms on the West Coast. The service is the initial valuation as well as annual updates. These valuations are often referred to as cheap stock engagements.

RM: *What are the growth opportunities for the industry?*

A: The panelists all believe that the Indian business valuation industry will grow significantly, especially domestically, given the acceptance of IFRS and fair value reporting in India, as well as in the global markets. "Given the above mentioned amendments providing significant growth opportunities to the valuation industry, we expect a Compounded Average Growth Rate (CAGR) of about 20%-25% over the coming five years," says Ramnani. Interestingly, two panel members also provide valuation capabilities in other services, such as real estate and plant machinery, for the domestic and foreign markets.

"There is immense opportunity for growth in this industry," says Cherian. "We see professionals being exposed to a wider variety of opportunities, thus enhancing their professional and career growth chances."

Regarding cross-border opportunities, all three panelists agree that Indian appraisal firms have been able to integrate with firms in the United States. Back-office operations of companies in the U.S. are ramping up operations as they maintain their cost arbitrage positions, while all of these firms provide enhanced responsiveness and turnaround given the time zone differentials and capability of working on client projects on a 24-hour basis. Services range from initial research and modelling to outsourcing valuations, while U.S. valuers maintain client relations.

RM: *What's your favorite worldwide travel story?*

A: All three panelists travel the globe and have interesting experiences, but we feature one from Ramnani. "My favorite travel story was when I traveled to Malaysia's Genting Highlands, which have some of world's best resorts and casinos," he says. "The fact that the entire property of Genting Highlands has been built by an idea of one single person on a vacant piece of land interested me the most."

Section VI. Data

Monthly Cost of Capital Data

Editor's Note: The charts in this section display the cost of capital data for each month of 2016 that were originally published in the Business Valuation Update *newsletter. These charts are included to provide readers with a reference point for cost of capital data as of a particular valuation date. Because Duff & Phelps data are published once a year, we've included the most recent data as of December 2016 in Exhibit 3.*

Exhibit 1. 2016 Month-by-Month Cost of Capital

	Jan-16	Feb-16	Mar-16	Apr-16	May-16	Jun-16	Jul-16	Aug-16	Sep-16	Oct-16	Nov-16	Dec-16
30-Day Treasury Yield	0.11%	0.17%	0.19%	0.29%	0.20%	0.11%	0.27%	0.24%	0.20%	0.27%	0.25%	0.24%
5-Year Treasury Yield	1.65%	1.73%	1.38%	1.31%	1.24%	1.32%	1.39%	1.00%	1.06%	1.18%	1.18%	1.30%
20-Year Treasury Yield	2.63%	2.64%	2.38%	2.28%	2.20%	2.31%	2.22%	1.81%	1.84%	1.90%	2.01%	2.24%
Long-Term Inflation Estimate	2.25%	2.25%	2.25%	2.25%	2.25%	2.25%	2.25%	2.25%	2.25%	2.25%	2.25%	2.25%
Long-Term Rate of Growth GDP	2.25%	2.25%	2.25%	2.25%	2.25%	2.25%	2.20%	2.20%	2.20%	2.20%	2.20%	2.20%
Dow Jones 20-Bond Yield	3.37%	3.43%	3.40%	3.25%	2.91%	2.80%	2.89%	2.64%	2.54%	2.51%	2.57%	2.76%
Prime Lending Rate	3.25%	3.50%	3.50%	3.50%	3.25%	3.50%	3.50%	3.50%	3.50%	3.50%	3.50%	3.50%
Barron's Intermediate-Grade Bonds	5.12%	5.15%	5.42%	5.37%	5.12%	4.93%	4.93%	4.66%	4.43%	4.26%	4.23%	4.37%
Dow Jones Ind P/E Ratio on Current Earnings	16.8%	16.2%	16.7%	17.1%	18.3%	19.1%	19.1%	19.2%	20.1%	20.0%	19.9%	19.5%
Dow Jones Ind P/E Ratio on 2015 Operating Earnings Estimate*	17.2%	17.2%	15.9%	16.4%	17.0%	16.9%	17.0%	17.5%	18.3%	17.5%	17.5%	17.4%
Dow Jones Ind P/E Ratio on 2016 Operating Earnings Estimate**	15.9%	15.8%	15.6%	16.4%	16.6%	15.9%	16.0%	16.1%	16.2%	16.1%	16.0%	15.9%

* Changes from 2015 Earnings to 2016 Earnings in June 2016
** Changes from 2016 Earnings to 2017 Earnings in June 2016

Exhibit 2. Month-by-Month Cost of Capital Data Chart

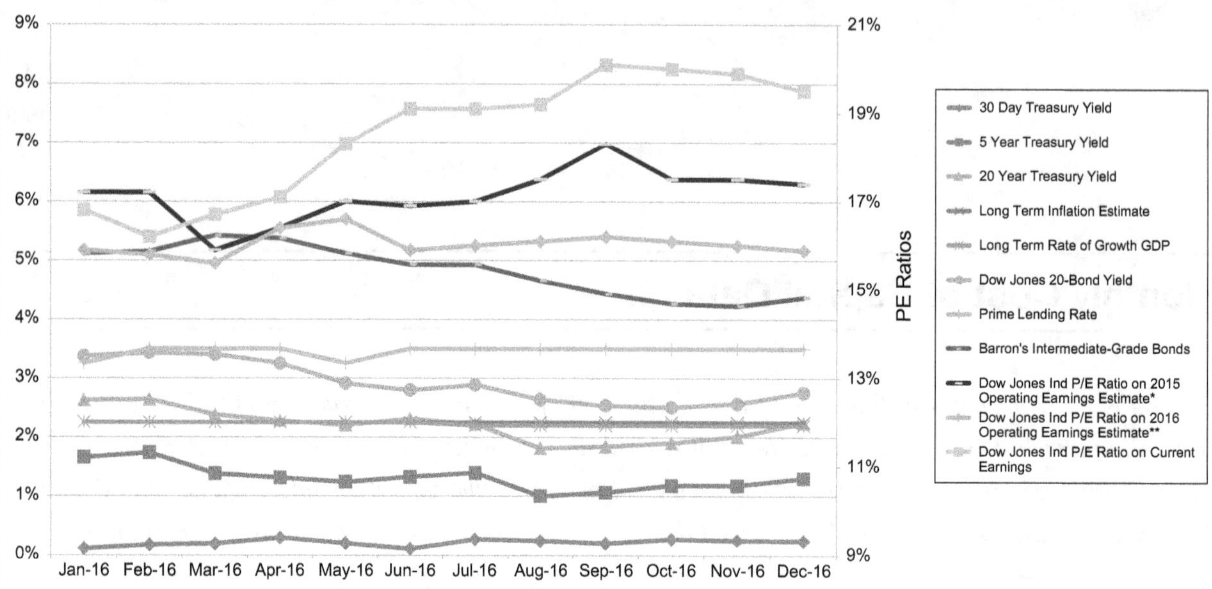

Exhibit 3. Duff & Phelps' 2016 Premiums Over Long-Term Risk-Free Rate[1]

Historical Equity Risk Premiums: Averages Since 1963 Data for Year Ending December 31, 2015.				
Measure Used for Size[2]	**Exhibit**	**1st**	**13th**	**25th**
5-Year Average EBITDA	A-6	4.6%	8.5%	12.0%
5-Year Average Net Income	A-3	4.3%	8.5%	12.3%
Sales	A-7	5.2%	8.8%	11.9%
Total Assets	A-5	4.4%	8.5%	12.2%

1 Source: *2016 Valuation Handbook – Guide to Cost of Capital* (A Exhibits) © Duff & Phelps, LLC. All rights reserved. Risk Premium Report cost of capital data include premiums where size is measured by eight size mea-sures: market value of equity, market value of invested capital, book value of equity, five-year average net income, five-year average EBITDA, sales, total assets, and number of employees. Complete current and historical Risk Premium Report cost of capital data are available at bvresources.com/dp.

2 Each measure of size is organized by Duff & Phelps, LLC in 25 portfolio ranks, with portfolio 1 being the largest and portfolio 25 being the smallest. Smoothed average premiums are present here because they are considered a better indicator than the actual historical observation for most of the portfolio groups. Premiums may be adjusted for differences between historic market risk premiums and expected equity risk premiums as described in the *2016 Valuation Handbook – Guide to Cost of Capital*. NOTE: The new *2016 Valuation Handbook – Guide to Cost of Capital* includes two sets of valuation data: (i) Risk Premium Report data; and (ii) CRSP Decile Size Study (previously published in the Morningstar/Ibbotson *SBBI Valuation Yearbook*).

Bob Dohmeyer, ASA; Pete Butler, CFA, ASA; and Rod Burkert, CPA/ABV, CVA developed a model designed to be more reliable than the build-up method for estimating the cost of capital of a small privately held business. This model uses the authors' new implied private company pricing line 2.0 (IPCPL) and is indexed directly to the IPCPL cost of capital. The model allows adjustments for differences in systematic risk (i.e., beta), diversifiable and total risk (i.e., total beta), liquidity, and debt capacity. Exhibits 4 and 5 summarize the IPCPL Index over 2016.

Exhibit 4. BVR's Private-Company Cost of Capital Index Based on Four Company Revenue Sizes in $ Thousands

	Jan-16	Feb-16	Mar-16	Apr-16	May-16	Jun-16	Jul-16	Aug-16	Sep-16	Oct-16	Nov-16	Dec-16
1,000	19.1%	19.1%	19.1%	18.9%	18.7%	18.8%	18.7%	18.3%	18.2%	18.3%	18.4%	18.8%
5,000	17.3%	17.3%	17.3%	17.2%	16.9%	17.0%	16.9%	16.5%	16.5%	16.5%	16.7%	17.0%
10,000	15.5%	15.6%	15.6%	15.5%	15.2%	15.2%	15.1%	14.8%	14.8%	14.8%	14.9%	15.3%
15,000	14.6%	14.7%	14.7%	14.6%	14.3%	14.3%	14.2%	13.9%	13.8%	13.9%	14.0%	14.4%

Exhibit 5. BVR's Private-Company Cost of Capital Index Based on Four Company Revenue Sizes in $ Thousands

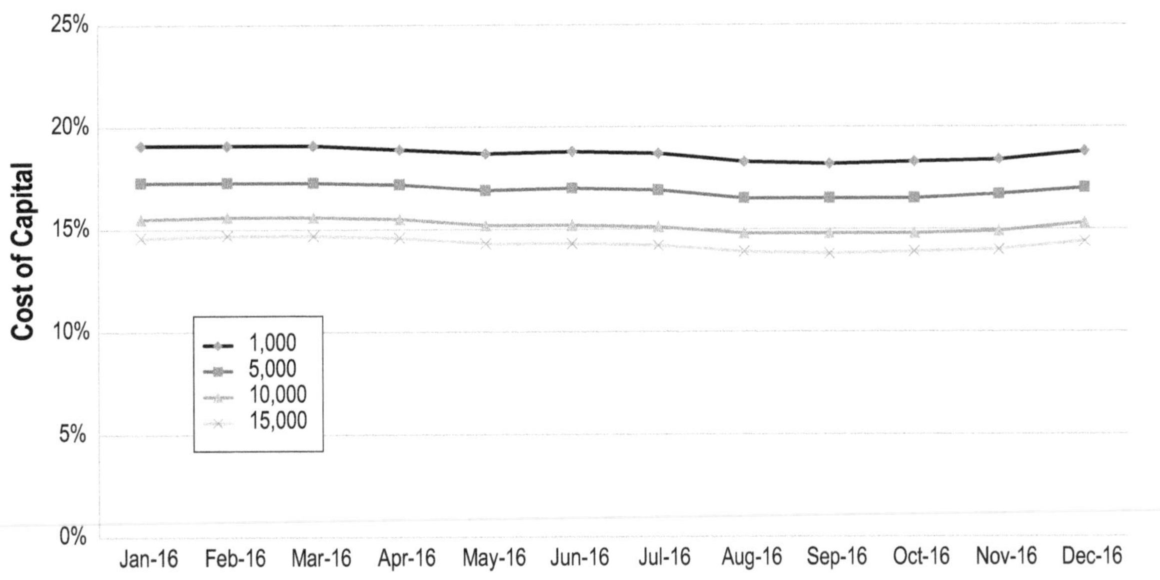

www.ingramcontent.com/pod-product-compliance
Lightning Source LLC
LaVergne TN
LVHW062140300926
849161LV00010B/2582
* 9 7 8 1 6 2 1 5 0 1 0 5 3 *